RFID in
the Supply Chain

A Guide to Selection and Implementation

Series on Resource Management

Titles in the Series

Handbook of Supply Chain Management, Second Edition
by James B. Ayers
ISBN: 0-8493-3160-9

The Portal to Lean Production: Principles & Practices for Doing More With Less
by John Nicholas and Avi Soni
ISBN: 0-8493-5031-X

Supply Market Intelligence: A Managerial Handbook for Building Sourcing Strategies
by Robert Handfield
ISBN: 0-8493-2789-X

The Small Manufacturer's Toolkit: A Guide to Selecting the Techniques and Systems to Help You Win
by Steve Novak
ISBN: 0-8493-2883-7

Velocity Management in Logistics and Distribution: Lessons from the Military to Secure the Speed of Business
by Joseph L. Walden
ISBN: 0-8493-2859-4

Supply Chain for Liquids: Out of the Box Approaches to Liquid Logistics
by Wally Klatch
ISBN: 0-8493-2853-5

Supply Chain Architecture: A Blueprint for Networking the Flow of Material, Information, and Cash
by William T. Walker
ISBN: 1-57444-357-7

ERP: Tools, Techniques, and Applications for Integrating the Supply Chain
by Carol A. Ptak with Eli Schragenheim
ISBN: 1-57444-358-5

Integral Logistics Management: Planning and Control of Comprehensive Supply Chains, Second Edition
by Paul Schonsleben
ISBN: 1-57444-355-0

Introduction to e-Supply Chain Management: Engaging Technology to Build Market-Winning Business Partnerships
by David C. Ross
ISBN: 1-57444-324-0

Supply Chain Networks and Business Process Orientation
by Kevin P. McCormack and William C. Johnson with William T. Walker
ISBN: 1-57444-327-5

Collaborative Manufacturing: Using Real-Time Information to Support the Supply Chain
by Michael McClellan
ISBN: 1-57444-341-0

The Supply Chain Manager's Problem-Solver: Maximizing the Value of Collaboration and Technology
by Charles C. Poirier
ISBN: 1-57444-335-6

Lean Performance ERP Project Management: Implementing the Virtual Supply Chain
by Brian J. Carroll
ISBN: 1-57444-309-7

Integrated Learning for ERP Success: A Learning Requirements Planning Approach
by Karl M. Kapp, with William F. Latham and Hester N. Ford-Latham
ISBN: 1-57444-296-1

Basics of Supply Chain Management
by Lawrence D. Fredendall and Ed Hill
ISBN: 1-57444-120-5

Lean Manufacturing: Tools, Techniques, and How to Use Them
by William M. Feld
ISBN: 1-57444-297-X

Disassembly Modeling for Assembly, Maintenance, Reuse, and Recycling
by A.J.D. Lambert and Surendra M. Gupta
ISBN: 1-57444-334-8

Back to Basics: Your Guide to Manufacturing Excellence
by Steven A. Melnyk and R.T. Chris Christensen
ISBN: 1-57444-279-1

Enterprise Resource Planning and Beyond: Integrating Your Entire Organization
by Gary A. Langenwalter
ISBN: 1-57444-260-0

Restructuring the Manufacturing Process: Applying the Matrix Method
by Gideon Halevi
ISBN: 1-57444-121-3

Inventory Classification Innovation: Paving the Way for Electronic Commerce and Vendor Managed Inventory
by Russell G. Broeckelmann
ISBN: 1-57444-237-6

RFID in the Supply Chain

A Guide to Selection and Implementation

Judith M. Myerson
IT Consultant
Philadelphia, Pennsylvania
USA

Auerbach Publications
Taylor & Francis Group
Boca Raton   New York

Auerbach Publications is an imprint of the
Taylor & Francis Group, an informa business

Auerbach Publications
Taylor & Francis Group
6000 Broken Sound Parkway NW, Suite 300
Boca Raton, FL 33487-2742

© 2007 by Taylor & Francis Group, LLC
Auerbach is an imprint of Taylor & Francis Group, an Informa business

International Standard Book Number-10: 0-8493-3018-1 (Hardcover)
International Standard Book Number-13: 978-0-8493-3018-6 (Hardcover)

Library of Congress Cataloging-in-Publication Data

Myerson, Judith M.
    RFID in the supply chain : a guide to selection and implementation / Judith M. Myerson.
        p. cm.
    Includes bibliographical references and index.
    ISBN 0-8493-3018-1
    1. Inventory control--Automation. 2. Radio frequency identification systems. I. Title.

TS160.R43 2006
658.7'87--dc22   2006045675

Visit the Taylor & Francis Web site at
http://www.taylorandfrancis.com

and the Auerbach Web site at
http://www.auerbach-publications.com

TABLE OF CONTENTS

Tables xvii
Figures. xix
Preface xxi

1 Supply Chain Overview 1
1.1 Paradigm Shift in Product Traceability. 1
    1.1.1 Transitioning to RFID Technology 1
    1.1.2 Tracking Problems. 5
    1.1.3 Supply Chain. 9
1.2 RFID Markets 12
1.3 Economic Feasibility of Rolling Out RFID 15
    1.3.1 Supply Chain Synchronization 16
    1.3.2 Customer Privacy Issues. 16
    1.3.3 Security Challenges 17
    1.3.4 Operational and IT Challenges (Hardware, Software,
        System Compatibility, People Expertise). 17
    1.3.5 Logistical Challenges 18
    1.3.6 Program Management Challenges. 19
    1.3.7 Education and Training 19
    1.3.8 Standard Implementation Challenges 20
    1.3.9 Lessons Learned. 20
        1.3.9.1 Iraq: Asset Visibility 20
        1.3.9.2 Wal-Mart: Implementation Training 23
        1.3.9.3 International Paper: Business Processes. 23
        1.3.9.4 Procter & Gamble: Docking Loading Throughput 23
1.4 RFID Technology Infrastructure. 24
    1.4.1 Open Architecture: Savant Server. 24
    1.4.2 Major Vendor Servers. 26
    1.4.3 Tags 27
    1.4.4 Antennas 29
    1.4.5 Readers 30
    1.4.6 Electronic Product Code. 31
    1.4.7 Object Name Service 33
    1.4.8 EPC Information Service. 34

    1.4.9 Scenarios 35
1.5 Web-Centric Supply Chain Management Challenges. 36
    1.5.1 Combining Web-Centric with RFID Technology 36
    1.5.2 E-Business Applications 36
    1.5.3 Advantages and Disadvantages. 37
References 38

2   RFID Technology 39
2.1 Primary Drivers. 39
    2.1.1 RFID Technology Deployment 39
    2.1.2 RFID Technology: Basics, Advantages, and Disadvantages 43
2.2 Selection Guidance on Tags, Servers, and Middleware 46
    2.2.1 EPC Tag Classes. 47
    2.2.2 ISO Standards 48
    2.2.3 RFID Device Selection Criteria 50
        2.2.3.1 What Are the Objects to Be Tagged?. 50
        2.2.3.2 What Are the Materials of the Objects and How
                 Do They Affect Reading Ranges?. 51
        2.2.3.3 What Are Chip Antenna Types?. 53
        2.2.3.4 What Readers Can Read Both Passive and Active Tags?. .55
        2.2.3.5 What Are Other Considerations that Could
                 Affect Externally the Optimal Location of Tags?. 56
        2.2.3.6 What Readers Can Read Both RFID Tags
                 and Bar Codes for Easy Transitioning? 56
        2.2.3.7 How Do Various Entities Organize
                 Frequency Types or Ranges?. 57
        2.2.3.8 What Standards Are the Vendors Using
                 for Their RFID Products?. 60
    2.2.4 Middleware Selection Criteria. 60
        2.2.4.1 RFID Plug-and-Play. 61
        2.2.4.2 RFID Supply Chain Execution Applications 62
        2.2.4.3 RFID Platform-Dependent Legacy Systems. 64
        2.2.4.4 RFID Integration Hubs 67
2.3 RFID Implementation Examples 68
References 73

3   RFID Applications in Supply Chain Management 75
3.1 Logistics 75
    3.1.1 SCM Logistics Maturity Model. 77
    3.1.2 Logistics: Reactive, Proactive, and RFID 79
3.2 Management. 82
    3.2.1 Oracle–PeopleSoft 82
    3.2.2 Microsoft RFID Council 83
    3.2.3 IBM. 84
    3.2.4 The METRO Group Future Store 85
        3.2.4.1 Inventory Management 86
        3.2.4.2 Information Management 86
        3.2.4.3 Check-Out 87

3.2.5   Chain Pharmacy Operations. 88
3.2.6   SAP 89
3.2.7   Web Services. 91
          3.2.7.1   Object Name Service. 93
          3.2.7.2   EPC Information Service 93
          3.2.7.3   Electronic Product Code .95
          3.2.7.4   Savant Servers. 96
          3.2.7.5   EPCglobal and the Auto-ID Center 97
References 100

4   Storing and Retrieving Data. 101
4.1   Two Big Questions. 101
          4.1.1   Relationship between Data Storage and Retrieval Issues. 101
          4.1.2   Understanding Risks Associated with RFID/EPC Technologies. . . 102
4.2   EPC Technology in Functional Areas. 103
4.3   Perceptions of Product Benefits 103
4.4   Database CD on Local Workstation. 105
4.5   Remote Database Servers 106
          4.5.1   How Can We Reduce the Number of Traffic
                   Bottleneck Incidents?. 107
          4.5.2   Why Do We Need to Divide the Database into the Static
                   and Dynamic Partitions?. 108
          4.5.3   What Kind of Database Management Should We Get
                   to Satisfy Our Requirements? 108
          4.5.4   What Is the Optimal Way of Increasing Throughputs
                   and Operational Efficiency? 109
                   4.5.4.1   Peoplesoft Enterprise Systems 110
                   4.5.4.2   IBM RFID Product. 110
          4.5.5   How Do We Reduce Loading Times Cost Effectively?. 111
          4.5.6   How Do We Migrate a Relational Database Management
                   System to Another? 112
          4.5.7   How Is Partitioning Emulated and What Are
                   the Partitioning Types?. 112
          4.5.8   How Do You Determine the Number of Partitions
                   for a Database? 115
          4.5.9   What Are the Factors You Should Consider in Your
                   Migration Planning? 116
4.6   Databases in Company Merger Processes 117
4.7   Hybrid Databases 117
4.8   Web Services 118
References 120

5   RFID Business Processes 121
5.1   Implementation Approaches 122
          5.1.1   Dual Shipping Faces 123
          5.1.2   Two Sides of the Mandates 124
          5.1.3   RFID Implementation Checklist 124

5.2 Business Process Reengineering 126
   5.2.1 Procter & Gamble: Dock Loading Throughput 127
   5.2.2 Canus: Changing Antenna's Orientation 128
   5.2.3 Unilever: Changing Tag Placement 128
   5.2.4 Heinz: Adapting Tag Requirements 128
   5.2.5 Gillette Scenario: Misplaced Case 129
   5.2.6 Canus: Adjusting Computer Speed 131
   5.2.7 Software Checklist 131
5.3 Organizational Maturity 132
5.4 Basic Multi-Layer RFID Business Process Model 135
5.5 Adaptive Multi-Layer RFID Business Process Model 136
   5.5.1 Adaptive Maturity 137
   5.5.2 Application Adaptors 138
   5.5.3 The METRO Group 139
5.6 Predictive Multi-Layer Business Process Model 140
5.7 RFID Business Processes Strategy 143
   5.7.1 IBM RFID Strategy 143
   5.7.2 Heinz RFID Strategy 144
   5.7.3 Canus RFID Strategy 144
   5.7.4 International Paper RFID Strategy 145
   5.7.5 Kayser-Roth RFID Strategy 145
   5.7.6 Philips Semiconductors RFID Strategy 146
   5.7.7 Intel RFID Strategy 148
   5.7.8 Unilever RFID Strategy 149
   5.7.9 Major Clothier Retailer RFID Strategy 149
   5.7.10 Marks and Spencer RFID Strategy 149
5.8 RFID Enterprise Supply Chain Systems 150
   5.8.1 Supply Chain Planning 150
   5.8.2 Supply Chain Execution 151
   5.8.3 Supply Chain Management 153
      5.8.3.1 SCM Logistics 153
      5.8.3.2 SCM Management 155
5.9 RFID Business Process Life Cycle 156
   5.9.1 Older Life-Cycle Models 158
      5.9.1.1 Waterfall Life Cycle 158
      5.9.1.2 Incremental Life Cycle 159
      5.9.1.3 Spiral Life Cycle 161
   5.9.2 Newer Life-Cycle Models 162
      5.9.2.1 Adaptive Linear Feedback Life Cycle 162
      5.9.2.2 Adaptive Dynamic Life Cycle 162
References 163

6 RFID Security, Privacy, and Risk Assessment 165
6.1 Security Policy 165
   6.1.1 Organizational Policy 166
   6.1.2 Issue-Specific Policy 166
   6.1.3 System-Specific Policy 167

6.2   Security of RFID Query 168
      6.2.1   Query Scenario 168
      6.2.2   Security Problems 169
6.3   Attacks on RFID Technology. 170
      6.3.1   War-Walking and Lifting. 170
      6.3.2   Counterfeiting 172
      6.3.3   Denial-of-Service 173
      6.3.4   Weak Cryptography 173
6.4   Defense in Depth. 176
6.5   Risk Assessment 177
      6.5.1   Risk Assessment Profile 178
      6.5.2   Internal Asset Risk Assessment. 178
      6.5.3   Risk Assessment Service. 182
References 183

Appendix A Passive RFID Technology 185
A.1   Avonwood (http://www.avonwood.com) 185
      A.1.1   Eureka 111 Systems 185
      A.1.2   Eureka 211 Systems 185
A.2   Escort Memory Systems (http://www.ems-rfid.com/) 186
      A.2.1   HMS Passive Read/Write Systems 186
              A.2.1.1   HMS100 Series Passive Read/WriteTags 186
              A.2.1.2   HMS800 Series Passive Reader/Writers. 186
              A.2.1.3   HMS827 Series Passive Reader/Writer 186
              A.2.1.4   HMS828 Series Passive Reader/Writer 187
              A.2.1.5   HMS820-04/HMS830-04 Series Passive Conveyor
                        Reader/Writers. 187
              A.2.1.6   HMS820-08/HMS830-08 Series Passive Wide-Plate
                        Reader/Writers. 187
              A.2.1.7   HMS820/HMS830 Passive Reader/Writers. 187
              A.2.1.8   HMS827-04 Passive Conveyor Reader/Writer 188
              A.2.1.9   HMS827-05 Passive Tubular Reader/Writer. 188
              A.2.1.10 HMS814/HMS816 Portable Reader/Writers 188
      A.2.2   Passive Read-Only Systems 188
              A.2.2.1   ES600-Series Read-Only Tags 189
              A.2.2.2   RS427 Read-Only Reader. 189
              A.2.2.3   RS427-04 Passive Read-Only Conveyor Antenna 189
A.3   Intermec (www.intermec.com) 189
      A.3.1   RFID Tags and Inserts 189
      A.3.2   RFID Readers. 191
      A.3.3   Intellitag PM4i Printer 194
      A.3.4   RFID Partners 195
A.4   Northern Apex (www.northernapex-rfid.com) 195
      A.4.1   Inlays and Tags 195
      A.4.2   Readers and Antennas 197
              A.4.2.1   900-MHz Readers and Antennas 197
              A.4.2.2   13.56-MHz Readers and Antennas 198

A.5 Philips (www.semiconductors.philips.com) 199
    A.5.1 I·CODE Transponder ICs 199
    A.5.2 MIFARE Reader Components 201
A.6 SAMSys...201
A.7 Symbol Technologies (www.symbol.com; formerly Matrics)..........202
    A.7.1 Tags 202
    A.7.2 Readers 202
    A.7.3 Antennas 203
A.8 TAGSYS (www.tagsys.com)..................................204
    A.8.1 Industry and Logistics Market..........................204
        A.8.1.1 RFID Chips...................................205
        A.8.1.2 RFID Tags....................................206
        A.8.1.3 RFID Readers 207
        A.8.1.4 RFID Antennas 208
        A.8.1.5 RFID Kits 209
    A.8.2 Industry and Logistics Partner Products 210
        A.8.2.1 Athelia 210
        A.8.2.2 Blackroc Technology (www.blackroc.com) 213
        A.8.2.3 DAP Technologies (www.daptech.com)............213
        A.8.2.4 EIA (www.eia-italia.com)........................214
        A.8.2.5 GIS (www.gis-net.de) 214
        A.8.2.6 ichain (www.ichain.co-za)......................215
        A.8.2.7 ICS (www.ica.nl)..............................215
        A.8.2.8 Microraab (www.microraab.hu)..................216
        A.8.2.9 Minec (www.minec.com) 217
        A.8.2.10 Nordicid (www.nordicid.com)...................218
        A.8.2.11 Northern Apex (www.northernapex-rfid.com) 218
        A.8.2.12 System Concepts (www.systemconcepts.com) 219
        A.8.2.13 Teraoka Seiko (teraoka.digi.co.jp) 220
        A.8.2.14 Toshiba (www.toshibatec-eu.com).................220
        A.8.2.15 Touchstar (www.touchpc.com) 220
    A.8.3 Products for the Library Market 221
    A.8.4 TAGSYS Partner Products for the Library Market 224
        A.8.4.1 Blackroc Technology (www.blackroc.com) 225
        A.8.4.2 Minec (www.minec.com) 225
        A.8.4.3 Vernon Library Supplies (www.vernlib.com) 225
        A.8.4.4 Gemsys (www.gemsys.no) 226
        A.8.4.5 VTLS Inc. (www.vtls.com)......................226
        A.8.4.6 Tech Logic (www.tech-logic.com) 226
        A.8.4.7 Teraoka Seiko (teraoka.digi.co.jp) 227
        A.8.4.8 Toshiba (www.toshibatec-eu.com).................227
    A.8.5 Textile Rental Industry 227
    A.8.5 TAGSYS Partner Products for Textile
        Rental Industry 232
        A.8.5.1 Laundry Computer Technics (www.LCT.nl) 233
        A.8.5.2 Jensen (www.jensen-group.com).................234

A.8.5.3 Positek RFID (www.positekrfid.com)..............234
A.8.5.4 Metalprogetti (metalpro@tin.il)...................235
A.9 Texas Instruments-RFID (www.ti-rfid.com) 236
A.9.1 13.56-MHz Products...........................236
A.9.2 Low-Frequency Products 237
A.9.3 Software 238

Appendix B Active RFID Technology 241
B.1 Alien Technology (www.alientechnology.com) 241
B.2 Axcess Inc. (www.axcessinc.com)...........................243
B.3 Escort Memory Systems 243
B.4 Microtec (www.ksw-microtec.de) 246
B.5 SAMSys (www.samsys.com) 247
B.6 Savi Technology (www.savi.com)...........................248
B.7 WhereNet (www.wherenet.com)...........................250

Appendix C Semi-Passive RFID Technology 253
C.1 Alien Technology (www.alientechnology.com) 253
C.2 Avonwood 254
C.3 KSW Microtec (www.ksw-microtec.com)...........................255

Appendix D RFID Middleware.........................257
D.1 Acsis Inc. (www.acsis.com) 257
D.2 Axcess Inc. (www.axcessinc.com) 258
D.3 Blue Vector Systems (www.bluevectorsystems.com) 258
D.4 ConnecTerra (www.connecterra.com).........................259
D.5 Data Brokers (www.databrokers.com) 259
D.6 EPCglobal (www.epcglobalinc.org).........................261
D.7 Franwell (www.franwell.com) 261
D.8 GlobeRanger (www.globeranger.com) 261
D.9 i2 Technologies (www.i2.com) 262
D.10 Manhattan Associates (www.manh.com).........................262
D.11 OATSystems (www.oatsystems.com).........................262
D.12 Oracle (www.oracle.com) 263
D.13 RF Code (www.rfcode.com).........................263
D.14 Savi Technology (www.savi.com).........................264
D.15 Sun (www.sun.com) 264
D.16 T3Ci (www.t3ci.com).........................265
D.17 TIBCO (www.tibco.com) 265
D.18 VeriSign (www.verisign.com) 265
D.19 webMethods (www.webmethods.com).........................266

Appendix E Network/Server Interfaces 267
E.1 Escort Memory Systems (www.ems-rfid.com) 267
E.2 WhereNet (www.wherenet.com).........................269
E.3 Blue Vector Systems (www.bluevectorsystems.com) 271

Appendix F Physical Markup Language
for RFID Applications 273
F.1 XML File Instances 273
    F.1.1 Instance 1: Multiple Tags with No Data 274
    F.1.2 Instance 2: Tags with Data 275
    F.1.3 Instance 3: Memory Tags with Data 276
    F.1.4 Instance 4: Tags with Mounted Sensors 277
    F.1.5 Instance 5: Observed Data in Hexbinary Format 278
F.2 XML Schemas 279
References 287

Appendix G Warehouse Management Systems 289
G.1 RT-Systems: RT-LOCATOR 289
G.2 Robocom 290
    G.2.1 Management Control 291
    G.2.2 Inbound 291
    G.2.3 Inventory Management 291
    G.2.4 Outbound 291
    G.2.5 RDT Subsystem 292
    G.2.6 Other RIMS Modules 292
G.3 HighJump 293
G.4 KARE Technologies 293
G.5 Daly Commerce 294

Appendix H Supply Chain Execution Systems 297
H.1 HighJump 297
H.2 Provia 302
H.3 Softeon 302
H.4 ClearOrbit 306
    H.4.1 Pro Series for Any ERP 307
    H.4.2 Pro Series for Oracle 10.7/11.0/11*i* 309
    H.4.3 Pro Series for SAP R/3 309
H.5 Peoplesoft (Formerly JD Edwards, Now Part of Oracle) 311

Appendix I Enterprise Intelligence: WebFOCUS 313
I.1 Data Sources 313
I.2 Reporting Server 313
I.3 Data Management 315
I.4 Microsoft Integration 317
I.5 Portal Integration 317
I.6 Reports as Web Services 318
I.7 Web Services Adapter 319
I.8 Miscellaneous 319

Appendix J Enterprise Databases 321
J.1 Base/One 321
    J.1.1 Base/One Foundation Class Library 322
    J.1.2 Database Command Processor 322

J.1.2.1 Common SQL Commands 323
J.1.2.2 Built-In Basic Commands 323
J.1.2.3 Built-In Commands That Use the Data Dictionary 323
J.1.2.4 DOS and WIN Command Lines. 324
J.1.2.5 Error Suppression Commands 324
J.1.2.6 Database Buffer Commands 324
J.1.2.7 Database Manager Commands. 325
J.1.2.8 Custom Commands 325
J.1.2.9 Macro Assignment Command Lines 326
J.1.3 Database Library 326
J.1.4 Systems Requirements 329
J.2 CodeBase 330
J.2.1 Windows CE 4.0 330
J.2.2 J2ME 331
J.2.3 JDBC 3.0 332
J.2.4 UNIX 334
J.2.5 Linux 334
J.2.6 Bundle for Windows and .NET 335
J.2.7 Delphi and Kylix 335
J.2.8 SQL 2.0 for Windows. 335
J.2.9 64-Bit Add-On 335
J.2.10 Maximum Limits 336
J.2.11 Slow Query Performance 337
J.2.11.1 Unique Tag. 337
J.2.11.2 Filtered Tag 337
J.2.11.3 Tag Using General Collating Sequence 339
J.2.12 Windows Registry 340
J.2.13 Using CodeBase from Microsoft Access 340
J.2.14 Running Visual Basic Example 341
J.2.15 Running Visual C++ Example 341

Appendix K Data Synchronization: GoldenGate 343
K.1 Primary Modules. 343
K.1.1 GoldenGate Capture Core 343
K.1.2 GoldenGate Delivery Core 344
K.1.3 GoldenGate Manager Core 344
K.2 Software Modules 344
K.3 Database Replication. 345

Appendix L Partitioning Large Databases: Oracle 347
Listing L.1 CREATE TABLE Example 347
Listing L.2 CREATE TABLE for Coded Unusable Items 350

Appendix M Software Engineering Standards 353
M.1 IEEE Standards 353
M.2 ISO/IEC Standards 356
M.3 Related Standards 358

Appendix N Business Process Automation: IBM Products. 359

Appendix O Commercial Assessment Products 363
O.1 HackerShield 363
O.2 NetRecon 364

Appendix P Risk-Related Software 365

Appendix Q Sample Security Policy Templates 377
Q.1   Acceptable Use Policy 377
       Q.1.1 Overview 378
       Q.1.2 Purpose. 378
       Q.1.3 Scope 378
       Q.1.4 Policy 378
              Q.1.4.1 General Use and Ownership 378
              Q.1.4.2 Security and Proprietary Information 379
              Q.1.4.3 Unacceptable Use 380
       Q.1.5 Enforcement 382
       Q.1.6 Definitions 382
Q.2   Acquisition Assessment Policy 382
       Q.2.1 Purpose. 382
       Q.2.2 Scope 382
       Q.2.3 Policy 382
              Q.2.3.1 General 382
              Q.2.3.2 Requirements. 383
       Q.2.4 Enforcement 384
Q.3   Audit Vulnerability Scan Policy. 384
       Q.3.1 Purpose. 384
       Q.3.2 Scope 385
       Q.3.3 Policy 385
              Q.3.3.1 Network Control 385
              Q.3.3.2 Service Degradation or Interruption. 385
              Q.3.3.3 Client Point of Contact during the Scanning Period . . 386
              Q.3.3.4 Scanning Period 386
       Q.3.4 Enforcement 386
       Q.3.5 Revision History 386
Q.4   Automatically Forwarded E-Mail Policy. 386
       Q.4.1 Purpose. 386
       Q.4.2 Scope 386
       Q.4.3 Policy 386
       Q.4.4 Enforcement 387
       Q.4.5 Definitions 387
Q.5   Database Password Policy 387
       Q.5.1 Purpose. 387
       Q.5.2 Scope 388
       Q.5.3 Policy 388
              Q.5.3.1 General 388
              Q.5.3.2 Specific Requirements 388

        Q.5.4   Enforcement 389
        Q.5.5   Definitions 390
Q.6   E-Mail Retention Policy 390
        Q.6.1   Purpose. 390
        Q.6.2   Scope 391
        Q.6.3   Policy 391
                 Q.6.3.1   Administrative Correspondence 391
                 Q.6.3.2   Fiscal Correspondence. 391
                 Q.6.3.3   General Correspondence 391
                 Q.6.3.4   Ephemeral Correspondence 392
                 Q.6.3.5   Instant Messenger Correspondence 392
                 Q.6.3.6   Encrypted Communications 392
                 Q.6.3.7   Recovering Deleted E-Mail via Backup Media 392
                 Q.6.3.8   Enforcement 392
                 Q.6.3.9   Definitions. 392
                 Q.6.3.10   Revision History 393
Q.7   Extranet Policy. 393
        Q.7.1   Purpose. 393
        Q.7.2   Scope 393
        Q.7.3   Policy 394
                 Q.7.3.1   Prerequisites 394
                 Q.7.3.2   Establishing Connectivity 395
                 Q.7.3.3   Modifying or Changing Connectivity and Access 395
                 Q.7.3.4   Terminating Access 395
        Q.7.4   Enforcement 396
        Q.7.5   Definitions 396
Q.8   Information Sensitivity Policy 396
        Q.8.1   Purpose. 396
        Q.8.2   Scope 397
        Q.8.3   Policy 397
        Q.8.4   Enforcement 400
        Q.8.5   Definitions 400
Q.9   Password Policy. 402
        Q.9.1   Overview 402
        Q.9.2   Purpose. 403
        Q.9.3   Scope 403
        Q.9.4   Policy 403
                 Q.9.4.1   General. 403
                 Q.9.4.2   Guidelines. 404
        Q.9.5   Enforcement 406
        Q.9.6   Definitions 406
Q.10   Remote Access Policy. 407
        Q.10.1   Purpose. 407
        Q.10.2   Scope 407
        Q.10.3   Policy 407
                 Q.10.3.1   General. 407
                 Q.10.3.2   Requirements. 408

Q.10.4 Enforcement 409
Q.10.5 Definitions 409
Q.11 Risk Assessment Policy 411
  Q.11.1 Purpose. 411
  Q.11.2 Scope 411
  Q.11.3 Policy 412
  Q.11.4 Risk Assessment Process 412
  Q.11.5 Enforcement 412
  Q.11.6 Definitions 412
Q.12 Router Security Policy. 412
  Q.12.1 Purpose. 412
  Q.12.2 Scope 413
  Q.12.3 Policy 413
  Q.12.4 Enforcement 413
  Q.12.5 Definitions 414
Q.13 Server Security Policy. 414
  Q.13.1 Purpose. 414
  Q.13.2 Scope 414
  Q.13.3 Policy 414
    Q.13.3.1 Ownership and Responsibilities 414
    Q.13.3.2 General Configuration Guidelines 415
    Q.13.3.3 Monitoring. 416
    Q.13.3.4 Compliance. 416
  Q.13.4 Enforcement 416
  Q.13.5 Definitions 416
Q.14 Virtual Private Network (VPN) Policy 417
  Q.14.1 Purpose. 417
  Q.14.2 Scope 417
  Q.14.3 Policy 417
  Q.14.4 Enforcement 418
  Q.14.5 Definitions 418
Q.15 Wireless Communication Policy 418
  Q.15.1 Purpose. 418
  Q.15.2 Scope 419
  Q.15.3 Policy 419
    Q.15.3.1 Register Access Points and Cards. 419
    Q.15.3.2 Approved Technology 419
    Q.15.3.3 VPN Encryption and Authentication. 419
    Q.15.3.4 Setting the SSID 419
  Q.15.4 Enforcement 419
  Q.15.5 Definitions 420
  Q.15.6 Revision History 420

Index **421**

TABLES

Chapter 1 Supply Chain Overview
    1.1 RFID Markets
    1.2 Tag Classes
    1.3 Three 64-Code Versions
Chapter 2 RFID Technology
    2.1 Tag Classes
    2.2 Defining Air Interface for RFID Devices in ISO/IEC 18000 Series
    2.3 Range of Intermic 915-MHz Materials in Feet
    2.4 Range of Intermic 2450-MHz Materials in Inches
    2.5 Matrics Read-Only Tags with One Antenna
    2.6 Matrics Read-Only Tags with Dual Antennas
    2.7 Frequency Bands in Multiples of Three
    2.8 RFID Types by Radio Frequency Ranges
    2.9 Global Areas by Frequency Ranges
Chapter 3 RFID Applications in Supply Chain Management
    3.1 Success Metrics
    3.2 EPC Partitions
Chapter 4 Storing and Retrieving Data
    4.1 Risks Associated with RFID/EPC Technology
    4.2 EPC Technology in Functional Areas
    4.3 Perceptions of Retail Product Benefits
    4.4 Speeds of 1-Mb File Transfer
Chapter 5 RFID Business Processes
    5.1 Software Checklist
    5.2 Application Adaptors
    5.3 Four-Stage Implementation Model
Appendix A Passive RFID Technology
    A.1 Intermec Range of 915-MHz Materials in Feet
    A.2 Intermec Range of 2450-MHz Materials in Inches
    A.3 RFID Partners
    A.4 Phillips Transponder IC Features

A.5 Phillips Smart Card Overview
A.6 Symbol Technologies Read-Only Tags with One Antenna
A.7 Symbol Technologies Read-Only Tags with Dual Antennas
A.8 TAGSys Products for Logistics and Industry
A.9 TAGSys ARIO RFID Reading Distance for Small and Large Modules
A.10 TAGSys Industry and Logistics Partner Products Sorted by Company
A.11 Athelia Industry and Logistics Products
A.12 Microraab Industry and Logistics Products
A.13 Northern Apex Industry and Logistics Products
A.14 TAGSYS Library Market Products
A.15 TAGSYS Partner Products for Library Market
A.16 TAGSYS for Textile Rental Industry Products
A.17 TAGSYS Partner Products for Textile Rental Industry
Appendix B Active RFID Technology
B.1 Eight Levels of Configurable Ranges
Appendix D RFID Middleware
D.1 RFID Middleware, Vendors, Firms, and Companies
Appendix H Supply Chain Execution Systems
H.1 Data Collection Advantage Options
Appendix I Enterprise Intelligence: WebFOCUS
I.1 Direct Data Interfaces
I.2 Platforms Supported
Appendix J Enterprise Databases
J.1 Features Supported by Windows CE
J.2 Processors Supported by Mobile PCs
J.3 Comparing J2ME Implementations
J.4 UNIX Platforms
J.5 Windows and .NET Bundle
J.6 Add-On Features
J.7 Maximum Limits
Appendix M Software Engineering Standards
M.1 IEEE Standards
M.2 ISO/IEC Standards
M.3 Related Standards
Appendix N Business Process Automation: IBM Products
N.1 IBM WebSphereR Adapters (Application)
N.2 IBM WebSphereR Technology Adapters

FIGURES

Chapter 1 Supply Chain Overview
    1.1 RFID versus Bar Technology
    1.2 Suppliers and Customer Interaction
    1.3 Supply Chain Management Conceptual Model
    1.4 RFID Technology Infrastructure
    1.5 Header Partition
    1.6 EPC Manager Partition
    1.7 Object Class Partition
    1.8 Serial Number Partition
Chapter 2 RFID Technology
    2.1 Object hierarchy
    2.2 RFID technology overview
Chapter 3 RFID Applications in Supply Chain Management
    3.1 Web services middleware
    3.2 RFID Web services
Chapter 4 Storing and Retrieving Data
    4.1 No Bandwidth Issues
    4.2 Possible Bandwidth Issues
    4.3 Dynamic Load Balancing
Chapter 5 RFID Business Processes
    5.1 Basic Multi-Layer RFID Business Process Model
    5.2 Adaptive Multi-Layer Business Process Model
    5.3 Visual Representation of the RFID Implementation Model
    5.4 Predictive Multi-Layer Business Process Model
    5.5 Waterfall Life-Cycle Model
    5.6 Incremental Life-Cycle Model
Chapter 6 RFID Security, Privacy, and Risk Assessment
    6.1 RFID Defense-in-Depth

PREFACE

It was the publisher's idea that I write *RFID in the Supply Chain: A Guide to Selection and Implementation*. Not only am I editor of *Enterprise Integration System, Second Edition Handbook* and author of *The Complete Book of Middleware*, I also had some innovative business process and project management ideas on improving the effectiveness of integrating enterprise systems with information on product traceability, the scope of which has been widened by the RFID technology mandates. In this book I applied them to both passive and active RFID technology in the supply chain.

This book starts with a discussion on the major paradigm shift in product traceability, which began with transitioning to RFID technology from barcode technology. This shift has contributed to the ability of the RFID technology to resolve tracking problems in a more effective and faster way, and has resulted in significant economic, operational, technological, and logistical impacts on supply chain infrastructures. It moves on to the discussion of economic feasibility of rolling out RFID with a focus on supply chain synchronization, customer privacy issues, security challenges, operational and IT challenges, logistical challenges, program management challenges, education and training, standard implementation challenges, and what lessons have been learned.

In response to the paradigm shift, the book addresses the RFID business processes (as discussed in Chapter 5) needed to analyze and resolve problems suppliers have faced when dealing with multiple customers, each with a different mandate policy and with their own set of suppliers. The external suppliers may have their own complex set of relationships with the customers. The customers, which both the originating suppliers and external suppliers deal with, may be the same or different. The customers and suppliers may have multiple systems that require the same RFID information.

Many top suppliers implemented RFID infrastructure in response to initial mandates from large customers such as Wal-Mart, the Department of

Defense, Target, Albertsons, and Best Buy in the United States, and the METRO Group in Germany. These customers mandated the suppliers provide their own RFID equipment and infrastructure and deliver RFID-tagged cases and pallets of items by January 1, 2005. Other large retailers provided their top suppliers with RFID equipment and technology to help them to get started. Some suppliers who did not receive the mandates or the RFID equipment from their customers decided to invest voluntarily in RFID technology rather than waiting for the "second" mandates and for opportunities to reap profits from RFID technology later on.

There are suppliers who have received the mandate from a customer, and the RFID equipment from another customer and have introduced or already introduced emerging RFID technologies into their companies without waiting for either a mandate or RFID equipment from a third customer. There are some suppliers who have received mandates from customers each requiring different RFID infrastructure implementation, depending on the type of item and package to be tagged.

There are suppliers who have implemented or planned to implement RFID technology in a portion of the supply chain with the intention of implementing it to the remaining part of the supply chain. This will happen when RFID technology gets more sophisticated, or the customers issue new mandates, or provide suppliers with more advanced RFID equipment.

The supplier–customer relationship in selecting and implementing the RFID technology can get very complex in the supply chain. Issues of what implementation approaches are used, how business process should be reengineered, and how organizational maturity affects reengineering projects should be addressed in one or more business process models I developed. They are (1) Multi-Layer RFID Business Process Models (basic, adaptive, and predictive), and (2) RFID business process life cycles including the adaptive linear feedback, and adaptive dynamic life-cycle models.

For background materials on business processes models, the reader should have a basic understanding of the supply chain overview as discussed in Chapter 1. Then the reader should move on to the next chapter on RFID selection guideline and implementation examples, such as speed of tag reads versus quality of computer inputs, and optimal tag location.

An understanding of the RFID application in Supply Chain Management as discussed in Chapter 3 should be acquired before the reader proceeds to the implementation of a business process model. The reader should be aware that the business and IT executives have different concerns on implementing the RFID applications. The business executives are concerned with customers and vendors and about the business processes that need to be adapted to SCM logistics in response to changing customers' demand for supplies and information about them. The IT executives, on the other hand, are concerned about what information systems and services can be implemented and shared across the organization.

These executives do not care which server is hosting a database operating system or even a particular database, whether it is spanning across the servers or restricted to a certain server. All they care is that they get the RFID data quickly to make important decisions. This means getting data in real-time from different database applications running on different platforms in a global network. For more details, read Chapter 4 on storing and retrieving data.

A security program needs to be in place before the RFID in the supply chain is implemented (see Chapter 6). The program should include security policies, procedures, standards, guidelines, and baselines. It also should include security awareness and incident handling, a compliance program, a risk assessment program, and a system accreditation program and types of attacks against RFID technology. More important is the integrated control management linked to the corporate strategy to ensure laws and regulations are followed through.

I wish to acknowledge the kindness of individuals, including the publisher, who suggested reference material and in many instances furnished it to me. I also wish to thank the editors and other individuals for considering my innovative ideas on selecting and implementing the RFID technology.

1

SUPPLY CHAIN OVERVIEW

This chapter begins with compelling reasons for transitioning to RFID technology from bar-code technology, and gives an overview of the RFID market. It moves on to the discussion of economic feasibility of rolling out RFID with a focus on supply chain synchronization, customer privacy issues, security challenges, operational and IT challenges, logistical challenges, program management challenges, education and training, standard implementation challenges, and what lessons have been learned. After this, we cover what RFID technology infrastructure is and should be, and then the future of Web-centric Supply Chain Management (SCM).

1.1 PARADIGM SHIFT IN PRODUCT TRACEABILITY

A major paradigm shift in product traceability began with transitioning to RFID technology from bar-code technology. It has contributed to the ability of the RFID technology to resolve tracking problems in a more effective and faster way, and has resulted in significant economic, operational, technological, and logistical impacts on supply chain infrastructures.

1.1.1 Transitioning to RFID Technology

This section gives a compelling reason for transitioning to RFID technology from bar-code technology. The advantages of the RFID technology over bar codes and other automated data collection technologies are reliability in heavy moisture, noisy, or dirty environments, and greater flexibility in reading the tags in a wider scanning area. We can attribute these advantages to the fact that radio frequency RFID technology has what bar-code technology does not.

In contrast to RFID tags (also known as transponders), in which a small radio-power microchip is embedded, bar-coded labels are pieces of paper with varying thicknesses of black lines. RFID readers (also known as inter-rogators) and bar-code scanners read the tags or labels affixed to items in four different ways.

The first difference is that a bar-code scanner reads printed labels containing identifying information about a product, case, or pallet. The second difference is that an RFID reader creates a radio-frequency field to activate multiple passive tags or to interrogate multiple active tags, whereas the bar scanner relies on the line of sight for communication with a single bar-coded label. Multiple RFID tags can be read all at once (e.g., up to 50 per second), whereas bar-coded labels can only be read one at a time. Some RFID tags automatically change data when the items are repackaged whereas bar-coded labels cannot change data at all. See Figure 1.1 on field areas.

Unlike bar-coded labels, the RFID tags can include information on where in the supply chain the packages, items, and pallets were physically moved, how they were tracked, and when the tracking took place at each point of

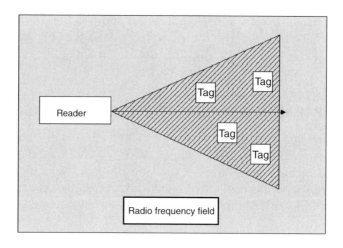

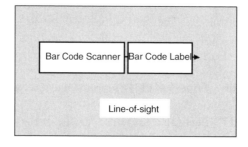

Figure 1.1   RFID versus Bar-Code Technology

the chain. RFID tags for a case hold a wider range of data about the product and the manufacturer than the tags for individual items. This saves time and cost of opening the case, taking out each product to read its label, putting back the products, and repacking the case, as the cases or pallets move from one end to another in the supply chain.

Tags work as long as they do not fall off cases or pallets, are not adversely affected by the offending materials, and are highly visible during transport. The antennas embedded in or attached to tags must be in proper orientation, as some cannot be easily reoriented to receive the reception of radio wave signals.

Unlike RFID tags, bar-coded labels are not programmable at all. Once the information is printed on the labels, it cannot be added to or be over-written. This means bar codes cannot be printed again to add new infor-mation. Even if the bar-coded labels are printed once, they are not able to contain information on what may have happened as the items physically moved from one point to another in the supply chain. The labels exclude tracking information and contain only the information about the product and manufacturer.

Programmable RFID tags, on the other hand, can track and record every movement, such as arrival, reshipment, and departure times at certain locations and on specified dates, and changes in environmental conditions, depending on the circuitry of the tags. The amount of data a tag can read depends on the memory size in the tag, and the frequency range for it.

An RFID tag with more advanced capabilities can be programmed to determine who can read certain parts of the data—not just the product and manufacturer—and what new information a user can write to the tag. It is almost like assigning user privileges to individuals or groups as to who can access what portion of a file or directory, who can receive and send alerts of various supply chain events, what level of data sensitivity can be assigned to users, groups, files, and directories, and how often the passwords need to be changed. Label programmability is another function that bar-code technology cannot do, as the information on the labels is limited to the product and manufacturer, and the programmer cannot add new informa-tion. The labels are printed once.

RFID technology comes in three flavors of frequency ranges: low, medium, and high. The tags with the lowest frequency range are passive with a very short reading range. Next in line are the tags with the middle frequency range that are also passive but reading range is not as short. Higher up in the scale of RFID technology is the active beacon RFID with longer reading range. Even higher are the two-way active tags.

All readers create a radio frequency field when they are turned on. When a reader detects passive tags, it activates them. These tags draw their power from the radio frequency field; they do not require battery power. Because they have no battery, the passive tags are smaller and lighter in weight than active tags. Some are as light as or even lighter than the bar-coded labels.

When active tags with battery power come into the field of a reader, the reader switches to the read mode and interrogates the tag. Although these tags are suitable for longer distance, they are more expensive than passive tags due to more complex circuitry of the tags and the battery's weight. Tag prices, however, will be less as the demand increases.

Passive RFID technology works well with individual and packaged items. Both passive and active RFID are used on conveyance units transporting and loading packaged items. Active RFID is applied to heavier items such as containers, pallets, and cases. Vehicles carrying these containers, pallets, and cases may be affixed with an active RFID tag at most times. In other words, passive RFID tags are more appropriate for smaller objects such as clothes, books, and other individual items and active RFID tags target larger objects such as the containers, pallets, and cases.

Another advantage of bar-coded labels is that they are readable regardless of what materials or ingredients are in the product or packaging and what materials are used to package the product. In contrast, RFID tags do not work with all material types; they work well as long as the packaging material and its contents do not contain offending materials, such as metal and liquid that can adversely affect the tag readability.

Ferrous metals are known to be the worst offenders. RFID and canned foods or soda bottles are not a good combination, although RFID has been used in some aspects of the food industry where the packaging and its contents do not have the offending material, such as labeling of plastic bags containing chicken. Economic alternatives to metal or metallic packaging, particularly where airtight storage is required, may not be feasible for smaller companies. Only very large companies may be able to absorb large overhead costs of researching alternative packaging schemes.

One way of getting around the problem with some offending packaging materials is to detune or attenuate the signals the tags emit. This can be done, however, in a very short reading range or other limited ways. Another way is to keep metallic content of the packaging material very low and place the tag away from the metallic content. The third way is to move the tag to another area of the product, case, or pallet away from the offending materials. For now, bar-coded cans requiring air tight storage (e.g., canned chicken soup) are here to stay until the time when alternatives to metallic packaging become available and marketable.

One issue with RFID technology is that the reader cannot communicate with a tag that is oriented perpendicular to the reader antenna. It is similar to the situation when you need to change the orientation of the antenna of your radio or TV to get better reception for a radio or TV station. You change the antenna's orientation again for other radio or TV stations when it receives poor reception of signals. This happens when you hear noise on your radio or see fuzzy images on your TV. This should not be a problem as the RFID-tagged items, cases, and pallets are not perpendicular to the antenna. The scanning area is much wider for the radio frequency field than for the bar-code counterpart.

The antenna in tags usually cannot be reoriented, either automatically or manually. When you place the products in a shopping cart in a random orientation, the reader may or may not be able to read all the tags in the cart. The antenna orientation in some tags may interfere with the orientation in other tags. When a shopper uses a reader to get information on all items in the cart, the information on some tags may not show up or may get distorted on a check-out computer screen. This means the tagged items in the shopping cart must be taken out on the check-out counter for proper alignment of the items' orientation.

Another issue is that even if the tagged items are placed in a proper orientation order in the cart to prevent signal interference, mobile RFID handheld readers (e.g., the shoppers) in close proximity to another may garble data while scanning the tags. The radio frequency field generated by one reader used to scan the items in one cart may overlap the field of another reader used to scan different items in another cart that happens to be in close proximity to the first cart.

To date, this problem is not significant, as there is not much opportunity for readers to interfere with one another. Mobile RFID handheld readers are expensive. As the demand for tags and mobile devices increases, RFID tags and readers will be cheaper to buy, making RFID more common in many areas of government, educational, and private sectors. Standards will be needed to allow the systems to share common radio frequency fields and bandwidths.

For this reason, RFID is more suited in manufacturing, retailing, and logistics supply chains where the readers are placed at strategic points in the supply chain such that one reader will not interfere with another reader while reading the items.

1.1.2 Tracking Problems

Several years ago, it was not at all uncommon to encounter problems of tracking certain items as they physically moved from one point to another in the supply chain. Some got lost, stolen, or misplaced during the transport. Others did not originally get shipped out due to a back order, an order cancellation, or a failure to pass quality inspection. Some got damaged or spoiled during their transport to final destinations. Others were found improperly configured or packaged or to have missing parts or inadequate data sensitivity labels when they arrived at a distribution center. A portion of the items lacked the required instructions on handling hazardous items or assembling nonhazardous parts in a complex unified whole. Some were subject to transportation constraints.

Sometimes the items got backlogged, backordered, recalled, or bull-whipped. Items that were cannibalized, discontinued, or returned were not properly recorded in the system. Excess, idle, and duplicate items piled up in the warehouse. Cases of counterfeited items went to security people but were not recorded in any RFID systems, as there were no reporting standards. Items were delivered too late when the customer ordered a similar item from another source that arrived more quickly. Then there were vapor items that did not exist at all. Problems of tracking over-shipped, under-shipped, user-dissatisfied, and wrong items occur almost on a daily basis.

Solving tracking problems without RFID technology requires a great deal of human intervention for one primary reason. Humans are needed to track down manually the information that cannot be added to the bar-coded labels. These labels are limited to product and manufacturer information. It is not possible at all to add new information to the labels, as the labels are printed once. On the other hand, RFID tags that can be read and written many times can track every movement, such as arrival, reshipment, and departure times at certain locations and on specified dates, and changes in environmental conditions, depending on the circuitry of the tags. The data can be changed as the RFID technology allows new information to be added to EPC in existing tags. The amount of data a tag can read depends on the memory size in the tag, the reading range, and the frequency range for it.

The human intervention needed to resolve tracking problems depends on the complexity of the interfaces among the Enterprise Application Integration (EAI), SCM, SRM, virtualized databases, legacy systems, wrap-systems, and various middle technologies. It is labor intensive to analyze a huge base of information about and in the files and databases, collect a portion of the needed data in a standard format, and analyze data in logging files, just to find out if items have been lost, damaged, or delivered, for example.

It is not possible to track physical movement of items in real-time without RFID technology. There is no way for the bar-coded labels to check with the databases in real-time if the items are delivered in terms of size, weight, kind, type, and other attributes and to send online alerts to the executives on possible order and shipment discrepancy.

If the information could not be found in any system, the alternative is for humans to place phone calls with key people, arrange meetings, or attend conferences locally or nationwide to get viewpoints from other stakeholders in the supply chain on resolving tracking problems. Papers acknowledging the receipt or delivery of items are not always available when there is no guideline to set the standards for recording and reporting the arrival and shipment of items, cases, and pallets.

The gaps in information are enormous in the RFID-less interconnected supply chains that now operate in the marketplace. Tracking the physical movements cannot keep up with the speed of getting the items to the market in response to the ever-increasing demand for supplies, especially on the national and global levels and with the speed of rapidly moving troops in the battlefields.

So how are some companies using the RFID technology to tackle problems encountered in pre-RFID days? Let's take a look at how Procter & Gamble in Spain used RFID technology to solve the problems with physical movements of items in a limited space. In 2001, the company experienced bottlenecks at the loading dock where forklift drivers would run of room on the dock for stacking pallets to be shipped. To make room, pallets were moved twice or production stopped for the loading dock to be cleared. To save time, the company moved the pallets to the trucks from the dock. However, these pallets were sometimes sent to the customers by mistake when they were supposed to reload back to the dock from the trucks. To increase throughput and eliminate costly mistakes, International Paper developed an RFID-based system to identify the pallets. This has allowed the plant to shift to direct loading, increase the speed of loading, and reduce the number of forklift truck drivers needed.

Although RFID technology better controls inventory loss and discrepancy though real-time visual asset tracking of the items, from item packaging in the chain to a customer's purchase of the items and sometimes beyond the point of sale, it does not account for tracking problems beyond the control of the supply chains, such as a supermarket clerk who, for instance, ordered wrong RFID products and did not properly record their status in an online database. The tags contain a whole lot of data, including how long they have not been used for a specified period of time. To counter these problems, the enterprise systems should consider updating supply information systems or integrating them with other EAI systems.

Yet tracking problems with RFID technology are far fewer than those without RFID technology. Solving problems with tracking RFID-tagged items can be done in real-time requiring less human intervention. More important are how humans interface with the RFID technology infrastructure and associated back-end systems and how humans can report inventory loss and discrepancy.

Also important are RFID Web services providing integration among heterogeneous systems (internal and external) and business-to-business communications, as long as Simple Object Access Protocol (SOAP) is fully interoperable between systems. With RFID Web services, a customer or even a supplier can synchronize data between SAP, PeopleSoft, Oracle,

Computer Associates, Baan, IBM, Microsoft, a CICS application, and a homegrown COBOL legacy system and the back-end systems for the RFID infrastructure.

To get the benefits of RFID technology, the organization must consider the people—the managers and the workers—behind the technology. This is particularly true for the technology's impact on organizational behavior, business processes, and ultimately consumer perception of the way the enterprise solves tracking problems and operates its SCM from one end to another.

To protect their image, large enterprises have striven to find better, more cost-effective, and more efficient ways of selecting and implementing RFID technology in supply chains. The enterprises must find ways to incorporate RFID into existing IT and logistics infrastructure without adversely affecting business processes at the enterprise level. Should they find it is necessary to change business processes to implement RFID technology, they must develop initiatives on organizational change management in the entire SCM life cycle, so people can accept the changes while maintaining high work productivity levels..

In September 2004, International Paper signed an agreement with Globe Ranger's iMotion Edgeware platform for RFID supply chain solutions. The company has recognized the importance of optimizing business processes using process and workflow management to deliver user-defined business rules for immediate visibility and exception alerts of the items being transformed and moved from one point to another in the supply chain. International Paper is number one in its industry for the second year.

Companies that offer Web services products include big names: IBM, Microsoft, Sun Microsystems, and Hewlett-Packard. All have incorporated Web services capabilities into their development tools and server software. Microsoft has incorporated XML into its .NET architecture. IBM offers Emerging Technologies Toolkit for Web Services and Autonomic Computing. It works with IBM WebSphere SDK for Web Services, WebSphere Application Service AE or AEs, or Apache Tomcat 4.06. HP Openview includes Web services management capabilities such as capturing Web services transactions and actively manages Web services over WSDL/SOAP. Sun offers the Java Web Services Developer Pack.

Shoppers will be able to point their scanner-equipped cell phones at a product and learn about its features from a RFID Web service on the manufacturer's Web site while they are in the store. Shopping will no longer involve long tedious lines at the check-out counter because items are scanned and billed to shoppers' preselected personal accounts as they leave the store. And smart shelves will tell manufacturers when to restock items so that consumers will always have access to the things they want to buy.

1.1.3 Supply Chain

In the days of supply chains without RFID technology, SCM, Supply Chain Planning (SCP), Supply Chain Execution (SEM), and Supply Chain Optimization (SCO) were discussed and debated in the growing global network of supply chains. Also discussed and debated were Supply Chain Visibility (SCV), Supply Chain Process Management (SCPM), Supply Chain Event Management (SCEM), and Supply Chain performance Management (SCpM). We have entered the age of supply chains with RFID technology.

Supply chain with RFID technology is a global network of integration hubs of suppliers and clients that create, track, and deliver RFID-tagged finished products manufactured from raw materials and semi-finished parts to multiple destinations from multiple supply sources. A supplier may serve as the primary or coordinating supplier or the secondary supplier depending on others for the raw materials and semi-finished product parts.

A client may be a retailer, wholesaler, warehouse manager, manufacturer, or even a senior executive. The client may serve as the primary or coordinating client or the secondary client depending on other clients to receive the finished products in the right quantities with the right specifications at the right time at the right locations.

Each player has a role in the physical movement of materials and products from one point to another in the supply chain. The supply chain, as a whole, involves all facilities, functions, and activities in manufacturing the product, coding basic information in RFID tags, reading and writing in real-time tracking activities of the product in the RFID technology infrastructure, and delivering the product to the customer who initiated the order. This infrastructure is integrated with back-end systems such as ERP, SCM, virtualized databases, legacy systems, and new wrap-up systems.

Figure 1.2 gives an example of how a supplier is related or coordinates with other suppliers in a hierarchy of different levels. It begins with a supply chain at level 0 receiving the semi-finished products from the two supply chains at level 1, one of which receives another semi-finished product from a third supply chain at level 2, that in turn gets raw materials from the fourth supply chain at level 3. The other supply chain at level 1 transports semi-finished products to the supply chain at level 0 and finished products to a customer at level 1.

The level 1 customer that bypasses the level 0 supply chain to get the finished products from the level 1 supply chain can deliver the products to customers at lower levels. One of these customers can receive a batch of finished products from the level 3 supply chain that also sends the semi-finished products to the level 0 supply chain.

Whereas the level 0 supply chain focuses on, say, consumer packaged goods, the supply chains at the other levels may focus on one of the three

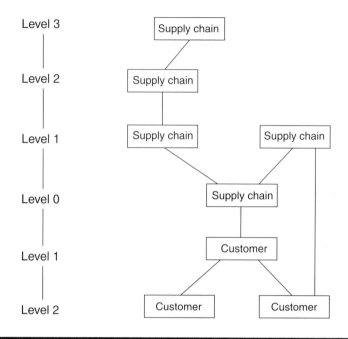

Figure 1.2 Supplier and Customer Interaction

models of consumer packaged goods, mass production or mass customization, or a combination of two or more models. The interaction of suppliers and customers gets more complex as the supply chains become more global and collaboratively communicate with one another over the Web in a standard way that spans interorganizational and geographical boundaries.

One way of handling the complex interaction between the customers and suppliers is to manage business processes of the supply chain interactions. This can be accomplished through SCM that involves business processes of planning, coordinating, integrating, managing, scheduling, controlling, producing, tracking, and delivering the product throughout the RFID technology infrastructure. SCM aims at increasing product visibility and speed via optimizing techniques used in the RFID infrastructure to read and write tracking information in real-time while integrating internal supply chain resources with external resources.

Business processes, however, are one part of the SCM strategy. Management techniques and product visibility make up the other parts of the SCM. To better visualize the SCM, we build a conceptual model of SCM as shown in Figure 1.3, which says that SCM starts with visibility and speed of the items as the base for the model. To make the base work, we move up to the next layer which focuses on techniques used in the RFID technology infrastructure. How the techniques are selected and chosen depends on

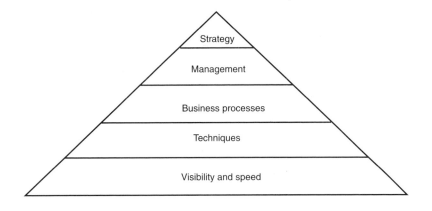

Figure 1.3   Supply Chain Management Conceptual Model

business processes in the third layer. What business processes to use and implement largely depends on what management philosophy and style is used to run the supply chain organization.

For instance, if the organization favors participative management, then we have a set of business processes that the participants and stakeholders are more inclined to accept collaboratively. On the other hand, if the organization chooses another type of management style, then we have a different set of business processes that may take a different set of participants and stakeholders a longer or shorter time to accept. Whatever the business processes and associated management philosophy are, the strategy must be spelled out clearly to help in translating the philosophy into business processes (and other actions to be taken by managers and other decision makers) in various parts of the supply chain organization.

Associated with SCM is the SCP [1] with RFID technology that involves the collaboration of demand and supply using the RFID infrastructure to track multiple products at various points in the supply chain for delivery of the items to satisfy the demands of multiple customers. It often is involved with planning network planning, capacity planning, demand planning, manufacturing resources, scheduling, distribution, and deployment resources.

More important is the forecasting of demand and supply changes while the executives are involved with managers on planning production. SCP is concerned with creating a set of suppliers in response to buyer forecasts, and with coordinating RFID technology assets to optimize the delivery of products in order to balance demand and supply at a given point of time.

Let's take a quick look at SCE, SCO, SCV, and SCPM. SCE [1] provides a framework of applications that enable procurement and supply of products through the RFID technology infrastructure integrated with the enterprise integration hub of SCM systems, ERP systems, virtualized databases, legacy systems,

Manufacturing Execution Systems (MESs), Warehouse Management Systems (WMSs), Transportation Management Systems (TMSs), and middleware technologies. The RFID infrastructure is a possible replacement for the Supply Chain Inventory Visibility (SCIV) system as the RFID tracking activities in real-time can contribute to increase the visibility of the products being tracked.

SCO with RFID technology aims at the best operating performance while optimizing schedules to reduce manufacturing and logistics bottlenecks in the supply chain. It employs the use of operations research techniques to maximize or minimize item tracking, production, and transportation capacity.

SCV is a means of capturing and analyzing the data from logistics activities to enhance the visibility of supply chains with RFID technology. The RFID infrastructure allows tracking and tracing inventory globally on a line-item level, as well as a case or pallet level. It also permits sending alerts when events deviate from expectations or unforeseen incidents.

The visibility into orders and shipments on a real-time basis as provided by the infrastructure and associated enterprise integration hubs gives enterprises advance knowledge of not only when the products will arrive, but also if a discrepancy occurs between the order and shipments of items, for example. The infrastructure would provide executives with timely and accurate information on the location, movement, status, and identity of units, personnel, equipment, material, and supplies in real-time. This would give the executives the capability to make changes in plans, policies, and procedures.

SCPM employs event and performance alerts to allow supply chain parties to detect, resolve, and solve problems in real-time. For instance, the RFID infrastructure triggers an event alert when a shipment has not left the supplier as scheduled and a performance event when the order fulfillment throughput has fallen below a certain threshold level.

Depending on the size of the RFID infrastructure and the organization, it may be feasible to split SCPM into SCEM and SCpM, each handling a large base of event triggers. This allows SCEM and SCpM to collect real-time data from multiple sources across multiple supply chains over heterogeneous systems. It also allows them to launch workflows and issue alerts to appropriate parties not only on the RFID infrastructure laptop screen but also via e-mail, phone, fax, personal digital assistant, or other devices.

Some vendors, however, specialize only in SCEM, whereas others have added SCEM components to their enterprise systems. Some vendors treat SCEM as one of the SCPM components. For others, SCPM is the SCEM. So, read the fine print about them.

1.2   RFID MARKETS

To get an idea of how RFID technology is used, the list shown in Table 1.1 is gleaned from TagSys' video demonstration at www.tagsys.com on each market category of supply items: waste, gas, food, containers, rentals,

Table 1.1   RFID Markets

Category	Data type	Processes	Benefits
Waste	Waste bin	As a waste bin is emptied and parked, information in the tag affixed to the bin is updated.	Waste collection is optimized. Bin parking is followed up.
Gas	Customer site	Cylinders are automatically filled. Movements of the cylinders to customer sites are fully traced and recorded in a tag on the cylinder. Inventories of empty cylinders are better controlled.	Gas cylinder losses are reduced. Delivery is more timely.
Food	Turnkey	At each step of the food transformation process, the label is updated and reused.	Losses are reduced. Inventory is better controlled. Quality control of the product is maintained at certain levels.
Containers	Content information of individual items	The processes of filling, cleaning, and maintaining a container to which a tag is affixed are automated. They are processed throughout the supply chain.	Labels are resistant to rough handling. Container flow and contents are better managed.
Video rentals	DVD/video CD cassette	The cassette is distributed while updating the database about the client and the rental type: traditional storefront video rental or DVD vending machine rentals. A tag is affixed to the cassette's package.	The tag is counterfeit-proof. Identification on the rented item is secured. Losses and thefts are reduced.

(continued)

Table 1.1   RFID Markets (Continued)

Category	Data type	Processes	Benefits
Animal ID	Cow	Data is updated throughout animal life cycle. Processes are automated and tracked throughout the slaughterhouse.	Animal feeding, medical follow-up, and proof of ownership are followed up.
Automotive	Car	Immediate access to vehicle information is provided, such as registration number, owner, insurance policy, shipping date, receiving date, and final destination.	Maintenance operations are better managed and controlled. Service and satisfaction are improved. Stolen cars can be rapidly be identified.
Maintenance and security	Fire extinguisher	Processes of tracking the product in the supply chain are automated.	Inventory of hazardous materials is very reliable. Maintenance of materials is better secured, and programmed not to alter data.

Source: Tagsys' video demonstration of RFID markets at www.tagsys.com.

animal identification, automotive, and maintenance/security. The process of attaching a tag to a supply item begins with entering the data into a tag via a computer and then attaching the tag to a product or a container. The tag must be positioned on the product or container so that it can be visible and at a certain distance between it and a reader. Each is assigned a unique identification number. A reader is portable, affixed to a vehicle window shield or installed at a control point.

The list also indicates how RFID technology automates the process of updating the label information while tracing the product, case, or container in a supply chain and what the benefits of automated processes are.

In Table 1.1, we mentioned that we can affix an RFID tag containing information about the contents of a container without opening it and viewing the products inside it. For some applications, we can use TagSys' RFID tunnel technology [2] to read the tags affixed to the items inside a container without opening it. To get this technology to work, we must first position RFID antennas and then connect them to an RFID reader (the TagSys Medio™ L200), and, in turn, link the reader to an information system. As all tags pass through the tunnel, they are simultaneously read either in bulk, or placed in containers, boxes, crates, or bags (e.g., laundry). A computer picks up tag ID numbers for display on the screen and then automatically updates the database [2], providing the speed of reader inputs is optimized or synchronized with the speed of a laptop and does not affect the tag readability.

Oracle chose TagSys RFID technology for its demonstration held during the World Economic Forum in Davos, Switzerland in January 2004. It used this technology to simulate retail applications in detecting counterfeited products, tracing and profiling products, and managing inventory.

1.3 ECONOMIC FEASIBILITY OF ROLLING OUT RFID

When conducting a study on economic feasibility of rolling out RFID, you must ensure that the risks have been mitigated to tolerable levels. Examples include no labor reduction, increased maintenance costs without data synchronization, inaccurate replenishment or reduction of out-of-stock, inaccurate pricing, and potential for increased transaction management costs.

Factors you should consider in your cost/benefit analyses include

- Supply chain optimization
- Customer privacy issues
- Security challenges
- Operational and IT challenges
- Logistical challenges
- Program management challenges
- Education and training
- Standard implementation challenges

Also important is how you calculate the ROI to determine the best potential return of various investment options. To implement RFID, net value present method-based ROI (also known as the time-value ROI) is a preferred method as the cash flows will most likely fluctuate from one year to another and the RFID technology and standards continue to evolve for faster product visibility and traceability due to improved business processes that the technology brings.

In addition to cash flow fluctuations, the time-value ROI is useful when the company makes additional capital expenditures after the project has started (e.g., a pilot study project to a full production project). This type of calculation is also useful when the company invests in building a large facility to accommodate the RFID infrastructure over a period of time; that is, investments do not occur at once. The choice of investment options depends on whether the company is mandated to implement RFID technology, the sophistication of the RFID technology the company needs to implement, and the company's dependencies in a complex network of multi-suppliers (e.g., first-level suppliers depend on the second-level suppliers, and so on).

1.3.1 Supply Chain Synchronization

The key to global supply chain synchronization is the global open standards for interoperable RFID technologies. The standards organizations contributing to the RFID standards are EPCglobal Inc., International Standards Organization (ISO), and the American National Standards Institute (ANSI). However, the nature of SCM networks makes the synchronization complex. The executives need to identify which players in the synchronization are leaders, challengers, or visionaries and which players are leading-edge or mainstream technology adopters.

The foundation of enabling synchronization is business process management as the basis for RFID visibility and traceability, business activity monitoring, analytics, and optimization. RFID business processes, as discussed in Chapter 6, are vital factors in reaching the goal of successful optimization of supply chain synchronization. In addition to implementation approaches and business process reengineering examples, Chapter 6 presents new approaches with adaptive and predictive multi-layer business process models, and briefly covers RFID business processes strategies by major RFID vendors to help you develop a strategy for your organization. The chapter explains how you can incorporate these processes into the supply chain systems and discusses the new adaptive dynamic and linear feedback life cycles.

1.3.2 Customer Privacy Issues

The costs of protecting privacy are far cheaper than the costs of lawsuits on the loss of privacy protection. One way of keeping the costs low is to develop a mechanism to deactivate the security function of the RFID tag while a self-check-out station scans the merchandise. This allows the customer to carry the merchandise outside the store even while walking in another radio frequency field generated by another RFID reader. If the tags are not properly deactivated, a war-driver can read and get the information from the RFID tags of purchased goods that a passerby carries in a shopping bag.

Let's take a look at a Gillette RFID tracking system at a Massachusetts Wal-Mart supermarket. It worked [3] but was eventually replaced with a new version because of privacy issues. The older tracking system sensed when a product was removed from the shelf. It then took a photograph of the shopper, compared to another snap taken when the product reached the check-out. The new system excludes the photography feature.

Another privacy issue that Dixon [3] has raised is what flashes up on a scanner as someone walks near the interrogator (especially the active interrogators that have a much wider scanning region that those of passive interrogators). The scanner could show

- Clothing origins
- Contents of materials
- Contents of briefcase or handbag
- Which credit cards being carried
- Linkage to RFIDs that identify the user of passport in suit pocket

The challenge is to ensure that privacy issues are not overlooked and consumer privacy is protected when rolling out RFID technology.

1.3.3 Security Challenges

War-walking is more bold than war-driving. War-walkers do not need a wireless device to find the RFID tags. With fake credentials or cards, they can bypass physical checks and find the system that uses RFID tags to monitor the movements of conference attendees. This is not a fiction. It actually happened in December 2003 at the WSIS Meetings at a conference center [4]. These crackers, or more likely the activists, did not like the idea of being monitored of where they were at the conference. They wanted to show that these tags raised loss of privacy issues without regard for physical security. This, however, is not the right way to handle loss of privacy issues.

Let's assume the cracker goes beyond finding the system. The cracker either runs away or removes the passive RFID tags from the objects, say, inside one case by sawing or etching the tags away. The cracker replaces them with the counterfeited tags, and reattaches the tag with original RFID data to the like objects in another case, all without being detected. This technique is known as lifting.

In another instance, a corporate spy walks around, scans the entire stock of a competing retail outlet, rewrites the tags of cheap products and replaces them with better product labels and even hides products in a metal-lined tag and replaces them with new tags on the shelf. Passive tags do not work very well when they come into contact with a metallic surface.

The challenge is to ensure that physical security is in place when rolling out RFID technology.

1.3.4 Operational and IT Challenges (Hardware, Software, System Compatibility, People Expertise)

Some challenges a Chief Technology Officer (CTO) faces are that governance structure of the company may not provide the IT staff the authority and support to do their jobs, the policy makers lack the vocabulary to communicate with various stakeholders, and the vision for the role of RFID technology in improving product traceability is lacking. The CTO also faces the challenges of rapid pace of technology change, inadequate funding, inadequate staffing, enterprise integration issues, and inadequate agreement on enforcement in standardization in equipment, software, procedures, and policies.

Also on the CTO's agenda are inadequate reviews and updates of standards, goods, policies, procedures, expectations, the lack of quality standards on adjustments in the speed of tags via software and hardware to improve the quality of input reads into laptops, and the interoperability problems among diverse platforms, software, and hardware although the interoperability standards are evolving. Added to the agenda are the lack of standards on the proximity of the antennas for active RFID technology, and the lack of standards on sharing the reading area by multi-readers, the emerging global EPCglobal standards more compatible with the ISO standards on RFID technology, and the issues of integrating unstructured data (e-mail, videos, and XML) with the RFID input reads.

1.3.5 Logistical Challenges

Setting up logistics of supply chains depends on how complex the vertical and horizontal the supply chain integration is, what business processes are used, what material management regulations the enterprise running the SCM system must comply with, and what type of enterprise the organization is. It depends on what information the customers are looking for, how fast they want the information, and how high the visibility of item movements they want.

It also depends on what material requirements the organization needs to get its SCM system to satisfy, such as make-to-order, engineer-to-order, make-to-stock, continuous replenishments, or seasonal replenishment. Some requirements are well suited for mass production whereas others fit into the mass customization category. The remaining portion may be a hybrid of both.

Also important is how serviceable material items to be returned should be handled for repair, overhaul, and maintenance and who should bear the costs of packing and transporting these items to the intended warehouses to accept these items for further processing.

Not to be overlooked is a model of organizational maturity. No matter how components are modularized, arranged, prioritized, and optimized, they may not work properly if the organization is not sufficiently mature to design, develop, and implement a SCM subsystem, say the SCM logistics system. To test for the maturity of the organization in incorporating RFID technology infrastructure into the logistics, we divide the system into five life stages and then assess each stage if it meets certain criteria before we proceed to the higher-level stage. The first stage indicates the organization is immature. As we proceed to the next higher level, the organization becomes more mature until its reaches maturity in the final stage. This model has five stages: pilot studies, logistics projects, organizational operations, logistics visibility, and logistics optimization. Chapter 4, "RFID Applications in SCM" gives more details.

1.3.6 Program Management Challenges

An enterprise should create an RFID Program Management Office (PMO) before developing RFID strategies. This office should by run by a person who can oversee the RFID selection and implementation program and have the ability to give a strategic option of building the RFID infrastructure and connect with the legacy systems via middleware platforms. This person should have the ability to integrate projects throughout the organization and achieve the desirable ROI in the long run. More important, a checklist of the following activities should be developed to determine the degree of involvement by the PMO to gauge the potential success of the RFID implementation program.

- RFID strategic plan for the entire organization
- Project plan
- Security and consumer privacy issues.
- Budget: initial, performance, and changes
- Staffing
- Methodologies and processes
- Training programs
- Funding
- Standards
- Risk management

Other activities can be added as needed, such as:

- Project dependencies
- Change management
- Checklists for project activities
- Constraints
- Enterprise and IT integration issues
- Post implementation review
- Configuration management
- Business process reengineering

1.3.7 Education and Training

This book partially fills the need for education and training in RFID technology by providing C-level executives and senior managers with selection guideline criteria on RFID devices and middleware to connect the RFID infrastructure with enterprise legacy systems. It is not a supplement to the

CompTIA RFID+ certification that addresses the shortage of RFID technical skills and knowledge needed for successful implementation of the technology in the areas of (1) installation, configuration, and maintenance of RFID hardware and device software; (2) site surveys and site analysis; and (3) tag selection, placement, and testing. The text does not cover the challenges of enterprise integration via middleware between the RFID infrastructure and legacy systems. The challenge is to provide education and training for C-level executives and senior managers on vendor-neutral selection and implementation of RFID technology.

1.3.8 Standard Implementation Challenges

Standards are critical for many RFID applications in supply chains. Much work has been done to develop standards for different RFID frequencies and applications. RFID standards—existing and proposed—fall into these types:

- *Air interface protocol:* the way the tags and readers communicate
- *Data content:* the way data is organized or formatted
- *Conformance:* ways to test that products meet the standard
- *Applications:* how standards are used on shipping labels

The trend is toward single global standards. For instance, in the air interface protocol category, EPCglobal developed a second-generation protocol (Gen2), which is not backward-compatible with either Class 1 or Class 0, as a global standard that is more closely aligned with ISO standards. Gen 2 was approved in December 2004. RFID vendors that had worked on the ISO UHF standard also worked on Gen 2.

The higher the EPCglobal class standards that the vendors can implement and the more global they are, the vendors who were not given the mandates are more willing to implement RFID technology as their products may need to be interfaced with products from other vendors for operational efficiency. The challenge is to develop global standards for RFID technology in four categories: air interface, data content, conformance, and applications.

1.3.9 Lessons Learned

In this section, we talk about lessons learned from Iraq, Wal-Mart, International Paper, and Procter & Gamble. The latter three were sponsors of the Auto ID Center.

1.3.9.1 Iraq: Asset Visibility

Prior to the mandate from the U.S. Department of Defense (DoD) on passive RFID tags for logistical items by 2005, RFID tags were underutilized within the United States for items shipped to the theater during the Operation Iraqi Freedom (OIF). Reasons for the under-utilization were that users did not understand how passive RFID technology worked, combat commanders did not require items with RFID tags, and the tag failed because it got separated from a pallet or damaged, or the batteries stopped working during the transit overseas and in Iraq.

The handler did not have the proper training to use the interrogator thinking it could be used just like a bar-code reader. The tag was not visible in the in-transit visibility (IVT) system, as the interrogator was not available or got misplaced at a location to scan the tag. Another reason was that the interrogator malfunctioned due to insufficient power, inability to connect, or mechanical failure.

In a report, the U.S. GAO [5] gives several reasons. Hundreds of material containers were backlogged at distribution points because of identification and transportation problems and inadequate asset visibility. The difference between material shipped to Army forces in the region and material they received resulted in accounting discrepancies in terms of billion dollars. Late fees were incurred on leased or lost shipping containers because of distribution chokepoints or losses.

Usable vehicles were stripped because of lack of spare parts or poor container identification. Products and product requests were duplicated because of bad management and accounting procedures and inadequate container identification. Supplies were not configured to meet Army unit requirements. Communications infrastructure was inadequate.

Theater distribution capability was insufficient and ineffective. The distribution of supplies was also delayed because cargo arriving in shipping containers and pallets had to be separated and repacked several times for delivery to multiple units in different locations. The U.S. DoD's lack of an effective process for prioritizing cargo for delivery precluded the effective use of scarce theater transportation assets. Assets got lost or taken by unauthorized personnel due to insufficient physical security at distribution points.

Other factors that may have contributed to the logistics support problems include the following.

- *Poor Asset Visibility.* DoD did not have adequate visibility over all equipment and supplies transported to, within, and from the theater of operations in support of OIF. For example, although the U.S. Central Command issued a policy requiring, whenever feasible, the use of RFID tags to track assets shipped to and within the theater, these tags were not used in a uniform and consistent manner. In addition, units operating in the theater did not have adequate access to, or could not fully use, DoD's logistics and asset visibility systems in order to track equipment and supplies because these systems were not fully interoperable and capable of exchanging information or transmitting data over required distances. Bandwidth and communications infrastructure were not adequate to allow access to asset visibility and other logistics information systems.

■ *Insufficient and Ineffective Theater Distribution Capability.* DoD did not have a sufficient distribution capability in the theater to effectively manage and transport the large amount of supplies and equipment deployed during OIF. For example, the distribution of supplies to forward units was delayed because adequate transportation assets, such as cargo trucks and material handling equipment, were not available within the theater of operations. The distribution of supplies was also delayed because cargo arriving in shipping containers and pallets had to be separated and repackaged several times for delivery to multiple units in different locations. DoD's lack of an effective process for prioritizing cargo for delivery precluded the effective use of scarce theater transportation assets.

■ *Failure to Apply "Lessons Learned" from Prior Operations.* The failure to effectively apply lessons learned from Operations Desert Shield and Desert Storm and other military operations may have contributed to the logistics support problems encountered during OIF. GAO's prior reports, as well as DoD and military service after-action reports and other studies of prior military operations, have documented some of the same problems that appear to be occurring in Operation Iraqi Freedom (OIF).

■ *Shortages of Spare or Repair Parts.* At times there were shortages of some spares or repair parts needed by deployed forces. Military personnel noted shortages of items such as tires, tank track, helicopter spare parts, and radio batteries. As a result, units resorted to cannibalizing vehicles or circumventing normal supply channels to keep equipment in ready condition.

■ *Inadequate Configurations.* Army prepositioned equipment used for OIF was not adequately configured to match unit needs. For example, parts inventories contained in the prepositioned stocks were not sufficient to meet the needs of the units that relied on them.

■ *Ineffective Logistics Support.* DoD contractors used for logistics support during OIF were not always effective. For example, we were told that some commercial shippers were unable to provide "door-to-door" delivery of supplies to units in the theater, as was required by their contracts.

■ *Inadequate Physical Security.* Physical security at ports and other distribution points in the theater was not always adequate to protect assets from being lost or taken by unauthorized personnel. For example, Army officials noted cases where vehicles and expensive communications and computer equipment had been lost from various distribution points in Kuwait.

Lesson learned: Solve logistics problems by applying "lessons learned" from this and prior operations, including asset visibility, spare and repair parts availability, and physical security.

1.3.9.2   Wal-Mart: Implementation Training

In late Spring 2004, Wal-Mart appeared to be cutting back on the mandate that all its suppliers comply with RFID tracking of cases and pallets by the beginning of 2005. Few suppliers had the experience in implementing RFID technology. Many had just the basic understanding of this technology and had been working on the issues. The rest were just starting out and needed time to learn technologies. Prior to its mandate, Wal-Mart apparently did not send out a survey to its suppliers to determine its readiness for RFID implementation, and appropriateness of its testing facility and provide or recommend RFID implementation training for those who needed it. Wal-Mart just gave the mandate without ever providing RFID technologies to the suppliers to help them get started.

Lesson learned: Consider supplier's readiness for RFID implementation.

1.3.9.3   International Paper: Business Processes

In September 2004, International Paper (www.internationalpaper.com) signed an agreement with Globe Ranger's iMotion Edgeware platform for RFID supply chain solutions. The company has recognized the importance of optimizing business processes using process and workflow management to deliver user-defined business rules for immediate visibility and exception alerts. International Paper is number one in its industry for the second year.

Lesson learned: Consider business processes in selecting and implementing RFID technologies.

1.3.9.4   Procter & Gamble: Docking Loading Throughput

In 2001, Procter & Gamble (P&G, www.pg.com) in Spain experienced bottlenecks at the loading dock where forklift drivers would run out of room on the dock for stacking pallets to be shipped. To make room, pallets were moved twice or production stopped for the loading dock to be cleared. To save time, the company moved the pallets to the trucks from the dock. However, these pallets were sometimes sent to the customers by mistake when they were supposed to reload back to the dock from the trucks.

To increase throughput and eliminate costly mistakes, P&G developed an RFID-based system to identify the pallets. This has allowed the plant to shift to direct loading, increase the speed of loading, and reduce the number of forklift truck drivers needed.

Lesson learned: Eliminate the costly mistake of delivering the pallets to the wrong distributors and customers.

1.4 RFID TECHNOLOGY INFRASTRUCTURE

This section talks about the complete structural arrangement supporting RFID technology. Electronic Product Code (EPC) Network model includes the following infrastructural elements:

- Tag
- Tag reader
- EPC
- Savant server
- Object Name Service (ONS)
- EPC Information Service, formerly called Physical Markup Language (PML)

As shown in Figure 1.4, the infrastructure begins with a laptop or desktop using Savant software to turn itself into a Savant server as the nervous network gateway (LAN) for tags, readers, an ONS server, and EPC middleware/application servers.

The Savant server interacts with different types of readers, collects data in a standard format, monitors events, and manages tasks of getting, expanding, filtering, logging data, and requesting ONS and PML activities. The information the Savant collects for each tag includes EPC of the tag read, EPC of the reader scanning the tag, time stamp of the reading, and temperature or location position.

We expect an increase in manufacturers, retailers, logisticians, and suppliers adopting EPC Network as the representative of the RFID technology infrastructure when EPCglobal sets the standards for Class 2 tags (rewritable passive tags) [6]. These tags carry more memory and data than Class 0 tags which are factory programmable, Class 1 tags that can be programmed by the retailer or supplier, and Class 1, v2 tags that have best features of the first two tag classes. EPCglobal has been working with manufacturers on passive and active tag standards beyond Class 2, and has continued its efforts to build a protocol based on synchronizing and incorporating ISO data standard.

1.4.1 Open Architecture: Savant Server

Savant software can turn a laptop or a desktop computer into a server. One of the things the software does is that it fixes incorrect or duplicate data gathered from readers before it stores and forwards data to any point of the chain. It allows customized filters to smooth data, providing the capability

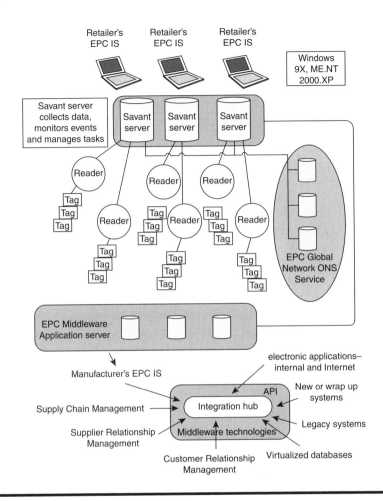

Figure 1.4   RFID Technology Infrastructure

to log data into a database or remote servers, monitors for event changes, and sends alerts to its intended recipients.

The Savants then forward data to the ERP systems, including SCM and Supply Relationship Management (SRM), virtualized databases, and SAP via middleware technologies through a full-time connection to the readers, or synchronizing data on an "as needed" basis. The Savant's real-time in memory database (RIED) structure is used to store event information, support SQL queries, and take "snapshots" of the database at different times.

Savant software works with Windows 9X, NE, NT, 2000, and XP and can be downloaded at no cost from Savant Web Server's Web site at http://savant.sourceforge.net/. The original version of this software running on distributed servers was designed by the Auto-ID Center for its EPC network infrastructure. For the software to work properly, the Internet Information Services (IIS), at least, must be turned off.

The Savant server can be customized to receive all the different data communications among readers, RS232, RS485, TCP/IP, and Ethernet. You can connect mini-servers to communicate with the main Savant server or mini-Savants. These mini-servers can convert all data signals to an Ethernet that has the ability to multiplex 900 readers or more—passive and active—at a time. The time elapsing between the client request and the server response is extremely fast and can serve over 100 simultaneous connections. These two features allow a reader to scan multiple tags at one time in a second or two.

Sun's version of Savant is available for managing the flow of RFID information between the readers of RFID tags and the back-end enterprise system. It contains reader failover features to allow the RFID information to continue to flow to its intended destination. Resource [7] gives details on Sun's EPC Networking Architecture.

ConnecTerra is another company that offers a middleware RFTagAware 1.0, the first version of its EPC Savant and reader management software. This software provides an Application Programming Interface (API) for data filtering and integration in various formats with enterprise software. RFTagAware also monitors the health of remote readers, upgrades software, runs diagnostics, and performs other maintenance operations.

1.4.2 Major Vendor Servers

When a Savant server reaches its disk capacity limit, the organization needs to consider RFID servers from major vendors, such as IBM, Oracle, and MS SQL Server.

Some issues to be considered are whether the organization should treat RFID technology as one of the sensor-based services or it should focus on a RFID database middleware that collects and interprets RFID events and escalates them to critical operational events or both. Oracle and IBM are examples of each, respectively.

Oracle Sensor-Based Services [8], an RFID-ready Oracle Warehouse Management was demonstrated at the RFID Journal Live! Conference in late March 2004. Based on Oracle Database 10g, Oracle Application Server 10g, Oracle Enterprise Manager 10g, and Oracle E-Business Suite 11i, Oracle Sensor-Based Services enable companies to integrate sensor-based information into their enterprise systems to achieve supply chain visibility in real-time.

Making up the Sensor-Based Services are primarily two middleware components: the Compliance Package and RFID Pilot Kit. The Compliance component allows companies to address the specific and unique reporting requirements coming down from major retailers and the U.S. Department of Defense. The Pilot Kit is more suited for smaller companies that only need drivers for the major RFID readers, and some reporting and analytic tools to process RFID data.

Oracle Sensor-Based Services provide capabilities to capture, manage, analyze, access, and respond to data from sensors such as RFID, location, and temperature. It allows users to query and audit specific events occurring in the system, and to receive alerts on recalls of a bad batch of products.

IBM, known for providing the overall systems integration for RFID at the METRO Group, is integrating RFID with DB2 Information Integrator for Content. It provides structured enterprise information via connectors to DB2 relational databases. The IBM product is made of three different elements: Devices, WebSphere RFID Premises Server, and a WebSphere integration server.

Readers, scanners, and printers are embedded with the first element, WebSphere RFID Device Infrastructure. They also include other sensor devices that come with RFID, such as temperature. The second element, IBM WebSphere RFID Premises Services is a middleware product that interprets RFID events to detect operational events, such as the sudden change in temperature of perishable products while being transported in a vehicle. The third element is an IBM integration server, such as WebSphere Business Integration Server or Server Foundation, unlike Oracle that offers an application server and E-Business Suite applications for a variety of data types across the enterprise.

As of January 2005, IBM has planned for a SAP-specific database, that is, DB2 specifically tailored to run SAP applications (e.g., DB2 for SAP). So what is the relationship between Oracle and IBM as a result of the PeopleSoft acquisition? Because PeopleSoft includes J.D. Edwards, with a strong legacy of applications running on IBM's iSeries (or AS/400) platforms, even though the bulk of PeopleSoft applications run on Oracle databases, Oracle has made commitments to support customers running Oracle/Peoplesoft wares on IBM middleware and databases. Improving Oracle's rapport with IBM is a number one priority.

1.4.3 Tags

RFID tags for a case hold a wider range of data about the product and the manufacturer than the tags for individual items. This saves time and cost of opening the case, taking out each product to read its label, putting back the products, and repacking the case, as the cases or pallets move from one end to another in the supply chain. The amount of data a tag can read depends on the memory size in the tag, the frequency range for it, and the tag class it is assigned.. Tags work as long as they do not fall off cases or pallets, are not affected by the offending materials, and are highly visible during the transport.

When active tags with battery power come into the field of a reader, the reader switches to the read mode and interrogates the tag. Although these tags are suitable for longer distance, they are more expensive than passive tags due to more complex circuitry of the tags and the battery's weight.

However, RFID tags do not work with all material types. They work well as long as the packaging material and its contents do not contain offending materials, such as metal, liquid, and dense materials (frozen meat and chicken parts) that can adversely affect the tag readability. Readers will also have a hard time detecting tags that are near the nylon conveyor belts. The frozen meat and chicken parts will need to be packaged in plastic bags to which the tags can be affixed. The tags will need to be repositioned on bottles containing liquid, so that a tag would be optimally located (e.g., further away) on the dishwashing bottle from the liquid.

To distinguish tag types from each other, EPCglobal has established five tag classes to indicate capabilities a tag can perform as indicated in Table 1.2. For instance, Class 0 tags are factory programmable. The EPC number is encoded onto those tags during manufacture and can be read by a reader. Class 1 tags can be programmed by the retailer and supplier. They are manufactured without the EPC number which can be encoded onto the tag later in the field (i.e., by retailer and supplier).

The Class 3 tags have the Class 2 capabilities plus a power source to provide increased range or advanced functionality. The Class 4 tags have the Class 3 capabilities plus active communication and the ability to communicate with other active tags. The Class 5 tags have the Class 4 capabilities plus the ability to communicate with passive tags as well.

Not mentioned in the table are the Class 1, Gen. 2 tags which take into account the interoperability issues between Class 0 and Class 1 tags. It is not possible for the retailer or supplier to duplicate the EPC number in Class 0

Table 1.2 Tag Classes

EPC tag class	Tag class capabilities
Class 0	Read only (i.e., the EPC number is encoded onto the tag during manufacture and can be read by a reader)
Class 1	Read, write once (i.e., tags are manufactured without the EPC number which can be encoded onto the tag later in the field)
Class 2	Read, write many times
Class 3	Class 2 capabilities plus a power source to provide increased range or advanced functionality
Class 4	Class 3 capabilities plus active communication and the ability to communicate with other active tags
Class 5	Class 4 capabilities plus the ability to communicate with passive tags as well

Source: *Hardware Program Configuration*, EPCglobal, 2004 at www.epcglobalinc.com.

tags in Class 1 tags; that is, the EPC number in Class 0 tags is not transferable to Class 1 tags. Generation 2 consolidates multiple protocols specified in Generation 1 as a single protocol.

Obviously the Class 0 through Class 2 tags are passive communication types and Class 3 tags are semi-passive types which are the passive tags with a power source. The Class 4 and Class 5 are active communication types.

To sum it up, the complexity of an EPC tag depends on the functionality of the tag, how it communicates with the readers and other devices, and whether it has a power source. Increasing the complexity of tags also increases the cost. Tags with advanced functions require more expensive microchips, and tags with a power source require a battery.

1.4.4 Antennas

Of importance to antennas are orientation, position, proximity, and reading zone. All are related to one another. None can be isolated without considering the other two. Chip antenna is not the same as the reader or conveyor antenna. If the vendor talks about an antenna, you may need to double-check to which antenna type the vendor is referring.

For instance, read-only RFID tags from Matrics (now known as Symbol Technologies) that come preprogrammed with customer-supplied EPC codes are available with one or two antennas. These tags have the read rate of up to 1000 tags per second and long read range of up to 30 feet. Read-only tags with one antenna are available in five types (see Chapter 2, "RFID Technology"). Each tag type indicates what materials it can be applied to, in what forms are available, and what the maximum reading distance is.

The read-only tags with one antenna of general-use type work best with general-purpose use on plastic, corrugated cardboard, bagtag, and plastic. They are in the form of inlay, adhesive inlay, and label. Next in line are rubber encapsulated and UV-protected glass tags that have reading ranges of 15 feet for metal, and glass and windshield, respectively. The glass bottle and concrete tags have the lowest reading ranges.

The read-only tags with dual antennas can be read from any orientation and are available in three types (see Chapter 2). Each type indicates what materials it can be applied to, what forms are available, and what the maximum reading distance is. The smaller the tag, the more likely it is limited to one antenna.

The tags (generally passive) with one antenna must be in proper orientation, as some cannot be easily reoriented to receive adequate reception of radio wave signals. The antenna in tags usually cannot be oriented as you can do with the TV antenna to get better reception for a channel. When you place the products in a shopping cart in a random orientation given the restriction that the antenna cannot be reoriented, the reader may or may not be able to read all the tags in the cart. The antenna orientation in some tags may interfere with the orientation in other tags. When a shopper uses a reader to get the information on all items in the cart, the information on some tags may not show up or may get distorted on a check-out computer screen. This means the tagged items in the shopping cart must be taken out on the check-out counter for proper alignment of the items' orientation.

Even if the tagged items are placed in a proper orientation order in the cart to prevent signal interference, mobile RFID handheld readers (e.g., the shoppers) in close proximity to another may garble data while scanning the tags. The radio frequency field generated by one reader used to scan the items in one cart may overlap the field of another reader used to scan different items in a second cart that happens to be in close proximity to the first cart.

For active tags, the reader cannot communicate with a tag that is oriented perpendicular to the reader antenna. A minimum of one antenna must be located in one zone. Although several antennas enable more accurate tag positioning, improper positioning due to reflections from walls and equipment can adversely affect the transmission from the batteries. The tags that are not located in the correct horizontal or vertical levels in buildings also affect the transmission quality.

Let's look at how Canus resolved the antenna problem. The Canus docking door allowed only three antennas to be set up. It found the third antenna did not allow enough reading area. Adjustments were made to this antenna by changing its orientation and position to provide a greater reading area for the antenna. A fourth antenna was added to ensure that a tag can be read regardless of its location on the pallet.

In sum, the antenna, orientation, position, proximity, and reading area as well as tag placement are important to ensure optimal reads provided, for instance, the tags are not attached or near the offending materials, and the speed of tags does not affect the quality of input reads into a laptop.

1.4.5 Readers

Readers come in four types: handheld, vehicle-mount, post-mount, and hybrid. The first three are dedicated to reading of the tags, active or passive. The fourth type has the active/passive mode allowing it to switch from the passive to active mode and vice versa. Both handheld and hybrid readers are more expensive than the vehicle-mount and post-mount. Next generation readers are expected to have less power consumption and fewer voltage requirements.

Passive RFID readers create a radio frequency field when they are turned on. When a reader detects passive tags, it activates them. These tags draw their power from the radio frequency field; they do not require battery power. Because they have no battery, the passive tags are smaller and lighter in weight than active tags. Some are as light or even lighter than the bar-coded labels.

When the active tags with power come into the reader's field, the reader switches to the read mode and interrogates the tag. Although these tags are suitable for longer distance, they are more expensive than passive tags due to more complex circuitry of the tags, and the battery's weight. Tag prices, however, will be less as the demand increases.

The proximity of the RFID-tagged items, cases, and pallets to the vehicle-mounted or post-mounted readers is predetermined for input reads optimization. The proximity of the RFID-tagged items, cases, or pallets to a mobile RFID reader can vary if the reader is within the acceptable reading zone. If the proximity of this reader is too close to the RFID-tagged items, say, in a shopping cart, collisions may occur, as standards to share common radio frequency fields and bandwidths are either unavailable or not officially approved for industrial application. For this reason, RFID is more suited in manufacturing, retailing, and logistics supply chain where the readers are placed at strategic points in the supply chain such that one reader will not interfere with another reader while reading the items.

1.4.6 Electronic Product Code

So, what does an EPC look like? An EPC is a unique 96-bit or 64-bit number embedded onto an individual RFID tag. It divides the information into four partitions in respective order:

- Header
- EPC Manager
- Object Class
- Serial Number

The first two are assigned by EPCglobal and the last two by EPC Manager [9]. Each partition is assigned a range of bits and separated with a dot something like this:

```
01.0000A13.0005E.000158DC0
```

As shown in the first highlighted portion of the code in Figure 1.5, the Header partition identifies the EPC's version number and defines the number, type, and length of all subsequent data partitions. Particularly for the 64-bit version, the Header partition specifies how the EPC coding scheme should be expanded, changed, or modified [10].

The second highlighted portion of the code in Figure 1.6 is the EPC Manager partition. It is concerned with the name of the enterprise, such as the name of the manufacturer. Your company reference number in your bar code should be consistent with what you would use in your EPC Manager Number.

In Figure 1.7, the third highlighted portion is the Object Class partition. It refers to the class of product, such as the manufacturer's laser paper item of certain brightness, weight, color, and number of sheets.

```
01.0000A13. 0005E.000158DC0

EPC version number 01
```

Figure 1.5   Header Partition

```
01.0000A13. 0005E.000158DC0

Manufacturer's name
(Office Paper Supply, Inc.)
```

Figure 1.6   EPC Manager Partition

```
01.0000A13. 0005E.000158DC0

Class of product, usually the
stock keeping number (SKU)
Laser paper
```

Figure 1.7   Object Class Partition

```
01.0000A13. 0005E.000158DC0

Serial number unique
to the item
```

Figure 1.8   Serial Number Partition

Table 1.3 Three 64-Code Versions

Partition	Version 1	Version 2	Version 3
Manager numbers	Few	Many	Few
Object types	Many	Few	Few
Serial numbers	Many	Few	Many

In Figure 1.8, the fourth partition is the serial number unique to the item.

The 96-bit EPC provides unique identifiers for 268 million companies. Each company can have 16 million object classes, with 68 billion serial numbers in each class. Because we do not need so many serial numbers, a 64-bit code, proposed by the Auto-ID Center (now EPC Global), has been used to help keep down the price of RFID chips. It costs somewhat more to encode additional bits on the RFID tags. Although the 64-bit code seems to be a good way to lower the costs, it may not "meet all the requirements of manager, object and serial numbers" [10]. To get around this problem you would need multiple versions of the compact version, as shown in Table 1.3.

Versions 1 and 3 are more appropriate for a single organization and Version 2 is better suited for a large global organization. The single organization may have many object types and serial numbers. Not shown in the table is a possible version for a single organization with few object types and many serial numbers.

When RFID technology matures and the increased demand lowers the costs of implementing the technology, we will see the 96-bit code for more items, cases, and pallets, as it may be advantageous to encode additional information about the product. In the years to come, we may see a 128-bit code for all items around the world only if a new technology will help to keep down the costs of encoding many bits on electronic tags. How this code will interface with IPv6 which also has an identifier length of 128 bits in the world of grid computing is a good question.

1.4.7 Object Name Service

ONS is an automated networking service similar to the Domain Name Service (DNS). What DNS does is that it directs a computer's Web browser to the correct Web server for the Web site an Internet user attempts to access. DNS is an Internet service that translates domain names that we can easily remember (www.yourdomain.com) into IP addresses (e.g., 134.137.234.35). Every time we use a domain name, a DNS service must translate the name into the corresponding IP address. The DNS system is its own network. If one DNS server does not know how to translate a particular domain name, it asks another one, and so on, until the correct IP address is returned.

If you are using a modem under Windows XP Professional running the Savant Server, you will find that DNS has been automatically assigned for you by default. If you are using a network rather than a modem and find that your network does not support automatic IP address and DNS server assignment, you will need to ask your network administrator for appropriate IP server address.

The following is an example of how to set up a typical ONS query using DNS for looking up information about an EPC. The query and response formats must adhere to the DNS standards, meaning that the EPC will be converted to a domain name and the results must be a valid DNS Resource Record. The following steps describe a typical ONS query that helps resolving EPC to a URL [11].

Step 1. A sequence of bits containing an EPC is read from an RFID tag:

```
(01 00000000000000000000010 00000000000011000
00000000000000110010000)
```

Step 2. The reader sends that sequence of bits to a local Savant server.
Step 3. That local Savant server converts the bit sequence into the Uniform Resource Identifier (URI) Form and sends it to the local ONS server for resolution:

```
urn:epc:1.2.24.400
```

Step 4. The ONS server converts the URI form into a domain name and issues a DNS query:

```
24.2.1.onsroot.org
```

Step 5. The DNS infrastructure returns a series of answers that contain Uniform Resource Locators (URLs) that point to an EPC Information Service (EPCIS) Server.
Step 6. The local ONS strips the URL from the DNS record and presents it back to the local Savant server:

```
http://pml.ourexample.com/ pml-wsdl.xml.
```

Step 7. The local server contacts the correct PML server found in the URL for the EPC in question.

1.4.8 EPC Information Service

EPC Information Service (formerly called the PML Server or Service), uses common, standardized XML vocabularies. Based on the Auto-ID PML Core specification 1.0, PML provides a standardized format for the exchange of the data captured by the readers in the RFID technology infrastructure with back-end systems, such as SCM, SRM, ERP, Material Management (MM), virtualized databases, and legacy systems This specification 1.0 was developed by the Auto-ID Center [12] to enable computers to understand the size, weight, and type of materials (liquid, metal, or nonmetallic solid) of EPC Network-enabled objects to which the RFID tags are assigned.

The PML contains all other information about the tagged items, such as what the item is, when it was or will be shipped, and, if applicable, what the drastic changes in temperature or other aspects of the environment are. The company's EPC Information Service can relay the information about its product to partners and customers with proper credentials.

With PML, a consumer, for example, could find out how to recycle a product's packaging, a retailer could set a trigger to lower prices on yogurt as an expiration date approaches, or a manufacturer could recall a specific lot of cars. PML can be used to monitor how a RFID reader reads multiple tags, how a RFID reader reads the tag ID and data from such a tag, and how data observed by a mounted sensor on the tag is read when such a tag is in the vicinity of a RFID reader.

1.4.9 Scenarios

In one scenario, here are the steps needed to be taken as the item moves from one end to another: from reading the tag at the manufacturer's site to sending alerts on inventory updates on both the warehouse manager and manufacturer's laptop screen, using the Savant server as the central nervous system in the RFID technology infrastructure.

The first step is to code the item with RFID tags of small, radio-powered microchips that can broadcast EPC at the factory's site. As the item leaves the factory, readers—portable and fixed—pick up its EPC. As the next step, the new location of the item is recorded in the EPC in the tag. Then, as the item one by one is placed on a pallet, a reader on the forklift picks up the EPC from the tag affixed to each unit.

In the fourth step, the reader transmits the information to the warehouse manager's confirming receipt of the pallet. A copy of this receipt is shown on both the warehouse manager's and manufacturer's screens. Next, the reader transmits serial numbers via Savant software that sends them to an ONS server. The ONS uses DNS to match the EPC code to information about the product.

Once a Savant server receives EPC data, it can query an ONS server to find out where product information is stored on other servers on the Internet. This points the RFID software to a database confirming information about the product and the shipment's contents. A copy of the confirmation is shown on both the warehouse manager's and manufacturer's screens. Finally, inside the store, each time an item moves off the shelf, inventory is updated and both the warehouse manager and the manufacturer get the alerts on their screens.

1.5 WEB-CENTRIC SUPPLY CHAIN MANAGEMENT CHALLENGES

Now today's SCM is mostly Web-centric, rather than Internet-based that saw E-business applications as a dynamic way of getting information from and sending it to the SCM, virtualized databases, legacy systems, middleware technologies, and other enterprise systems. These applications effectively provide an information system that links multiple companies in the chain. Web-centric SCM shifts analysis of a single unit to a much bigger picture of the analysis of companies contributing to the integration of systems over several thousands of hubs in a single hub to accomplish a single goal of the SCM: getting the finished goods to the targeted destination in a globally collaborative network.

1.5.1 Combining Web-Centric with RFID Technology

Web-centric SCM combined with RFID technology infrastructure will provide the enterprises with tighter control of real-time tracking activities within the framework of enterprise integration. This Web-centric hub would be most likely a Web site across the enterprises in a global network based on open standards and the OASIS standards to support procurement, maintenance, and manufacturing functions within the supply chain, such as:

■ Electronic Procurement Standardization (EPS)
■ Materials Markup Language (MML)
■ Product Life Cycle Support (PLCS)
■ Production Planning and Scheduling (PPS)
■ Universal Business Language (UBL)

Although the future of Web-centric SCM looks promising, it should be noted that not all parts of the chain are related to data. Consider the following.

■ What about the way the employees handle the RFID-tagged items?
■ How are these items protected from loss and people not authorized to have access to them? What about those RFID-tagged items recorded properly in the information systems?
■ What about improvement alternatives in business processes that we need to address for the RFID-based SCM?
■ How are the event and performance alerts to be incorporated into a Web? What role would SCPM play in the development of a RFID-based supply chains?

1.5.2 E-Business Applications

E-business applications [13,14,5] have evolved as Internet tools that have been used to execute front-end and back-end operations in a supply chain.

E-business applications provide an information system to allow multiple companies to share data in the chain.

E-business applications traditionally consist of three groups. They are E-commerce (e.g., retail consumers), E-procurement (e.g., RFID tags, readers and so on), and E-collaboration (e.g., group information sharing).

E-commerce starts when a customer places an order. When a supply chain gets it, the back-end information systems process the order in various business transactions throughout the chain. To complete the tasks of processing the order, the RFID technology infrastructure must process other transactions such as tracking the status of orders and recording performance measures linked to the supply chain.

Managing a large volume of orders, each of which can contain a long list of products to be acquired can be a very complex process. To better handle the complexity or procuring the items, many industries have electronic marketplaces for buying and selling products over the Internet. The mechanism these industries use is known as E-procurement with links to public market and well as trading partners. This makes it possible for the suppliers to be linked to various parts of the chain via the information hub.

In addition to various transactions, the information hub may also serve as a bridge between the partners to share information. For example, XYZ Technology offers a Web-based platform that provides a real-time link/messaging platform across the supply chain partners. Everything from purchase orders, sales orders, invoices, checks, and other business documents may be shared over the Internet, providing security is not compromised inside and outside the firewalls.

With E-collaboration, the information hub could be used to provide information needed to develop new products in response to consumer demands for them. This hub has been viewed as a way to shorten product life cycle in a highly competitive market.

1.5.3 Advantages and Disadvantages

In a global network, the information hub might be extremely difficult to implement. One reason is that the parties each with proprietary standards may or may not agree about sharing the hub. To overcome part of this problem, the parties should agree to open standards for the RFID infrastructure. Another problem is the distributors compete for the ownership of customers. The distributors do not like the idea of having the manufacturers in direct communication with the customers via the hub.

The third problem is that the physical implementation of a global Web-centric Web site with RFID technology infrastructure as one of the back-end systems could be daunting. Another problem is that it would be costly to implement an enterprise Web-centric information hub, given that different partners use different technologies even though open standards are intended to be platform-independent.

Furthermore, the EPC global tag class standards are still evolving and not all industries are using the latest standard updates. For instance, some suppliers use Class 0 tags (factory setting) whereas others use Class 2 tags (programmable to read and in some cases to write depending on the memory in the passive tag circuitry). There might be some suppliers who are waiting for better passive tag technology if they are not mandated to provide RFID-based products. Other problems include the nondata aspects of the supply chain the hub cannot handle. Then we must consider security and information assurance issues of the Web-centric supply chain that have not been addressed.

REFERENCES

1. Glossary of Industry Terms, Ryder at http://www.ryder.com/resources_got.shtml#s.
2. "The RFID-enabled Tunnel from TAGSYS; one-pass identification of boxes and crates full of items," February 2, 2004, TAGSYS at http://www.tagsys.net/modules.php.
3. Dixon, Dr. Patrick, "RFIDs: Great New Business or Brave New World?" presentation slides by Global change at http://www.globalchange.com/ppt/rfid/index.htm.
4. "WSIS Physical Security Cracked," posted by Cowboy Neal on Thursday, December 11, 2003, 10:56 PM at the Slashdot Web site.
5. *Preliminary GAO Observations on Effectiveness of Logistics Activities during Operation Iraqi Freedom. Bringing to the Subcommittee on Defense, House Appropriations Committee*, November 6, 2003.
6. Kabachinski, Jeff, "An Introduction to RFID," *Biomedical Instrumentation & Technology*, March/April 2005.
7. "The Sun EPC Network Architecture," February 2004 at http://www.sun.com.
8. Schwartz, Ephraim, "Oracle unveils next round of RFID solutions," *Infoworld*, March 29, 2004.
9. "Implementation Notes: How to Obtain Your EPC Manager Number," EPC global, U.S., July 15, 2005 at http://www.epcglobalus.org.
10. Brock, David L., "The Compact Electronic Product code: A 64-bit Representation of the Electronic Product Code," Auto-ID Center, 2001 at http://www.autoidlabs.org.
11. "The Compact Electronic Product Code: A 64-bit Representation of the Electronic Product Code," Auto-ID Center, November 1, 2001. Distribution.
12. "The Sun EPC Network Architecture," February 2004 at http://www.sun.com.
13. Definitions, Locio Net at www.locio.net.
14. ERPConsultant on E-business applications at http://www.erpconsultant.com.

2

RFID TECHNOLOGY

This chapter consists of three sections: RFID technology primary drivers, selection guideline criteria, and RFID implementation examples. The first section discusses RFID technology deployment and the advantages and disadvantages of the technology. The second section explains EPC, tag classes, and applicable ISO standards. It also gives a general, criteria guideline to help executives choose RFID tags, readers, middleware, and network/servers. In the last section, we cover some RFID implementation examples, such as speed of tag reads versus quality of computer inputs, automatic reorders, tag location for dishwashing liquids, and item-level tracking.

2.1 PRIMARY DRIVERS

Although it is true that Wal-Mart and the U.S. Department of Defense (DoD) mandates are the immediate reason for the increasing adoption of RFID technology, there are other more substantial reasons for it such as the urgent need to close the information gaps in a firm's closed-loop supply chain in order to expedite turnaround time of cases and pallets. They have felt if the technology is good enough, the demand for it will increase, and technology deployment will drive the prices down.

2.1.1 RFID Technology Deployment

When Wal-Mart and the U.S. DoD announced their mandates in 2004 or earlier, they required all their top suppliers, regardless of their size and revenues, to undertake expensive investments in the deployment of the RFID technology infrastructure with a promise of ROIs in a few years. In some pilot studies the quality of RFID labels, readers, and the software arose, and have led some suppliers to customize technologies to suit their environments. Whether the technology infrastructure had to be customized, some suppliers were ahead of the schedule in meeting the mandated deadline. Most other suppliers were ready to meet the deadline by the first day of January in 2005 whereas the remaining suppliers were still in the pilot stage, and needed further testing and guidance before they would begin deployment later on.

For Wal-Mart, the deployment appeared to slow down when the company announced it was deluged with data. This occurred because the company did not take the incremental approach the German retailer, METRO Group, did. In contrast with the Wal-Mart mandate for its top 100 suppliers on the same day, the METRO Group started with 20 suppliers in the initial rollout in November 2004 and continued to take in additional suppliers. The METRO Group would expand the rollout to include 300 suppliers in 2006.

The success of METRO group is attributed not only to their incremental approach but also their focus on the initial deployment of pallets and cases. Another success factor is some suppliers' use of automatic pallet-labeling device for Ultra High Frequency (UHF) RFID tags for shipments to the METRO Group. Nestlé worked with Sato and UPM Rafsec, an RFID tag headquartered in Tampere, Finland, to develop this device. The METRO Group's early deployment success in the initial rollout in November 2004 does not mean the deployment has been flawless. Rather it means it started the deployment earlier than originally anticipated or planned.

The METRO Group has taken not only the incremental approach to deployment but also the top-down approach in a hierarchy of tag objects with the pallets at the peak of a pyramid (see Figure 2.1). In the pyramid, the pallet level is followed by the case level and then the item level. This means each pallet consists of cases, each of which in turn consists of items.

Rather than requiring all major suppliers to use RFID tags on the same day as mandated by Wal-Mart, Albertsons, a large supermarket chain in the United States took an incremental collaborative approach, not just the METRO Group's incremental approach. The company wanted to learn as the technology matures, meaning that it strived to prepare for initial rollout of

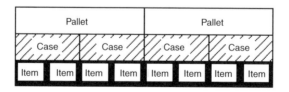

Figure 2.1   Object Hierarchy

deployment with no or little problems. It needed to collaborate with suppliers to consider, for example, what unanticipated factors could affect tag reads. Albertsons aimed to have all of its suppliers tag shipments by October 2005.

Target Corp., the fourth largest retailer in the United States targeted June 1, 2005 for RFID compliance. Its top suppliers have been required to apply RFID tags on pallets and cases. The company wants all suppliers to tag pallets and cases by the spring of 2007.

Whatever the deployment dates and issues are, one goal of many executives is to generate higher ROIs and favorable profit margins with less capital by improving inventory management control, replenishing shelved items, taking stock orders in real-time, and better utilizing space. Although the demand for RFID technology has resulted in cheaper tag prices, some large retailers selling their merchandise at bargain prices may find current tag costs high.

As the demand for RFID technology increases, more and more off-the-shelf software packages will become available at cheaper prices. Automating the production of RFID hardware (readers and tags) will become more widespread for less money. New middleware standards and strategies will emerge allowing vendors to work together on leveraging and integrating tag data from diverse sources in a common format.

While waiting for the RFID item technology to mature, you should consider a model monitoring the maturity of your organization to gauge the effectiveness of your investments in an RFID technology infrastructure. For instance, the Capability Maturity Model has five levels of organizational maturity [1]. It starts with ad hoc, the initial level of maturity, and then proceeds to higher levels in respective order: repeatable, defined, managed, and optimizing. We discuss them each in a supply chain model later on in this book.

Another area to gauge the effectiveness of your investments is better inventory management and control. It, as a matter of fact, got the highest number of scores as the most important benefit from RFID technology from the survey participants who responded to an online survey conducted by Computing Technology Industry Association (Comp TIA) in September 2004 [2]. More important than easier tracking and recalls that took fourth place were reduced product tampering, theft, and counterfeiting, and improved collaborative planning with supply chain partners, respectively. This makes sense as better inventory management and control aims at reducing the risks of tampering, theft, and counterfeiting. It also means it requires better planning of collaboration among trading partners.

The third area to gauge is the effectiveness of the automated process of manufacturing passive tags. One example is Alien Technology's "fluidic self-assembly" techniques of integrating all tag production steps into one automated manufacturing process. This technique already has dramatically increased Alien's capacity to two billion tags per year.

In addition to Alien Technology, Gillette, a key player in the Massachusetts Institute of Technology's Auto-ID Center, used OAT's RFID middleware in a pilot study to connect and integrate with various readers, to filter and route data, and, of course, to track and trace goods from one point to another in the supply chain. Once the middleware transforms the data into a common format, it sends them to Provia warehouse management software, the core of its Supply Chain Execution (SCE) applications.

In view of high costs of RFID technology investment, Gillette cautiously moved from pilot studies to limited scope reality as of November 2004, the same time when METRO Group announced Gillette is one of the suppliers in the initial deployment. Gillette's scope of RFID implementation will be broader when the company is able to scale consumer its item-level products to a mass production environment and produce an extremely high accuracy of product tracking.

Even if RFID technology eventually takes a major share of the market of automated data collection at the pallet, case, and item levels, bar-code technology may still be used in certain situations where passive RFID tags (with a frequency of 13.56 MHz) cannot easily read through metal or foil packaging or at great distances. As radio waves bounce off metal (and are absorbed by water), RFID tags may not be embedded within metal objects (with high water content). Those tags have been adapted to read through metal but at a distance far shorter than the distance at which most tags can be read. One recommendation is to use lower-frequency tags that have better penetration capabilities but have other drawbacks not inherent in the 13.56 MHz tags.

The U.S. DoD, however, has a different reason for issuing RFID mandates for passive RFID technology in its attempt to close some information gaps to expedite faster turnaround times. It has found that active RFID technology better tracks and manages the shipment of assets in real-time from supply chains to the battlefields overseas, down to the soldier level, although it has met with some logistics problems due to fast-moving battlefields.

The U.S. DoD has been using active RFID tags in Operation Iraqi Freedom (OIF) on an ad hoc basis to manage shipments in transit. It has implemented the use of active RFID across the board to be integrated into the supply information systems.

Over the past decade, the military has spent millions of dollars in implementing the RFID technology as a way of reducing the loss or misplacement of supplies (such as those items that were never used during the 1991 Gulf War) and the shortages of ammunition, fuel, and water that plagued American troops during and after the invasion of Iraq a year ago. One implementation goal is to maintain a smoother flow of supplies to the front lines given transportation constraints. Another goal is to allow a rapidly moving force to continuously replenish its supplies through better inventory management control. The military must know what they have, where the supplies are, and how they are used.

In 2003, the U.S. DoD began to implement passive RFID program while asking suppliers to start attaching passive tags to their supply items for a better control of inventory systems at the soldier level, so that the inventory systems of record could be automatically updated while under fire. The U.S. military learned a lesson that using active RFID worked well in Kuwait in 1991, but with the rapidly moving force in Iraq, the process of delivering the supplies at the soldier level became more difficult.

The U.S. DoD claimed to have not used any passive RFID in OIF. Although it has used the active RFID, it decided to mandate suppliers to attach passive tags to their merchandise, except liquids, metals, and bulk commodities that interfere with transmission of radio signals. It is important for soldiers to receive the supplies continuously replenished in order to move about in battlefields. When the supplies were not available, the soldiers used American ingenuity to replace them with makeshift versions or cannibalized parts from larger unused supply items.

2.1.2 RFID Technology: Basics, Advantages, and Disadvantages

Now the U.S. DoD and Wal-Mart have taken the initiatives to mandate suppliers to put passive RFID tags on cases and pallets as the technology is seen to save costs and time in better inventory and item tracking management. Although the suppliers are finding ways to implement or have implemented the technology, the market for active RFID technology continues to grow but at a slower pace.

The market for passive RFID products is growing faster than the market for active RFID products primarily because the passive products are smaller and easier to handle than their active cousins. Because they are smaller, the data storage capacity for the passive tags is smaller than that for the active products. For example, each passive tag can store about two kilobytes of information, such as how to care for the item, details about its supply chain history, and even data about the customer who purchased it.

The storage capacity for active tags is much larger to allow multiple files of larger size on the server database via a laptop. For both RFID technologies, the readers can be either mounted on a surface or something you can wave in the air with more flexibility in orientation than is possible with barcode technology. The data transfer rate for active products is much faster than that for passive products.

RFID tags can be programmed to send, receive, and modify data, and may contain protocols on who can read part of the data. Bar codes, on the other hand, are visual presentations of the data to be read by an optical scanner. Once printed they cannot be modified.

The degree of programmability is contingent on how much power the passive RFID readers can generate to the tags, and the active and semi-passive RFID readers can wake up the tags. The more power the tags can have or receive, the more possibilities there are for programming read/write capabilities of a reader. In active tags (and perhaps some programmable passive tags), data may be secured, and only certain individuals assigned passwords to read them.

Passive RFID tags draw their power from the silicon chip from radio waves reflected by an RFID reader within the short scanning range of the radio frequency field. When the tags are outside the radio frequency field, they will not work. The power to the chip must meet the minimum voltage threshold needed to turn on the chip. When the chip is turned on, it can send back information on the same radio frequency wave. Range is usually limited to several meters. So ask about the voltage threshold if this information is not available in a technical specification.

Yet, the possibilities of programming are not realized unless the readers are connected to a laptop via a communication interface, LAN, or a wireless or cellular network. Even with the connected readers, the memory size of the RFID chips (usually 128 bytes) greatly limits how much they can be programmed.

Although the read/write tags are more expensive than the read-only versions, they may provide better anti-theft deterrence and other security features. For some applications, they could be used for quality assurance. Although passive RFID tags do not require batteries, passive handheld readers contain rechargeable batteries that may be charged directly through the RS-232 or USB port.

Active RFID tags draw power from batteries from a reader with a maximum of up to ten years or so of continuous battery life. The reader is both a transceiver and a decoder. This means when it transmits a signal though the antenna, the tag answers or reflects the information embedded. The memory size is configurable up to eight Kbytes, allowing more programming options than offered by passive tags. Although heavier in weight, the active RFID technology is better in programming asset tracking in mobile environments.

Unlike passive tags lacking battery power, semi-passive tags (also known as semi-active tags or smart label tags) are tags with a power source such as a laminar, flexible, low-cost, and small battery to run a chip's circuitry (e.g., on-tag temperature sensor). These tags may rely on a reader to power the transmitted signal that can be used for on-tag temperature or other types of sensing. They can be used to monitor inputs from sensors to detect drastic changes in temperature (e.g., too hot or too much moisture) or any other aspects of the environment that could adversely affect the quality of the tagged object.

Unlike active tags that come with much stronger battery power, semi-passive tags do not boost the radio frequency range. Semi-passive tags offer a better read range (e.g., more than 100 meters) than their passive counterparts.

Unlike passive tags, active tags can receive a weaker signal from the reader at a wider field frequency range at a greater distance. These tags get their energy from the batteries that when activated transmit a signal to a reader. The power source on these tags boosts the return signal. These tags have ranges anywhere from tens of meters to hundreds of meters. They, however, cost more than the passive and semi-passive types because of the complexity of the circuitry. Like semi-passive RFID technology, active RFID technology can be combined with sensor applications to detect environment changes that could result in, for example, spoiled chicken or damaged computers.

Some reasons for the slower growth of active RFID technology are that the batteries may unexpectedly die out long before the battery life is scheduled to cease, and that the geographical zone for the antennas must be defined. A minimum of one antenna must be located in one zone. Although several antennas enable more accurate tag positioning, improper positioning due to reflections from walls and equipment can adversely affect the transmission from the batteries. The tags that are not located in the correct horizontal or vertical levels in buildings also affect the transmission quality (see implementation example 3 on Canus in the latter part of this chapter).

Although most industrial, retail, and supply chain sectors require only the simplest, lowest-cost tag, the potential value of more complicated tags justifies their increased cost in certain industries. For example, the food industry may want to add temperature tracking by adding a temperature sensor on tags. If one or more tags detect a sudden increase in temperature during shipment or some other means of transport, the tag will send an alert regarding the unexpected mechanical breakdown of a refrigeration system during the transport or in a warehouse via a fixed, portable, or even Palm-mounted reader to a manager. After getting an alert, the executive or manager can remotely turn on the backup system in a warehouse, redirect a moving vehicle to the nearest supply chain location or send an emergency crew to fix the refrigeration system.

The executives should get a report or two on these alerts, so that they can prevent a similar situation form happening again. It is far cheaper to consider, evaluate, and choose backup refrigeration or other system than to pay the high costs of replacing spoiled foods, the packaging materials, and even thousands of tags affixed to them.

If the tags do not need a sensor, you'd be better off with the cheaper passive tags for other merchandise. On the other hand, if you need a reader that can read both active and passive tags, consider a hybrid reader allowing a handler to easily switch from a passive mode to an active mode with a click. You must determine what data you really need. Unwanted data creates information system bottlenecks adversely affecting the turnaround times for cases and pallets.

2.2 SELECTION GUIDELINE ON TAGS, SERVERS, AND MIDDLEWARE

This section focuses on a general guideline to help executives know what RFID tags, readers, middleware, and network/servers to look for (see Figure 2.2) and how to select them from the following appendices.

- Appendix A: Passive RFID Technology
- Appendix B: Active RFID Technology
- Appendix C: Semi-Passive RFID Technology
- Appendix D: Network/Server Interfaces
- Appendix E: Middleware

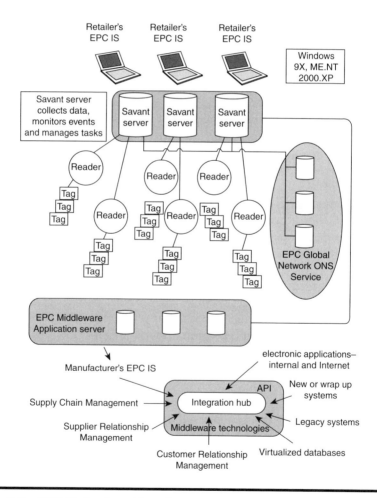

Figure 2.2   RFID Technology Overview

A Web site address is provided for each vendor if the executives wish to request additional information to help them make better decisions on increasing asset visibility in real-time throughout the supply chain. The problem is that data from a vendor's middleware software, product, or platform may not be in the same format as the data from another vendor's. This means a higher level of middleware software, product, or platform is needed to resolve this problem. As the demand for the RFID-tagged products increases, we will see more of the middleware products that can take in data from systems running on diverse platforms and bring them together in a common format for transmission to trading partners.

Even with the most efficient RFID middleware software you can get for your organization, you should know what to do with the data, otherwise you as the supplier will be deluged with data you do not want. Just be sure you have specific data requirements needed to meet RFID mandates.

Meanwhile, you should consider tradeoffs in your economic analysis feasibility studies on cheaper passive tags versus more expensive active tags, with particular attention to compliance with EPCglobal standards. You should consider how much data and programming you will need.

We expect a significant increase in the number of executives, manufacturers, retailers, logisticians, and suppliers adopting EPCglobal Network as part of the RFID technology infrastructure when EPCglobal sets the standards for the read/write Class 2 passive tags (see the next section on tag classes) that carry more memory and data than the earlier class versions. Additional memory means more opportunities to add data that the executives may want to better control and manage inventories in order to expedite turnaround times of pallets and cases.

For instance, Texas Instruments, a provider of ISO-compliant RFID products, has adopted EPC standards for its TI-RFid™ technology. In December 2004, the company confirmed plans to deliver EPC UHF Generation 2 RFID to the market based on the ratified EPCglobal Gen 2 specification. The plan calls for working samples in the second quarter of 2005 and volume production in the third quarter of 2005.

As of this time of writing, EPCglobal is currently working on tag classes higher than Class 2 and on incorporating some International Organization for Standardization (ISO) standards that we discuss later on in this section.

2.2.1 EPC Tag Classes

As indicated in Table 2.1, Class 0 tags are factory programmable. The EPC number is encoded onto those tags during manufacture and can be read by a reader. Class 1 tags can be programmed by the retailer and supplier. They are manufactured without the EPC number which can be encoded onto the tag later in the field (i.e., by retailer and supplier).

Table 2.1 Tag Classes

EPC Tag Class	Tag Class Capabilities
Class 0	Read only (i.e., the EPC number is encoded onto the tag during manufacture and can be read by a reader)
Class 1	Read, write once (i.e., tags are manufactured without the EPC number which can be encoded onto the tag later in the field)
Class 2	Read, write many times
Class 3	Class 2 capabilities plus a power source to provide increased range or advanced functionality
Class 4	Class 3 capabilities plus active communication and the ability to communicate with other active tags
Class 5	Class 4 capabilities plus the ability to communicate with passive tags as well

Source: Hardware Program Configuration, EPCglobal, 2004 at www.epcglobalinc.com.

The Class 3 tags have the Class 2 capabilities plus a power source to provide increased range or advanced functionality. The Class 4 tags have the Class 3 capabilities plus active communication and the ability to communicate with other active tags. The Class 5 tags have the Class 4 capabilities plus the ability to communicate with passive tags as well.

Not mentioned in Table 2.1 are the Class 1, Gen 2 tags that take into account the interoperability issues between Class 0 and Class 1 tags. It is not possible for the retailer or supplier to duplicate the EPC number in Class 0 tags in Class 1 tags; that is, the EPC number in Class 0 tags is not transferable to Class 1 tags. Generation 2 consolidates multiple protocols specified in Generation 1 as a single protocol.

Obviously the Class 0 through Class 2 tags are passive communication types whereas Class 3 tags are semi-passive types which are the passive tags with a power source. The Class 4 and Class 5 are active communication types.

To sum it up, the complexity of an EPC tag depends on the functionality of the tag, how it communicates with the readers, and other devices, and whether it has a power source. Increasing the complexity of tags also increases the cost. Tags with advanced functions require more expensive microchips, and tags with a power source require a battery.

2.2.2 ISO Standards

Avonwood, Northern Apex, Philips, Tagsys, Texas Instruments, and others offer RFID products that conform to ISO 18000 air interface standards or ISO 15693 standards on identification cards. ISO/International Engineering

Consortium (IEC) 18000 series contains six parts. The first part, ISO/IEC 18000-1:2004, defines the parameters to be determined in any Standardized Air Interface Definition in the ISO/IEC 18000 series.

The subsequent parts of ISO/IEC 18000 series provide the specific values for definition of the Air Interface Parameters for a particular frequency or type of air interface, from which compliance (or noncompliance) with ISO/IEC 18000-1:2004 can be established.

Table 2.2 indicates what part of the series refers to a frequency type or range for use in item management applications. The third part, in addition, provides physical layer, collision management systems, and protocol values for item identification. Note that the fifth part is not available.

ISO/IEC 15693 series contain three parts, all of which pertain to identification cards, contactless integrated circuits, and vicinity cards. The first part covers physical characteristics and the second part looks at air interface and initialization. The third part focuses on anti-collision and transmission protocol.

ISO standards unfortunately do not give much information on the amount of minimum memory needed for each part number. It would be helpful to determine what and how much data should be in a tag. Some standards, however, will be incorporated into future EPCglobal standards for easier transition from or coexistence with ISO/IEC standards.

Texas Instruments, a provider of ISO-compliant RFID products, has adopted EPC standards for its TI-RFid™ technology. In December 2004, the company confirmed plans to deliver EPC UHF Generation 2 RFID to the

Table 2.2 Defining Air Interface for RFID Devices in ISO/IEC 18000 Series

Part Number	Frequency Type	Purpose
ISO/IEC 18000-2	Below 135 kHz	For use in item management applications
ISO/IEC 18000-3	13.56 MHz	Provide physical layer, collision management systems, and protocol values for item identification
ISO/IEC 18000-4	2.45 GHz Industrial, Scientific, and Medical (ISM) band	For use in item management applications
ISO/IEC 18000-6	860 MHz to 960 MHz ISM band	For use in item management applications
ISO/IEC 18000-7	433 MHz band	For use in item management applications

market based on the ratified EPCglobal Gen 2 specification. The plan called for working samples in the second quarter of 2005 and volume production in the third quarter of 2005.

2.2.3 RFID Device Selection Criteria

To begin the processing of selecting a tag type with an associated reader, you should consider answering the following questions as part of the selection criteria in your economic analysis or a feasibility study.

- What are the objects to be tagged?
- What are the objects made of and how do they affect reading ranges?
- What are chip antenna types?
- What readers can read both passive and active tags?
- What readers can read both RFID tags and bar code labels for easy transitioning?
- What are other considerations that could affect externally the optimal location of tags?
- How do various entities organize frequency types or ranges?
- What other standards are the vendors using for their RFID products?

You can modify or expand the selection criteria to suit your strategies, requirements, and budgets.

2.2.3.1 What Are the Objects to Be Tagged?

The objects to be tagged are pallets, cases, and items in a hierarchical order. For our own purpose, this order is arbitrarily based on the hierarchy of three layers of object levels, as follows.

- Object Level 0: item level
- Object Level 1: case level
- Object Level 2: pallet level

The Level 0 layer at the bottom of the hierarchy pertains to products on the item level. The Level 1 layer refers to cases stacked on a pallet and the Level 2 layer pertains to the pallet.

Given the above hierarchy, let's assume the information stored in a case tag coincides with the information in the database about the products the case holds. We find information stored in a pallet tag points to the information in the database about the cases stacked on the pallet. If the pallet tag gives information different from that in the database about the cases, then we know the reader did not scan all the cases.

One possible reason is that the reader may have some problems in reading individual products inside the cases arranged in the center of a pallet, particularly when even rather than odd number of cases are stacked horizontally and vertically on the pallet. It is because in part the reader could not emit enough power to activate tags affixed to cases of items stored in the middle of a pallet stacked with say, 150 cases.

Another possible reason is that the shape and size of the product can affect the optimal location for tags on cases and pallets. For instance, if the product is a bottle of dishwasher liquid tapering at the top, it leaves much air space at the top. The tag should be placed at the upper third of the case, so it will encounter less or no interference from the liquids.

The third reason is that according to Kimberly-Clark, a Wal-Mart supplier, it is better to put tags not on the outside of a case, but on the interior wall of the case or inside the flap. Kimberly-Clark had trouble reading tags on the outside of cases when those cases were stacked on pallets in such a way that the case butted up against the metal of a lift truck. Other reasons for less than optimal reading of tags include white noise from a moving nylon conveyance, the large metal beams in a warehouse, and the steel bar in the foundation of a floor.

Some pilot studies or demonstrations give mixed status on consumer item-level products. For instance, Gillette, a maker of razor blades, has indicated that scaling the products on the item level to a mass production environment is several years away. On the other hand, Texas Instruments reported that a major clothing retailer of jeans successfully conducted the first major field test of RFID for consumer item-level tracking. RFID tags produced 99.9 percent inventory tracking accuracy in distribution centers. So if you are planning or mandated to issue RFID tags for your products on the item level, consider materials of your products when you set up a pilot study.

2.2.3.2 What Are the Materials of the Objects and How Do They Affect Reading Ranges?

If various materials, such as fish, paper products, water, gasoline, and the steel used by rifles are bundled within a pallet, expect an interference with radio signals as it is difficult to transmit radio signals through liquid and metals. The U.S. DoD gets around this interference problem by excluding sand, gravel, liquids, or other types of bulk commodities from its RFID tagging plan.

Passive tags made of certain material work well with certain materials other than metals and liquids. Some active tags, such as Alien's EPC Class 1 UHF tags, can be applied to metallic and liquid environments to a limited extent.

Passive tags affixed to materials containing metals, high carbon content, or high water content can reduce their read ranges. Collision of radio signals between tags, and distance between tags that are outside the frequency field range can interfere with emitted radio signals. The metal of a lift truck against which the passive-tagged cases may be butted up, the large metal beams in warehouses, and the steel bar in the foundation of a floor can reduce the accuracy of tag reads.

Another factor influencing the accuracy of tag reads is the difference in radio frequencies the tags can hold. For instance, 915 MHz and 2.45 GHz Intermec tags give different reading ranges for both metallic and nonmetallic materials. As shown in Table 2.3, 915-MHz passive container tags work best with free space, cardboard, and plastic materials in respective order whereas reusable plastic container tags are well suited for plastic, plywood, and cardboard materials.

Encapsulated metal mount stick tags work best with glass, cardboard, and "free space" materials although their reading ranges are higher than those of the reusable plastic container bags. "Free space" tags work better with "free space," cardboard, and plywood materials but not at all with metallic (direct contact and 06-in. standoff) material. Container tags perform poorly with metallic materials.

Now, let's take a look at the reading range of Intermec 2.5 GHz in inches as shown in Table 2.4. Metal mount tags work well with metallic materials whereas the other two tags either perform poorly or not at all with metallic. CIB Meander tags and metal mount inserts are well suited for plastic, cardboard, "free space," and plywood materials. Metal mount tags have the lowest reading range of all materials for glass and the other two tags have the second lowest reading ranges of materials for glass.

Table 2.3 Range of Intermic 915-MHz Materials in Feet

	Plastic	Metal, Direct Contact	Metal, .06" Stand-off	Glass	Cardboard	Free Space	Plywood
Container insert	4.5	.5	.5	8	3.5	3.5	6
Container tag	9.5	.25	.75	5	9	13	8
Intelligent ID card	3.5	0	0	1.5	7.5	9	1.5
Reusable plastic container tag	10	1	3.5	4	6.5	6	7
Encapsulated metal mount stick tag	12.5	10	8	13	13	13	12
"Free space" tag	4	0	0	4	11	12	10

Source: Intermec.

Table 2.4   Range of Intermic 2450-MHz Materials in Inches

	Plastic	Metal, Direct Contact	Metal, .06" Stand-off	Glass	Cardboard	Free Space	Plywood
CIB Meander Tag	22	0	9	5	16	16	17
Metal Mount Tag	21	38	43	1.5	28	28	29
Metal Mount Insert	24	0	11	7	19	18	16

Source: Intermec.

What the results show is that although tags—metallic and nonmetallic—can be used with metallic materials, their reading ranges are either shorter, little, or none. So if you have metallic materials to which the tags are to be affixed, you need to test tags' reading ranges. If it is economically and physically feasible, you may wish to change the material to another to get a better reading range.

2.2.3.3 What Are Chip Antenna Types?

Chip antenna is not the same as the reader or conveyor antenna. If the vendor talks about an antenna, you may need to double-check to which antenna type the vendor is referring.

For instance, read-only RFID tags from Matrics (now known as Symbol Technologies) that come preprogrammed with customer-supplied EPC codes are available with one or two antennas. These tags have the read rate of up to 1000 tags per second and long read range of up to 30 feet.

Read-only tags with one antenna are available in five types as shown in Table 2.5. Each tag type indicates what materials it can be applied to, what forms are available, and what the maximum reading distance is.

As you saw, the read-only tags with one antenna of general-use type work best with general-purpose use on plastic, corrugated cardboard, bagtag, and plastic. They are in the form of inlay, adhesive inlay, and label. Next in line are rubber encapsulated and UV-protected glass tags that have reading ranges of 15 feet for metal, and glass and windshield, respectively. The glass bottle and concrete tags have the lowest reading ranges.

On the other hand, the read-only tags with dual antennas can be read from any orientation and are available in three types as shown in Table 2.4. Each type indicates what materials it can be applied to, what forms are available, and what maximum reading distance is.

Table 2.5 Matrics Read-Only Tags with One Antenna

Type	Application	Form	Maximum Reading Distance(feet)
General use	General-purpose use on plastic, corrugated cardboard, bagtag, and plastic	Inlay, adhesive inlay, and label	25
Rubber encapsulated	Metal	Converted only	15
UV-protected glass	Glass and windshield	UV-protected inlay only	15
Glass bottle	Glass bottles	Inlay, adhesive inlay, and label	5
Concrete	Embedded in concrete floors	Adhesive inlay only	5

Source: Symbol Technologies.

For instance, in Table 2.6, carton tags with dual antenna have the highest reading ranges when applied to corrugated cardboard, paper, or plastic. General plastic tags with dual antenna have the lower reading ranges, when applied to plastic or wood pallet. The reading range is the same for the paper roll tags when applied to garments, paper, and wood.

For some other tag manufacturers, the higher frequency tags (13.56 MHz) may have a primary advantage over the lower-frequency counterparts (134.2 kHz). For instance, the antenna in a higher-frequency tag may make

Table 2.6 Matrics Read-Only Tags with Dual Antennas

Type	Application	Form	Maximum Reading Distance (feet)
Carton	Corrugated cardboard, paper, or plastic	Inlay, adhesive inlay, or label	25
General plastic	Plastic or wood pallet	Inlay, adhesive, or label	15
Paper roll core II	Garments, paper, wood	Inlay, adhesive, or label	15

Source: Symbol Technologies.

fewer turns than the antenna in a lower-frequency tag. For this reason, the higher-frequency tags may have better capabilities to penetrate nonmetallic materials. This means radio waves of higher frequency can bounce off metal and are absorbed by water. Higher-frequency tags may not be embedded within metal objects with high water content. One way of getting around this problem is to use lower-frequency tags that may have better penetration capabilities. To find out more, check with the manufacturers.

2.2.3.4 *What Readers Can Read Both Passive and Active Tags?*

Active tags can be combined with passive tags to create a hierarchical visibility of asset tracking in the supply chain. For example, both passive and active RFID are used on conveyance units transporting and loading packaged items. Active tags' longer read range provides effective coverage of double doors, dock doors, package counters, wide corridors, and other broad areas that passive systems cannot cover. One caution is that white noise produced by moving nylon conveyor belts may affect the optimal reading of tags.

You need a multi-frequency, multi-protocol reader (also known as "agile" reader) to read both active and passive tags. This type of reader was pioneered by SAMSys when standards were not well formed. Even with EPCglobal standards in place, agile readers are useful for reading both tag types next to each other. It is particularly useful to switch the mode with the same reader. For instance, in the passive mode with a certain frequency, Wal-Mart was able to read 30 percent of the tags on cases of consumer soap containing moisture. By switching to another mode, Wal-Mart was able to read the tags with 100 percent accuracy.

SAMSys, however, is not the only one offering this type of device. As of July 2003, Savi technology, provider of active tags has collaborated with Matrics (now Symbol Technologies), the producer of passive tags based on EPC standards to develop a handheld device of tracking the shipping containers, trailers, and other conveyances. This would provide a better way of collecting information in real-time on how, say, the container has been broken into and what items are missing or damaged. This information could also include how the items have been shipped.

The handheld device reads Matrics' passive tags up to 33 feet and writes the data to Savi's 433 MHz active RFID tags. It can also read active tags up to 330 feet. Matrics offers fixed readers for dock doors, forklift trucks, and conveyor systems. Both readers are based on Savi's Universal Data Appliance Protocol (UDAP). Although this protocol is proprietary, it is the open communications to enable interoperability with other automated data collection systems, such as bar-code, RFID, Global Positioning System (GPS), and other hardware-based systems as well as wireless application development and integration services that can be linked to Web-based Savi

SmartChain applications. Savi UDAP partners include Alien, Brooks, LXE, Symbol, Intermec, and WhereNet.

As of September 2004, AXCESS Inc. and GlobeRanger entered into a partnership to provide capabilities to incorporate active, passive, and sensor-based systems in one package and manage the infrastructure for enterprisewide, multi-site deployments. AXCESS' active RFID tags and sensors can enable businesses to monitor, control, and track personnel, assets, inventory, and vehicles enterprisewide and deliver tag data over the network to GlobeRanger's iMotion™ Edgeware™ platform. Data from passive RFID systems can be incorporated with data from sensor data such as temperature, pressure, and motion. As an added feature, an anti-tamper option is available for AXCESS' active tags. This means when the tag is tampered, it sets off an alert to the appropriate parties in the supply chain.

In response to the trend toward the interoperability of tracking networks of passive and active tagged pallets and cases among NATO networks, Denmark's Ministry of Defense announced in November 2004 that it contracted with Savi Technology to deploy a software platform linked with RFID technologies for tracking and managing supply chain shipments in real-time. This software platform is designed to be interoperable with RFID-driven networks already developed by Savi Technology for NATO's Afghanistan Supply Chain, the United Kingdom Ministry of Defence, and the U.S. DoD.

2.2.3.5 What Are Other Considerations that Could Affect Externally the Optimal Location of Tags?

You need to look around in your warehouse or another supply chain facility to see if there are metals affecting the reading of tags. For instance, one of Wal-Mart's suppliers, Kimberly-Clark, has noted that it is better to put tags not on the outside of a case, but on the interior wall of the case or inside the flap, particularly when the cases are butted up against the metal of a lift truck.

The large metal beams in warehouses and the steel bar in the foundation of a floor can also reduce the accuracy of tags. The white noise produced by moving nylon conveyor belts may affect the optimal reading of tags. If other suppliers do not follow the Kimberly-Clark example, reading tags will not be accurate and it will be very costly to resolve tag location problems.

2.2.3.6 What Readers Can Read Both RFID Tags and Bar Codes for Easy Transitioning?

Bar codes will not disappear overnight when RFID technology is in use as the RFID technology is not fully mature. For easier transitioning to RFID tags for manufacturers and retailers currently using bar-code technology, some vendors are offering hybrid RFID/bar-code scanners and others offer hybrid self-check-outs. These hybrid devices allow the executives to evaluate the benefits of RFID technology without disrupting their existing bar-code system. It also allows them to try out various RFID readers, tags, and other devices, and perhaps RFID specific applications and middleware within their existing infrastructure without making major changes to the system.

For example, PSC (www.pscnet.com) offers Falcon® 5500 Mobile Hybrid Terminal capable of scanning both RFID labels and bar codes. This handheld device running on the Windows CE-NET Operating System can scan bar-code and RFID-tagged shipments on the same pallet and track them throughout the supply chain, warehouse, distribution center, transportation, and retail store. When the device gets the information, it transfers it to legacy systems possibly via middleware in open system architecture. EPC Class 0 and Class 1 tags can be configured for scanning.

In another example the NCR FastLane™ self-check-out that allows shoppers to scan both RFID-tagged and bar-coded items was installed in METRO Group's RFID Innovation Center when it opened in August 2004 in Germany. In response to privacy concerns, the security function of the RFID tag is deactivated while a self-check-out station scans the merchandise. This allows the customer to carry the merchandise outside the store even while walking in another radio frequency field generated by another RFID reader. This way the information on the merchandise will not be inadvertently picked up by that reader. The NCR FastLane, manufactured by FEIG ELECTRONIC GmbH, supports EPCglobal standards for both Class 0 and Class 1 tags.

In November 2004, the hybrid RFID/bar-code technology was introduced into the logistics operations of METRO Group's Cash & Carry, Real, and Kaufhof stores. In January 2005, NCR Fastlane supplemented conventional check-out lanes in 50 of its Real and Extra stores in Germany.

Some other hybrid devices you might want to consider are the Memor2000 from MINEC, the 4X terminal, and a handheld device that does not require a shift key to change the mode, Gemini HF 210, a handheld terminal from Blackroc Technology.

An alternative to the hybrid devices is Savi's UDAP, that allows multiple devices and applications to share information from various Savi partners. Alien Technology, Intermec Technologies, LXE, Symbol Technologies, RFcode, SAMSys Technologies, and WhereNet are UDAP certified partners.

2.2.3.7   How Do Various Entities Organize Frequency Types or Ranges?

RFID systems come in a spectrum of radio frequencies ranging from 125 KHz through 5.8 GHz. Specifying what frequencies RFID products can carry varies from one vendor to another, from one standard-governing body to another, and from one market research firm to another. In this section, we show how each of the following gives a list of frequency bands: Texas Instruments, AIM Global Network, Forrester Research, EPCglobal, and ThinkMagic.

Table 2.7 Frequency Bands in Multiples of Three

Very low frequency	3 kHz to 30 kHz
Low frequency	30 kHz to 300 kHz
Medium frequency	300 kHz to 3 MHz
High frequency	3 MHz to 30 MHz
Very high frequency (VHF)	30 MHz to 300 MHz
UHF	300 MHz to 3 GHz

Texas Instruments, the vendor of both passive and active RFID systems, divides the spectrum into frequency bands in multiples of three as shown in Table 2.7. It considers the RFID systems operating at 13.56 MHz as a high-frequency band.

AIM Global Network refers to an ISO standard that divides the spectrum of frequency bands into 135 KHz (or below), 13.56 MHz, 2.45 GHz, 5.8 GHz, and UHF. It does not specifically say whether 13.56 MHz is a high- or low-frequency band.

Forrester Research gives four main RFID types organized by radio frequency usage (see Table 2.8). For each frequency type band assigned to a device, maximum reading range of the device using this band and its uses or applications are included. Again, Forrester Research treats the devices operating at 13.56 MHz as having a high-frequency band.

In addition to EPCglobal Tag Data Standard, Version 1, EPCglobal makes available on its Web site the following specifications.

- 900 MHz Class 0 Radio Frequency (RF) Identification Tag Specification
- 13.56 MHz ISM Band Class 1 Radio Frequency (RF) Identification Tag Interface Specification
- 860 MHz–930 MHz Class 1 Radio Frequency (RD) Identification Tag Radio Frequency and Logical Communication Interface Specification

Table 2.8 RFID Types by Radio Frequency Ranges

Low frequency	125–134 KHz	Range: less than 5 feet	Animal identification, car anti-theft systems, key tracking
High frequency	13.56 MHz	Range: less than 5 feet	Library inventory, parts tracking
UHF	868–928 MHz	Range: 15–18 feet	Pallet and container tracking
Microwave	2.45 GHz	Range: 18–20 feet	Car toll tags

Table 2.9 Global Areas by Frequency Ranges

	United States and Canada	European Union Countries	Japan
Low frequency	125 kHz	125 kHz	125 kHz
High frequency	13.56 MHz	13.56 MHz	13.56 MHz
UHF	902–928 MHz	868–870 MHz	950–956 MHz

The basic rule of thumb is that, for instance, if a low frequency tag has the capability to read many and write once then it is considered a Class 1 tag.

According to ThingMagic, RFID market is grouped into three global areas by three frequency ranges as shown in Table 2.9.

As you saw, the low- and high-frequency types are de facto standard whereas the UHF type varies somewhat from one global area to another. One reason for this variation is that the RFID technologies employing the low and middle frequency are more mature than those using the higher frequency.

Savi Technology groups RFID technologies into five categories. They are Very Short Range Passive RFID (e.g., 125 kHz), Short Range Passive RFID (e.g. 13.56 MHz), Active Beacon, Two-way Active, and Real-Time Locating Systems (RTLS).

The biggest advantage with very short range passive tags is that they are very inexpensive and are used globally. However, it requires significant process changes and has limited multi-tag capability. Short-range passive tags are also inexpensive and have sufficient range for dock doors and similar portals. However, many readers and antennas are required for a complete coverage, and multi-tag collection can be slow although tags are known to be read almost simultaneously by a good reader. Two-active tags are more expensive but have more highly reliable communication and better support for add-on memory and sensors. One problem is that these tags have limited portal capability.

Active Beacon Long Range RFID is inexpensive and has wide-area monitoring (a distance of 50 to 100 meters). With this long range, a chokepoint implementation is difficult or impossible. For example, assets on a conveyor belt cannot be distinguished from assets sitting in storage and applications are therefore limited to scenarios of continuous tag collection such as taking inventory when collecting all tag data is required or searching for a specific tag. Unlike the two-way active tags, Active Beacon RFID has no ability to write to the tag and has no means of disabling the beacon. You need compelling reasons to employ this technology.

Real-Time Location Systems have long-range communication of 50 to 100 meters. RTLS has the ability to locate tags to within ten feet but resolution decreases in crowded environments and it is difficult to translate the data information to a logical location such as the specific parking slot where a trailer might be located. It is not possible to write to the tag due to the long-range distance and also involves a costlier infrastructure due to the number of readers required and the expensive processing equipment. Another drawback is that this infrastructure is very expensive to install and implement. You need compelling reasons to use this technology.

2.2.3.8 What Standards Are the Vendors Using for Their RFID Products?

EPC-compliant and ISO-compliant tags do not complete the list of RFID standards for compliance. For instance, Intermac, an RFID technology vendor, gives the following list of standards. Not all standards are applied to each RFID product.

- ISO/International Engineering Consortium (IEC) 18000 Part 6: Air interface for item management at UHF
- ISO/IEC 15961 and 15962: Information interface for object-oriented use of RFID in item management
- American National Standards Institute/InterNational Committee for Information Technology Systems (ANSI/INCITS) 256:2001: American RFID standard for item management
- European Article Numbering Association.Uniform Code Council Global Tag (EAN.UCC GTAG): Application standard for use of RFID in the macro supply chain
- ANSI MH10.8.4: Application standard for RFID on reusable containers
- ISO/IEC 18000 Part 4, Mode 1 (2.45 GHz)
- ISO 18185 Electronic Seal Tags
- ISO 22389 RFID Read/Write for Containers
- Automative Industry Action Group (AIAG) B-11 Tire and Wheel Identification

The list shows ANSI/INCITS, AIAG, and various ISO standards but does not show any EPC compliance. Even though the vendors may just list the most important standards in their promotional literature, they may not mention other RFID compliance or related standards for lack of space, time, and money. So, it is wise to contact the vendors to ask for a complete list of standards for their RFID products and about upgrading to higher-level or other standards when they become available. It does not hurt to ask them if they are migrating to EPC tag classes as the EPCglobal is working on incorporating some ISO standards.

2.2.4 Middleware Selection Criteria

The key to your selection of one or more middleware products is how they integrate or optimize businesses and event-driven processes in the RFID technology infrastructure. You should also consider how fast the executives can receive the alerts on environmental and physical changes in the RFID-enabled supply chain.

Another factor you should consider is to determine whether to have the RFID technology infrastructure as an open architecture or part of a closed-loop information system that would expedite turnaround times for pallets and cases. This depends on what the size of your organization is, how complex your legacy, ERP, and SCM systems are, and how the presence of offending materials in your warehouse or another facility can affect tag reads. It also depends on how an RFID infrastructure can fit into the existing floor plan of your warehouse, what equipment you use to transform a product in various stages, and what the optimal number of cases and pallets is to fulfill customers' orders.

If you opt for an open architecture, the Savant Web servers (see Figure 2.2) are recommended as it is a software technology that acts as the central nervous system of the EPCglobal Network (see Chapter 1) or another network infrastructure. It turns any desktop running Windows 95 or above into a server as long as you have an Ethernet connected to it. You can download it for free from http://savamt.sourceforge.net. You will need to determine which middleware products can support the Savant Web server, how they can be integrated into and affect your existing IT infrastructure, and whether more costly server software packages will do a better job of tracking pallets, cases, and items; integrating business processes; and optimizing the number of tags to be read per second, while not slowing down the server.

RFID middleware market indicates there might be at least these categories:

- RFID plug-and-play
- RFID SCE applications
- RFID platform-dependent legacy systems
- RFID integration hubs

2.2.4.1 RFID Plug-and-Play

Some packages are platform-dependent and others are more platform-independent. Some packages offer a library or reusable codes and components for software customization whereas others do not yet provide configurable options.

Some packages provide almost virtual walkup to physically change the configuration of reader tags whereas others give visual representation of the objects on the screen. Some packages offer broad filtering options and others do not at all. Regardless, the main point of this middleware type is to send the data to an enterprise system.

For instance, ConnecTerra's RFTagAware Edge Server gets incoming data from the tags affixed to the items, cases, or pallets. The core of the RFID TagAware server is the console that is used to filter, aggregate, transform data into a common format, and monitor it. Then the filtered and reformatted data is exported via Application Programming Interfaces (APIs) into Supply Chain Management (SCM), Enterprise Resource Planning (ERP), Warehouse Management System (WMS), Logistics, and other EAI applications. Any of these systems can be developed as a .NET application, Java application, a Web service, or another type of application.

GlobeRanger takes a different approach; it's more of an open architecture yet more platform-limited than ConnectTerra. GlobeRanger is built entirely on a .NET Framework whereas ConnecTerra exports data from the server into a Web service, Java applications, .NET applications, and .NET Framework.

GlobeRanger's iMotion running on the Edgeware platform, provides a library of reusable codes and components for device adapters and standard-based integration that the third-party developers can use to develop applications to suit a RFID organization's requirements. The developers can also customize visual workflow management to identify critical events and send alerts not only to developers but also to executives who wish to keep informed of all events. Users can customize business rules as the basis of the workflow management to manage the device network of hybrid technologies (bar codes, RFID readers and tags, and sensors). iMotion supports the integration of multiple RFID protocols on one application.

OATSystems' OATmw, running on a Java platform, has the walkup interface to configure deployment of readers, label printers, alerts, and filters, and even change locations. It also allows you to administer and monitor reader networks, such as enabling or disabling readers, turning antennas on and off, and adding, changing, or deleting algorithm parameters. OATmw also has the capability to manage RFI interferences by scheduling algorithms, changing priority and proximity, and setting limits.

EPC Middleware enables data exchange between an EPC Reader or network of readers and business information systems. EPC Middleware manages real-time read events and information, provides alerts, and manages the basic read information for communication to EPC Information Services (EPCIS) or the company's other existing information systems. EPCIS enables users to exchange EPC-related data with trading partners through the EPCglobal Network. It may be used as a bridge to other middleware products that have workflow and other features that EPC Middleware does not have.

Northrup Grumman launched its Illuminos RFID software-development kit, a light version of RFID middleware. It delivers data from RFID applications in the format each application requires without any filtering or other additional functionality.

2.2.4.2 RFID Supply Chain Execution Applications

In this category, application vendors focus on SCE applications on business operations and rules to transform the way the information has been collected, filtered, and distributed from readers to SCM, other EAI, and database systems in the RFID technology infrastructure. SCE applications include WMSs, Transportation Management Systems (TMSs), Logistics Management Systems (LMSs), and Supply Chain Inventory Visibility Systems (SCIVSs).

SCE applications focus on performance management based on the integration tradeoffs between the demands from the customers and the supplies from trading partners in the supply chain, but do not involve procurement activities characteristics of the SCM. SCE applications also may extend and synchronize business processes to trading partners across the network in the supply chain.

Some vendors treat this type of middleware as a separate application, integrate it into a larger part of the SCM, or add it as a module to a SCE application. Further SCE applications may be part of a SCM system or be considered as separate from it as RFID-centric. The SCM system that contains SCE applications may also include other supply chain applications such as Supply Chain Planning (SCP).

If a SCE application is external to a SCM system that a company internally runs, it will require appropriate interfaces. Some vendors integrate SCE applications to Supply Chain Performance Management (SCPM) applications to send alerts on various events. Even if the vendors do not integrate, SCPM applications may be available as separate packages from other vendors or part of the SCM system. Some vendors provide support for collaborative messaging exchange between Web services and non-Web services involving the use, filtering, and deployment of RFID data collected from RFID tags.

As of this writing, Provia, Manhattan Associates, RedPrairie, SAP, and High-Jump Software are the major players in SCE applications. Each has its own benefits and advantages of running an SCE system, application, or module, as middleware. They give you an example what to look for when you compare application vendors, even those vendors that are not mentioned in this section.

ViaWare WMS is the core of Provia's platform independent SCE solution and coexists with RFIDAware to leverage the visibility of RFID items in warehouses. This database-independent (Oracle, SQL, Informix) system includes Yard Management functionality (ViaWare YMS) of tracking carrier performance, scheduling dock doors, and doing other things to improve performance. Also included in the SCE solution are ViaWare TMS and ViaWare Optimize. Provia's FourSite, as a stand-alone or part of the ViaWare suite targets toward managing customer inventories in many warehouses.

Manhattan Associates offers WMS as part, not as a core, of its Integrated Logistics Solution™. Like WMS, Manhattan Associates also offer other supply chain applications as a separate package or with an integrated whole. They include Transportation Management, Performance Management, and RFID in a Box™ to enable RFID connectivity with existing systems. Unique to Manhattan Associates are Trading Partner Management, Reverse Logistics Management, and Distributed Order Management. Trading Partner Management aims at synchronization across the trading partner network whereas Reverse Logistics Management automates the process of product returns.

RedPrairie offers RFID-MAX™ to enable RFID technology within its SCE suite of products including WMS, transportation management,and labor-productivity management. This makes the SCE RFID-centric, although WMS is not the core of the product suite. Unlike Provia and Manhattan Associates, RedPrairie integrated RFID-MAX with its Supply Chain Process Management to manage events, send alerts on various events, and improve performance based on the information gained from the events.

Included in mySAP SCM is the SAP RFID application running on SAP NetWeaver that provides interoperability with Microsoft .NET, Java 2 Platform Enterprise Edition (J2EE) and SAP's ABAP. It provides RFID supply chain networking, planning and coordination of EPC-compliant RFID readers, tags and other products SCE including data warehousing, and enterprise asset management.

SAP RFID application also provides event/exception management via SAP Event Management, the goal of which is to support an adaptive supply chain model that is responsive to changing demands and supplies. Through the SAP Web Application Server, SAP provides the interoperability of Web services technologies. SAP also provides open integration technologies to support messaging exchange between Web services and non-Web services. ERP adaptors are provided for integration into existing SAP R/3 supply chain execution processes.

Supply Chain Advantage, HighJump's RFID technology-enabled product suite, includes advanced, tightly integrated solutions for warehouse management, yard management, transportation management; supply chain visibility, event management, trading partner enablement/collaboration, and automated data collection.

Data Collection Advantage from HighJump Software, a 3M company, allows you to configure the collection of RFID-enabled data. It is designed to be integrated into any ERP system (including PeopleSoft, soon to be merged with Oracle), Oracle, MAPICS, and SAP), With Data Collection Advantage, you can tailor predefined transactions to meet the unique needs of your enterprise.

2.2.4.3 RFID Platform-Dependent Legacy Systems

This middleware category focuses on the way the big names' platform-dependent legacy systems are used to transfer RFID data from readers for filtering and deployment to an integration hub of back-end SCM, ERP, other EAI systems, and database systems. This includes RFID middleware platforms, solutions, or even a council using existing technologies.

Some software giants "have baked" RFID into their mainstream applications and servers whereas others developed a middleware platform for use with mainstream applications and databases. One relies on a strategy approach for a flexible approach to installing, testing, implementing, and deploying the RFID technology infrastructure. Another uses a partnership alliance approach to using the mainstream applications and databases. Depending on your existing technologies and organizational strategies, you may make the choice that suits best with regard to ROIs: short term and long term whether you are required to comply with RFID mandates or you wish to reorganize logistics operations to realize performance and asset visibility gains from transitioning to the RFID infrastructure.

In this section, we cover Sun, Microsoft, IBM, and Oracle. For each, specific technologies used in their RFID technology infrastructure to run a RFID middleware platform or solution are highlighted. A middleware platform is not the same thing as middleware software. The middleware platform is platform dependent whereas middleware software packages may be platform independent.

For some potential customers who may be smaller companies that need to comply with various RFID mandates, investment in RFID deployment can be high depending on the size and complexity of increasing asset visibility in real-time. For this primary reason, the big names have offered potential customers RFID strategies, software trials, test centers, and other means of testing and evaluating middleware platforms, software, and technologies for the RFID technology infrastructure.

2.2.4.3.1   Sun Microsystems: RFID Middleware Software

Sun Java System RFID software is the Sun's middleware platform based on open industry standards included those defined by EPCglobal. It consists of two components: the Java System RFID event manager and the Java System RFID information server. Both are available for download.

The RFID Event Manager in the role as the supply chain event manager processes large amounts of EPC data coming from readers into the system. The Event Manager then transfers the data to the supply-chain back-end systems such as a SCM or an ERP system and to the RFID Information Server to log EPC data and events. The information server stores and aggregates associated business data regarding various EPC events using the following platforms: Solaries 9/SPARC, Solaris 9 (x86) 12/03 and RedHat Enterprise Linux 3.0. Sun has deployed The Dallas RFID Test facility as the first in the series of Sun RFID Test Centers for the purpose of allowing the companies to test and evaluate various configurations before investing in RFID technology infrastructure.

2.2.4.3.2   Microsoft: RFID Council

On April 5, 2004, Microsoft RFID Council was formed to look at RFID requirements and how Microsoft technologies can be used in the RFID infrastructure to increase asset visibility in the supply chains. The Council has several partners including Accenture, GlobeRanger, HighJump Software, Intermec Technologies, Intellident, Manhattan Associates, Provia Software, and Reqio.

Microsoft technologies used to collect, filter, transform, integrate, and store RFID data and events include Microsoft Windows CE, SQL Server™, and BizTalk® Server. Also included are Visual Studio® and Web Services Enhancements (WSE) for Microsoft .NET to create Web services-enabled RFID solutions.

As of September 2004, Jack Link's Beef Jerky, a U.S.-based, midmarket segment international snack manufacturer worked with Microsoft. and partners ABC Computers, Avery Dennison (smart labels and RFID label compliance services), SAMSys (readers and antennas), and SATO America (RFID label printers) to implement RFID. As an example of good project planning and management process, the company decided to start early on RFID implementation, even though the deadline for trading partner mandates would be at least 2006.

This early start enabled the company to plan for a project of four phases. Completed in less than three weeks, the first phase involved tagging cases and pallets for selected beef jerky items destined for the Wal-Mart distribution center in North Texas.

The second phase used Microsoft Navision, a middleware, to leverage RFID for manufacturing tracking. RFID tags were attached to totes and racks in a closed-loop system; they automated recoding ingredient lot and finished products tracking. The third phase of the project extended the process to raw-material supplies, to record lot information as part of the receiving and picking processes.

The fourth and final phase involved the use of RFID technology to track the movement of inventories from the company's manufacturing sites to its central distribution center. During each of the last three phases, any problems that would surface were analyzed, evaluated, and corrected long before the 2006 mandates.

2.2.4.3.3   IBM: RFID Middleware Strategy

IBM's approach is to develop a flexible RFID middleware strategy using a middleware to accept incoming data from readers, filter it, and then send it into business processes and enterprise applications. The strategy includes SCE and SCP as two of the four business processes for a flexible framework according to the customers' requirements, strategies, and technologies.

As of December 2004, IBM's Sensor and Actuator Solutions business unit introduced two new WebSphere-based servers to help enterprises to automate business processes using RFID and middleware for retail store operations. They are IBM WebSphere RFID Premises Server and IBM WebSphere RFID Device Infrastructure.

METRO Group used an IBM RFID middleware based on the IBM Web-Sphere RFID Premises Server in its initial deployment in November 2004. The software aims at integrating RFID tags and RFID readers in networks with customers' IT systems. This provides the retailer with a virtual view of RFID-tagged pallets and cases shipped to its distribution centers. IBM WebSphere RFID Device Infrastructure is designed for RFID manufacturers who need a platform for integrating RFID data collection.

In conjunction with these two software packages, IBM WebSphere Remote Server aims at managing, for example, retail store locations. Retailers can link new or current in-store RFID-enabled applications and Point-Of-Sales (POS) systems with one another and the enterprise.

2.2.4.3.4   Oracle: Sensor-Based Services

According to Oracle, RFID is just one type of sensor-based technology; others include moisture, light, temperature, and vibration sensors. Increasingly, Oracle is combining RFID tags with sensors and tracking technologies such as Global Positioning System (GPS) to give companies greater visibility into their supply chains for reduced risk and optimized business processes. GPS is used to calculate the position of a GPS receiver anywhere on the earth as long it is used in the open and semi-blocked areas. It, however, may fail in urban and blocked areas. We are only concerned with RFID, not GPS, readers with regard to SCE applications.

Oracle builds RFID into its mainstream applications making it a platform-dependent middleware platform. It draws sensor-based RFID data including location and temperature from primarily Oracle Database 10g, and Oracle Application Server 10g. Using Oracle Enterprise Manager 10g, and Oracle E-Business Suite 11i, *Oracle integrates* sensor-based information into the enterprise systems. Oracle's solution includes a Compliance package, an RFID pilot kit to help companies connect readers to Oracle applications.

2.2.4.4   RFID Integration Hubs

webMethods focuses on the integration of event-driven components into the Services-Oriented Architecture (SOA). TIBCO takes a different approach by overlapping its Event-Driven Architecture (EDA) on the SOA.

2.2.4.4.1   webMethods: SOA RFID Middleware

Prior to 2005, the U.S. DoD told its suppliers to start using RFID so it can track the goods it receives. It has used webMethods to put the data in a common format from more than 30 enterprise systems it operates. webMetnods integrates heterogeneous home-grown applications by integrating them into a service-oriented architecture. This gives the DoD high levels of asset visibility.

webMethods' Enterprise Services Platform, a component of webMethods Fabric combines proven application integration capabilities and event-driven technology with a distributed service-oriented architecture to create an integration infrastructure. The Enterprise Services Platform can incorporate all Web services, including those exposed using proprietary integration products from other vendors, application servers, and SOA modules being developed by packaged application vendors.

2.2.4.4.2   TIBCO: EDA Middleware

TIBCO's Track and Trace Solution gives managers and executives a real-time view of order and inventory information by incorporating EPC and business information across organizations and their network of suppliers and distributors. This enables them to better monitor the changes in supply and demand.

Behind this solution is TIBCO's Event-Driven Architecture (EDA) that TIBCO overlaps with SOA in an architectural framework to increase asset visibility across the supply chain. This framework is particularly important for better inventory control and management based on faster turnaround times of alerts in real-time on problems with tracing and tracking the cases and pallets.

2.3 RFID IMPLEMENTATION EXAMPLES

The first eight implementation examples pertain to retailing and logistics. METRO Group was the first retailer in the world to start rollout of RFID-tagged pallets and cases. Gillette presented a demo on how it could redirect a misplaced case to its intended destination. Canus showed how tag reading at a certain speed can slow down a computer.

International Paper offers customers automatic reorders when they move a roll of paper onto their equipment. Unilever focuses on tag location on cases for less interference. Procter & Gamble used RFID technology to solve docking loading throughput problems. A major retailer succeeded to achieving a 99.9 inventory tracking accuracy in its first major field test of RFID. Marks and Spencer shows how employing RFID technology reduces the system's capital cost less than 1/10 of the annual cost of using bar codes for perishables throughout the supply chain from pick-up to distribution.

The last implementation example pertains to the library and textile garment markets. Although they may appear to target a limited audience, they could be used as lessons to learn in retailing and logistics.

Example 1: METRO Group: IBM RFID Servers in Early Deployment

METRO Group hired IBM to provide middleware and installation services for the RFID rollout that began in November 2004 with shipments of warehouse pallets and cases from 20 product suppliers, including Unilever, Procter & Gamble, Gillette, Johnson & Johnson, Kraft Foods, Colgate-Palmolive, GlaxoSmithKline, Nestlé, and Esprit. METRO Group has used an IBM RFID middleware based on the IBM WebSphere RFID Premises Server to provide the retailer with a virtual view of RFID-tagged pallets and cases shipped to its distribution center and exchange data with METRO's merchandise management system.

METRO's RFID rollout is expected to grow to about 100 suppliers by December and about 300 suppliers by 2006, along with additional METRO warehouses and stores in Germany. Early deployment in November 2004 was influenced by METRO'S belief that the results of the Future Store Initiative indicated that process efficiency and merchandise availability increased by about ten percent and losses and theft were reduced about fifteen percent. Smart Chips were affixed to the pallets.

Example 2: Gillette: Redirecting Misplaced Case

One demonstration in late September 2004 linked Gillette's RFID network to a reader at the Baltimore Convention Center where the EPCglobal U.S. Conference was held. The scenario showed how a tagged case of Gillette Venus razor blades got separated from the shipment it was part of, and how the company used EPCglobal Network to identify the misplaced case, and how a discovery station responded to a query and displayed the information about the case. A Gillette warehouse employee used the information to reorder and redirect the case to the correct Gillette dock door for correct shipping. Gillette's discovery station used the EPCglobal Network Object Name Service (ONS) offered by Verisign to provide authentication services.

Example 3: Canus (Speed of Tag Reads versus Quality of Computer Input)

Canus, a maker of goat's milk, is meeting Wal-Mart's tagging requirements ahead of schedule. The RFID technology monitors temperature of its products in real-time to keep the products from spoiling in transit. The deployment uses UHF readers and tags from Alien Technology.

Adjustments had to be made to software and hardware. For instance, the speed of tags affected the quality of input reads into the computers. It found that reading tags at one-second intervals was the optimal speed. Anything less than one second slowed down the computer.

In another instance, the Canus docking door allowed only three antennas to be set up. It found the third antenna did not allow enough reading area. Adjustments were made to this antenna by changing its orientation and position to provide a greater reading area for the antenna. A fourth antenna has been added to ensure that a tag can be read regardless of its location on the pallet.

Example 4: International Paper (Automatic Reorders)

In September 2004, International Paper signed an agreement with Globe Ranger's iMotion Edgeware platform for RFID supply chain solutions. The company has recognized the importance of optimizing business processes using process and workflow management to deliver user-defined business rules for immediate visibility and exception alerts. The customers will take advantage of the RFID technology to trigger reorders automatically when they move a roll of paper onto their own equipment to produce cartons or items.

Example 5: Unilever (Tag Location for Dishwashing Liquids)

Unilever found the shape and size of the product can affect the optimal location for tags on cases and pallets. It placed the tags at the top third of the case of dishwashing liquid bottles that taper at the top. This tapering feature of these bottles has allowed air space at the top of the cases where tags can experience less interference as it is known that tags do not work very well in close proximity to liquids.

Example 6: Procter & Gamble (Dock Loading Throughput)

In 2001, Procter & Gamble in Spain experienced bottlenecks at the loading dock where forklift drivers would run out of room on the dock for stacking pallets to be shipped. To make room, pallets were moved twice or production stopped for the loading dock to be cleared. To save time, the company moved the pallets to the trucks from the dock. However, these pallets were sometimes sent to the customers by mistake when they were supposed to reload back to the dock from the trucks.

To increase throughput and eliminate costly mistakes, Procter and Gamble developed an RFID-based system to identify the pallets. This has allowed the plant to shift to direct loading, increase the speed of loading, and reduce the number of forklift truck drivers needed.

Example 7: Major Clothier Retailer (Item-Level Consumer Tracking)

In the first major field test of RFID for consumer item-level tracking, a major clothing retailer according to Texas Instruments showed how EPC-complaint RFID tags produced 99.9 percent inventory tracking accuracy in tests in distribution centers and boosted in-stock sales significantly compared with stores in the area not using RFID.

RFID readers were wired into shelves to alert store staff when any item became out-of-stock on the shelf so it could be replenished immediately. Other foreseeable benefits of RFID include assisting POS operations by allowing mass scanning at checkout and instantly processing returns, loss prevention, and loyalty discounts.

Example 8: Marks and Spencer (RFID versus Bar Codes for Perishables)

Marks and Spencer, one of Europe's largest retailers, decided to move from bar codes to reusable RFID smart labels. The company is pioneering a very large RFID supply deployment with 3.5 million tags using EPC-compliant TI-RFID technology.

Fifty chilled food suppliers are linked or to be linked to more than 350 stores across the United Kingdom. This way, the company can move perishable refrigerated foods more quickly and accurately through the supply from dispatch and sorting to pick-up and distribution. The system's capital cost is less than 1/10 of the annual cost of using bar codes, reading food trays, dollies, and roll cages 83 percent faster at each point in the supply chain.

Example 9: Library and Textile Markets

The library market extends from the supply chain of publishing books, from raw materials or semi-finished parts to the delivery of books as finished products for the libraries to purchase to which RFID tags can be affixed. Likewise, the textile rental industry serves as an extension to the much larger supply chain of raw materials or semi-finished items to the delivery of garments for use in hospitals, labs, and other large enterprises that require daily laundry of garments in compliance with local, state, and standard-governing regulations. For both scenarios, the RFID technology keeps track of all processes from one primary supply chain to an extended supply chain. The technology works as long as there are no offending materials nearby.

RFID tags in finished products (e.g., library books) delivered to customers such as libraries may be reused as "library" tags. With these tags, the libraries have a choice of keeping some information (e.g., ISBN, title, author, publisher's name and location), removing other information that the libraries do not need such as location of raw materials, and adding the check-in and check-out dates, the location of the books, and patron's name.

Once a library receives the books it ordered or received from the returning patrons, the extended supply chain begins with the book checked in on a shelf after it is read by a RFID transponder nearby. The extended library chain ends with the book checked out when the product is delivered. At this point, the tag has been updated to show the date it was checked out, the date it is to be checked in, the location of checking in or out, the name of the borrower, the title, author, publisher, and date of the book, and other essential information to track the book in the library.

The book to be checked out is placed on a reading station to read and update the tag, say, inside the back cover without having the librarian open it. The station can read the tags inside the books stacked on the station platform simultaneously, as long as there are no offending materials nearby.

In existing libraries, RFID tags can co-exist with existing EM anti-theft systems. The RFID tags affixed to books should have enough memory and data to allow a librarian to track the process of loaning out books to patrons (with RFID reading station or portable reader), recording books returned by patrons (also with RFID reading station or portable reader), and placing them on the shelves mounted with a smart fixed RFID reader).

Now, let's look at the textile market. The consumers, particularly the medical and hospital staff, for example, send bags of dirty things to a cleaning store or a control point to have tags sewed in the clothes, if not done before, and to begin the process of automatically updating information in the sewn-in tags on unsorted garment without opening the bags that the clothes have been checked in and sorted in preparation for loading.

At each stage of the garment handling process, the clothes are placed on the station platform to record the status of each process. At the final process new information is entered on the tags that clean clothes are ready to be checked out and sorted out before they get loaded onto a truck on its way to an intended destination. The retailer receiving them records the receipt and delivery of clothes on the tags, and the database is updated each time the tag information is read.

REFERENCES

1. Hoffman, Michael, Brian Cheung, and Douglas Peterson, "A Framework to Measure and Improve Your Virtual Prototyping Process, MSC Software at http://www.mscsoftware.com.
2. Various surveys conducted by Comp TIA at http://www.comptia.org.

3

RFID APPLICATIONS IN SUPPLY CHAIN MANAGEMENT

This chapter is grouped into two parts: logistics and management. The first part, the logistics aspects of Supply Chain Management (SCM), pertains to any supplies that can be procured, managed, and transported from one point to another in the supply chain. Examples include hospital supplies, pharmaceutical supplies, clothing supplies, aircraft supplies, subsistence (food), vehicle part supplies to field troops overseas, clothing supplies, office supplies, computer supplies, furniture, and shoe supplies.

The second part, the management aspects of the SCM covers the integration with ERP Systems, Web Services, loyalty cards, handheld devices, smart shelves, and POS terminals.

Business executives are concerned about the interactions of SCM logistics with customers and vendors and about the business processes that need to be adapted to SCM logistics in response to changing customers' demand for supplies and information about them. IT executives on the other hand are concerned about what information systems and services can be implemented and shared across the organization. Let's take a closer look at the differences between logistics and management aspects of SCM.

3.1 LOGISTICS

Setting up logistics of supply chains depends on how complex the supply chain is vertically and horizontally, what business processes a SCM system uses, what material management regulations the enterprise running the SCM system must comply with, and what type of enterprise the organization is.

75

It depends on what information the customers are looking for, how fast they want the information, and how high the visibility is of item movements wanted.

It also depends on what material requirements the organization needs to get its SCM system to satisfy, such as make-to-order, engineer-to-order, make-to-stock, continuous replenishments, or seasonal replenishment. Some requirements are well suited for mass production whereas others fit into the mass customization category. The remaining portion may be a hybrid of both.

Also important is how serviceable material items to be returned should be handled for repair, overhaul, and maintenance, and who should bear the costs of packing and transporting these items to the intended warehouses to accept for further processing.

Not to be overlooked is a model of organizational maturity. No matter how components are modularized, arranged, prioritized, and optimized, they may not work properly if the organization is not sufficiently mature to design, develop, and implement a SCM subsystem, say the SCM logistics system. To test for the maturity of the organization in incorporating RFID technology infrastructure into the logistics, we divide the system into five life stages and then assess each stage if it meets certain criteria before we proceed to the higher-level stage. The first stage of course indicates the organization is immature. As we proceed to the next higher level, the organization becomes more mature until its reaches maturity in the final stage.

For our own purpose, we give each stage a name as follows.

- Pilot studies
- Logistics projects
- Organizational operations
- Logistics visibility
- Logistics optimization

To measure the success of each stage, we need to devise some kind of metrics system in terms of performance from one stage to another. The standard way is to divide the metrics into three parts: low success, average success, and high success based on an agreed probability for each. In Table 3.1, we arbitrarily give low success a probability in the range of

Table 3.1   Success Metrics

Low success	0.0–0.3
Average success	0.4–0.7
High success	0.8–1

0.0–0.3. We assign average success and high success a probability in the range of 0.4–0.7 and 0.8–1.0, respectively.

3.1.1 SCM Logistics Maturity Model

Let's give a brief description of each maturity stage, so you can better understand what each stage entails. Here they are.

■ *Pilot Studies Stage:* The organization typically does not provide a stable environment for developing a new logistics management system for an RFID technology infrastructure. At this stage the organization undergoes a pilot case study of implementing and executing the infrastructure. The organization may not have sound management practices if the pilot study is not planned properly. The focus on optimizing the logistics management system is little. Because a pilot study does not guarantee the development of a logistics management system for the RFID, infrastructure will not be stable because the process of testing the infrastructure keeps changing particularly when the flaws of the infrastructure and associated logistics system are discovered. Performance depends on the capabilities of individuals or teams and varies with their job skills and knowledge.

■ *Logistics Projects Stage:* At this stage, policies for managing an RFID infrastructure project and procedures to implement those policies are established only after a pilot study has been successfully tested and implemented several times. At this point, the organization uses these policies to allow it to repeat successful practices developed on pilot projects. However, successful practices do not mean the same processes to be implemented by the projects must be used. Whatever process is used, it must be measured and able to contribute to the better practices. In order to achieve effective process, project and management controls must be installed. In building a logistics management system, the costs, schedules, and requirements are tracked. Controls are necessary to prevent unauthorized changes to the process, practices, and policies. This means some sort of project configuration policies should be established. Performance is based on how the team interacts with its subcontractors and warehouse managers.

■ *Organizational Operations Stage:* The standard process for developing a new logistics management system is documented, based on integrated system development practices. An organizationwide training program is implemented to ensure that the staff and managers have the knowledge and skills required to fulfill their assigned roles in the logistics management system. This means the documentation on the system must contain readiness criteria, inputs, standards, and procedures for performing the logistics of RFID-based supplies, verification mechanisms (such as team reviews), outputs, and destination criteria.

■ *Logistics Visibility Stage:* The organization establishes metrics to test for logistics visibility from one point to another in the supply chain. This allows the process of developing logistics with the acceptable measured limits. When the limits are exceeded, action is taken to correct the problem. The range of variations within the limits must be carefully monitored.

■ *Optimized Level:* The entire organization is focused on continuous process improvement. The organization has taken proactive actions to prevent defects in the system from recurring. Cost/benefit analyses of new technologies to improve the process of the development of logistics visibility system are performed. The development process is continually evaluated using new technologies and methods.

Logistics maturity is low when, for example, the items have been out of stock too long causing the customers to turn to a competitor's similar items that can be delivered on time. The returns to distributors and manufacturers are too high in terms of the percentage of those actually sold to retailers. They do not include returns for repair, overhaul, or periodic maintenance. Here are some reasons for the returns.

■ Overstock due to poor planning
■ Recalls of items found to be defective at the retailer stores
■ Cancelled items (at a preprocurement stage)
■ Items that got damaged during transport
■ Items that are no longer in demand
■ Items that have been tampered
■ Items that failed to comply with regulations
■ Items that got separated from the transport for reassignment

To make logistics more mature, we need to reduce the number of returns to an acceptable level. To begin, we enter first the Pilot Studies stage and then progress to the higher levels of the logistics maturity model.

Logistics maturity is high when, for example, there are ideally no recalls within a specified period of time, and the customers are satisfied with the information that they have found easily and accessed quickly. It is also high when the executives are satisfied with the way business processes have been adapted to customers' changing demands and with the proactive actions to prevent defects, minimize recalls, and avoid reactive logistics. The organization has taken a proactive action to prevent defects. The maturity has reached the Optimized level.

Now, we have come up with a question that we need to answer. Is logistics part of SCM or the other way round? When we say SCM logistics SCM is one of the many components of logistics. Actually SCM is an element of the Pilot Study stage of the maturity model. Even the SCM may be well developed conceptually and can be successfully implemented and executed; it is still a pilot study. The reason is that SCM is a separate entity from the RFID technologies. It is a back-end system to the RFID infrastructure.

Although interfaces or connectors connect these entities via middleware technology, variations in performance, reliability, and speed are not measured and optimized in the Pilot Study Stage. Let's go to the next stage: Logistics Projects. Here we need to optimize the inventory via an optimization system. The SCM cannot alone optimize the inventory; it only tracks the movements from one point to another in the supply chain. Another important aspect of this maturity stage is the monitoring of real-time exceptions.

We need to focus how the inventory tracking and transport should be monitored and what measurements or statistics should be used in monitoring. Of course at this point, you would be concerned about your budget and your ability to tell the company why it is important to have real-time monitoring whether or not they like to hear it.

Let's suppose the company does want to hear in part or fully what you have to say about your logistics program; you can convince them of the strategic importance of managing suppliers from different sources. You can also go on to say that there will be no duplicate orders, lost items, or anything else you do not want to see in your report showing lower profit margins or a poor image of how your company operates its supply chain.

At the next stage, Organization Operations, we should be concerned with the quality of the logistics training of personnel to improve their skills in management logistics and SCM, so that appropriate roles and responsibilities can be assigned to team members to improve the flow of materials and supplies while reducing costs. This means people have the appropriate skill sets for their jobs. This includes the ability to optimize resources and to integrate logistics functions.

Higher up in the maturity model is the Logistics Visibility stage. Here we are concerned with optimizing the entire supply chain using various techniques. This includes effective cross-organization team relationships and measurement techniques. We reach the Logistics Optimization stage at the apex of the maturity model. We get involved with long-term planning, so that the supply chain, optimized in previous model stages, can be flexible enough to quickly respond to changing logistics demands.

3.1.2 Logistics: Reactive, Proactive, and RFID

Let's give a historical background on how reactive logistics has evolved into proactive logistics and then RFID-based logistics, most of which are still in the lower end of the maturity model. It is always more cost effective to establish a policy on proactive logistics before an incident occurs than a policy on reactive logistics occurring after the incident. Even better is the proactive logistics based on the RFID technology infrastructure.

To illustrate the differences of all three logistics types, let's consider the impact of federal Medicare cuts in 1997 on major hospitals in major cities and rural areas that saw profit margins drop as much as 40 percent. Hospitals were closing, went into bankruptcy, sent personnel home, or to look for other jobs. Many surviving hospitals saw their credit ratings slide. In sum, the Medicare cuts intended to create a surplus that the Congress spent on highways, airport, and defense, caused the nations' health infrastructure to deteriorate.

In a few years Congress acknowledged the Medicare cuts were too drastic and gave back some money over a period of time; the hospital logistics infrastructure was already a mess in response to sudden Medicare cuts. The hospitals were totally unprepared for the impact of the cuts on hospital logistics.

To save the once-proud hospitals particularly in big cities from sliding any further, they reacted to the cuts by hastily establishing policies on logistics hoping to cut costs to make up for the gaps created by the cuts. However, this reactive logistics not only saved some money, it also laid off personnel, merged or realigned departments, eliminated redundant research work, and cut back unnecessary supplies. Hospital personnel who survived the cuts were resistant to organizational changes. There was too much reliance on individuals rather than team work to make the changes work. Communications between merged or aligned departments were not satisfactory.

One obvious drawback of the reactive logistics approach is that logistics was not planned, not proactive, not reliable, and not optimized across the organization rather than in each department as a separate unit. Logistics operations were still costly, were inefficient, and resulted in duplicate orders, lost supplies, missing supplies, and supplies that got separated from a transport facility. That is because there was no system to track in real-time hospital supplies. Information was not available that hospital personnel wanted. Information, if available, was difficult to find.

There were many instances when a patient needed special equipment and supplies that were not immediately available. The nurses did not know the exact location of the equipment and supplies and wasted their time on non-patient care looking for them. When they could not find the equipment and supplies, orders were placed. While waiting for the orders to arrive, the nurses finally found the equipment and supplies. Blame this on reactive logistics that left little time for the C-level executives to think things through on how logistics should be planned, implemented, and optimized in each stage of the logistics life cycle, especially the information that the nurses wanted but was unavailable.

Then, some hospitals took proactive actions to advance logistics over the past few years. However, logistics has tended to be fragmented with little visibility over ordering stock availability and status of supply chain activities. They drain patient care resources and the costs continued to increase even after the affected hospitals took measures to cut operation costs in response to Medicare cuts. The nurses continued to waste their time on nonpatient care looking for equipment and supplies that a patient immediately needed, but to a lesser extent due to some non-real-time control over the flow of supplies in the supply chain management.

As a way of getting around some of these issues, RFID-based logistics is recommended to increase inventory visibility, simplify existing business processes, eliminate costly processes, create leaner processes, and to release unnecessary, duplicate, or wasteful resources as part of a more effective supply chain management in real-time. Some purposes of the RFID-based logistics are to reduce drastically or entirely eliminate the time the nurses spend on nonpatient care, to ensure correct materials are ordered by the procurement department, and to reduce storage, transport, and support costs.

When we talk about hospital logistics, we are referring to the logistics of creating cost economies among multiple hospitals and the supply base to ensure the right product—hospital or pharmaceutical—gets to the patient in the right hospital at the right time based on the right information that can be accessed quickly and easily in real-time. Enforcing the policy of leaner logistics without RFID technology infrastructure would not make economical sense. RFID technology is needed to better track the consumption level at the product, location, and patient levels. It increases the visibility of the materials management component of the supply chain management system to allow the hospital staff to focus on patient case. It permits warehouse/distribution centers to consolidate deliveries in limited space relieving of traffic congestion in hospitals.

Had RFID infrastructure been implemented in hospitals prior to Medicare cuts, the hospital margin loss would have been less as the C-level executives would have better visibility of what and how many supplies were ordered and how they were packaged, at the product, case, and pallet levels. The executives would also know in real-time where the supplies went, when the warehouse/distribution centers got them, stored them, and delivered them to the customers, and whether the supplies that arrived at the intended destinations remained intact, not damaged, not spoiled, or not counterfeited.

In the year of 1997 the hospitals were not ready for the RFID technology infrastructure. Now the hospitals are ready or have started to implement this technology as part of their SCM system. RFID technology allows a better link between end users and suppliers and allows logistics and SCM systems to be better adaptable to changing user or demand requirements for supplies and information and supplier innovations to streamline logistics. As suppliers deal with more and more hospitals, they can offer cost economies for a wider scope of supply base and even predict to a certain degree future demands of the hospitals and resulting leaner logistics for the supplies.

3.2 MANAGEMENT

This section looks at intervening mechanisms to integrate with ERP Systems (e.g., Oracle-PeopleSoft), Web Services, handheld devices (e.g., The METRO Group Future Store), smart shelves (e.g., Chain Pharmacy Operations). The intervening mechanism, whatever it is, cannot always close the enterprise system gaps without considering the opportunities and limitations of the mechanisms used in connecting the services via a network of business processes over the intranet and Internet. An organization may find that it is more practical, less costly, and more timely to connect via application calls or to wrap a legacy application to Web services that requires frequent changes.

Changing code in a Web service is far faster than recompiling an updated application that takes a long time to complete its run. Although faster changes to code look more attractive, there are other considerations we should look at that could affect the speed of getting the work done, such as poor project management planning, and the limitations of contractual obligations of running Web services on different platforms and customers' demand for certain information not readily available.

3.2.1 Oracle–PeopleSoft

As of Winter 2004, SAP became the leading provider for enterprise business software in the world market with Oracle with its purchase of Peoplesoft trailing behind. SAP has provided tools for creating, managing, and changing Web services in the Enterprise Services Architecture, a term used to convey the architecture for integrating applications. Yet, SAP is all out to be the dominant provider shortly after Oracle's acquisition of PeopleSoft in its quest for a larger share of the market.

PeopleSoft® EnterpriseOne is a complete suite of modular, preintegrated industry-specific business applications (e.g., SCM, Customer Relationship Management (CRM), and Financial Management), designed for rapid deployment on the Internet. The EnterpriseOne has a heavy SCM slant with a focus on advanced planning, customer order management, logistics, and manufacturing, particularly the warehouse management logistics whereas Enterprise looks at just inventory management.

It is interesting to note that prior to the platform giant Oracle's business software acquisition, warehouse management was Oracle's platform logistics and PeopleSoft EnterpriseOne SCM placed warehouse and transportation management under the business software Logistics category.

Evidently PeopleSoft could not meet the competition of other players in the RFID-based enterprise business middleware market.

Just because Oracle bought PeopleSoft does not mean Oracle DBAs have a smooth ride working with PeopleSoft databases. Performance-related and SQL optimization issues arise from time to time. So, if the executives expect quick turnarounds of reports or answers to customer's queries, they must ensure the Oracle DBAs either have a background in PeopleSoft database issues or attend training classes.

Bringing PeopleSoft's SCM suite of business processes to Oracle Sensor-Based Services aims at better leveraging competition with SAP's mySCM business suite. Oracle Sensor-Based Services draws sensor-based RFID data including location and temperature from primarily Oracle Database 10g, and Oracle Application Server 10g. Using Oracle Enterprise Manager 10g, and Oracle E-Business Suite 11*i*, *Oracle integrates* sensor-based information into the enterprise systems.

Both SAP and Oracle have their own architecture for creating and managing Web services: external and internal. Nevertheless the scene of enterprise business software with particular focus on RFID will change in the years to come. Nothing remains the same as the market is ever fluctuating in response to new demands, new supplies, new technologies, and new sets of business processes. The executives must pay attention to customers' changing demands for information.

Oracle is not the only platform giant, however. The other player is IBM which builds RFID solutions on its existing WebSphere. This platform supports large-scale application integration of business processes.

3.2.2 Microsoft RFID Council

Microsoft held the first Microsoft RFID Council meeting in April 2004. Partners who signed up include Accenture, GlobeRanger, HighJump Software, Intermec Technologies, Manhattan Associates, and Provia Software, all using the Microsoft platform to collect, manage, and integrate RFID data via Microsoft Windows CE, SQL Service, and BizTalk Server. These partners are working with Visual Studio and Web Services Enhancements (WSE) for Microsoft .NET to create Web services-enabled RFID solutions. Microsoft is collaborating and coordinating with RFID partners to adapt financial management and supply chain management solutions for small and midsize businesses that may have different requirements for information from those of the much larger enterprises.

RFID Council met again in February 2005 to determine how to make it easier for customers to request or get supply and inventory information via RFID technologies on Microsoft platforms. The customers want to reduce errors in collecting data and improve the visibility of where the products are, how they are shipped and stored, and when they are delivered.

One customer's goal is to reduce the level of inventories by allowing the suppliers to respond to changing demands in real-time, so that the supplies can be delivered at the item, case, and pallet labels to retail stores on time.

The U.S. Federal Drug Administration in response to customers' demand for reducing counterfeiting, theft, and diversion of drugs recommends RFID technology at the item inventory level. This allows the retail stores to track the movement of the item, to determine if the shelf is empty or nearly empty, so it can replenish the shelf immediately, and to the information in real-time as the items move from one point to another in the supply chain.

Customers' concerns and issues are not explicitly addressed in Microsoft's Deployment Model as described in Microsoft Smarter Retailing Initiative Whitepaper (January 2005). The model places four approaches—Big Bang, Function by Function, Location by Location, and Combination—in the cost/risk of introducing new changes in the framework of a two-dimensional matrix. It does not consider the maturity (organization, logistics, or SCM) as another variable that could transform the model to a three-dimensional matrix by which the customers' concerns may be better addressed. This would give the executives much better perspective of how RFID technology would meet the customer's demand for information that was difficult to get in older technologies, and would contribute to feedback on how the SCM logistics systems should be developed. Communications on this feedback work better in the environment that allows open communications and collaboration between departments and executives in the organization.

Among Microsoft's product offerings to implement Web sites based on smarter retailing initiatives, Microsoft Windows Sharepoint services could be used to share RFID information and create RFID collaboration and information-sharing SCM applications. Microsoft Office Live Meeting is also offered to enable real-time online collaboration with employees, executives, and RFID vendors on the issues of RFID technology and information systems.

3.2.3 IBM

There is one thing all executives are concerned about: an uncertainty element when new RFID technology infrastructure is incorporated into the existing supply chain or used to build a new one for integration with their legacy ERP, including their SCM systems. No matter what information the customers need and how fast they want it, every shipment adds an element of uncertainty: items that got lost, unexpected recalls, items that got separated from shipment but were found in another destination, items that got damaged while in transit, duplicate items, and so on.

To better control this uncertainty, IBM has come out with a business RFID strategy to better track the movements of items throughout the supply chain with a higher degree of certainty. To make their strategy work, IBM offers their customers their RFID product line. The primary portion of this line is the WebSphere RFID Premises Server, a middleware product that monitors RFID events as a way of determining critical operation events in real-time thus reducing the element of uncertainty to a more acceptable level while keeping the company's positive profit margins.

The product line is divided into:

- Devices, such as readers, scanners, and printers embedded with WebSphere RFID Device Infrastructure
- IBM WebSphere RFID Premises Server, a middleware product to detect critical operational events
- IBM WebSphere Business Integration Server or Server Foundation to be integrated with enterprisewide business operations

IBM helped METRO Group develop an integrated RFID solution for its prototype Extra Future Store. As the RFID system integrator, IBM led the strategy for implementation of the project. To ensure each supplier is interoperable with RFID technologies, IBM established a lab for that purpose. Since then IBM has climbed the ladder from one layer to another in the maturity model for pallets and cases of products. Once METRO Group gets to tagging of the products at the item level on a massive scale, it will fully mature with its RFID technology infrastructure.

Along the way, RFID technologies have reduced labor by eliminating manual scanning of pallets and physical inventory counts, improved returns management with fast access to purchase data obtained from RFID tags, and optimized production and distribution plans between manufacturers and retailers in real-time regarding the tagged products at the pallet, case, and item levels.

3.2.4 The METRO Group Future Store

The METRO Group Future Store Initiative in Rheinberg was found as a cooperation project between METRO Group, SAP, OAT systems, Oracle, Intel, and IBM as well as other partner companies from the information technology and consumer goods industries. They all aim at promoting innovations in retailing on a national and international level. In the long run the initiative sets the stage for creating or implementing existing standards for retailing that can be implemented on an international scale.

The technologies that the METRO Group Future Store Initiative used in a test store were aimed at making shopping more convenient for consumers through better service and at improving processes in retailing. Different combinations of RFID applications were tested in which a completely integrated system was implemented for inventory management, information management, and check-out.

Let's take a look at each of the three aspects of the integrated system. They are inventory management, information management, and check-out.

3.2.4.1 Inventory Management

The Future Store Initiative focuses on the development of new processes in inventory management using RFID technology. Merchandise goods can be tracked at various locations as they move from one end of the supply chain to another in the central warehouse and for the delivery and storage of goods and shelf filing. Using the data captured from the RFID tags, goods can be reordered according to demand and inventory safety check.

All goods are sorted on RFID-tagged pallets in a central warehouse before they are delivered to the Future Store. Data captured from RFID tags are transferred to an electronic RFID merchandise management system, allowing the goods to be registered with the respective information in the system. Once registered, the locations of goods can be tracked throughout the entire logistic chain.

When ready, the loaded pallets are moved to the exit zone of the central warehouse, where an electronic gate is installed with an RFID reading device. When passing this gate, the data in the chips of the tags affixed to the cartons and pallets is transmitted to the merchandise management system.

When goods are received at the Future Store, employees transport the pallets from the truck through an RFID gate at the backstore entrance. The data of the chips on each pallet and crate are read. Once the merchandise management system is updated, the supermarket employees can compare the received goods with the order to determine if the order was met or if the items were over-shipped, under-shipped, or missing.

After the goods are delivered for storage in the back room of the Future Store, each storage position is affixed with an RFID tag. When storing the goods, the employees use a handheld scanner to read this tag into the system.

When taking goods to the sales room to refill the shelves, the employees pass an RFID gate at the exit of the backstore area, where the data on the RFID chips affixed to the cartons is captured for transmission to the merchandise management system. Cartons that could not be emptied due to a lack of shelf space are returned to the backstore area. As they pass at the gate, tag data is updated and then transferred to the system. When the merchandise is emptied from the carton, the RFID tags are deactivated. But what happens when the executives need the information from those tags that have been deactivated?

3.2.4.2 Information Management

Innovative technologies and devices offer a whole new range of information possibilities in the Future Store. The Personal Shopping Assistant, information terminals, and advertising displays, for example, help customers to find products and advise them with comprehensive information when choosing the goods. A customer can also take advantage of intelligent scales, electronic shelf labels, and smart shelves. Let's take a brief look at each device.

Personal shopping assistants are handheld mobile computers, each of which is given to a customer with a personal loyalty card when the customer enters the store. After using the loyalty card, the customer gains access to a range of individual services, such as shopping list recall, product shelf map, and product price search. In the first instance, the customers can recall their own shopping list comprising the purchases of the last few weeks. In the second instance, the customers can search a product on this device to find out exactly where it is located in the store. In the third instance, customers can check out the price of and other information about the product. When the customer is finished with shopping, the list is transferred to the check-out (automatic or cash).

Info-Terminals are touch-screen displays, serving as shopping aids. They offer an array of information on product lines such as meat, wine, fruit and vegetables, or baby products. Customers also receive updated recipe suggestions.

An intelligent scale is capable of recognizing fruit and vegetables and distinguishing the different products. The scale uses an integrated camera to identify the product and prints out an adhesive tag containing the price and other information that the customer sticks on the plastic bag.

Electronic shelf labels will make conventional price labels a thing of the past in the Future Store. The goods are placed on shelves equipped with electronic shelf labels. On a small display, the customer sees the base and product prices. Next to the display is a paper label showing product name. The system sends information on price changes directly to the displays (and check-out systems as well) via a wireless local data network. The check-out systems are also provided with data from this source.

Smart shelves in the Future Store are equipped with RFID reading devices on the bottom and linked to the merchandise management system. They recognize when goods are misplaced or missing. When it happens, they send a message to the system. When the employees receive them, they can rearrange or refill the goods.

3.2.4.3 Check-Out

The customers have new options for paying their shopping fast by scanning the products using the Personal Shopping Assistant or using the self-check-out allowing customers to act as cashiers. They draw their articles with a scanner with RFID reader. They may pay as usual, either cash or with credit card. Those who do not wish to take advantage of new technologies can take advantage of paying in cash at the check-out.

3.2.5 Chain Pharmacy Operations

It is anticipated that item level adoption of RFID technology by the pharmaceutical industry will be complete by 2006. Now, let's take a look at how an RFID application in SCM could be used in the chain pharmacy operations. Let's divide the operations into four parts: manufacturer's plant, manufacturer's distribution center, wholesale distributor, and retail distributor center. For each we briefly take a look at the input and output process [1].

Keep in mind the following scenario is really a "marketing" talk on how chain operations should be done without regard of assessing a pharmaceutical organization on what maturity stage it is or would be. As of this writing, it appears to be in the Pilot Study Stage as no information is provided on the measurement data on the effectiveness of the RFID application in pharmaceutical SCM systems.

At a manufacturing plant, the tag is embedded with the following data: product description, lot number, batch number, expiration date, and case EPC number. At the exit gate, a reader scans a tag, captures the product information, and records when and where the data capture took place. It sends the recorded data to a middleware and then to an application via PDA, laptop, or a desktop computer. Next, the plant ships the product to a manufacturer's distribution center.

When the product arrives, a reader records the date, time, and receiving location, at the manufacturer or distribution center's entrance gate. When a notification of a purchase order from a wholesale distributor is received, the product is prepared for outbound shipment. A reader at the exit gate captures the data, time, and shipping location.

When the product arrives at the wholesale distributor, the date, time, and receiving location are captured. The wholesale distributor then executes new order receiving processes to verify a purchase order shipment receipt. It first conducts Rapid Read of Electronic Product Code (EPC) on the product and prints an EPC Pharma Receiving Summary report. It then validates the receiving information through cross-reference validation among packing slip, the purchase order, and EPC Pharma Receiving summary report. This can be accomplished with an RFID application that automates the cross-reference process.

When a retail distribution center receives the product, it executes new order shipping processes. It first conducts Rapid Read of EPC on the product being shipped, and prints an EPC Pharma Shipping Summary Report. It then validates the shipping information through cross-reference validation between the purchase order and EPC Pharma Shipping Summary Report. This can be accomplished with an RFID application that automates the cross-reference process.

When the retail distribution center receives a purchase order from a retail pharmacy, it ships out the product. At the exit gate of the center, the date, time, and shipping location are captured. When the product arrives at the retail pharmacy, the date, time, and receiving location are recorded. Recording information, however, does not end here. The reader (affixed to a shelf) records when a product is placed on the shelf and when it is removed from the same shelf by a customer for a possible purchase. The customer then takes it to the check-out. A handheld reader scans the tag of the product, deactivates it, and then transfers the updated information to a database.

Let's suppose a shipment to the wholesale distributor contains a counterfeit product. At the wholesale distributor, an EPC is automatically validated. When the results show that no match was found, the RFID application sends an alert to check the shipment for authenticity. During the transport, the authentic product was stolen from a case. When the retail distribution center gets the case with the missing item, the reader scanning the tags on the case and the units within the case sends an alert that there is a discrepancy in the information on the case tag and on the unit tags in the case. When this happens, the theft is investigated.

Now let's assess the scenario with the following questions on the maturity of the organization.

1. How fast and reliable was RFID information read from the tags?
2. Did the supplies encounter traffic bottlenecks on their way to a warehouse or distribution center? If so, how long was there a delay for each incident of the bottleneck?
3. Did the plant ship all of the products to fulfill the order and deliver on time?

3.2.6 SAP

SAP has been integrating with built-in RFID capabilities in its SCM applications since the late 1990s long before Wal-Mart and the U.S. DoD mandated their suppliers to comply. It was one of the first software suppliers to join the Auto-ID center (now EPCglobal). The METRO Group and Procter & Gamble are using SAP as part of their RFID technology infrastructure.

SAP modules are built upon one another in a certain order and interface with one another to send data and messages and receive them. Its programming language is English-like, although there were some problems of translating certain terminologies from German to English for use in certain American business or organizational cultures.

Being an enterprise application leader does not ensure SAP will be freed from project failures that may arise from implementation of SAP applications. Myerson [2] pointed out that FoxMeyer Drug, once a profitable wholesale drug distributor, filed for bankruptcy in 1996 and led lawsuits against SAP (and Andersen Consulting for $500 million each). Shortly FoxMeyer Drug was acquired by a competitor.

Myerson further stated that organizational culture is one key success factor as evident with Dow Corning's success in implementing SAP R/3, the same software FoxMeyer Drug used. According Scott and Vessy [3], "Dow Corning's success can be attributed to organizational culture in three areas that FoxMeyer Drug did not provide. They are open communication, empowerment, and realistic expectations."

Today, SAP applications are bundled to provide support for packing and unpacking, goods issue, receiving, and track and trace business processes. They include SAP's Web Application Server, SAP Auto-ID Infrastructure, Supply Chain Event Management (SCEM), and SAP Enterprise Portal. As the name implies, the Auto-ID Infrastructure links RFID data to disparate back-end systems. It is a component of SAP NetWeaver application and integration platform. It includes a Business Rule Configurator for creating new business processes and SAP Event Management for monitoring exceptions to business processes triggered by data captured from RFID tags affixed or embedded in individual items, pallets, and cases.

In conjunction with the Auto-ID Infrastructure is SAP Warehouse Management that has been configured to handle nested RFID tags at various levels (e.g., palette, case, individual) via its Handling Unit Management module. SAP has added RFID adaptors to integrate the RFID captured data with SAP Advanced Planning & Optimization (SAP APO), SAP Inventory Collaboration Hub (SAP ICH), and other SCM Event Management (SAP EM).

mySAP SCM supports RFID-enabled execution scenarios within warehouse and logistics processes. It provides planning, execution, coordination, and collaboration capabilities of transforming traditional supply networks into adaptive supply networks. mySAP SCM is part of mySAP Business Suite. An adaptive supply network allows cooperating and collaborative companies to share information and knowledge in response to changing market conditions via planning, executing, sensing, responding, and learning.

Planning tools help to build a SCM model, including SCM design, demand and supply planning, manufacturing planning, and transportation planning. Execution tools aim at integrating planning, logistics, and transactional systems through materials management, manufacturing and transportation execution, and warehouse management. Coordination tools focus on supply event management and performance management whereas collaboration tools focus on sharing information to achieve supply goals through Collaborative Planning, Forecasting, and Replenishment (CPFR), support for Vendor-Managed Inventory (VMI), and support for Supplier-Managed Inventory (SMI).

Specifically, mySAP SCM contains nine modules.

- Strategic planning
- Demand planning

- Supply planning
- Procurement
- Manufacturing
- Warehousing
- Order fulfillment
- Transportation
- Visibility

Details on each are available on the SAP's Web site.

3.2.7 Web Services

How do we get a SAP application to communicate with an application from Oracle-PeopleSoft, Microsoft, IBM, Computer Associates, Baan, or even a COBOL-based and database-driven legacy system from a smaller company? One way of doing it is to develop and deploy a set of Web services using the XML (eXtensible Markup Language) for business-to-business E-commerce applications. As shown in Figure 3.1, Web services acts as a middleware between a SAP application and enterprise applications or legacy systems from major vendors.

Now, let's take a look at how RFID can be linked with Web services regardless of the vendors, seen as a new way of "helping organizations integrate new RFID applications into existing supply chain systems and share data about product location, ordering and inventory with suppliers and customers" according to [4]. Just make sure your organization is matured enough or can grow in maturity to accept RFID technology in a SCM system. Your cost/risk measurement is worthless if you do not include the maturity factor in your measurement.

To link up with RFID, Web services must work directly or indirectly with at least two components, Object Name Service (ONS) service and EPC Information Service (EPC IS), of the Auto-ID Center technology infrastructure to support the integration of RFID applications into the enterprise supply chain systems and to share product data, including EPCs. As shown in Figure 3.2, RFID Web services get inputs from EPC IS and RFID applications.

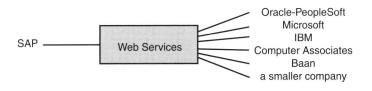

Figure 3.1   Web Services Middleware

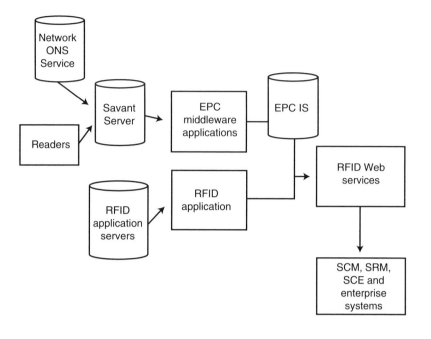

Figure 3.2   RFID Web Services

We already have covered what RFID tags and tag readers are, what they do, and how they are used in Chapter 2. We discuss briefly what ONS is, how EPC IS is used, what EPC is, how EPC is used, and then what Savant servers are and do, so you can better understand how information is transformed or processed from one place to another in the supply chain based on a set of business rules. This is important when the customers complain about the wrong or truncated information they got or even the omission of the right information they never got. You need to know what processes were that resulted in incorrect or omission of information about which the customers complained.

Keep in mind Savant servers are not the only types of servers to be used with RFID readers and EPC Network ONS Service. They serve as an example of how a server other than the Savant can be used to work with the readers in an open environment. The workflow of readers, servers, ONS service, EPC IS, and other aspects of RFID applications differ from one company to another, from one vendor to another, and from one supplier to another. The degree of the openness of the environment in which the RFID servers and associated infrastructure runs varies among vendors and suppliers.

The nature of the RFID requirements should not be overlooked, either. For example, the storage capacity of the Savant server may be less than that of the servers from the major vendors. It may be useful to start with the Savant server and then migrate to servers of much larger capacity offered by major vendors as the capacity of the Savant server approaches the maximum. On the other hand, you might want to start with a major vendor's server on a smaller scale to take advantage of other services offered by the vendor.

As with other Web Services, RFID Web services will provide integration among heterogeneous systems and business-to-business communications, provided that SOAP is fully interoperable between systems, and the servers run in an open environment. With an RFID Web services, a customer or even a supplier can synchronize data between SAP, Oracle-PeopleSoft, Computer Associates, Baan, IBM, Microsoft, a CICS application, and a home-grown COBOL legacy system without the more expensive handling of the back-end systems with complex middleware layers.

3.2.7.1 Object Name Service

ONS is an automated networking service similar to the Domain Name Service (DNS) that directs a computer's Web browser to the correct Web server for the Web site an Internet user attempts to access. DNS is an Internet service that translates domain names that we can easily remember (www.yourdomain.com) into IP addresses (e.g., 134.137.234.35). Every time we use a domain name, a DNS service must translate the name into the corresponding IP address. The DNS system is its own network. If one DNS server does not know how to translate a particular domain name, it asks another one, and so on, until the correct IP address is returned. If your network does not support automatic IP address and DNS server assignment, you will need to ask someone in an internal network department for appropriate IP server address, Preferred DNS address, and Alternate DNS address.

The ONS matches the EPC code to information about the product. Once the EPC data is found, it is sent to a Savant server (remember, it is a server in an open architecture). The server then queries the ONS server to find the information. Once the information is found, the Savant server can be programmed to send the information to an EPC IS server and then a SCM system for further processing. Once a Savant receives EPC data, it can query an ONS server to find out where product information is stored.

3.2.7.2 EPC Information Service

EPC Information Service (EPC IS) used to be called the PML (Physical Markup Language) Server or Service, based on common standardized XML vocabularies. The core part of the PML Core provides a standardized format for the exchange of the data captured by the sensors in the Auto-ID infrastructure, for example, RFID readers. The Auto-ID PML Core specification 1.0 defines the syntax and semantics of PML Core. It was developed by the Auto-ID Center to enable computers running on different platforms to understand the size, weight, and type of materials (liquid, metal, or nonmetallic solid) in common format on various objects to which the RFID tags are assigned.

The PML contains all other information in common format about the tagged items such as what the item is, when it was or will be shipped, and, if applicable, what the drastic changes in temperature or other aspects of the environment are. Other examples include information from multiple tags with and without a memory chip, and data observed by a mounted sensor on the tag within the vicinity of a RFID reader (see Appendix F for samples). The company's EPCIS can make the information about its product available to partners and customers with proper credentials.

With PML, a consumer, for example, could find out how to recycle a product's packaging, a retailer could set a trigger to lower prices on yogurt as expiration dates approach, or a manufacturer could recall a specific lot of cars [5]. Companies that offer Web services products include big names: IBM, Microsoft, Sun Microsystems, and Hewlett-Packard. All have incorporated Web services capabilities into their development tools and server software to provide customers with information quickly and easily. Microsoft has incorporated XML into its .NET architecture, offering ASP.NET as a way of developing Web services.

In addition to the Savant server software for Microsoft Windows from http://savant.sourceforge.net, major vendors are offering XML-based Web service software for servers. For example, IBM offers Web Services Toolkit (renamed Emerging Technologies Toolkit) in several Java-based IBM products. It provides WebSphere SDK for Web Services for WebSphere Studio Application Server and WebSphere Application Server. HP Openview Captures includes Web services management capabilities such as capturing Web services transactions and actively manages Web services over WSDL/SOAP. It also enables provisioning, user profile registration, real-time SLA enforcement, access control, subscription management, and prepaid billing.

Free software is available for implementing Web services, such as Java Web Services Development Kit from Sun. There are wizard tools for a fee to set up a Web service for a particular service.

So which Web services tool to use? Your people may want a certain tool and you may opt for another for greater operational efficiency for less cost and less risk for better integration with databases. Different databases have different ways of sending a query for the same information. Make sure your people are aware of the pros and cons of the databases, especially how the data is stored virtually across the servers in an enterprise. Check the maturity level of implementing and integrating a Web service into your enterprise systems, from an organizational, but by department by department.

3.2.7.3 Electronic Product Code

Although the executives are interested in what information the customers want easily and quickly, they should have some knowledge of what constitutes a basic EPC data and how much it can be expanded to hold additional data that might be of use to the customers. This knowledge is important when communicating with IT managers and other players in the building or reorganizing of the supply chain for a more efficient operation with less number of recalls for less cost.

An EPC is a unique 96-bit number embedded onto an individual RFID tag. Another difference is that the bar-coded data labels do not allow for additional data and scanning in real-time whereas the EPC leaves enough room for a reader to write and read additional data on the tag in real-time.

The EPC divides the information into four partitions each separated with a dot something like this:

```
01.0000A13.0005E.000158DC0
```

As shown in Table 3.2, each partition is assigned a block of bits and describes how it is being used. In Table 3.2, we briefly describe for each partition.

From the leftmost side, the code starts with a header followed by a manager partition and then an object class followed by a serial number. The header identifies the EPC's version number and defines the number, type, and length of all subsequent data partitions. The header assists in expanding, changing, or modifying the coding scheme in the maximum–minimum range, including the compact version of the EPC [6]. EPC Manager is the name of the manufacturer, such as Johnson & Johnson whereas the object class refers to the class of product, such as bandages. The serial number is unique to the item instance.

Table 3.2 EPC Partitions

Partition	Bits	Description	Example
Header	8	EPC version number	01
EPC manager	28	Name of the enterprise (e.g., manufacturer's name)	RFID Company (000A13)
Object class	24	Class of product, usually the stock keeping unit (SKU)	Arrowroot Water, 250-ml plastic bottle (0005E)
Serial number	36	Unique to the item instance (e.g., identify a specific brand, size, and bottle of drinking water)	000158DC0

The Auto-ID Center proposed and implemented both 64- and 96-bit EPCs [5]. The 96-bit EPC provides unique identifiers for 268 million companies. Each company can have 16 million object classes, with 68 billion serial numbers in each class. Because we do not need so many serial numbers, a 64-bit code has been proposed to help keep down the price of RFID chips and tags. This is something that the executives like to hear: the leaner the better for less cost.

Let's take a look at an example of setting up a typical query using DNS for looking up information about an EPC. This means that the query and response formats must adhere to the DNS standards, meaning that the EPC will be converted to a domain name and the results must be a valid DNS Resource Record. The following describe a typical ONS query.

1. A sequence of bits containing an EPC is read from an RFID tag:

   ```
   (01 0000000000000000000010 00000000000011000
   000000000000000110010000)
   ```

   As you saw, each partition is separated with a space.
2. The TAG Reader sends that sequence of bits to a local server:

   ```
   (01 0000000000000000000010 00000000000011000
   000000000000000110010000)
   ```

3. That local server converts the bit sequence into the URI (Universal Resource Indicator) Form (TAG Data Standards) and sends it to the local ONS Resolver which then converts the URI form into a domain-name and issues a DNS query for records for that domain.
4. The DNS infrastructure returns a series of answers that contain URLs (Universal Resource Locators) that point to one or more servers.
5. The local resolver than strips URL from the DNS record and presents back to the local server in the following form:

   ```
   http://pml.example.com/ pml-wsdl.xml.
   ```

6. The local server contacts the correct EPCIS server found in the URL for the EPC in question.

3.2.7.4 Savant Servers

In a geographically distributed environment, the Savant gathers, stores, and processes EPC data from one or more readers that can read tags of individual items without opening the case or container. It corrects duplicate reader entries, forwards data up or down the chain, and monitors for events when, for example, the stock level is low. After this, the Savant servers forward data to the SCM or other ERP systems, on an always-on basis or through synchronizing data when needed.

The Savant consists of three major software modules.

■ Event Management System (EMS): A Java technology-based system provides an API with various types of readers, collects data in a standard format, allows customized filters to smooth data, and provides the capability to log data into a database or remote servers using standard protocols (HTTP, Hypertext Transfer Protocol; SOAP, Simple Object Access Protocol; JMS, Java Message Service; and Java Message Queue).

■ Real-time, in memory database structure (RIED): The RIED can be used to store event information. Applications can access RIED using JDBC technology or a native Java technology interface. RIED also supports SQL operations and maintains "snapshots" of the database at different time stamps.

■ Task Management System: This system provides an external interface to schedule tasks. In addition to data gathering and transmission, it can be used to request PML and ONS activity.

3.2.7.5 EPCglobal and the Auto-ID Center

EPCglobal is a joint venture between EAN International and the Uniform Code Council (UCC). Governed by the EPCglobal Board of Governors, it is a not-for-profit organization entrusted by industry to establish and support the EPC Network as the global standard for automatic identification of any item in the supply chain of any company, in any industry, anywhere in the world. Its objective is to drive global adoption of the EPCglobal Network developed by the Auto-ID Center, an academic research project headquartered at the Massachusetts Institute of Technology (MIT) with labs at five leading research universities around the globe.

After October 31, 2004, the administrative functions of the Auto-ID Center ended and the research functions evolved into Auto-ID Labs. EPCglobal continued to work very closely with Auto-ID Labs to refine the technology and meet needs identified in the future. As part of the Auto-ID Center transition to the EPCglobal organization, pertinent content and archived background information from the Auto-ID Center's Web site was relocated to a new site at www.EPCglobalinc.org on November 1, 2003.

The following is a list of members of the Board of Overseers at the Auto-ID Center as of August 23, 2003. As indicated above, the administrative functions of the Auto-ID Center migrated to EPCglobal in a few months. After October 31, 2003, the Board of Overseers was replaced by the EPCglobal's Board of Governors which initially started with 15 seats and is expected to expand to 21 seats. Those members of the Board of Overseers who were not included in the Board of Governors based on a new criterion apparently have remained as EPCglobal members.

Abbott Laboratories
Ahold IS
Best Buy Corporation
Canon Inc.
Carrefour
Chep International
Coca-Cola
CVS
Dai Nippon Printing Co., Ltd
Department of Defense
Ean International
Eastman Kodak
Home Depot
International Paper
Johnson & Johnson
Kellogg's Corporation
Kimberely Clark Corporation
Kraft
Lowes Companies, Inc.
Metro
Mitsui & Co, Ltd.
Nestle
Pepsi
Pfizer
Philip Morris USA
Procter and Gamble Company
Sara Lee
Smurfit-Stone Container Corp
Target Corp.
Tesco Stores Ltd.
The Gillette Company
Toppan Printing
Uniform Code Council
Unilever
United States Postal Service
UPS
Visy Industries
Wal-Mart Stores, Inc.
Wegmans Food Markets, Inc.

Westvaco
Yuen Foong Yu Paper Mfg. Co., LTD.

The following is a list of Technology Board members as of August 23, 2004.

ACNielsen
Alien Technology
Avery Dennison
AWID
British Telecommunications (BT)
Cash's
Catalina Marketing Corp
Checkpoint Systems, Inc.
ConnecTerra, Inc.
Ember Corporation
Embrace Networks
Flexchip AG
Flint Ink
GEA Consulting
GlobeRanger
IBM Business Consulting Serivces
IDTechEx
Impinj, Inc.
Information Resources, Inc.
Intel
Intermec
Invensys PLC
Ishida Co, Ltd.
KSW Microtec AG
Manhattan Associates
Markem Corp.
Matrics
Morningside Technologies
NCR Corporation
Nihon Unisys Ltd.
NTT
NTT Comware
OATSystems
Philips Semiconductors
Rafsec
RF Saw Components

SAMSYS
SAP
Savi Technology
Sensitech
Sensormatic Electronics Corp
Siemens Dematic Corp.
STMicroelectronics
Sun Microsystems
Symbol Technologies
TAGSYS
ThingMagic
Toppan Forms
Toray International, Inc.
Vizional Technologies
Zebra Technologies Corporation

REFERENCES

1. Lyle Ginsburg (Accenture), "The Impact of Electronic Product Code (EPC)/Radio requency Indentification (RFID) on Chain Pharmacy Operations," Pharmacy and Technology Conference, National Association of Chain Drug Stores, Philadelphia, Pennsylvania, August 23–27, 2003 at http://meetings.nacds.org/rxconference/2003/presentations/Tues_ImpactofEPC_Ginsburg.pdf.
2. Myerson, Judith M. Enterprise project failures and solutions, In: *Information Management: Strategy, Systems and Technologies*, Boca Raton, FL: CRC, 2002. This paper is the most popular in the category of project failures and successes.
3. Scott, Judy E. and Iris Vessey, "Managing risks in enterprise system implementation," *Communications of the ACM*, 45(4):77–81, April 2002.
4. Violino, Bob, "Linking RFID with Web services," *RFID Journal*, October 6, 2003 at http://www.rfidjournal.com.
5. "Enabling Smart Objects: Breakthrough RFID-enabled supply chain Execution Infrastructure," Sun Microsystems at www.sun.com.
6. "The Compact Electronic Product Code: A 64-bit Representation of the Electronic Product Code," Auto-ID Center, November 1, 2001. Distribution restricted to sponsors until February 1, 2002.

4

STORING AND RETRIEVING DATA

Enterprise, medium-sized businesses, and small businesses use various database applications to create, retrieve, store, and manage virtualized data in geographically distributed servers. The executives do not care which server is hosting a database operating system or even a particular database, whether it is spanning across the servers or restricted to a certain server. All they care is that they get the RFID data quickly to make important decisions. This means getting data in real-time from different database applications running on different platforms In a global network.

4.1 TWO BIG QUESTIONS

But the biggest two questions are: how well do CEOs, CIOs, and executives understand the relationship between data storage and retrieval issues and RFID/EPC technologies? How well do they understand the risks associated with RFID/EPC technologies?

4.1.1 Relationship between Data Storage and Retrieval Issues

One way of finding out the answers for the first question is to take a look at an interview's findings of the executives' understanding of the current industry perspectives on data synchronization and RFID/EPC technology [2]. Another way is to take a look at some products that would address the issues the executives may raise, and compare advantages and disadvantages of each product based on their perceptions.

Let's first take a look at the three interview findings or how well the executives understand industry perspectives on data synchronization and RFID/EPC technology:

Finding 1: "When asked whether or not data synchronization was a prerequisite to RFID/EPC implementation, there was a mixed bag of answers. Those organizations only familiar with data synchronization of RFID tended to see the initiative more separately than those that had a solid understanding of the benefits of both technologies. Additionally there seemed to be confusion in the industry about what the potential issues were if RFID/EPC implementation proceeded without data synchronization. This was evident regardless of the organization's position on the connection between the two."

Finding 2: "Companies tended to understand that there were applications that could proceed with EPC without data synchronization; those internal applications could theoretically be implemented with some benefit and without syncing with trading partners Concerns were expressed among retailers and manufacturers about collaborative benefits being realized."

Finding 3: "Seventy-five percent of manufacturers indicated that data synchronization should come before EPC either some or all of the time, depending on the type of implementation. Only 25 percent of manufacturers did not see a connection between the sequence of implementation of data synchronization and EPC."

What do these findings mean? Data synchronization should come before the RFID/EPC technology. It would benefit collaborative efforts between trading partners before the selection and implementation of an RFID technology infrastructure take place.

4.1.2 Understanding Risks Associated with RFID/EPC Technologies

Helping the executives gain understanding is important as RFID and EPC selection and implementation require relatively high investment, and they need to be able to get ROIs that would help their balance sheets show a profit margin. The risks of going forward with the RFID and EPC technologies with uncleaned synchronized data between trading partners in the supply chain are high. Table 4.1 lists what each risk is and what factors may contribute to the risk.

Not included in the table is the risk of not having records to track excess, unshipped, over-shipped, lost, idle, damaged, and spoiled items. They require increased handling in communications, including record reconciliation, packaging to return items, and providing transportation to dispose spoiled items.

Table 4.1   Risks Associated with RFID/EPC Technology

Lack of labor reduction	If human intervention is still required to validate EPC information, labor will not be reduced to an optimum level. In fact, labor requirements could even intensify to deal with the increased volume of incorrect data.
Increased data maintenance costs	In the case that trading partners are attempting to use EPC information to track product without having synchronized their data, they may need to map different product information from one format to another to make use of the information.
Inaccurate replenishment or no reduction of out-of-stock	If supplier and retailer data is not synchronized, incorrect product may land on the shelf, or required replenishments may be missed, even when product is available in the backroom.
Inaccurate pricing	If a system identifies a product incorrectly, the wrong price could be associated with it. If this is not addressed, the product could be priced incorrectly on the shelf.
Potential for increased transaction management costs	Inconsistent data formats traded between partners for EPC use may require increased handling in everyday communications, including purchase orders and receiving of goods.

Source: ATK/KSA. All rights reserved. Reprinted with permission.

4.2 EPC TECHNOLOGY IN FUNCTIONAL AREAS

The executives would need to know how RFID/EPC technology would be used physically, culturally, and organizationally, to form a cross-functional EPC core team of manufacturers, transportation crew, distributors, packaging people, information technology specialists, merchandisers, and other players in the supply chain.

Table 4.2 shows how the role of EPC technology would contribute to the following functional areas, each of which is given a reason for it.

4.3 PERCEPTIONS OF PRODUCT BENEFITS

The executives might be also interested in the findings of a survey on how each supplier and retailer has perceived their products benefiting from the item-level adoption of the data synchronization foundation. Table 4.3 shows

Table 4.2   EPC Technology in Functional Areas

Manufacturing	Tags will likely be applied during the manufacturing process. The tag application and cost must be incorporated into manufacturing operations. In addition, the information initially stored in the RFID tag should be written according to the requirements of the rest of the value chain.
Transportation	If the EPC is to provide better overall supply chain visibility, the transportation network will need to use tags correctly to update the supply chain monitoring system at critical points. Additionally, if transportation is to be held liable for any inaccurate shipments due to EPC information, it will need to understand how the tag information is used and how it affects the transportation network.
Distribution	As benefits within the distribution network are key for most companies considering EPC use, distribution must be heavily involved in determining which applications of the EPC would be most beneficial, including which data carried in the EPC is most useful.
Packaging	Incorporating RFID tags into product packaging, at all levels, will be critical for companies deploying RFID/EPC.
Information technology	RFID and EPC implementation requires systems development and support. Work will be required in areas such as database selection, capacity, interface creation, data summarization, and item data management tools.
Store operations	The EPC code can have a significant impact on store operations, from learning to use the system for accurate receiving, backroom storage, and shelf replenishment, to the use of smart shelves for theft deterrence and no-scan checkout.
Merchandising	It is crucial to determine where EPC tags will be applied to merchandise, which merchandise they will be applied to, and how the tags may be perceived by the customers.
Sales	Sales personnel can be a source of great ideas of using the enhanced information available through EPC use. Additionally, suppliers in particular will benefit from sales personnel focusing on sales rather than addressing product identification and invoicing issues.
Human resources	Two key components of realizing the full potential with this implementation are proper training and change management. HR should be involved early to communicate and understand the impact of these changes on corporate policy and regulations.

Table 4.3 Perceptions of Retail Product Benefits

Retail Product	Item Cost (%)	Time-Sensitive Product (%)	Risk of Out-of-Stock (%)	Risk of Theft (%)	Risk of Counterfeit or Smuggling (%)	Product Safety/ Recall Concerns (%)	Overall (%)
Razor blades	75	0	100	100	25	0	100
Cereal	50	25	50	0	0	50	0
Ground beef	25	100	25	0	25	100	50
Cigarettes	50	25	75	100	75	25	50
Soda	25	25	100	25	25	50	50
High-end apparel	100	100	75	75	50	0	100
CDs & DVDs	75	50	75	100	100	0	100

Source: ATK/KSA.

seven items, each showing the suppliers' and retailers' perceptions of product characteristics.

As shown in Table 4.3, razor blades, high-end apparel, and CDs and DVDs are perceived to have a better chance of taking advantage of data synchronization for RFID technologies. The risk of an item being out of stock is the highest with razor blades and soda meaning that they are popular items. The risk of an item being stolen is the highest with razor blades and CDs and DVDs.

4.4 DATABASE CD ON LOCAL WORKSTATION

There are certain advantages of storing data on and retrieving them from the CDs as long you take precautionary measures on securing them. If a CD is run on a local workstation, it will not create network traffic bottlenecks characteristic of the connections between the workstation and remote servers.

We need to address how well a database during a pilot study stage would perform in a production environment. Although the database is on the local disk, there is no bandwidth or any other network issues to be concerned about (see Figure 4.1), so the retrieval can be done in a matter of seconds.

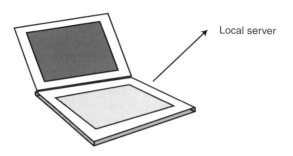

Figure 4.1   No Bandwidth Issues

4.5 REMOTE DATABASE SERVERS

Once the database is moved to a networked server—many miles—away from the local machine, we will have storage and retrieval issues (see Figure 4.2).

To discuss them, we first ask questions, such as:

- How can we reduce the number of traffic bottleneck incidents?
- Why do we need to divide the database into the static and dynamic partitions?
- What kind of database management should we get to satisfy our requirements?

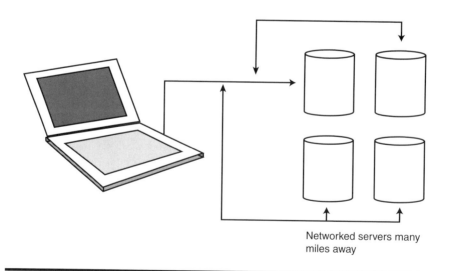

Figure 4.2   Possible Bandwidth Issues

- What is the optimal way of increasing throughputs and operational efficiency?
- How do we reduce loading times cost effectively?
- How do we migrate a relational database management system to another?
- How is the partitioning emulated and what are the partitioning types?
- How do you determine the number of partitions for a database?
- What are the factors you should consider in your migration planning?

4.5.1 How Can We Reduce the Number of Traffic Bottleneck Incidents?

When a database becomes too huge for the local server, updating it frequently may cause the performance to go downward below the minimum acceptable level. Migrating the database to a remote server will not solve the problem. It is more efficient to access the database on a CD than across the Internet. By putting the data closer to the user, the bandwidth can be decreased by many orders of magnitude, so this is the preferred approach when monthly or quarterly CD updates will suffice.

You can eliminate the bandwidth by putting the database on an internal disk or reduce the bandwidth by putting the database on a local server connected directly to your computer without going across the Internet. You can convert your desktop computer or laptop into a local server (e.g., IIS and Savant) and connect it directly with the other local servers in an intranet network. You can plug in an external hard drive as a local server into your desktop computer or laptop.

To give you an idea, Table 4.4 compares the speeds of doing 1-Mb file transfer to a hard disk from a CD or from broadband cable access (assuming there is no delay in message delivery across the Internet caused by other Internet users). Keep in mind the technology used in manufacturing a CD-ROM could affect its performance. As shown in the table, the CD with the speed of 8x is the fastest.

Table 4.4 Speeds of 1-Mb File Transfer

8x CD-ROM	.8 seconds
4x CD-ROM	1.7 seconds
1.5 Mbps cable modem	5 seconds
256 Kbps DSL	31 seconds
56 Kbps modem	143 seconds or 2 minutes and 23 seconds

4.5.2 Why Do We Need to Divide the Database into the Static and Dynamic Partitions?

Let's suppose the database reaches the maximum capacity of a CD-ROM; a most likely event will occur when a RFID database outgrows its smaller size for the pilot study's testing environment. As a way of getting around this problem, the traditional approach has been to move the entire database onto a networked server, which may be far removed from the end users who frequently send updates across the Internet.

Although this approach assures that users see or store up-to-date information, it also implies a much lower level of performance. This is particularly true when the network is the Internet and the risk of a large number of traffic bottleneck incidents is high. To reduce the risk to a more tolerable level, we need to consider which portion of the database should be static that does not need to be updated and which portion of the same database should be dynamic that needs to be frequently updated.

In the real world, the vast majority of information in most databases is relatively static, and a relatively small, but nevertheless important, subset of the data is updated frequently. This means the RFID database system needs to be designed in such a way that the database can be divided into static and dynamic partitions. The static partitions can remain on a local server and the dynamic partitions can be moved to a remote server for frequent updates by the users. The bandwidth, on an overall basis, can be decreased by many orders of magnitude.

4.5.3 What Kind of Database Management Should We Get to Satisfy Our Requirements?

The executives need to consult with the requirements specialist to take a look at the requirements specification for a database management system for the RFID technology infrastructure. Not only the specification should conform to a specific standard such as those provided by the IEEE or other standard-body organization; the executives should raise any issues regarding the requirements that may have been overlooked due to the emerging RFID technologies.

Some issues to be considered are whether the organization should treat RFID technology as one of the sensor-based services or it should focus on an RFID database middleware that collects and interprets RFID events and escalates them to critical operational events or both. Oracle and IBM are examples of each, respectively.

Oracle Sensor-Based Services [1], an RFID-ready Oracle Warehouse Management was demonstrated at the RFID Journal Live! Conference in late March 2004. Based on Oracle Database 10g, Oracle Application Server 10g, Oracle Enterprise Manager 10g, and Oracle E-Business Suite 11*i* - Oracle

Sensor-Based Services enable companies to integrate sensor-based information into their enterprise systems to achieve supply chain visibility in real-time.

Making up the Sensor-Based Services are primarily two middleware components: Compliance Package and RFID Pilot Kit. The Compliance component allows companies to address the specific and unique reporting requirements coming down from major retailers and the U.S. Department of Defense. The Pilot Kit is more suited for smaller companies that only need drivers for the major RFID readers, and some reporting and analytic tools to process RFID data.

Oracle Sensor-Based Services provide capabilities to capture, manage, analyze, access, and respond to data from sensors such as RFID, location, and temperature. It allows users to query and audit specific events occurring in the system, and to receive alerts on recalls of a bad batch of products.

4.5.4 What Is the Optimal Way of Increasing Throughputs and Operational Efficiency?

One of the ways to answer this question is to provide two scenarios that would show how the RFID technology can be used to increase throughputs and operational efficiency. They are spoiled chicken and separated item scenarios.

Let's start the first scenario with a truck equipped with an RFID device that monitors the temperature of plastic-wrapped chicken it is transporting to a supermarket. The chicken must be transported at a certain range of cool temperature and will get spoiled when the temperature goes beyond that range. If the temperature reaches the danger level due to some kind of breakdown in the refrigeration component inside the truck, the device will send an alert to the driver, the warehouse manager, and the executive in real-time. The driver will immediately stop the truck, quickly fix the problem, or turn on the back-up refrigeration, and go to the nearest facility to transfer the chicken to another truck to complete the trip.

Of course, if it took too long for the problem to be fixed, the chicken already got spoiled after being exposed to high temperature. Meanwhile the RFID device collected data on the time and location the temperature began to deviate from the normal range, how long the chicken was subject to high temperature, and when the temperature was finally put under control when the problem was fixed or when the back-up refrigeration was turned on.

Let's consider the separated item scenario. As a pallet of nonperishable items was loaded onto a truck at a warehouse distribution center, the pallet passed by a RFID reader that picked up data: item type, time location, and so on. More pallets followed. When the truck was full, the back door of the truck was closed, and the driver drove away from the loading truck to begin a long trip.

During the transit, the RFID reader periodically updated the time and location it scanned the pallets of items. Somehow, the back door got loose, and the driver was not aware of what was happening. When the truck went over a bumping spot on the road in the process of being reconstructed, an item fell out of the truck. When the truck got to its final destination, the driver was not aware that the item got separated. Then he got a call from the distribution center about the separated item based on the information the RFID reader collected and sent back to the distribution center from time to time during the transit. The distribution center assured him that someone found the separated item and returned it to the center using the address found on the item.

If the items, however, get separated very frequently, we have another problem. To resolve part of the problem we need to take a closer look at the ways we can improve the business processes to increase higher visibility of the items. Improving the processes will assist in reducing the risk to a more tolerable level of having the items separated during the transit from one point to another in the supply chain.

4.5.4.1 PeopleSoft Enterprise Systems

Let's assume the problems with spoiled chickens and items getting separated during the transit have been fixed, the RFID data is then sent to back-end legacy systems, such as an Oracle's PeopleSoft Enterprise Supply Chain Management and IBM RFID product for further processing.

PeopleSoft enterprise systems have encountered some database optimization problems before they came under Oracle's umbrella. Oracle's purchase of PeopleSoft along with the Oracle Sensor-based services have helped gain additional share of the database market. As of March 2005, it held 41.5 percent share of the market. However, it may change in the future as new technologies emerge for high visibility of RFID items.

4.5.4.2 IBM RFID Product

IBM, known for providing the overall systems integration for RFID at the METRO Group, is integrating RFID with DB2 Information Integrator for Content. It provides structured enterprise information via connectors to DB2 relational databases. The IBM product is made of three different elements: Devices, WebSphere RFID Premises Server, and a WebSphere integration server.

Readers, scanners, and printers are embedded with the first element, WebSphere RFID Device Infrastructure. They also include other sensor devices that come with RFID, such as temperature. The second element, IBM WebSphere RFID Premises Services, is a middleware product that interprets RFID events to detect operational events, such as the sudden change in temperature of perishable products while being transported in a vehicle. The third element is an IBM integration server, such as WebSphere Business Integration Server or Server Foundation, unlike Oracle that offers an application server and E-Business Suite applications for a variety of data types across the enterprise.

4.5.5 How Do We Reduce Loading Times Cost Effectively?

Reducing loading times in a cost-effective way is another issue about which executives are concerned. Several vendors offer a new way of resolving long loading times that could be caused by heavy Internet traffic at certain times and even network bottlenecks High-speed bandwidths or even high-compression files do not always guarantee fast loading times, a factor that could have an impact on remote database performance.

Let's take a look at how Base One's Rich Client Architecture solves the loading problems. In the Rich Client model, the client PC can have a large library of programs and data files. It transfers over the network the instructions to these programs to create the rich content using the CPU and local storage resources of the client computer. The transmitted instructions might include a small amount of valuable dynamic data to fill in certain details of the content not available in the client data files.

For example, a military application might keep large detailed maps resident on a hardened laptop, with the latest locations of available targets picked up across slow communication lines and displayed as little flags on the map and may not have certain data needed for adequate implementation. To fill in the data needed, it gets the data from a remote server: the latest locations of available targets picked up across slow communication lines. These targets are displayed as little flags on the map.

This scenario might be useful in determining where the RFID items need to be distributed as the target locations changed, or even putting a flag on a map where RFID-based items got accidentally separated while they were in transit to a warehouse distribution center. The back door of the vehicle was not tightly secured and became loose.

The information on the location is obtained from a fixed reader in the interior of, say, a truck that periodically scans these items. When the reader scans again at its preassigned time interval, it sends an alert to the distribution center where the remote server wirelessly receives data from that reader. The alert may contain information, for example, that an item got separated and might be found at a certain location.

In the third scenario, the remote server gets an alert on the sudden drop in temperature in the interior of a truck carrying perishable items. It then sends data as flags to be placed on a map on a laptop or a PDA of an emergency worker and an executive to keep posted on the visibility of the RFID-based items in transit.

It is so much faster for the application to use local disk to manage previously downloaded large, high-resolution graphics. It can run faster than the Web site running through the same phone line.

A database library can be used to create Rich Client architecture. The library provides a useful middleware layer between the application and the database. It supports databases from IBM, Microsoft, Oracle, and Sybase.

4.5.6 How Do We Migrate a Relational Database Management System to Another?

Another issue of concern to the executives is the migration of a relational database management system to another. The source database table, report, form, and query objects may be different from their target counterparts. This problem can be alleviated with migration toolkits provided by major database vendors Oracle, Microsoft, and IBM. These toolkits display the target equivalent of the source tables, reports, forms, and queries.

Third-party tools, such as those offered by Bunker Hill Corporation, allow conversion of MS Access databases to Oracle (Scriptoria), and DB2 (ei-O), so the enterprises can take advantage of better network performance and larger capacities of Oracle and DB2 databases, especially when a MS Access database is reaching its capacity limits. (The size of a MS Access database that can be converted is limited to 2 GB.)

There are few things you should keep in mind when converting or migrating from MS Access. Migrating views from MS Access to Oracle may be limited depending on the complexity and the number of the MS Access databases and applications. MS Access and MySql do not have the groups/roles features of the other more heavy-duty RDBMSs. Not supported by MS Access and MySql are stored procedures and event triggers.

Although MS SQL Server is seen as the default choice for migration to Oracle, migration issues are automatically resolved when Oracle Migration Workbench is used. Automatic resolution, however, does not mean inherent incompatibilities do not exist. For example, MS SQL Server focuses on accessing multiple databases whereas Oracle consists primarily of a system tablespace and multiple user-defined tablespaces. What this means is that MS SQL Server is built upon multiple databases and does not understand what a tablespace is all about. However, there are some workaround solutions to make the migration work.

4.5.7 How Is Partitioning Emulated and What Are the Partitioning Types?

Let's take a look at the way Microsoft SQL Server tries to emulate the partitioning of Oracle tablespaces striped across multiple disks that appear as one logical disk drive. For Microsoft SQL Server, let's first look at file-groups and then RAID and show how both can be used to make the partitioning emulation.

Microsoft SQL Server uses filegroups at the database level to control the physical placement of tables and indexes. Filegroups are logical containers of one or more files, and data contained within a filegroup is proportionally filled across all files belonging to the filegroup. File groups allow you to distribute large tables across multiple files to improve I/O throughput.

Distributing data can also be done with hardware-based RAID (Redundant Array of Independent Disks) or Windows NT software-based RAID. Windows NT software-based RAID or hardware-based RAID can set up stripe sets consisting of multiple disk drives that appear as one logical drive. The recommended RAID configuration for SQL Server is RAID 5 (stripe sets with an extra parity drive, for redundancy) and RAID 10 (mirroring of stripped sets with parity).

When a database gets very large, you might want to consider both the RAID and filegroup options. For instance, if you have a database that spans multiple physical RAID arrays, you might want to consider filegroups to further distribute your I/O across multiple RAID arrays. Just remember two key words regarding Microsoft SQL Server: filegroups and RAID.

For MS SQL Server, RAID is one example of hardware partitioning that can be achieved without splitting tables by physically placing them on individual disk drives. Having a table on one physical drive and other tables on separate drives can improve query performance. Alternatively, a table striped across multiple drives can be scanned faster than the same table stored on a drive.

Hardware partitioning, however, is not the only partitioning type. Horizontal partitioning and vertical partitioning are some other types you might want to consider. Partitioning data horizontally based on age is common. You can, for example, partition the data into ten tables, with each table containing data for each of ten years. You can also divide a table into multiple, say twelve, tables, each containing the same number of columns but with fewer rows. Each carries one month of data for a given year.

Vertical partitioning divides a table into multiple tables containing fewer columns. Normalization and row splitting are some examples of vertical partitioning. You probably heard about normalization. What normalization does is that it removes redundant columns from a table and places them in secondary tables. Primary key and foreign key relationships link secondary tables to their primary counterparts. Row splitting is what it says. It splits the original tables with fewer columns. Each logical row in a split table matches the same logical row in the others.

You need to decide which types of partitioning—hardware-based, vertically, or horizontally—will make economic sense to generate ROIs short-term and long-term. You should include in the calculations your comparison of:

- Response times for complex queries such as those associated with online analytical processing (OLAP) applications
- Partitioning types within a single system or across a cluster of systems
- Scalability ranges to support very large databases or complex workloads along with increased parallelism for administrative tasks such as index creation, backup, and restore

Although major database vendors offer parallelism and partitioning to increase throughputs and operation efficiency, you should do your homework on how benchmarks should be conducted, what the best price/performance ratios would be. It is more efficient and less costly to distribute a large database over multiple medium-sized machines than to run it on one large machine.

IBM DB2 UDB is capable of partitioning a tablespace into multiple tablespaces horizontally and vertically, quite useful for the warehouse of RFID data, the scope and range that could grow over a period of time. IBM points out the fact that the physical design of a database must meet certain operational requirements, such as:

- How many times can a database be loaded and refreshed within a given period of time?
- What is the best way of loading the data?
- How are we going to update the tables?
- Are we going to append data at the end of the data set or in a new partition? After appending the data in a partition, how much time is reduced to refresh and maximize the database availability during the updates?
- How much time is allowed for reloading a table?
- Which is more effective in restoring data, from operation data sources or from image copies?
- What backup site should we consider for backing up and restoring critical data? This site should be outside the facility in which a computer/network infrastructure system runs a database system, and other legacy systems, including SCM, as well.

IBM DB2 UDB allows partitioned tablespaces to perform complex queries in parallel. In addition to partitioned tablespaces, DB2 also offers simple and segmented tablespaces, the features not available in other RDBMSs. A simple tablespace can contain more than one table and is composed of pages, and each page can contain many rows from many tables. A segmented tablespace is composed of groups of pages called segments. Each segment can hold rows from a single table. In the real world, where an RFID-based database is expected to grow, requiring the database tables be split across multiple disks, partitioning tablespaces have advantages of accommodating the growth that simple and segmented tablespaces are not capable of handling.

Although you may not care about the partitioning key, you should know that the proper choice of this key can maximize availability, allow load and refresh activities, increase parallelism for queries and utilities, and accommodate growth of data.

4.5.8 How Do You Determine the Number of Partitions for a Database?

Given the basic information about partitioning, how do you determine the number of partitions for a database? According to IBM, there are several factors to consider:

- Business considerations
- Utility processing
- Size of the data
- Barch window availability
- CPU and I/O configuration
- Query parallelism

Of these six factors, business considerations, CPU and I/O configuration, and query parallelism are the most important for executives. We already talked about query parallelism. Keep in mind that this feature is related to the other two factors. If CPU and I/O configuration are not sufficient, then response times of query parallelism will be not what you have expected. In the same way, if business considerations are not well thought out, the response times of query parallelism will be less than the expected norm.

Now, let's take a look at business considerations and CPU and I/O configuration factors.

Business considerations. You may have a good reason to keep data together in a partition. For instance, you may want to organize data by week and by month, so the weekly or monthly data marked can be deleted according to some date or age criteria. You also need to consider:

- How much space you need for a partition to allow for growth of data within that partition
- What type of alert you want to receive and send when the data reaches the maximum capacity of the partition
- How the data should be overflowed into another partition
- How the affected partitions should be reorganized; what the processes are involved in reorganizing the partitions

CPU and I/O configuration. To determine the number of partitions, you need to know how many partitions the I/O subsystem can produce and CPU can consume. To support new data requirements that require an increase in hardware capacity, you need new hardware configurations that would better support the growth of data to be produced by the I/O subsystem and consumed by the CPU.

4.5.9 What Are the Factors You Should Consider in Your Migration Planning?

Whatever the source database you choose to migrate to a target database via a IBM Migration Tookit or manually, you need to carefully consider several factors that could affect your business. Some factor example factors to consider as suggested by IBM are:

- Allocation of resource required to get the database objects, stored procedures, and physical database from the original database to DB2 UDB
- The person-hours, downtime, and human error
- The extent of customizing objects according to your business migration specification
- The extent of complex features that require manual modification

The factors to be considered should be part of migration planning and project management. Good project management practices, however, do not always ensure the success of a migration project. They must be in the collaborative environment where executives, project managers, and IT specialists can work together on a common ground. The executives speak a business language different from the language spoken by the project manager and IT specialists. For instance, from a project management standpoint, a business process chart addresses business requirements that the executives understand whereas a more technical model focuses on system capabilities. Combining both business process and technical charts in some kind of a common format will assist in formulating a policy on migration process.

According to IBM, a migration process could consist of five steps: specify, convert, refine, generate, and deploy. The convert step can be used to change the default mapping between the source and target databases. The convert stop is used to view the conversion and error messages. Both the convert and refine steps can be repeated until the conversion results you get automatically or manually in the refine step are accurate and complete. The generate and deploy steps transfer the object to the target database.

4.6 DATABASES IN COMPANY MERGER PROCESSES

I have previously mentioned that Oracle has chosen to compete against SAP for a greater share of the market even after Oracle purchased PeopleSoft to beef up its ERP (including SCM) offerings. In contrast, IBM and SAP have been alliance partners for 30 years in delivering enterprise solutions even though at this time of writing SAP has run databases in the Oracle environment.

It is interesting to note that IBM is also a SAP customer, and SAP is an IBM customer. In 1999, SAP extended their relationship with IBM by adopting DB2 UDB as the strategic platform for SAP production systems, particularly the SAP Business Warehouse and mySAP.com (E-procurement, SCM, etc.). DB2 UDB provides support for AIX, OS/400, z/OS, Windows 2000, Windows Server 2003, SUN, HP-UX, and Linux. IBM also offers a database migration from IBM Informiz Dynamic Server to DB2 UDB in an SAP environment.

As of January 2005, IBM has planned for a SAP-specific database; that is, DB2 specifically tailored to run SAP applications (e.g., DB2 for SAP). So what is the relationship between Oracle and IBM as a result of the PeopleSoft acquisition? Because PeopleSoft includes J.D. Edwards, with a strong legacy of applications running on IBM's iSeries (or AS/400) platforms, even though the bulk of PeopleSoft applications run on Oracle databases, Oracle has made commitments to support customers running Oracle/Peoplesoft wares on IBM middleware and databases. Improving Oracle's rapport with IBM is a number one priority.

What does this all mean? It means that executives need to take a closer look at the hardware and software acquired in the merger process and how the acquisition could affect existing relationships between major vendors, that is, whether former enemies will become strategic alliance partners and so forth.

4.7 HYBRID DATABASES

RFID technology would greater benefit from linking data to hybrid databases that provide native support for the coexistence of both relational and unstructured data. As of February 2006, IBM offered the DB2 "Viper" release, in beta, as a hybrid database. This appears to be a way of overcoming the limitations of relational databases in searching and sorting huge amount of data.

Viper (now known as DB2 9) stores both structured and unstructured data in their respective native formats and allow both types of data to be queried via SQL or Xquery statements. The idea is to be able to write an XML statement to query native XML interspersed with relational data. This is in contrast to relational databases that currently offer some support for XML data and store it as relational. Expect responses and challenges from their competitors: Oracle and Microsoft on hybrid databases.

4.8 WEB SERVICES

Although the development of hybrid databases is in the works, Web services technologies have evolved and grown due to the popularity of modularization that characterizes Web services that have been used to retrieve and store data and databases.

Some executives, however, are reluctant to change their legacy systems or migrate their databases for a simple reason that it is not cost effective to do so. In this case they many want to consider Web services to bridge the gap between RFID technology infrastructure and legacy systems including SCM and databases from major vendors.

Several vendors, such as WebFocus, provide Web services offerings to bridge the information gap. According to Myerson's article [3], Web services are seen as a way of lowering development and integration costs and improving customer and supplier relationships while expanding relationships. Web services, on the other hand, can be defined as application components capable of collaborating with each other on integration and aggregation of applications between enterprises over multiple networks on different platforms in a standard way. The exposed Web services can be done within an enterprise and between one enterprise having the SCM system and another enterprise maintaining an RFID database over the Internet.

In the real world, not all enterprises offer all aspects of EAI applications (SCM, ERP, etc.). To get around this problem, an enterprise lacking the SCM application can use Web services to link up dynamically to an external SCM provider that, in turn, points to an external ERP provider in an alliance partnership with SAP.

One major difference between EAI and Web services should be noted. The EAI is tightly coupled and can be either synchronous or synchronous, whereas Web Services are loosely coupled and the consumers of synchronous Web services must be available at all times.

Let's take a look at some WebFocus product suites that address some issues. The WebFOCUS enterprise business intelligence suite provides the capability to consume Web service information and incorporate it as a data source, and present data as a Web service.

WebFOCUS exposes reports as Web services, allowing external applications to consume them via standard Simple Object Access Protocol (SOAP). WebFOCUS' data access and integration capabilities provide access to relational data sources and legacy applications. WebFOCUS reports can incorporate information from any enterprise system and then be published as a Web service. One issue here is that SOAP is not completely interoperable industrywide, although industries have been working together to remove incompatibilities.

The WebFOCUS Web Services Adapter enables Web services created and deployed using any Web-services authoring tool to be directly consumed by the WebFOCUS report server and manipulated as though it were relational data. The same Web service may be manipulated in conjunction with RDBMSs, DBMSs, and legacy file systems accessible through the WebFOCUS enterprise adapter architecture. WebFOCUS can also read a Web service as a data source when creating a data warehouse or mart using WebFOCUS ETL Manager.

So, how does WebFocus handle load balancing?

WebFOCUS Maintain's accomplishes scalability (see Figure 4.3) in two ways: by exploiting load balancing to grow and shrink dynamically as the load increases and decreases, and by supporting "n-tier" processing, which enables developers to partition application logic over one or more platforms. The server can be distributed and linked to WebFOCUS servers on any other platform.

WebFOCUS Maintain provides closed-loop business intelligence with the ability to update information stored in databases. It also provides an object-oriented 4GL for structured, object-oriented, and hybrid programming.

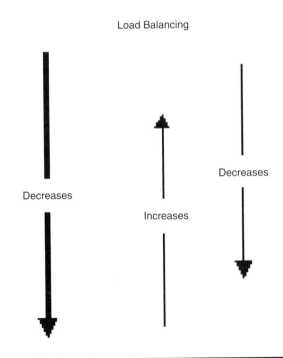

Figure 4.3　Dynamic Load Balancing

There are other Web services you might want to consider. You need to ask questions on how well their Web services link up with external Web services or EAI applications over the Internet. There are issues of how much bandwidth is needed and how to handle network traffic bottlenecks created either up expected surge in the traffic or when the traffic passes over from a larger bandwidth to a smaller bandwidth in a busy time. Although there have been talks about mixing bandwidths of different sizes and types in a four- or six-lane traffic lane in which a faster packet can easily go move over to the adjacent lane rather than be forced in the same lane in front of the slower packet from a different application. But this will not happen for a while.

REFERENCES

1. Connect the Dots: Harnessing Collaborative Technologies to Deliver Better Value to Consumers, A.T. Kearney and Kurt Salmon Associates, February 2004 at http://www.fmi.org/supply/Connectthedots.pdf.
2. Myerson, Judith, Web Services: A Supplement to Enterprise Application Integration, *Information Management: Strategy, Systems and Technologies*, Boca Raton, FL: Auerbach, 2003.
3. Schwartz, Ephraim, "Oracle unveils next round of RFID solutions," *Infoworld*, March 29, 2004.

5

RFID BUSINESS PROCESSES

Many top suppliers implemented RFID infrastructure in response to initial mandates from large customers such as Wal-Mart, the Department of Defense, Target, Albertsons, and Best Buy in the United States and the METRO Group in Germany. These customers mandated the suppliers provide their own RFID equipment and infrastructure and deliver RFID-tagged cases and pallets of items by January 1, 2005.

Other large retailers provided their top suppliers with RFID equipment and technology to help them to get started. Some suppliers who did not receive the mandates or the RFID equipment from their customers decided to invest voluntarily in RFID technology rather than waiting for the "second" mandates and for opportunities to reap profits from RFID technology later on.

There are suppliers who have received the mandate from a customer, and the RFID equipment from another customer and have introduced or already introduced emerging RFID technologies into their companies without waiting for either a mandate or RFID equipment from a third customer. There are some suppliers who have received mandates from customers each requiring different RFID infrastructure implementation, depending on the type of item and package to be tagged. Some items and packages can be tagged with minimal problems whereas others can be tagged after much experimentation on where on the product, case, or pallet the tag should be placed to avoid close proximity to offending materials.

There are suppliers who have implemented or planned to implement RFID technology in a portion of the supply chain with the intention of implementing it to the remaining part of the supply chain. This will happen when RFID technology gets more sophisticated (e.g., from pallet RFID tagging to individual RFID item tagging), or the customers issue new mandates, or provide suppliers with more advanced RFID equipment.

Things can get very challenging when a supplier is dealing with multiple customers and rely on other suppliers to supply certain parts to complete the assembly or multi-layer packaging at the originating supply distribution center. These external suppliers may have their own complex set of relationships with the customers. The customers that both the originating suppliers and external suppliers deal with may be the same or different. The customers and suppliers may have multiple systems that require the same RFID information.

In this chapter, we take a look at implementation approaches, and business process reengineering, and briefly cover how organizational maturity affects reengineering projects. After this, we discuss three types of Multi-Layer RFID Business Process Model: basic, adaptive, and predictive. Next, we show instances of RFID business process strategy that various companies have used: IBM, Canus, International Paper, Kayser-Roth, Philips Semiconductors, Intel, Unilever, a major IT clothier retailer, and Marks and Spencer. We talk about Supply Chain Planning (SCP) and Supply Chain Execution (SCE) as they pertain to RFID business processes. We finish the chapter on various RFID business process life cycles including the adaptive linear feedback, and adaptive dynamic lifecycle models.

5.1 IMPLEMENTATION APPROACHES

Implementation approaches can be broadly divided into one-dimensional, two-dimensional, and multidimensional, each of which affects business processes of supply chains in some ways. Each group can have variants to suit organizational needs for improving business processes of RFID implementation at the site, package, and network levels.

One scenario for the one-dimensional approach is a customer that relies on suppliers who have no other customers to sell and who have implemented RFID technology in their entire supply chain and distribute the tagged cases and pallets to a limited number of distribution centers. A scenario for the two-dimensional approach is the supplier who deals with one or more customers who mandate RFID implementation in various maturity phases and another customer who does not until a later time. A scenario for the multidimensional approach is a supplier selling their products to multi-customers and getting supplies from other suppliers to complete the business processes of the RFID infrastructure of emerging technologies at the pallet, case, and item levels. Not all suppliers who provided equipment to the requesting supplier have RFID infrastructure in place completely or partially, or will reach the item level due to the nature of products to be packaged.

Whatever the approach is used, and whatever the complexity of the supplier–customer relationship is, the RFID implementation is seen as a better way of tracking and increasing the visibility of items throughout the supply chains, and improving business processes not otherwise possible with bar-coding technology. Some benefits include:

- Real-time recovery of mis-shipped items or items that got separated from shipment while in transit
- Reallocation of personnel within the operation of supply chain
- Elimination of lost sales opportunities due to massive recalls of items that have not been RFID-tagged
- Prevention of theft allowing for faster handling of the items: loading and distributing from a supply chain and replenishing popular items at a retailer's store
- Automated real-time alerts for all exceptions via mobile devices and faster response with corrective actions wirelessly or wired
- Better traceability when errors occur in tagging RFID labels to the items, cases, and pallets

RFID implementation requires integration with servers, storage devices, and EAI applications: between units within an organization, and between an originating enterprise and external partners. It also requires on the part of the executives to select carefully which implementation approach to use particularly when they receive mandates from different customers, each requiring different RFID infrastructure whether customers offer RFID equipment or not.

Even though the first mandates do not mean the RFID technology has matured, so much of the success of emerging technological implementations hinges on undertaking the appropriate business process reengineering work. Business processes will become more sophisticated and complex as technology implementations evolve.

Let's take a look at dual shipping faces of some suppliers as a way of starting the RFID implementation and at two sides of the mandates of providing the suppliers with RFID equipment and requiring the suppliers to provide their own equipment.

5.1.1 Dual Shipping Faces

In response to initial mandates from customers, some suppliers succeeded in RFID implementation and others did not. Some of those who succeeded may have dual shipping faces of their supply chain. One portion of the cases and pallets are to be shipped with RFID tags to large retailers that mandated RFID implementation, and the other portion of the cases and pallets with bar codes are to be shipped to other customers that did not issue the mandates but may do so at a future date. Those suppliers with a dual shipping face will eventually extend incrementally the RFID implementation to the remaining cases and pallets to derive benefits and competitive advantage of RFID for all of the shipping components of the supply chain.

5.1.2 Two Sides of the Mandates

It would have been far more beneficial if the larger retailers that mandated RFID implementation provided their largest suppliers with RFID equipment, so there would be a greater number of suppliers succeeding in RFID implementation. The British retailer Marks and Spencer just did that, as compared to Wal-Mart and others that issued the mandate that its 100 suppliers provide their own RFID equipment. Marks and Spencer equipped its 200 biggest suppliers with RFID equipment after convincing them that the benefits of implementing the RFID technology would exceed the costs of doing so [1]. What this means is that the suppliers are more receptive to implementing RFID technology when they are provided with equipment than when they are not.

The kinds of equipment the suppliers get depends on the size and type of business the customer is engaged in and also depends on whether the benefits can exceed the costs of RFID implementation. It is very important that customers also provide the suppliers with RFID experts, business process analysts, and software integrators to assist in implementation and to resolve any technical issues that may arise during pilot studies.

The suppliers who received the mandates and did not initially succeed in implementation lacked time to develop the checklist, and thus did not have much choice in selecting and testing the RFID technology. Under these circumstances, they were forced to adopt a "tag and ship" approach to RFID tagging to keep large retailers happy at the expense of automated business processes and ROIs that they could realize in later years.

These suppliers were in a hurry to implement the RFID technology without regard for improving business processes in a product's life cycle, from parts assembly to case or pallet delivery. Many of the processes were still done by humans rather than the systems that can automatically track the flow of business processes more efficiently. This means the approach to business processes these suppliers were using in implementing RFID was based on the tag and ship approach rather than the automatic tracking system approach to achieve efficiency and productivity gains in the entire supply chain.

5.1.3 RFID Implementation Checklist

You need to develop a checklist of questions for which you and your staff can provide answers to help you better plan for an RFID implementation. So, you would be in better shape, for instance, to deal with a retailer that mandates you provide your own equipment and another retailer that provides you with the equipment. The checklist should focus on the impact of the implementation of RFID infrastructure on your enterprisewide organization. You can determine from the answers what business processes need to be improved in order for the implementation to succeed.

Here is a sample checklist that you could use as a guideline.

1. What the size and elements of RFID infrastructure are
2. How SCM, ERP, and other EAI applications should integrate with the RFID infrastructure
3. What the means of connecting the EAI applications with the RFID infrastructure are
4. What RFID middleware should be used to accomplish the integration
5. What RFID middleware vendor types should be considered: integration specialist or major platforms
6. How much stock-outs can be reduced
7. How much administrative errors can be reduced
8. How much the costs of direct labor can be reduced
9. How much higher the sales would be by increasing product availability
10. How much loading time and faster check-out at the distribution center can be reduced
11. How much the costs can be reduced by eliminating or reducing cycle counts
12. How better planning can be accomplished
13. In what ways thefts can be prevented by using RFID
14. How exception management can be accomplished

Other factors in your checklist that you should include are:

1. How long the organization has been in business
2. How complex manufacturing, supply chain, and distribution are
3. How effective change management is
4. What the leadership style is. Examples include participative management and online collaboration
5. How effective internal controls to comply with various regulations are
6. What skills the RFID personnel should have
7. What training the RFID personnel should have
8. How much the RFID training would be
9. How a data model should be developed
10. How mature the organization is in implementing RFID technology

Expand your checklist as needed so you can adequately plan for improvement to business processes to be brought about by RFID technology. Consider both intangible and tangible benefits. Avoid the temptation to jump directly to reengineering business processes without adequate preparation. To do so will result in longer decision cycles and implementation time, solving the wrong problem, doing over the work, poor risk mitigation, and longer return on investments [3]. Because the RFID technology continues to evolve, you need to be flexible in reengineering business processes. As enterprise-level business processes consist of processes on a smaller scale, you need to be able to send feedback from higher-level processes to the lower level, so that the business processes as a whole will continue to improve.

5.2 BUSINESS PROCESS REENGINEERING

The suppliers who initially succeeded in RFID implementation reengineered business processes before they embarked on the implementation. They reengineered to improve and automate business processes that they used to integrate RFID data into SCM, ERP, and other enterprise applications via middleware technologies. The integration of the processes was done in a loosely coupled environment where messages were exchanged between enterprise applications across the diverse platforms within the enterprise and with external organizations.

What the suppliers thought they could improve business processes with RFID technology may not always have gotten expected outcomes. For instance, Canus, a maker of goat's milk had to adjust or optimize the speed of a laptop as it was affecting the quality of RFID input readers into the laptop. Some data could not be recorded or stored in the laptop because of the differences in speed between the laptop and the readers connected to it (see section on Canus RFID Strategy). The technique Canus used to resolve the problem is called network business process reengineering.

Some suppliers were wise to set up an RFID infrastructure pilot study to determine how much it would improve business processes, productivity, and operational efficiency. They tested servers and networks from large platform vendors such as IBM, Oracle, SAP, and Microsoft before they started RFID implementation. They also tested data synchronization from various readers into the servers.

As some small suppliers do not have the overhead costs of installing these expensive servers, they may start with server software of smaller scale such as Savant Server that can turn a desktop into a server provided that no other servers are running on the same machine. The Savant server is an open source Web server for a Windows platform. If they find that the pilot study will result in ROIs in later years, they may consider more expensive servers from platform vendors or even middleware technologies to store an increase in RFID data for the remaining portions of their supply chains.

In addition to network business process reengineering we already discussed, we need to consider business process reengineering at the package level (also known as the package business process reengineering), and at the site level (also known as the site business process reengineering). For instance, some suppliers have found the shape and size of the product can affect the optimal location for tags on cases and pallets. Close proximity of tags to the liquid portion of each product inside the pallet and case will experience more interference from the liquid than the tags placed farther away from the offending material. Packaging reengineering has been used to reduce the amount of interference by finding optimal location of tags on cases and pallets.

We now give two instances of site business process reengineering (Procter & Gamble and Canus), two instances of package business process reengineering (Unilever and Heinz), and network business process reengineering (Gillette and Canus).

5.2.1 Procter & Gamble: Dock Loading Throughput

Let's take a look at how Procter & Gamble (P&G) in Spain implemented RFID technology to increase dock loading throughput as a way of reengineering and improving site business processes. The problem was that in 2001, P&G, a supplier for Wal-Mart (and others as well) experienced bottlenecks at the loading dock. The forklift drivers ran out of space on the dock for stacking pallets to be shipped. To solve the problem, the workers and drivers made room on the loading dock by stopping production so they could clear the dock.

Because stopping the production often resulted in a waste of time and productivity, the company decided to move twice the pallets. First, the workers moved the pallets to the trucks from the dock, and then reloaded them onto the same dock. The drawback of this solution was that the drivers sometimes became confused and sent these pallets to the customers by mistake instead of reloading them onto the dock from the trucks. The labels had the wrong information, not appropriately marked, or fell off. Productivity and profits declined. Business processes were chaotic and prone to human errors.

To increase throughput and eliminate costly mistakes, P&G developed an RFID-based system to identify the pallets as they are loaded on the dock. This has allowed the plant to shift loading, increase the speed of loading, and to reduce the number of forklift truck drivers needed. As a result the loading time was reduced by as much as 40 percent by eliminating unnecessary or erroneous loading. This led to reduction in labor and process times in handling everyday tasks of loading pallets onto and from the dock. This allowed for better utilization of personnel for loading and unloading operations. Business processes improved.

With more efficient truck and yard management, P&G no longer afforded the costly mistakes of loading the pallets that were sent elsewhere when the workers were supposed to reload them on the dock. Other benefits of the RFID technology are that it immediately sends alerts on extraordinary conditions and that reduction of threat results in fewer insurance claims and fewer out-of-stock situations. All these have contributed to the efficiency gains realized through reengineering of existing business processes by eliminating those processes that were not necessary and by enhancing those processes that were needed. By reengineering and automating site business processes, P&G succeeded in RFID implementation.

Now that the docking throughput problem has been solved, P&G went further in increasing product visibility into the store sales floor and back-room via software developed by TIBCO and IBM that have engineered separate Inventory Management applications at a live demonstration at the EPCglobal U.S. Conference 2004. These applications were used to query a retailer's EPC IS to gain product visibility through the supply chain. EPC IS interfaces are Web services that come with encryption and other security measures to protect trading partners.

It is obvious that P&G has benefited from real-time recovery of items that almost went to the wrong customer. Personnel that were found to be in the "excess" category after the RFID implementation were reallocated to other areas of the supply chain. P&G has gained sales opportunities that were lost during mis-shipments, slow responses to exceptions, and massive recalls that were not necessary when limited real-time recalls would be sufficient. Prevention of theft allowed for faster handling of the items. Loading and distributing items, cases, and pallets from a supply chain were done more efficiently.

5.2.2 Canus: Changing Antenna's Orientation

The Canus docking door allowed only three antennas to be set up. It found the third antenna did have enough reading area in order to work properly. One solution was to employ site business process reengineering to make adjustments to this antenna. The company changed its orientation and position to provide a greater reading area for the antenna. A fourth antenna has been added to ensure that a tag can be read regardless of its location on the pallet.

5.2.3 Unilever: Changing Tag Placement

Unilever has found the shape and size of the product can affect the optimal location for tags on cases and pallets. It has employed package business process reengineering to place the tags at the top third of the case of dishwashing liquid bottles that taper at the top. This tapering feature of these bottles allows air space at the top of the cases where tags can experience less interference as it is known that tags do not work very well in close proximity to liquids. This has improved business processes of tagging the RFID labels to the product, reducing the incidents of readers not working properly with the tags and picking up the wrong data from the tags due to frequency interference from the liquids.

5.2.4 Heinz: Adapting Tag Requirements

Heinz hired the IBM Business Consulting Services to determine how to use the technology in the most effective manner to keep the retailers happy.

Heinz wanted to make sure its RFID strategy would be in line with the changing market trends while maximizing its potential ROIs. IBM recommended to Heinz top of the line vendors and the way RFID infrastructure should be built in the entire supply chain, not just a portion of the supply chain. Due to contents of many cans and packages, IBM experimented with different label placements on the product in various environmental conditions and conducted a RFID pilot using the application from Heinz to reengineer package business processes.

5.2.5 Gillette Scenario: Misplaced Case

Sometime in 2005, Gillette merged into the family P&G. Both are considered leaders on RFID and global data synchronization. Before the merger Wal-Mart accounted for about 15 percent of sales from P&G. The merger resulted in sales to Wal-Mart for another 15 percent. The merger also raised the issues of merging the automated business processes as P&G and Gillette individually have different sets of automated business processes. Although this is not much of an issue at the present time, it could be later on as RFID technology becomes more sophisticated in changing the way the items are identified, packaged, and distributed to achieve productivity and operational efficiency gains.

Now let's take a look at Gillette's premerger demonstration of how it could solve the problem of a misplaced case by redirecting it to the correct dock door for reshipping to the warehouse that ordered the case. The demonstration took place in late September 2004 at the Baltimore Convention Center where the EPCglobal U.S. Conference was held.

Gillette started the demonstration by linking the RFID network to a reader at the convention where the conference was held. The scenario showed how a tagged case of Gillette Venus razor blades got separated from the shipment it was part of, and how the company quickly solved the problem in real-time and business processes.

First it used EPCglobal Network to identify the misplaced case. Second, it showed how a Discovery Workstation responded to a query and displayed the information about the case that the case needs to be reassociated with the purchase order given that the location specified in the query matches a shop-to-location recorded in the manufacturer's enterprise system. The manufacturer may also return other information such as an expiration date and other business processes. Third, a Gillette warehouse employee used the information to reorder and redirect the case to the correct Gillette dock door for correct shipping. To provide authentication services, Gillette's Discovery Workstation used the EPCglobal Network Object Name Service (ONS) offered by Verisign.

A misplaced case is not the only possibility of how EPCglobal network can be used to identify it for reshipping. Other possibilities include using the network to identify items that have been sitting idle in a warehouse because a customer did not get a notification that they have arrived. In pre-EPCglobal network days, these excess items could not be easily returned to the supplier for redistribution to other customers that needed them. This would not happen with the RFID infrastructure in place. The Discovery Workstation would send an alert in real-time when the items in the warehouse were not distributed within a certain timeframe or when the items were shipped to the wrong warehouse. Instead of the items piling up, eventually crowding the warehouse like sardines, only a few RFID-tagged items would be returned to the supplier for reshipping, thus saving the supplier lost time, lost sales, and lost profits.

Now what if the EPC number has not been properly recorded in the manufacturer's EPC repository? The response would indicate the item has been stolen, counterfeited, or got lost during the transit. For each response, it recommends what actions to take based on some predefined set of business processes. The actions to take depend who the requester is.

For this reason, it is important to verify the EPC has been properly recorded at periodic times in case a cyber-attacker finds a way to change the EPC number wirelessly. It is also important to encrypt the EPC number. This must be done at an authorized location and time and by an individual or group with proper credentials.

Let's suppose the item has been mis-shipped and it is not possible to reassociate with the purchase even if the EPC number has been properly recorded in the manufacturer's EPC repository. If the requester is a customer (e.g., retailer or warehouse manager) for which the pallet is intended and the manufacturer's enterprise system matches the ship-to-location in its record with the location specified in the customer's query, the Discovery Workstation will deliver a response for product reassociation with the purchase order. On the other hand, if the location specified in the query does not correspond to a product distribution area linked to the shop-to-location in the manufacturer's enterprise system, the Discovery Workstation will respond with a "gray market" condition and actions to take based on a set of predefined business processes.

If the product is sent to the wrong customer, that the other intended customer who requested a response to the query, the requestor gets a response to take a suggested appropriate action, such as returning the product. The response might contain additional useful information, such as name, contact information, and account number.

Another possible use of the Discovery Workstation is to track certain batches of items that need to be recalled after the manufacturing firm discovers a flaw in one of the raw materials and determines that this would create a potential health hazard [2]. Using the Discovery Workstation, the manufacturer can establish which production batches were affected by the flawed material. Upon discovery, the system generates a report of the affected items and the cases containing the affected items that need to be recalled.

The manufacturer checks the reported items or cases against the existing inventories on hand.

If the inventoried items match those items in the report, the manufacturer eliminates them. Then, the manufacturer continues to use the Discovery Workstation to check with the transportation department to determine how many of the remaining items were shipped to distributors, wholesalers, and retailers. For each item or for each case containing the affected items, a logistical path is established. From this, the manufacturer contacts each recipient and recalls the items or cases one by one.

This selective approach is far better than the old approach of recalling all items and all cases containing items, both affected and unaffected, from all recipients who bought the items within a given timeframe. The selective approach also increases the amount of ROIs than would have been possible with the old approach.

5.2.6 Canus: Adjusting Computer Speed

Canus discovered the speed of tags affected the quality of input reads into the computers in a pilot study. The company found that reading tags at one-second intervals was the optimal speed. Anything lower, less than one second, slowed down the computer. The computer could not keep up with the lightning speed of the readers. To get the computer to read below one second, the company would have to buy a more expensive computer with faster CPU and disk speeds. For the pilot study, it felt it could use network business processes to reengineer the adjustments to get the RFID readers and the computer to talk to each other happily. This shows how the company used an innovative approach to create business processes without breaking the IT budget while realizing ROIs in later years.

5.2.7 Software Checklist

Replenishing items at the customer's store can be done in real-time without having the customer check manually what is needed to be replenished. Real-time alerts for all exceptions are sent to mobile devices for faster corrective actions. When errors occur, the items or packages can be better traced in less time for less cost than with human's manual tracing. Suppliers want to reduce out-of-stocks, unsalable products, product loss due to theft, and the costs of management used to move and monitor inventory. Suppliers want early return of investment through applications from Wal-Mart, P&G, IBM, Sun, TIBCO, Verisign, and others.

Let's take a look at the applications from TIBCO and IBM to help you meet the challenge of asking questions in a checklist. You can use the checklist to compare like applications from other vendors in addition to

IBM and TIBCO and determine which ones offer the flexibility to perform a range of functions and turn information in real-time, to achieve the most improvements in business processes and get earlier return of investments. Table 5.1 is a suggested checklist along with response examples.

Other questions you want to ask are related to what kind of process flow you need to accomplish a series of tasks both on the screen and behind it.

1. How do you want the initial query screen to appear?
2. How do you want locations and products to be listed?
3. How do you want a manager to select a location?
4. How do you want the application to use EPCGobal to return information about the customer?
5. Do you want the application to automatically specify target quantities based on a predetermined criterion?
6. Does the application allow you to determine what level the inventory should be maintained at specific locations?
7. What types of target quantities of the application can you specify at distribution center, store backroom, store sales floor, and even real-time shelves?
8. Does the application allow you enter custom types of target quantities?

Other questions you should consider in the checklist include:

1. To what extent will the application allow you to tailor the way the information appears on the screen?
2. How well and how fast can the application look up the appropriate EPC information?
3. How well can the application perform with a complex set of queries?
4. What databases are to be used with the application?
5. Does the application provide you with query templates?
6. Can you enter own query specifications?

5.3 ORGANIZATIONAL MATURITY

By giving the demonstration, Gillette showed how the organization is attempting to evolve in the maturity life cycle by reengineering and automating business processes regardless of the implementation approach. P&G showed how it has evolved in organizational maturity when it increased dock loading throughput. Unilever showed its organizational maturity has improved somewhat when it reconsidered tag placement on their products.

What this means is that the maturity of an organization is contingent on how well it is reengineering business processes, that is, how well it attempts to overcome the shortcomings of existing business processes and

Table 5.1   Software Checklist

How does the inventory screen appear? Does it apply to your situation?	TIBCO application focuses on inventory reports for the retailers. It divides the Retailer Inventory Report Screen into three distinct zones. They are Product Search, Locations, and Current View of Inventory Level. On the other hand, IBM application shows the Management of Inventory Targets screen of three parts. They are Target Structure Detail, Target Inventory Level Alerts, and Last Check Levels. Although the TIBCO application provides the Locations zone on the Retailer Inventory Report Screen, the IBM application offers P&G a list of locations (and products) in response to the Retail Inventory Query Screen within the Manufacturer Supply Chain Inventory Reporting Application. After the selections are made, the applications bring up the Management of Inventory Targets.
How do you want to search the product? Will you be able to search the product on the opening screen? Will you need to use a screen to query a product and see the inventory levels in the next screen?	TIBCO runs a query on one screen to show P&G inventory levels at requested locations in the Retailer Inventory Report Screen. The Product Search zone gives a hierarchy of the product found. If the inventory is below the specified target, the report offers a button to send an e-mail to the retailer selected (Wal-Mart). IBM application on the other hand will show P&G the selected products, locations, and SKUs. It will ask the user to specify inventory targets. Locations with inventory below target levels are highlighted. In both applications, the last time the inventory checks were done is available. There is one difference, however. The IBM application categories the locations into backroom and selling for each location whereas the TIBCO application lists all backroom and selling locations into a single column without categorizing them.
How do you want the alerts to be sent? Where and to whom do you want to send them? What types of alerts do you want to be triggered?	TIBCO software allows a supplier to send an e-mail request to a customer to move "excess" items to another location where inventory is below specific targets. IBM takes a different approach. It selects from a list of locations and products, specifies inventory inputs for the locations, and creates an alert if a location does not match the target inventory levels. The alert takes two forms: active and passive. The active form is an alert sent to mobile users and the passive form is the locations below target levels are highlighted on the screen.

accommodate future RFID technologies and emerging applications. It also is contingent on how the organization takes actions as defined not only by business processes but also by existing contracts and legislations.

If the organization is not mature regardless of how long it has been in business and how successful the pilot studies were in implementing the RFID technology, there will be some problems of reengineering business processes. The less mature organizations would focus on meeting the base requirements of the mandates from the large customers without considering the potential ROIs of RFID deployment, the changing standards, and the capabilities of existing storage facilities to expand for growing RFID data.

The mandates that the suppliers provide their own equipment or accept them from the customer only require them to begin a foundation for building a RFID infrastructure. These mandates did not give suppliers opportunities for developing business strategies on reengineering of business processes. The mandates also require the suppliers to comply with existing standards without considering the possibilities of new or emerging standards (see Appendix M) for technologies that could affect future implementation of RFID infrastructure.

To better control and monitor future implementation impacts, the more mature organizations build business strategies on top of the base requirements of the mandates to allow for adapting the RFID infrastructure to changing standards, compliance regulations, and changing network scenarios. It is the network and storage infrastructure that should receive the most attention in business strategies as the RFID technology allows the collection of a wider range of data on the labels than its bar-coding technology counterpart can. This requires the use of middleware to integrate the RFID data into various legacy systems, ERP, CRM, databases, and so on.

The problem here is that not all mature organizations have the legacy systems they need to communicate with the RFID infrastructure. Most medium-sized and small businesses may find it necessary to link up with the external legacy systems. This means a loosely coupled environment of middleware technologies connecting, for example, via a gateway to a closed-loop system to an open system that can be adapted to meet changing business process requirements. One most popular middleware technology is Web services seen as bridges among disparate platforms, applications, and systems. It is useful when the supplier has to deal with multidimensional approaches particularly when the supplier sells their products to multi-customers and gets supplies from other suppliers to complete the business processes of the RFID infrastructure of emerging technologies. Not all suppliers who provided supplies to the requesting supplier have RFID infrastructure in place completely or partially.

Keep in mind organizational maturity is not the same thing as the technology maturity. An organization can be mature while it is handling and implementing an emerging technology. That is because the organization already has business strategies in place and continually updates it as technology changes or emerges.

However, assessing organizational maturity of an organization is not enough to meet the challenge of RFID implementation. It needs to be supplemented with a Multi-Layer RFID Business Process Model of three types: basic, adaptive, and predictive.

5.4 BASIC MULTI-LAYER RFID BUSINESS PROCESS MODEL

While continuously adding new technologies and standards to the ever-expanding mix of RFID infrastructure, categorizing and improving business processes for existing and emerging implementation plans become more challenging. One way of meeting this challenge is to create a multi-layer RFID business processes model. With this model, the maturity evolution starts from the core of the process model and continues until it reaches the outermost layer of the model. As new elements of the RFID infrastructure are added, the maturity evolution starts over from the core. Let's start with an illustration with a basic Multi-Layer RFID Business Process Model, as shown in Figure 5.1.

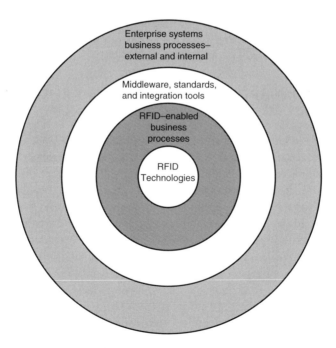

Figure 5.1   Basic Multi-Layer RFID Business Process Model

As shown in the figure, the core of this model is strategy, plan, goals, and objectives on changing and automating business processes the organization must set before it begins to implement RFID. If the strategy, plan, goals, and objectives are not adequately developed, the RFID implementation project whatever the implementation approach is used will most likely fail. Once the strategy and plan are in place and the goals and objectives are set, we then proceed to the next layer, RFID-enabled business processes. This means the RFID technologies enable and automate new business processes. For example, by implementing RFID technologies, P&G was able to streamline and automate business processes that have resulted in productivity and efficiency gains.

To connect to the rest of the enterprise systems, you need middleware technologies, Web service standards, and integration processes to streamline business processes. For example, you need a leading Web service based on one or more business processes to orchestrate other Web services. A data-centric Web service without business processes cannot do the orchestration. Business processes can be set to industrywide standards. The orchestrated Web services may work with other middleware technologies to connect to one or more enterprise systems.

Then you go from this third layer to the outmost layer to set up business processes for internal and external enterprise systems, such as supply chain planning and supply chain execution applications. This layer completes the Multi-Layer RFID Business Process Model. We also look at the business process issues of SCP, SCE, and SCM applications.

5.5 ADAPTIVE MULTI-LAYER RFID BUSINESS PROCESS MODEL

Business processes will become more adaptive (better known as the adaptive business processes) in response to emerging technologies, changing customer demands, new external threats, and new market opportunities, as well as changes in the implementation approach (e.g., from two-dimensional to multidimensional). It is important to consider what the risk, return, and feasibility of the RFID infrastructure are and how they can be adapted to business processes over time starting from the inner layers of the adaptive model.

Some adaptive business processes can also be dynamic. This model is more suitable for supply chain organizations that initially split their shipping into two parts. The first part is those shipping cases and pallets that have been RFID-enabled to meet mandates from large retailers. The second part is those shipping cases and pallets that have not been RFID-enabled for customers that have not issued the mandates. These cases and pallets were eventually to be RFID-tagged with the goal of placing RFID tags on individual times on a massive scale, if technologically practical and feasible.

This model is suitable for a mid-sized or small supplier that voluntarily implements the RFID technology by providing their own equipment to meet the mandate.

5.5.1 Adaptive Maturity

Now let's revise the model to show how business processes could become more adaptive and more dynamic as they move from the inner core to the outermost layer. What this means is we have an adaptive maturity that starts from the core of the process model and continues until it reaches the outermost layer of the model. The maturity is adaptive as compared to the static version as you have seen in the previous model. Adaptive maturity dynamically responds to the changing consumer demands, implementation approaches, technologies, and regulations whereas static maturity linearity responds to the same conditions. Adaptive response means feedback into the previous layers to create and automate business processes in response to technology changes, competitive market changes, and shifts in the economy. Figure 5.2 shows that each stage of the adaptive maturity could send feedback to any of the previous stages for further improvements before it returns to a higher layer.

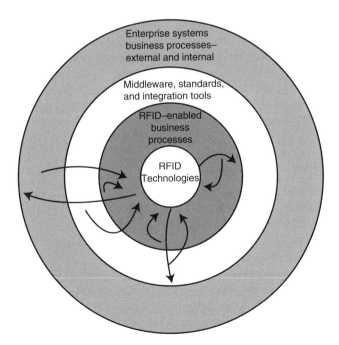

Figure 5.2 Adaptive Multi-Layer Business Process Model

As shown in the figure, if the maturity level reaches the second inner layer from the core layer, it can send feedback to the core layer and repeat the process. If the maturity level reaches the third layer, it can send feedback to either the core layer or the second inner layer and repeat the process if necessary. If the maturity level reaches the outermost layer, it can send feedback to one of the three ways: the core layer, the inner second layer, or the inner third layer.

As the maturity level moves to the next higher layer, the business processes mature from the strategy, plan, goals, and objectives layer spelling out what business processes to achieve to the enterprise layer. This spells out a complex set of enterprisewide business processes that you may need to implement when you move from the pilot study to a full-scale RFID implementation throughout the supply chain. The RFID benefits should result in the value perceived and expected by stakeholders in RFID implementation, such as [1]:

■ Increased revenue
■ Lower cost
■ Inventory reduction
■ Reduced capital assets

Overall, adaptive and dynamic business processes appear to be an effective mechanism in improving and automating the processes, integrating a complex, redundant process, and improving performance. However, improving these processes for a wide range of disparate applications becomes very complex due to, for instance, interoperability problems among enterprise systems (e.g., SCP, SCE, and SCM), and the issue of integrating and automating business processes arises.

5.5.2 Application Adaptors

Unlike the basic version, the adaptive model employs application adapters where necessary. Application adapters are useful in resolving certain types of interoperability problems of integrating disparate applications and automated business processes. Some software companies are offering product adapters to reduce or eliminate the time to customize adaptors to integrate disparate applications. For instance, IBM offers WebSphere Application Adaptors to allow users to exchange information between ERP, HR, CRM, and supply chain systems, such as those shown in Table 5.2.

A complete list of IBM Websphere Application Adaptors is available in the appendix. IBM is not the only vendor, however, to offer application, technology, or integration adaptors. Microsoft is another major player in its offerings of adapters for many of the Windows server systems.

Table 5.2 Application Adaptors

Oracle	SAP Software	Claify CRM
PeopleSoft Enterprise	Portal Internet	i2 Active Data Warehouse
SunGard FRONT ARENA	Websphere Commerce Adapter	CORBA
AdapterforEnterprise JavaBean (EJB)	Lotus Domino	Data Handler for EDI
Web Services	Java-based HTTP Adapter	WebSphere MQ Workflow Adapter

SAP NetWeaver comes with preintegrated business applications running on industry standard platforms, such as Java 2 Platform, Enterprise Edition (J2EE), Microsoft .NET, and IBM Websphere. Microsoft offers technology adaptors for Windows operating systems. However, IBM offers the Web-Sphere RFID Premises Server dedicated to aggregate, integrate, and monitor RFID data that you use to detect critical operational events.

5.5.3 The METRO Group

So how mature is the METRO Group? Before we can determine the maturity of this group, let's rehash a little bit on what it has done. METRO Group hired IBM Business Consulting Services to provide middleware and installation services for the RFID rollout that began in November 2004 with shipments of warehouse pallets and cases from 20 product suppliers, including Unilever, Procter & Gamble, Gillette, Johnson & Johnson, Kraft Foods, Colgate-Palmolive, GlaxoSmithKline, Nestlé, and Esprit. METRO Group has used an IBM RFID middleware based on the IBM WebSphere RFID Premises Server to provide the retailer with a virtual view of RFID-tagged pallets and cases shipped to its distribution center and exchange data with METRO's merchandise management system.

METRO's RFID rollout grew to about 100 suppliers by December 2004 and is expected to grow to about 300 suppliers by 2006, along with additional METRO warehouses and stores in Germany. Early deployment in November 2004 was influenced by METRO's belief that the results of the Future Store Initiative indicated that process efficiency and merchandise availability increased by about 14 percent and losses and theft were reduced about 15 percent.

Let's take a look at how the METRO Group uses the IBM WebSphere RFID Premises Server to improve adaptive business processes. This server is part of the IBM RFID product package. Completing the package are devices and a WebSphere Integration server. WebSphere RFID Premises

Server is designed to detect critical operational RFID events from various devices we have talked about in previous chapters. The server helps to reduce out-of-stock situations by increasing stock visibility, and reduce shrinkage, return, and reconciliation costs by visible tracking, rotating, and allocation of the products. It also allows collaboration and sharing of data within an enterprise and with trading partners.

To improve business processes and integrate business information, the WebSphere Business Integration Server, as its name implies, does the job. The server helps users to create business processes and integrate business information in multiple business applications across diverse platforms. It also allows the users to improve business processes in response to changes in a highly competitive market due to emerging technologies and shifts in the economy. The server comes with both preintegrated adapters and process templates. Additional information about the IBM integration servers and associated components is available in Appendix N.

Given the brief information about the technologies the METRO Group is using to improve and integrate business processes, the group is expected to reach its full maturity. The maturity will be adaptive rather than static as the METRO Group appears to be flexible in adapting to new technologies and business processes in each stage of maturity level.

5.6 PREDICTIVE MULTI-LAYER BUSINESS PROCESS MODEL

This predictive model goes a step further than the adaptive multi-layer business process model, although it is not yet available. When it is ready as a reference, a new ring will be added to the outermost ring of the adaptive model. Before we discuss what the predictive model is, let's take a look at TIBCO's four stage RFID implementation model as shown in Table 5.3.

Formulated in November 2003, the TIBCO model is divided by the years each stage covers and the level of maturity for each stage, as shown in Table 5.3. As you can see in the table, some stages overlap one another. Table 5.3 has been converted into a visual representation of the stage overlaps as shown in Figure 5.3.

Table 5.3   Four-Stage Implementation Model

2004–2005 *Stage 1*	2004–2006 *Stage 2*	2005–2007 *Stage 3*	2006–2010 *Stage 4*
Tagging and tracking	Integrating RFID data into the IT infrastructure	Leveraging RFID to improve business processes	Predictive business

Source: TIBCO [4].

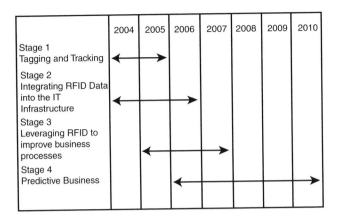

	2004	2005	2006	2007	2008	2009	2010
Stage 1 Tagging and Tracking	←——→						
Stage 2 Integrating RFID Data into the IT Infrastructure	←————→						
Stage 3 Leveraging RFID to improve business processes		←————→					
Stage 4 Predictive Business		←————————→					

Figure 5.3   Visual Representation of the RFID Implementation Model

The first two stages begin in 2004–2005. Although the larger firms' implementation of the tagging and tracking appears to be nearly with the expected timeframe, it may take longer for the medium-sized and smaller firms to catch up. Large retailers, such as Wal-Mart, gave RFID mandates to, say, 100 largest suppliers and the investments can be quite large to start the pilot study of RFID implementation.

Although the medium-sized and smaller suppliers are not mandated to comply, the number of these suppliers voluntarily complying with the RFID mandates is growing at a much slower rate. Some cannot afford the overhead of heavy investments in the RFID infrastructure. As the demand increases, the costs of tags and readers are expected to fall, making it more affordable for the medium-sized and smaller suppliers to change from bar coding to RFID technology. For these reasons, the start date for the tagging and tracking stage may be extended to 2006 and possibly the IT Integrating RFID data into the IT infrastructure stage to 2007.

The year of 2005 saw the first implementations of leveraging RFID to improve the business processes stage. It is projected to continue until 2007. RFID technology so leveraged should support reengineering so that the larger suppliers can analyze the data from reengineered business processes and use the data to implement new business practices. For the smaller suppliers the projection should be extended to 2008 or so. The fourth stage of predictive business is scheduled to begin 2006 through 2010. This means future business processes can be predicted based on historical RFID data obtained from various implementation approaches. Therefore it is important to back up data on a periodic basis at an offsite facility.

Now let's take a look at the Predictive Multi-Layer Business Process Model as shown in Figure 5.4. As shown in the figure, a predictive business

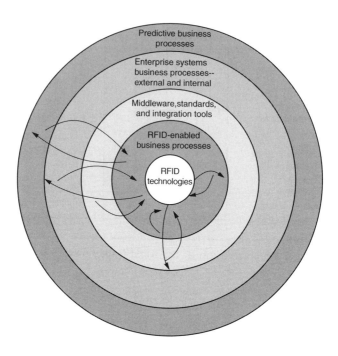

Figure 5.4 Predictive Multi-Layer Business Process Model

process layer is added to the outermost layer of the adaptive model. Each stage of the maturity model could send feedback to any of the previous stages for further improvements before it returns to a higher layer. If the maturity level reaches the second inner layer from the core layer, it can send feedback to the core layer and repeat the process if necessary. If the maturity level reaches the third layer, it can send feedback to either the core layer or the second inner layer and repeat the process. If the maturity level reaches the fourth layer, it can send feedback to the core, the second inner or the third inner layer, and repeat the process. If the maturity level reaches the outermost layer, it can send feedback to one of the four ways: the core layer, the inner second layer, the inner third layer, or the inner fourth layer.

As the maturity level moves to the next higher layer, the business processes mature from the strategy, plan, goals, and objectives layer spelling out what business processes to achieve to the enterprise layer, and then to the predictive layer. This spells out a complex set of predictive enterprise-wide business processes that you may need to implement when you move from the pilot study to a full-scale RFID implementation based on historical RFID data throughout the supply chain as long as the RFID benefits result in the value perceived and expected by stakeholders in predictive RFID implementation.

The historical data, however, can change over the years. Certain data needed in one year would be no longer needed in the following year. Some data that are considered predictive may also be used in the enterprise system business processes layer. This means the two outermost layers may overlap each other. The predictive layer may expand and the enterprise layer may become less or vice versa depending on the predicted emerging technologies, metric tools used, and projected RFID investments and ROIs.

5.7 RFID BUSINESS PROCESSES STRATEGY

Let's take a look at how IBM, Heinz, Canus, International Paper, Kayser-Roth, Philips Semiconductors, Intel, Unilever, a major clothier retailer, and Marks and Spencer have used RFID strategy to identify and reengineer business processes that will derive the most value for the emerging technology and then to develop an implementation plan that would bring in realizable ROI sooner. No business process strategies are the same in scope and approach at site, package, and network levels.

5.7.1 IBM RFID Strategy

IBM focuses on RFID strategy both for the enterprise and mid-business market as a way of choosing the right mix of implementation approach, technologies, and business processes. The company groups business processes into four components: SCP, SCE, inventory merchandise management, and customer experience. It pulls data from the RFID infrastructure by the way of data and process integration into these business processes. What this means is that the data from the infrastructure is operated on, aggregated, and filtered through process integration into the four components of business processes. IBM focuses on open communication required to connect among the RFID infrastructure, the process integration, and the business processes along with external integration via middleware technologies.

Once the business processes have been set, they are used to enable the RFID network and integration services. The final step is to establish strategy services in the five following areas: business case, strategy assessment, roadmap development, pilot development, and supply chain development. To develop a pilot study, you need to present first a business case (see Heinz Product Scenario Testing). Next, you proceed to strategy assessment using the findings as the background material and develop a roadmap over a period of time.

If the pilot study does not succeed, you need to return to the business case and strategy assessment to correct the flaws (e.g., RFID labels were put on the wrong places of certain food products; they were too close to the top containing the liquid component). Only when the pilot study shows a successful RFID implementation, can you then plan and develop supply chain facilities, networks, and applications. This indicates IBM has been using the Adaptive Multi-Layer Business Process Model with layers tailored to their business process components.

5.7.2 Heinz RFID Strategy

Now let's take a look at Heinz that did not know which vendors to use or which direction to take in implementing RFID. The first step the company undertook to develop a RFID strategy was to hire the IBM Business Consulting Services to determine how to use the technology in the most effective manner to keep the retailers happy. Heinz wanted to make sure its RFID strategy would be in line with the changing market trends while maximizing its potential ROIs.

In response, IBM recommended top of the line vendors and the way RFID infrastructure should be built in the entire supply chain, not just a portion of the supply chain. Due to contents of many cans and packages, IBM experimented with different label placements on the product in various environmental conditions and conducted a RFID pilot using the application from Heinz.

IBM used various models to compare alternative costs and benefits of each scenario over a period of ten years. Not only ROI was calculated; IBM used other financial tools to compare the costs and benefits of outfitting plants and warehouses with RFID technology and determining the best loading/unloading dock throughputs.

5.7.3 Canus RFID Strategy

Canus, a maker of goat's milk, has successfully implemented its RFID strategy. It has met Wal-Mart's tagging requirements ahead of schedule by focusing on inventory management, customer relations, and technology innovations. The RFID technology Canus is using temperature monitors of its products in real-time to keep the products from spoiling while in transit due to a sudden breakdown in the vehicle's thermostat circuitry or the vehicle's mechanics that affect the circuitry. The deployment uses UHF readers and tags from Alien Technology.

Adjustments had to be made to software and hardware. For instance, the speed of tags affected the quality of input reads into the computers. It found that reading tags at one-second intervals was the optimal speed. Anything lower than one second slowed down the computer. The computer could not keep up with the lightning speed of the readers. To get the computer to read below one second, the company would have to buy a more expensive computer with faster CPU and disk speeds. For the pilot study, it felt it could make the adjustments to get the RFID readers and the computer to talk to each other happily. This shows how the company used an innovative approach to create business processes without breaking the IT budget while realizing ROIs in later years.

In another instance, the Canus docking door allowed only three antennas to be set up. It found the third antenna did have enough reading area in order to work properly. One solution was to make adjustments to this antenna. The company changed its orientation and position to provide a greater reading area for the antenna. A fourth antenna has been added to ensure that a tag can be read regardless of its location on the pallet.

By making the adjustments to the third antenna and adding the fourth antenna, the company was able to further refine business processes. It did not use outside help to make a business case, develop a strategy, and a roadmap. It knew what to do when it implemented a pilot study. The company also shows it has unknowingly applied Adaptive Multi-Layer Business Processes model for RFID implementation. The company sends feedback to a prior layer before proceeding to the next higher one with the Adaptive Multi-Layer Business Process Model. It reached its maturity level when it moved the pilot study to a full scale production.

5.7.4 International Paper RFID Strategy

In September 2004, International Paper initiated an RFID strategy when it signed an agreement with Globe Ranger's iMotion Edgeware platform for RFID supply chain solutions. The company recognized the importance of optimizing business processes using process and workflow management to deliver user-defined business rules for immediate visibility and exception alerts (display and audio). The customers will take advantage of the RFID technology to trigger reorders automatically when they move a roll of paper onto their own equipment to produce cartons or items with the RFID reading area.

iMotion can correlate RFID data with business processes to create events that can be acted upon by the information systems when the events encounter exceptions. When an event is triggered, it may indicate that a business process needs to be improved. This means business processes can be changed and adapted by sending feedback to the prior steps in RFID implementation according to the Adaptive Multi-Layer Business Process Model.

One advantage of using iMotion's RFID Visual Device Emulator is that you can simulate how the readers, antenna fields, and tags would behave in the real world. If there is a problem with any of them, adjustments can be made right on the screen, including the tag reading speed.

5.7.5 Kayser-Roth RFID Strategy

Unlike other suppliers who were mandated to implement RFID technology, Kayser-Roth Corp., the maker of legwear and apparel volunteered to meet

Wal-Mart's compliance deadline by January 2005. It was not one of Wal-Mart's 100 largest suppliers. Kayser-Roth wanted to meet the larger retailer's requirements and ship cases and pallets to it from an RFID-enabled distribution center. It contacted IBM to help to set up the first pilot, and select vendors for the project to improve business processes. As IBM's offering aimed at much larger companies, it adapted its offering and scaled down its prices for the mid-market. Kayser-Roth was the first one to receive mid-market offering from IBM and took advantage of the IBM test center in Gaithersburg, MD.

Like IBM, the company groups business processes into four components: SCP, SCE, inventory merchandise management, and customer experience but on a smaller scale. It pulls data from the RFID infrastructure by the way of data and process integration into these business processes. The data from the infrastructure is operated on, aggregated, and filtered through process integration into the four components of business processes within the Adaptive Multi-Layer Business Processes Model.

5.7.6 Philips Semiconductors RFID Strategy

Philips Semiconductors engaged IBM Business Consulting Services to begin a trial project in November 2003 to monitor its own chip making, including the manufacture of RFID tags. The project included choosing vendors, reengineering more than 1000 business processes, and the building of custom components, plus training and project management. After a period of ten months, the implementation of the RFID technology was successful. The implementation included the integration of the IBM RFID Middleware software with legacy warehouse or order management software.

IBM and Philips tagged wafer cases and carton packages with RFID chips at Phillips' manufacturing site in Taiwan and its distribution center in Hong Kong. IBM fully implemented RFID in its East Fishkill plant, where more than 600 business processes were reengineered and driven by RFID. Philips also has implemented RFID technology at other manufacturing facilities and distribution centers in Asia Pacific, Europe, and the United States.

Let's take a closer look at how IBM has helped Philips in implementing the RFID technology in each of the plants. First, it divides each project into five stages:

- Assess
- Plan and design
- Pilot
- Implement
- Run

In the Assess stage, the project begins with the assessment of a business case, RFID feasibility study, and the roadmap of how RFID execution is. Then the project proceeds to the next stage of planning and designing an RFID technology infrastructure. This involves setting up a site survey, designing custom RFID components, choosing vendors, reengineering business processes, and improving new ones.

Then the project moves to the Pilot stage. Here, the requirements are defined; the pilot is built, tested, and monitored. The results are analyzed for further refinements, improvements, and reengineering if necessary. When the project comes to the Implementation stage, the process has been transformed, the applications have been integrated, and project implementation has been tested with the support for training. Change management is part of the Implementation stage to ensure that the people at Philips will accept the changes and implement them smoothly. When the project reaches the Run stage, it will maintain and provide on-site services for the RFID infrastructure.

The example of a business case that Philips along with IBM developed for the Assess stage does not apply to all companies, as each company offers products different from other companies on which the RFID tags are to be placed. Here is a checklist that IBM recommends in assessing the technology:

1. What technology is currently in use?
2. What is the current level of automation?
3. What are the minimal benefits of moving to RFID?
4. Is the current technology able to handle large volume of real-time data that RFID readers generate?
5. What are the costs of product relative to cost of RFID technology?
6. Will RFID technology realize ROI eventually?
7. Will the company be able to use investments for internal inventory management for future external supply chain applications as the industry adopts RFID?
8. How effective are the current business processes? How much do they need to be reengineered to be more effective in operating the RFID infrastructure?
9. Who should be the outsourcers of the supply chain? And how many?
10. How many steps are involved in manufacturing the product? How are the products handled and stored? How complex are the manufacturing, handling, and storage requirements?

Now, let's take a look at why it is very important to choose the right vendors for the RFID implementation project. Here is the checklist.

1. Improve customer service to enhance supply chain visibility and reduce cycle time.
2. Increase working efficiency in SCE, for example, to scan entire cartons without slowing down operations, and to reduce the incidents of repackaging.
3. Manage better space utilization in real-time to better manage stock and locations.
4. Confirm value of RFID technology.
5. Ensure success of pilot to support customers' plans to integrate RFID in their supply chain management processes.

There are other reasons as well, tangible and intangible.

5.7.7 Intel RFID Strategy

Intel has taken a different approach from Phillips. It set up the Intel RFID Technology Center in Germany as a showcase for suppliers on integrating SAP NetWeaver components with ERP applications on Intel architectures using Savant Server. As explained in a previous chapter the Savant architecture allows Savant Servers to be placed in allocations where information is needed to be captured. It includes a middleware component that monitors and receives the inbound information flow from all active and passive RFID devices. One variation of Savant-compatible middleware solutions is, for example, Oracle Edge Server and SAP components that can filter out redundant and erroneous data a Savant server receives before sending it to ERP applications.

The Intel RFID Technology Center Server Architecture can be quite complex. It starts with the core of RFID-Integration consisting of a Savant server running a SAP GUI that connects via a dial-up to a gateway of RFID readers on one end and to an Intel hub via TCP/IP on the other end. This hub also connects with servers running SAP CRM and other SAP applications and components and including an Intel RFID Technology Center with SAP router behind a firewall. At the other end of this firewall are notebooks and PDAs with RFID readers. The server that runs SAP R/3 is connected via a hub to a database server that is activated when needed.

Intel has presented a business case RFID on using SAP Netweaver connected to a mySAP ERP system. It starts with SAP CRM application creating a service order upon request for one from a mobile device, such as a laptop or PDA. The order is then checked for availability from an RFID inventory database. SAP NetWeaver transfers purchase orders for spare parts to mobile users.

If a supplier needs to integrate additional sensors such as temperature or air pressure sensors (e.g., checking temperature of packaged chicken parts while in transit), it should consider a sensor-based architecture such as offered by Oracle's Sensor Based Service Architecture (SBSA). With this architecture, it is possible to add RFID and other sensors without making changes to current applications.

5.7.8 Unilever RFID Strategy

Unilever has found the shape and size of the product can affect the optimal location for tags on cases and pallets. It has placed the tags at the top third of the case of dishwashing liquid bottles that taper at the top. This tapering feature of these bottles allows air space at the top of the cases where tags can experience less interference as it is known that tags do not work very well in close proximity to liquids. This has improved business processes of tagging the RFID labels to the product, reducing the incidents of readers not working properly with the tags and picking up the wrong data from the tags due to frequency interference from the liquids.

5.7.9 Major Clothier Retailer RFID Strategy

In the first major field test of RFID for consumer item-level tracking, a major clothing retailer according to Texas Instruments showed how EPC-compliant RFID tags produced 99.9 percent inventory tracking accuracy in tests in distribution centers and boosted in-stock sales significantly compared with stores in the area not using RFID.

RFID readers were wired into shelves to alert store staff when any item became out of stock on the shelf so it could be replenished immediately. Other foreseeable benefits of RFID business processes include assisting POS operations by allowing mass scanning at check-out and instantly processing returns, loss prevention, and loyalty discounts.

5.7.10 Marks and Spencer RFID Strategy

Marks and Spencer, one of Europe's largest retailers, decided to move from bar codes to reusable RFID smart labels to improve business processes. The company pioneered a very large RFID supply deployment with 3.5 million tags using EPC-compliant TI-RFid™ technology. Fifty chilled food suppliers have been linked to more than 350 stores across the United Kingdom. This way, the company can move perishable refrigerated foods more quickly and accurately through the supply from dispatch and sorting to pick-up and distribution, reading food trays, dollies, and roll cages much faster at each point in the supply chain.

5.8 RFID ENTERPRISE SUPPLY CHAIN SYSTEMS

Some companies such as IBM and Kayser-Roth, in the above instances, have referred to SCP, SCE, or SCM in their RFID strategy and those who did not will most likely expand their strategy to include those systems as they proceed to RFID implementation in the other portions of the supply chain. The enterprise supply chain systems have effects on business processes in varying degrees. In the Adaptive Multi-Layer Business Process Model, changes in any supply chain systems may send feedback to lower inner layers for continuous improvement of business processes. When the changes are incorporated or adapted, the model moves the process from a lower layer to a higher layer. This is also true of the Predictive Multi-Layer Business Process Model.

Let's take a look at each system as it pertains to RFID infrastructure, implementation, and deployment.

5.8.1 Supply Chain Planning

Initial planning starts the RFID life cycle and can be changed if it gets feedback from SCE and SCM systems in the Adaptive and Predictive Multi-Layer Business Process Models. SCP systems, also known as advanced planning and scheduling systems, were originally focused on the manufacturing shop floor, and used for planning and scheduling of the orders. They start with order demand, and determine how and when the demand can be satisfied. The modules that make up an SCP system include inventory planning, supply chain network, manufacturing planning, and demand planning. These functions are all integrated in order to maximize planning efficiencies and improve business processes.

As a subset of SCM, it is the process of coordinating assets to optimize the delivery of goods, services, and information from supplier to customer, balancing supply and demand. An SCP suite sits on top of a transactional system to provide planning, what-if scenario analysis capabilities, and real-time demand commitments. Typical modules include network planning, capacity planning, demand planning, manufacturing planning and scheduling, distribution and deployment planning, and transportation planning and scheduling.

SCP decisions will need to be rethought to gain the benefits of RFID in lowering labor costs, reducing theft, and increasing product visibility and how RFID would contribute to reengineered business processes in supply chains. SCP must be flexible enough to allow decision makers to respond to changes in planning at any point in the supply chain. Care must be taken when a provider of supply management software product suites, including SCP tools is acquired by another company. The acquiring company may choose to remake the products with additional features, to incorporate them into a larger back-end system, or to delete certain features that appear not to be profitable.

5.8.2 Supply Chain Execution

In this category, application vendors focus on SCE applications on business operations and rules to transform the way the RFID information has been collected, filtered, and distributed from readers to SCM, other EAI, and database systems. SCE applications include Warehouse Management Systems (WMSs), Transportation Management Systems (TMSs), Logistics Management Systems (LMSs), and Supply Chain Inventory Visibility Systems (SCIVSs).

SCE applications focus on performance management based on the integration tradeoffs between the demands from the customers and the supplies from trading partners in the supply chain, but do not involve procurement activities characteristic of the SCM. SCE applications also may extend and synchronize business processes to trading partners across the network in the supply chain.

Some vendors treat this type of middleware as a separate application, integrate it into a larger part of the SCM, or add it as a module to an SCE application. SCE applications may be part of a SCM system or be considered as separate from it as RFID-centric. The SCM system that contains SCE applications may also include other supply chain applications such as SCP.

If a SCE application is external to a SCM system that a company internally runs, it will require appropriate interfaces. Some vendors integrate SCE applications to Supply Chain Performance Management (SCPM) applications to send alerts on various events. Even if the vendors do not integrate them, SCPM applications may be available as separate packages from other vendors or part of the SCM system. Some vendors provide support for collaborative messaging exchange between Web services and non-Web services involving the use, filtering, and deployment of RFID data collected from RFID tags. Care must be taken when a provider of supply management software product suites, including SCE tools is acquired by another company.

As of this writing, Provia, Manhattan Associates, RedPrairie, SAP, and HighJump Software are the major players in SCE applications. Each has its own benefits and advantages of running an SCE system, application, or module as a middleware. They give you an example what to look for when you compare application vendors even those vendors that are not mentioned in this section.

ViaWare WMS is the core of Provia's platform-independent SCE solution and coexists with RFIDAware to leverage the visibility of RFID items in warehouses. This database-independent (Oracle, SQL, Informix) system includes Yard Management functionality (ViaWare YMS) of tracking carrier performance, scheduling dock doors, and doing other things to improve performance. Also included in the SCE solution are ViaWare TMS and ViaWare Optimize. Provia's FourSite, as a stand-alone or part of the ViaWare suite targets toward managing customer inventories in many warehouses. Gillette has used Provia's RFID products and solutions.

Manhattan Associates offers WMS as part, not as a core, of its Integrated Logistics Solution™. Like WMS, Manhattan Associates also offer other supply chain applications as a separate package or with an integrated whole. They include Transportation Management, Performance Management, and RFID in a Box™ to enable RFID connectivity with existing systems. Unique to Manhattan Associates are Trading Partner Management, Reverse Logistics Management, and Distributed Order Management. Trading Partner Management aims at synchronization across the trading partner network whereas Reverse Logistics Management automates the process of product returns.

RedPrairie offers RFID-MAX™ to enable RFID technology within its SCE suite of products including WMS, Transportation Management, and Labor-Productivity Management. This makes the SCE as the RFID-centric, although WMS is not the core of the product suite. Unlike Provia and Manhattan Associates, RedPrairie integrated RFID-MAX with its SCPM to manage events, sent alerts on various events, and improved performance based on the information gained from the events.

Included in mySAP SCM is the SAP RFID application running on SAP NetWeaver that provides interoperability with Microsoft .NET, Java 2 Platform Enterprise Edition (J2EE), and SAP's ABAP. It provides RFID supply chain networking, planning, and coordination of EPC-compliant RFID readers, tags, and other products SCE including data warehousing and enterprise asset management.

SAP RFID application also provides event/exception management via SAP Event Management, the goal of which is to support an adaptive supply chain model that is responsive to changing demands and supplies. Through SAP Web Application Server, SAP provides the interoperability of Web services technologies. SAP also provides open integration technologies to support messaging exchange between Web services and non-Web services. ERP adaptors are provided for integration into existing SAP R/3 SCE chain execution processes.

Supply Chain Advantage, HighJump's RFID technology-enabled product suite, includes advanced, tightly integrated solutions for warehouse management, yard management, and transportation management; supply chain visibility and event management; trading partner enablement/collaboration; and automated data collection. Data Collection Advantage from HighJump Software, a 3M company, allows you to configure the collection of RFID-enabled data. It is designed to be integrated into any ERP system [including

PeopleSoft (soon to be merged with Oracle), Oracle, MAPICS, and SAP], With Data Collection Advantage, you can tailor predefined transactions to meet the unique needs of your enterprise.

5.8.3 Supply Chain Management

SCP and SCE EW associated with SCM (see Chapter 3) consist of two parts of SCM: logistics and management. The logistics part pertains to any supplies that can be procured, managed, and transported from one point to another in the supply chain. Examples include hospital supplies, pharmaceutical supplies, clothing supplies, aircraft supplies, subsistence (food), vehicle part supplies to field troops overseas, clothing supplies, office supplies, computer supplies, furniture, and shoe supplies. The management part is concerned with the integration with ERP Systems, Web Services, loyalty cards, handheld devices, smart shelves, and POS terminals.

Business and IT executives look at SCM logistics differently. Business executives are concerned with how SCM logistics interacts with customers and vendors and about how business processes should be adapted to SCM logistics. IT executives on the other hand are concerned with how information systems and services can be implemented and shared across the organization. Business and IT executives need to collaborate with each other on what implementation approach (one-, two- or multidimensional) to use in order to improve business processes. The approach so selected at a point of time in the supply chain may change to another approach as business processes improve. The executives also need to consider the Adaptive Multi-Layer Business Process Model as a way of integrating ERP and SCM functionalities with the RFID-enabled applications. It may be possible to bypass the model's third layer of middleware technologies serving as a bridge between the SCM systems and RFID applications, only if the RFID-enabled SCM systems can be developed from scratch and packaged for delivery to the customers and suppliers.

5.8.3.1 SCM Logistics

The executives also need to consider a model of organizational maturity. No matter what implementation approach to use, and how well the Adaptive or Predictive Multi-Layer Business Process Model is applied, the SCM system components may not function or integrate properly in logistics if business processes have not improved due to organizational immaturity and other factors. To test for the maturity of the organization in incorporating RFID technology infrastructure into the logistics, consider the SCM Logistics Maturity Model. We divide the maturity model into five life stages and then assess each stage if it meets certain criteria before we proceed to the higher-level stage. The first stage of course indicates the organization is immature and the final stage indicates the organization is completely mature.

For our own purpose, we give each stage a name and then describe what each does or intends to do as follows.

■ Pilot studies
■ Logistics projects
■ Organizational operations
■ Logistics visibility
■ Logistics optimization

Pilot Studies Stage: The organization typically does not provide a stable environment for developing a new logistics management system for an RFID technology infrastructure. It undergoes a pilot case study of implementing and executing the infrastructure. A one-dimensional approach is being explored. The one-dimensional implementation approach needs to be worked out. The study of strategies, goals, and objectives, the core component of the Adaptive Multi-Layer Business Process Model is not applicable.

Logistics Projects Stage: At this stage, policies for managing an RFID infrastructure project and procedures to implement those policies are established only after a pilot study has been successfully tested for implementation. Successful practices do not mean the same processes to be implemented by the projects must be used. The organization takes a one- or two-dimensional implementation approach depending on the complexity of the RFID infrastructure and the customer–supplier relationships. After the organization has worked out and implemented the strategies, goals, and objectives, it then can proceed to the next layer of RFID-enabled business processes of the Adaptive Multi-Layer Business Process Model.

Organizational Operations Stage: The standard process for developing a new logistics management system is documented, based on integrated system development practices. An organizationwide training program is implemented to ensure that the staff and managers have the knowledge and skills required to fulfill their assigned roles in the logistics management system including the use of middleware technologies. The organization can move from one-dimensional to the two- or multidimensional implementation approach. It moves to the layer of middleware technologies of the Adaptive Multi-Layer Business Process Model only when the organization operations have satisfied some criteria.

Logistics Visibility Stage: The organization establishes metrics to test for logistics visibility from one point to another in the supply chain. This allows the process of developing logistics with the acceptable measured limits.

The implementation approach applies to the customers' all suppliers who send items to all designated distribution warehouses, and retail outlets. The Adaptive Multi-Layer Business Process Model proceeds from the feedback of previous layers to the outermost layer: enterprise systems business processes, internal and external, but are not yet optimized.

Optimization Level: The entire organization is focused on continuous process improvement. The organization has taken proactive actions to prevent defects in the system from recurring. The implementation approach applies to the customers' all suppliers who send items to all designated distribution warehouses or retail outlets. The Adaptive Multi-Layer Business Process Model remains in the outermost layer where enterprise systems business processes, internal and external, are optimized to gain productivity and operational efficiency.

When organizational maturity is high at the Logistics Optimization stage, the feedback of higher levels in the Adaptive Multi-Layer Business Process Model goes to the lower layers of the model for continuous business process improvement. High maturity does not mean organization maturity will stay high. The level of maturity may decline in response to emerging technologies and new legislative regulations.

When it begins to decline, the implementation approach needs to be changed, and all four components of the Adaptive Multi-Layer Business Process Model need to be revised to improve business processes until it reaches the outermost layer. Instead of waiting for the maturity level to decline, the state of organizational maturity, the implementation approach and the Adaptive Multi-Layer Business Process Model need to be reviewed on a periodic basis, say every three years or so.

5.8.3.2 SCM Management

This SCM aspect looks at the intervening mechanism to integrate with ERP Systems (e.g., Oracle-PeopleSoft), Web services, handheld devices (e.g., The METRO Group Future Store), and smart shelves (e.g., Chain Pharmacy Operations). The intervening mechanism, whatever it is, cannot always close the enterprise system gaps without considering the opportunities and limitations of the mechanisms used in connecting the services via a network of business processes over the intranet and Internet. An organization may find that it is more practical, less costly, and more timely to connect via application calls or middleware technologies, to wrap a legacy application to Web services that requires frequent changes.

Changing code in a Web service is far faster than changing and recompiling a long-running application. Although faster changes to code looks more attractive, there are other considerations we should look at that could affect the speed of getting the work done, such as:

- Poor project management planning
- Wrong implementation approach
- Low organizational and logistics maturity
- Static business processes
- Performance issues
- Limited contractual obligations of running Web services on different platforms
- Customer demand for certain information that not readily available

Just make sure your organization is mature enough or can grow in maturity to accept adaptively RFID technology in an SCM system using the right mix of implementation approaches. Your cost/risk measurement is worthless if you do not include the maturity factor and the components of the Adaptive or Predictive Multi-Layer Business Process Model in your measurement. Care must be taken when a provider of a supply management software product suite, including SCM tools is acquired by another company. The acquiring company may choose to remake the products with additional features, to incorporate them into a larger back-end system, or to delete certain features that appear not to be profitable.

5.9 RFID BUSINESS PROCESS LIFE CYCLE

This life cycle puts engineering discipline into the business process, so that it allows reengineering of each stage when it receives feedback from other stages in response to emerging technologies, organizational changes, and new legislation and regulations. In choosing a life cycle for your organization, you need to consider business process models, implementation approaches, methods and techniques, life cycle methodologies, processes and procedures, and automated tools. It is the responsibility of the executives to ensure the effectiveness of RFID business processes and the resulting ROI that would pay off the investment within a certain timeframe.

RFID business process reengineering is a form of systems engineering. Like system engineering, RFID business process reengineering begins with a study of what user needs are, and proceeds to the development of concept and a model (e.g., Adaptive or Predictive Multi-Layer Business Process Model) and determines what the new systems and hardware requirements will be to translate the concept and model to a concrete infrastructure. Next, you need to have the system design documented in a professional manner that can be easily understood by a team of executives, IT managers, and other members. If the document reveals flaws in the RFID business process reengineering, the team needs to revise the concept, model, system design, software requirements, and hardware requirements. The process continues until the executives and other team members are satisfied with how RFID business processes should be reengineered.

The executives would want to know how the RFID business process should be analyzed. This analysis should include how the requirements should be allocated, reviewed, and inspected, how trouble reports should be prepared, and what corrective actions should be taken. If the correction actions are not satisfactory or need to be improved, the process continues until the executives and team members agree to the analysis. Then they proceed to the design, implementation, and testing of the RFID business process reengineering. Upon completion of satisfactory tests, the RFID business process reengineering should be integrated in your company's overall IT infrastructure, and be verified and validated before proceeding to the formal acceptance of the documentation on RFID business process reengineering.

The executives must ensure a checklist is adequate for analyzing RFID business process reengineering. The checklist must show that the requirements are not ambiguous and the terminology used is understood by all team members. The checklist should state the assumptions that could affect the implementation of RFID business process reengineering. It should also prioritize the requirements, ensure the requirements are consistent with one another and with requirements in related documents, and ensure that testing methods are stated for each requirement.

As an RFID business process reengineering project gets more complex, it would make more sense to organize the group of objects that are related to one another in a hierarchy of several levels. The rationale behind it is that it is easier to locate in the hierarchy an object or two for review and changes than to scan, say, 2000 pages of the document in text format on the reengineering effort. An object could represent a text document of, say, 50 or 100 pages. If the number of objects is too few, then it would be more practical to apply RFID business processes reengineering in text format than the object-oriented version.

The documentation on object-oriented hierarchy should include data flow diagrams, and state diagram for each object, and show how requirements would be translated into objects and how an object model would be created from these objects. Then this model would serve as input into the system engineering requirements for further analysis in a life cycle of design, implementation testing, integration, maintenance, verification, validation, and documentation.

To make the RFID Business Process reengineering project a success, the executives need to determine if:

- The resources would be adequate for the entire life cycle of the process reengineering.
- The project would be within budget and delivered as scheduled.
- The plans for the following activities are adequate: acquisition, risk management, configuration management, and quality assurance.

To represent a life cycle, we need a model. So what life-cycle models are there that might be available for the RFID business process reengineering? There are waterfall, incremental, and spiral life-cycle models. Can they be adapted to the process reengineering? What about the adaptive linear feedback life-cycle model, and the adaptive dynamic life-cycle model? Of those life cycles, the adaptive life-cycle models are newcomers.

Let's take a look at each within the framework of RFID business process reengineering. We start with the older models. When we get to the discussion on the newer models, we show why they are better than the older versions.

5.9.1 Older Life-Cycle Models

Waterfall, incremental, and spiral models are briefly discussed, so we can compare them to the newer models in the next section.

5.9.1.1 Waterfall Life Cycle

The following steps show the stages are seen as sequential in the waterfall; the model does not allow for iteration of previous stages. As shown in Figure 5.5, all prior stages must be completed before the model proceeds to begin the next stage [5].

We do not see working versions of the product until late in the project. All objectives, requirements, and constraints must be clearly stated throughout the project; no ambiguity is allowed before the project begins. Because the waterfall model does not treat risk management as an important element or stage, the risks must be perceived to be low in order for the model to succeed. One example of low risk is when the company has experience in

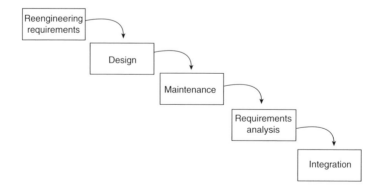

Figure 5.5 Waterfall Life-Cycle Model

building RFID infrastructure in one aspect of the supply chain, then use existing designs to build another such RFID infrastructure in another aspect of the chain. The resources do not change.

The linearity of this model is not practical in the real world of RFID business process reengineering. The projects are rarely sequential, and the resources, including the RFID designs and system interoperability are rarely constant. All objectives, requirements, and goals need to be reengineered at various times in a pilot study or in the SCM Logistics Maturity Model. The reengineering of RFID business processes on a large scale may require several iterations of prior stages of the model for continuous improvement. The waterfall model does not allow iterations of the stages.

It does not consider the impacts of the emerging RFID technologies on business processes or the impacts of reengineering business processes on each stage. The model does not consider that we need to manage risks of integrating RFID infrastructure with SCP, SCE, and SCM as a way of reengineering and improving RFID business processes.

For these reasons the waterfall model is out of the question. Let's take a look at the incremental life-cycle model.

5.9.1.2 *Incremental Life Cycle*

The incremental model does not require a complete set of requirements or well-defined objectives and constraints as the waterfall model does. The incremental model can begin with, say, one-third of the requirements in the first project (see Figure 5.6). For our own purpose, we restrict to three elements of the model: requirements, reengineering, and implementation.

When the first project moves to the second stage of reengineering, the next third of the requirements begin in the second project, as the first project moves to the implementation stage and the second project to the design stage.

The last third of the requirements begin in the third project. When the second project moves to the implementation stage, the implementation stage from the first project is incorporated into the implementation stage in the second project and the third project moves to the reengineering stage. When the third project moves to the implementation stage, the implementation stage from the second project is incorporated into the implementation stage in the third project.

Although the advantage of the incremental model is that it shortens the project time by providing usable functionality earlier, there may be a tendency to push difficult problems to the future just to show success to the management. This is something for which the executives have to watch out. They should ask if all requirements have been addressed no matter what time they have started or whether the objectives and constraints need to be well defined at the beginning of the project. Another area that should be of concern to the executives is whether the interfaces between the

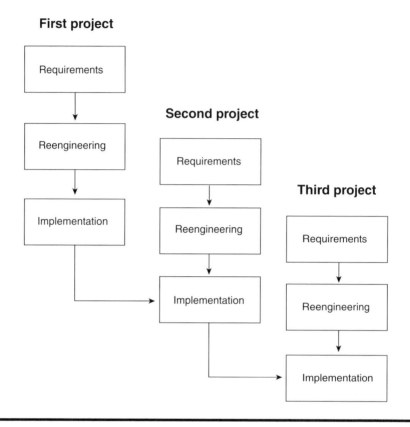

Figure 5.6   Incremental Life-Cycle Model

implementation stages will be free of bugs or did contain bugs but were not included in the report to the management. The model also assumes the resources are constant and do not contain a risk assessment element such as the Boehm Spiral Model [5] does.

In other words, if the incremental model is perceived to be risky, do not use it. Even if it is perceived not to be risky, it is not well suited for RFID Business Process Reengineering on a large scale as the reengineering effort may require several iterations of prior stages of the model for continuous improvement of business processes. The incremental model does not allow iterations of the model; it allows only the incremental of the implementation stages. Like waterfall models, incremental models do not treat risk management as an important component. They do not consider that we need to manage risks of integrating RFID infrastructure with SCP, SCE, and SCM as a way of improving RFID business processes.

5.9.1.3 *Spiral Life Cycle*

The spiral model is like the incremental model but with a difference. Unlike the incremental model, the spiral model allows the system to grow in size whether the resources are constant or expanding. Like those for the incremental model, objectives, alternatives, and constraints for the spiral model are not always well defined. The spiral model does not require a complete set of requirements, and there is a tendency to push difficult problems to the future to demonstrate to the management that the project was a success when it was not. Unlike the incremental model, the spiral model requires clean interfaces between modules: no bugs and no problems. This is not practical in the real world as interoperability problems between applications in a heterogeneous world are more likely to happen.

In Barry Boehm's proposed spiral model, prototyping is used to control costs and risks. Prototyping is used when risks are minimized in each of the four phases of the process from requirements to implementation. Can this spiral model be applied to the RFID business processes? Let's take a look at the steps of the spiral model [5]:

1. Determine objectives, alternatives, and constraints.
2. Plan next phases.
3. Evaluate alternatives, identify, resolve risks.
4. Develop, verify next level product.
5. Risk analysis.
6. Risk mitigation.
7. Concept of operation.
8. Requirements analysis.
9. Design implementation and test.

The spiral model does not allow iterations of risk analysis and risk management stages. It only allows phase iteration of the process. In other words, when the spiral model proceeds to risk analysis and risk management stages and then reaches the implementation stage, it repeats the process at the second step. The iteration ends when the model "spirals" to the fourth phase. For each phase, risk analysis and mitigation depend on whether the prototyping is well defined.

The spiral model is not well suited for RFID business process reengineering. The spiral model does not address business processes in any lifecycle phases. On the other hand, the adaptive and predictive models allow iterations of any stages for continuous improvement until the organization is mature to reach fully the business goals of the models. The strategies, objectives, and goals, the inner core of the adaptive and predictive models, are well defined. If the goals change in response to emerging technologies and new regulations, then the process of iterative improvements continues. For each improvement effort, we have a new set of well-defined strategies, objectives, and goals.

The difference between the adaptive linear and dynamic models is that the latter model can interact with other models for a different set of business process reengineering requirements. The former model is a stand-alone.

5.9.2 Newer Life-Cycle Models

We consider three new life-cycle models that can be used to improve RFID business processes. They are adaptive linear feedback life cycle, adaptive dynamic life cycle, and predictive.

5.9.2.1 Adaptive Linear Feedback Life Cycle

The adaptive linear feedback life cycle is based on the Adaptive Multi-Layer Business Process Model. Unlike the incremental and spiral models, the strategies, requirements, and objectives are well defined, so there would be no tendency to push difficult problems to the future. The impact of each stage on business processes is addressed as the model moves to a higher level linearly. Risk analysis and mitigation take place only at the implementation stage. In response to technology changes, the model sends feedback to the beginning of the first stage of the model. At this point, the process is repeated.

5.9.2.2 Adaptive Dynamic Life Cycle

The adaptive dynamic life cycle is based on the Adaptive Multi-Layer Business Process Model. Unlike the incremental and spiral models, the strategies, requirements, and objectives are well defined, so there would be no tendency to push difficult problems to the future. The impact of each stage on business processes is addressed as the model moves to a higher level. Unlike the linear feedback life cycle, risk analysis and mitigation take place only at each stage. In response to technology changes, the model sends feedback to not only the beginning of the first stage but also the other stages of the model. The process is dynamically iterative. Changes in strategies, requirements, and constraints are well defined. One example of this use of the adaptive dynamic life cycle is several adjustments to the speed of a laptop as it was affecting the quality of RFID input readers into the laptop.

REFERENCES

1. Hanebeck, Christina, Director Enterprise Applications, "Strategies for deriving value beyond RFID compliance," *GlobeRanger*, November 2003.
2. Hansbeck, Hanns-Christian, Director Enterprise Applications, "Process management and RFID: implications and considerations for process management," *GlobeRanger*, White Paper, 2004.
3. Zujkowski, Stephen, "RFID lessons learned: Its not all about the tag," Cap Gemini Ernst & Young, March, 2004.
4. TIBCO RFID Implementation and Integration Solutions, TIBCO Software.
5. Sorensen, Reed, A Comparison of Software Development Methodologies, Software Technology Support Center at http://www.stsc.hill.af.mil/crosstalk/1995/01/Comparis.asp.
6. DeGrace, Peter, and Stahl, Leslie Hulet, *Wicked Problems, Righteous Solutions: A Catalogue of Modern Software Engineering Paradigms*, Yourdon Press Computing Series, Prentice Hall, Englewood Cliffs, NJ, 1990.

6

RFID SECURITY, PRIVACY, AND RISK ASSESSMENT

A security program needs to be in place before the RFID in the supply chain is implemented. The program should include security policies, procedures, standards, guidelines, and baselines. It also should include security awareness and incident handling, a compliance program, a risk assessment program, and a system accreditation program. More important is the integrated control management linked to the corporate strategy to ensure laws and regulations are followed through.

In this chapter, we cover security policy, security in RFID query, a query scenario, attacks on RFID technology, and risk assessment.

6.1 SECURITY POLICY

The security policy starts at the top level where the executives and senior management determine the scope of RFID security and what RFID assets need to be protected. The assets not only include information systems, but also in-house personnel, contractors, facilities, software, hardware, documentation, and other things that the executives can add to meet the requirements of their organization. They need to make protecting these assets a high priority and provide various protection mechanisms with funds and resources in the most effective way.

In developing an RFID security policy, the executives must understand laws, regulations, and compliance issues not only within their own countries but with their trading partners in other countries. They need to know what to expect from the employees and the consequences of noncompliance. To what extent will the employees be cooperative? What happens when they do not comply? What assets are to be protected? Do they have any value? Will the policy be related to current or future activities?

The executives should determine who will be responsible for developing, approving, and enforcing the policy, and for reviewing deviations and incorporating them in an updated policy. They also should determine how frequently the policy should be reviewed and who is responsible for translating the strategic plans into mandatory standards, recommended guidelines, and detailed procedures to provide tactical support.

Then the management needs to determine whether a security policy will be organizational, issue specific, or system specific. For those who would like to have sample security policy templates, they are available in Appendix Q. The SANS Institute received permission to provide sanitized policies from a large organization. The templates form a good starting point and are easy to modify to meet your business needs.

6.1.1 Organizational Policy

When setting up an organizational security policy, the executives need to spell out a general statement to specify what the program's goals are, who should have the responsibilities, how to enforce the policy, and what the strategic and tactical plans are. The following are some policy examples with a description of each.

- Ethics policy to define the means to establish a culture of openness, trust, and integrity in business practices and spell out the responsibilities of key management people in the RFID infrastructure.
- Information sensitivity policy to define the requirements for classifying and securing the organization's information and spell out the responsibilities of key people in classifying the information.
- Audit vulnerability scanning policy to define the requirements and provide the authority for the information security team to conduct audits and risk assessments to ensure integrity of information/ resources, to investigate incidents, to ensure conformance to security policies, or to monitor user/system activity where appropriate.
- Risk assessment policy to define the requirements and provide the authority for the information security team to identify, assess, and mitigate risks to the organization's RFID information infrastructure associated with conducting business.
- Acquisition assessment policy to define responsibilities regarding corporate acquisitions and define the minimum requirements of an acquisition assessment to be completed by the information security group.

6.1.2 Issue-Specific Policy

An issue-specific policy addresses specific security issues, such as what management can and cannot do with employees' e-mail messages. The following are some examples with a description of each.

- Password protection policy to define the standards for creating, protecting, and changing passwords
- Acceptable use policy to define acceptable use of equipment and computing services, and the appropriate employee security measures to protect the organization's corporate resources and proprietary information
- Automatically forwarded e-mail policy to document the requirements that no e-mail will be automatically forwarded to an external destination without prior approval from the appropriate manager or director
- E-mail retention policy to define standards to prevent tarnishing the public image of the organization
- Extranet policy to define the requirement that third-party organizations requiring access to the organization's networks must sign a third-party connection agreement

Another example is an RFID issue-specific security policy [1] that includes the following elements. A template is not available.

- Labeling to show when RFIDs are used
- Tags that are visible, easy to remove, and in packaging not in product
- Tags that can be deactivated or wiped on sale
- Stores agreeing to returns of goods without their tags
- RFID payment systems allowing cash instead
- Consumers reading data on their tags if not destroyed or removed at purchase
- RFID payment systems allowing cash instead
- Consumers accessing personal data on your systems linked to tags that they own

6.1.3 System-Specific Policy

A system-specific policy spells out what software is to be installed, what databases need to be protected, and how firewalls and intrusion detection systems are to be implemented. The following are some examples with a description of each.

- Database credentials coding policy to define requirements for securely storing and retrieving database usernames and passwords
- Router security policy to define standards for minimal security configuration for routers and switches inside a production network, or used in a production capacity

- Server security policy to define standards for minimal security configuration for servers inside the organization's production network, or used in a production capacity
- VPN security policy to define the requirements for Virtual Phone Network (VPN) connections to the organization's network
- Wireless communications policy to define standards for wireless systems used to connect to the organization's networks

6.2 SECURITY OF RFID QUERY

Before we get any further on the security policy, let's take a look at the RFID infrastructure for supply chains as a small part of the bigger picture of secured commerce over the Internet. This big picture involves different RFID infrastructures of all trading partners—the manufacturers, retailers, and other parties of the supply chains—who have been authenticated and authorized to deal with one another over the Internet. This allows these partners to share, collaborate, and distribute RFID data. Although digital certificates authenticate the trading partners, all transactions and data must be encrypted when transmitted over the Internet.

The encryption mechanisms are of no value if the information in the RFID tags and database has been attacked, compromised, or counterfeited. To ensure that the information can be restored to its original format, the network administrator must ensure that an effective backup and recovery or business continuity policy is in place after it satisfactorily passes several tests. It is very important for the management to include in the security policy on what off-sites would be used for backing up and recovering data, and who will be responsible for scheduling backups and recovery. Also important is what access controls are to be used and who will be responsible for these controls.

6.2.1 Query Scenario

Now let's take a look at a simple scenario of a query between a manufacturer and a retailer [2], so the management could determine what else to put in the security policy. The scenario shows how the network administrator authenticates the trading partners and controls access to information and how the data is encrypted before the query is transmitted over the Internet. It assumes that RFID data have not been attacked, compromised, or counterfeited. The scenario only concerns itself with a secure Internet connection with digital certificates to authenticate the identity of the requester and sender of information and protect the data from those who cannot be validated with the certificates.

In the first step in securing the sharing of data, a network administrator receives a query from the retailer to ship the items. The administrator authenticates not only the user but also the device (e.g., RFID reader) and server (e.g., the Savant server) onto the manufacturer's network, and then issues a digital certificate. When the secure device gets the certificate, it reads the Electronic Product Code (EPC) compliant tags according to the contents of the query and stores data in the manufacturer's EPC Information Systems (EPC IS). The administrator must ensure that the data in the tags has not been attacked, compromised, or counterfeited before allowing the device to read the data and store it on the EPC IS. In this scenario the tags are affixed to a pallet of goods.

As long as the tag data is legitimate, the administrator encrypts the response to the query and sends it to the retailer that the goods have been shipped. When the retailer receives the pallet of goods, the retailer sends a query to the network to find out what goods are in the pallet without opening and repacking the pallet. The retailer's IT system relies on network ONS (Object Naming Service) to look up the manufacturer's EPC and point computers to information about the product, and the shipment time and location associated with the code.

The manufacturer and the retailer then use SSL to create a secure encrypted connection to allow the retailer to send the query to the manufacturer. Before the manufacturer's system can process the query, it must validate the identity of the requesting retailer via a digital certificate. If the validation is successful, the manufacturer grants permission to send or share RFID data based on the relationship between the trading partners.

6.2.2 Security Problems

We have two problems with this scenario. First, it does not take into account that "the 128 bytes of data on most tags are visible to anyone with a reader, no tags ... are read-protected and write-protected," according to Lukas Frunwalk, CTO DN-Systems Enterprise Internet Solutions in Germany in [3]. None of the tags are "alter-protected" as well.

This means that the RFID infrastructure could provide a new avenue of attack for terrorists especially when a remote wireless device can pick up the information from unsecured tags affixed particularly to individual items. This wireless device could bypass the more secured RFID readers: fixed, portable, or handheld. What is more is that these terrorists could disable the RFID deactivation mechanisms when the items leave the retail stores.

The origin of this security problem is the EPCs, a global standard that can invite hackers to attack the RFID technology system. According to [1], "one system fits all; one person cracks all."

The second problem is that it assumes the authentication requirements are the same for different parties from one manufacturer to another and from one retailer to another. It is most likely that one retailer will get pallets of goods from different manufacturers, and that one manufacturer will send pallets of goods to different retailers. In reality, the authentication requirements can be different for different manufacturers and retailers. This gets to be a headache for users who need to sign on each with a different password to access different RFID and non-RFID applications and network sessions. The solution is to employ a Web Single Sign On (WSSO) mechanism with a single password using SAML (Security Access Management Language) that is used to federate identities across the domains.

6.3 ATTACKS ON RFID TECHNOLOGY

The executives may say, "OK. What kinds of attacks on the RFID tags, data, and the network do you expect? We need to know what the threats, their impacts, and their frequencies are, so we can define the scope of RFID security in the policy."

Let's start with the first question: What are the security risks with RFID? Darren Suprina [4] gives some good answers. He points out, "The information inside [passive] RFID tags is vulnerable to alteration, corruption, and deletion" due to low processing speed and low memory. In contrast, some high-end active RFID readers and tags tend "to improve security through use of cryptography, challenge-response protocols, rotating passwords, and tamper detection technology" [5]. These devices have more processing power and more memory than their passive counterparts. They are more expensive and need a battery to give a boost to the processing power. The passive RFID devices do not need a battery. The tags wake up when they receive a signal from a reader.

Now let's go the second question: How can we categorize the attacks on RFID technology? The management can start with the four categories of the attacks that are unique to the RFID infrastructure: war-walking and lifting, counterfeiting, denial-of-service, and weak cryptography. The executives can expand the attack list to suit their organizational requirements and constraints.

6.3.1 War-Walking and Lifting

You probably have heard about war-driving, also known as the wireless LAN driving. It is a technique of using a Wi-Fi-based laptop or PDA to detect Wi-Fi wireless networks while driving in a vehicle, such as a small truck or an automobile. Legitimate war-drivers do not use services without proper authorization.

In the RFID technology arena, we add the wireless RFID driving to the description of war-driving. It is not necessary to have a LAN as an access point that a remote wireless device can pick up. A war-driver can use the device to pick up the information from unsecured tags affixed to an item, case, or pallet. What is more is that the war-driver could disable the RFID deactivation mechanisms when the items leave the retail stores.

In addition, the war-driver can read and get the information from the RFID tags of purchased goods that a passerby carries in a shopping bag. This can happen only if the tags are not properly deactivated when they leave a retail store or a warehouse.

War-walking is more bold than war-driving. War-walkers do not need a wireless device to find the RFID tags. With fake credentials or cards, they can bypass physical checks and find the system that uses RFID tags to monitor the movements of conference attendees. This is not a fiction. It actually happened in December 2003 at the WSIS Meetings at a conference center [6]. These crackers, or more likely the activists, did not like the idea of being monitored of where they were at the conference. They wanted to show that these tags raised the loss of privacy issues without regard for physical security. This, however, is not the right way to handle the loss of privacy issues.

Let's assume the cracker goes beyond finding the system. The cracker either runs away or removes the passive RFID tags from the objects, say, inside one case by sawing or etching the tags away. The cracker replaces them with the counterfeited tags, and reattaches the tag with original RFID data to the like objects in another case, all without being detected. This technique is known as lifting.

In another instance, a corporate spy walks around, scans the entire stock of a competing retail outlet, rewrites the tags of cheap products and replaces with better product labels and even hides products in a metal-lined tag and replaces with new tags on shelf. Passive tags do not work very well when they come into contact with a metallic surface.

Let's take a look at Gillette's RFID tracking system at a Massachusetts Wal-Mart supermarket. It worked [1] but was eventually replaced with a new version because of privacy issues. The older tracking system sensed when a product was removed from the shelf. It then took a photograph of the shopper, compared to another snap taken when the razors reached the check-out. The new system excludes the photography feature.

Another privacy issue that Dixon [1] has raised is what flashes up on a scanner as someone walks near the interrogator (especially the active interrogators that have a much wider scanning region than those of passive interrogators). The scanner could show:

- Clothing origins
- Contents of origins
- Contents of briefcase or handbag
- Which credit cards being carried
- Linkage to RFIDs that identify the user of passport in suit pocket

Make sure the RFID infrastructure is secured with physical security control mechanisms. If your company can afford it, you could use, for example, AXCESS's ActiveTag system, a single-system approach to automatic monitoring and tracking applications right from your desktop computer, including Asset Management, Personnel and Vehicle Access Control, Personnel Monitoring, Production and Process Control, and Inventory Tracking.

This system allows the information on tag identification and location to be forwarded over the network to a host computer running AXCESS' ActiveTrac software (for other risk-related software products, see Appendix P). The system allows you to integrate alert signals into existing alarm, access control, and surveillance systems. It would be nice to send an alert signal to an executive's multifunction watch that acts as a mini wireless device if there is one available.

You should determine what countermeasures you need to mitigate the risks of war-driving, war-walking, and lifting threats before RFID is fully implemented.

6.3.2 Counterfeiting

It is the semi-conductor companies who manufacture RFID tags. Unlike security firms, the semi-conductors have practically no experience in security [4]. These companies are more interested in getting the customers to buy their products rather than in the discussion of product vulnerabilities and countermeasures. Another problem is the vendors who become too overconfident that their products will not be easy to break.

According to Johnston and Warner [4], a clever person can counterfeit RFID tags and even switch RFID readers. With a switched reader, you will be not able to read the tags. Johnston and Warner also point out that an adversary can defeat an encryption by switching readers after gaining physical access to the location that sends encrypted communications.

Now, how does an adversary make the switch? One possibility is to switch with a fake reader. Another possibility is to tamper with the original reader. It is so easy to do so with a portable handheld device, particularly the ones that can fit into the palm of most hands. The tampered or replaced reader can be modified to allow the adversary to control a legitimate reader nearby from a distance and write counterfeit serial numbers on the RFID tags. It also can be modified to automatically change the original RFID numbers stored in the reader's database and replace it with invalid numbers.

That is why it is important to secure custody for the reader even when a RFID handler is not using the device. It is also important for the organizations to ensure that a legitimate reader can reject an invalid RFID number counterfeited on the tag or in the reader's database.

Better yet in the pharmaceutical industry is the Authenticated RFID Platform offered by 3M and Texas Instruments. This platform, as announced in June 2005 is a multi-layered, transaction-based security solution that allows the authentication of each item uniquely and securely. The Texas Instruments tags for this platform have more processing power and are more expensive than those with the lower frequency of the passive RFID tags. This additional processing power allows each tag when activated to generate a machine-readable security stamp containing a digital signature that is based on Public Key Infrastructure (PKI). To validate the RFID tag's digital signature as genuine, 3M's authentication system is used. Imagine when this type of technology becomes available for the passive RFID tags with more processing power at low cost.

You should determine what countermeasures you need to mitigate the risks of counterfeiting threats before RFID is fully implemented.

6.3.3 Denial-of-Service

RFID radio signals area also very easy to block or jam. This can cause denial-of-service not only to the RFID tags but also at the data and network level.

Hackers and crackers can launch a denial-of-service attack by using electromagnetic fog to block RFID scanning and flooding a retail outlet with radio waves at the same frequencies as RFID scanners, thus causing chaos at check-outs. They also can hide a transmitter in a cat at a parking lot. This transmitter can block radio signals, causing an RFID-enabled store to close, and send a malicious virus to an EPC IS server containing the RFID data. So when a passerby picks up a cat and takes it to the store for a treat in a restaurant, forget it!

You should determine what countermeasures you need to mitigate the risks of denial-of-service before RFID is fully implemented.

6.3.4 Weak Cryptography

Although we expect the price for passive tags to drop below five cents per unit in a few years, we must acknowledge that these tags are computationally weak for the standard basic symmetric key cryptographic operations. Because more expensive RFID tags have more processing power and memory they can perform advanced cryptographic functions. Most low-cost tags are readable; many have limited writeable capability. This is because these tags are designed with basic functionality to keep the costs low.

Although we can get around this problem in a limited way via minimalist cryptography and Elliptic Curve Cryptography (ECC), they are more appropriate for other RFID devices, smart cards. However, they are worth a brief discussion as we can point out how weak the cryptography can be for the RFID tags with low processing power.

Let's take a look at the issues with the kill and sleep/wake commands that led to the interest in minimalist cryptography and ECC. To keep the cost of passive tags low, small, and lightweight, Auto-Labs and EPCglobal specified only the basic functionality for the tag chip. These tags are designed to emit only static signals when a reader sends a query. Auto-ID Center had in mind to give chip designs the importance of privacy by allowing the tags to be killed even if the tags are not writeable. The kill command is done by sending signals to the tags to render them inoperable permanently.

However, security policy on RFID kill at sale can be confusing. For instance, Gillette will implement the policy only if requested whereas Wal-Mart will keep the policy always in place. On the other hand, Tesco as of Summer, 2004 does not have the policy on killable tags in place, but seems to have a preference for the policy on tag destruction. If the tags are hidden, the inability to destroy the tags could lead to major theft of the merchandise.

To overcome some of the confusing policies on when to use the kill command, the AUTO-ID Center and EPCglobal have proposed to put the chip tags to sleep for a while rendering them inoperable temporarily and then wake up these tags later on with a pair of sleep/wake commands.

For example, the check-out clerk at a supermarket kills the tag of purchased goods automatically or upon a customer's request. If the customer does not want the tag to be killed, this person can ask the check-out clerk to put the tag to sleep. After the clerk gets the tag to sleep, the customer leaves the store. The customer then gets home and wakes up the tags of purchased goods for, say, physical access control, theft-protection of belongings, and wireless cash cards.

The customer can also use the awakened tags to "make a range of smart appliances practical in the home ... and to return RFID-tagged items to shops without the need for a receipt." The war-drivers and war-walkers, however, may take advantage of the customers who find the sleep and wake commands inconvenient or forgot to put the tag to sleep by eavesdropping to the traffic between a reader and the tags of purchased goods.

Businesses have concerns about unauthorized monitoring of RFID tags before they are finally killed. A retail competitor could read tags inside the pallets or cases it ships to get business intelligence regarding the turnover rate of stocks, the shopping patterns of customers, and so forth. Businesses would like to have the sleep/wake commands to ensure the unauthorized monitoring of the tags does not take place. These commands should be properly implemented at the proper time at strategic locations of the supply chains and beyond.

Timing of these commands should be changed dynamically to frustrate the eavesdroppers. However, some supply chain workers and even managers, like the retail customers, may find the sleep/wake, even the kill, commands inconvenient, particularly when the check-out clerk, for instance, accidentally kills the tags of purchased goods that should have been put to sleep.

This is where the discussion on the potentials and drawbacks of the minimalist cryptography and ECC for the low-cost passive RFID tags comes in. Both aim to overcome some problems with the sleep/wake commands.

As mentioned previously, the basic functionality of the low-cost RFID tags does not allow the basic cryptographic operations, due to limited processing power and little memory and size of the chip. Juels [7] gives a security model to show privacy and authentication may be improved by enhancing their capabilities to a limited extent, better known as minimalist cryptography.

To make it work, the tag must have memory of several megabytes and be writeable. The scheme for this cryptography is pseudonym throttling. It stores a short list of random identifiers of pseudonyms and goes into a cycle. Very little computation, if any, is involved, as contrasted to standard cryptography that requires quite a bit of computation and more complex circuitry.

This is how the throttling works. Each time a reader queries the tag, the throttling emits the next pseudonym in the list, cycling to the beginning when the list is exhausted. The major advantage is that it prevents the guessing of kill codes. One disadvantage is that the memory is short and short memory in turn limits privacy: consumer and corporate. Another disadvantage is that the list is short and the cycle is static. The cryptography as discussed above is still weak. It does not involve computation that characterizes the stronger cryptography. It merely throttles though a short list of pseudonyms in a cycle.

The ECC is widely accepted for its efficient deployment of the public key mechanism. ECC is known for its compactness due to the novel way [8] it uses arithmetic units to perform complex computations. It is much more compact then RSA, allowing the low-cost tags to be RFID-enabled.

To get the ECC to work properly in RFID tags, we cannot overlook three important things: an adequate memory, the size of the area into which the ECC is installed, and the amount of power the tag can consume and emit signals to perform a simple computation. If the memory is too low, the ECC will not work. If the memory is adequate but the circuitry does not give enough power to consume, the ECC will not work. If the size of the area is too small regardless of memory size or the amount of power consumption, the ECC will not work. The memory, the area size, and power consumption must be set properly in order for all three to get the computation to work properly.

Then the executives would ask, "What about the security of a cryptographic device such as ECC-enabled RFID tag? In what ways can a competitor attack the tag to get the information about our product and our company?"

One possibility is an adversary monitoring power consumption while the tag performs a cryptographic operation. Another possibility is the adversary measuring how long it takes to do the cryptographic operation. The third possibility is to analyze how the tag behaves when the operation that did not work properly sends error messages.

You should determine what countermeasures you need to mitigate the risks of weak cryptography threats before RFID is fully implemented.

6.4 DEFENSE IN DEPTH

Let's assume light-weight cryptography for the RFID tag is well designed and is one of the protection mechanisms to defend the RFID infrastructure from attacks. In reality, 100 percent protection from cryptography is not possible. What is possible is the mitigation of risks to cryptographic attacks to an acceptable level. Another possibility is to let other protection mechanisms take over at the software/hardware level if one protection mechanism degrades or fails. They include firewalls, intrusion detection systems, scanners, RFID monitoring, failover servers, VPNs, and PKI.

As shown in Figure 6.1, these protections form the core of the Defense-in-Depth model of three rings. The middle ring focuses on access and audit controls. Access controls are best achieved with a WSSO for each user via SAML. Auditing is accomplished with an examination of security practices and mechanisms within the organization.

Overlapping the core and middle rings are the operating systems that include both, for example, firewalls and access controls, such as Windows 2000 security, Windows 2003 Server Security, UNIX and Linux security, and Web security. Also included are the automated tools and devices to assess network vulnerabilities.

The outer ring is a set of security policies including business continuity policy, risk assessment policy, password protection management policy, and server security policy.

Implementing the Defense-in-Depth is not as easy as it seems. For example, Myerson [9] points out that network administrators must often choose from among a dizzying array of specialized hardware and software products to meet their organizations' need for network security. Although individual products from different vendors are attractive as best-of-breed solutions in specific areas such as virus detection or authentication, businesses require assurance that the disparate products will work together to provide seamless, comprehensive network security.

Alternatively, administrators can choose to purchase a broad range of solutions from a single vendor as part of a product suite. Although this may

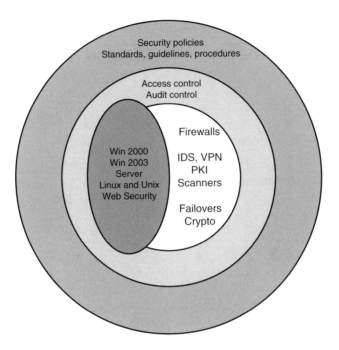

Figure 6.1 RFID Defense-in-Depth

alleviate some integration concerns, it can also limit the choice of application. It is unlikely any single vendor can provide the desired capabilities across a spectrum of security technologies.

To realize both best-of-breed application choice and full management integration, network administrators should consider an enterprise security solution built on an open architectural platform. With well-defined interfaces, this enables third-party security applications to plug in seamlessly with the overall security policy. In addition, an open architecture can leverage Application Programming Interfaces (APIs) to develop and deploy custom applications to meet specific network security needs.

6.5 RISK ASSESSMENT

In this section, we look at three types of risk assessment:

- Risk assessment profile of companies implementing the RFID deployments
- Internal asset risk assessment
- Risk assessment service

We also look at choosing a firewall product to be considered as a counter-measure in risk assessment.

Keep in mind risk assessment tends to be data-oriented. We need to make an assessment of how well business processes can be or have been applied to the RFID infrastructure. We need to develop countermeasures to mitigate the risks to the infrastructure as a result of an incorrect or inadequate sequence of business processes of having an impact on the effectiveness of the infrastructure.

6.5.1 Risk Assessment Profile

According to [10], AMR Research conducted its Risk Assessment Profile (RAP) study of major RFID implementation service providers on how well they have implemented their RFID deployments in the Consumer Products (CP) sector. Its findings indicated that none of the RFID implementors are all either medium or high risk; none are low risk. The reason is that none of the companies have completely integrated an RFID project into legacy systems.

AMR rated RFID service providers on their performance on four service attributes. The first one considers a service provider's RFID expertise and the second attribute looks at how well the provider can deliver RFID services in the CP sector. The next attribute measures the quantity and the quality of its past CP manufacturing RFID deployments and the final attribute looks at how well the provider can support a global RFID implementation for an international CP manufacturer.

According to AMR's report, global players IBM Global Services and Accenture offered the lowest risk. Yet, in late Winter 2004, the U.S. Department of Defense selected IBM Consulting Services [11] "to help manage and support the development of policy on use of RFID tags by 43,000 defense suppliers." Under a three-year contract, "IBM will assist the Department [of Defense] by identifying RFID commercial best practices, developing business rules based on analysis of RFID projects, educating and informing suppliers, and developing and executing a change management strategy..."

6.5.2 Internal Asset Risk Assessment

Should senior management decide on having an in-house security team conduct a risk assessment, they need to identify the assets and business rules that determine what needs to be protected. The assets include not only information, but also personnel, facility, hardware, software, and documentation. Then senior management assigns a value for each asset and determines the cost of maintaining physical assets and retaining the staff.

Other concerns of assigning value to assets include the value to the competitors, costs of recovering physical assets and hiring new staff, and the costs of developing or acquiring the assets.

The next step in risk assessment is to estimate potential loss per risk. This includes the cost of physical damage, loss of productivity, and unauthorized disclosure of confidential information. It also includes the cost of recovering from an attack or a disaster, and the calculation of the Single Loss Expectancy (SLE) for each risk. You get the value of SLE by multiplying the asset value by the exposure factor which is the percentage of loss as a result of a threat on an asset.

The third step is to assess vulnerabilities of each asset. Some vulnerabilities of an asset may overlap some vulnerabilities of another asset for the same threat. A vulnerability is an asset weakness that could be exploited. You can check network vulnerabilities with commercially available tools, some of which are listed in Appendix O.

The next step is to identify threats and then assess them by performing two calculations. First, calculate the probability of each threat that has been previously identified. Second, calculate the Annualized Rate of Occurrence (ARO) that determines how many times each threat could happen in a year.

After this, determine the overall loss potential per threat. Calculate the ALE for each threat by multiplying SLE by ARO. Choose cost-effective countermeasures to mitigate risks for each asset. Compare the ALE for each threat before the countermeasures are chosen with the ALE for each threat after the countermeasures are chosen. Next, calculate the ROI for installing countermeasures. Choose countermeasures to be installed that would generate acceptable ROIs,

Choosing a countermeasure is not always very easy. Let's take a look at the problems associated with the firewall as a countermeasure.

According to Myerson [9], firewalls have become an effective tool for protecting enterprise networks against intruders. As more computers become networked and are given access to the public Internet, the possibility of break-in attempts increases. Enterprise networks today contain valuable resources that provide access to services, software, and databases. For whatever reason, certain individuals exploit lax security as some network sites to download personal information, steal sensitive data, or even destroy files. Increasingly, companies are turning to firewalls to protect themselves against theft and mischief. By occupying a strategic position on the network, firewalls work to block certain types of traffic and allow the rest of the traffic to pass.

Myerson [9] states that even when the enterprise network is set up to provide effective firewall security, it must be checked periodically for possible weak spots. This can be done with risk assessment tools that identify potential security problems before they can be exploited by hackers. Using such tools can prevent customer information from falling into the wrong hands, which can result in lawsuits, financial penalties, and damage to corporate image.

A firewall enforces access control policies between two networks: an "untrusted" network, such as the Internet, and a "trusted" network, such as an enterprise network. It is designed to protect information resources of an organization. The firewall determines which inside services may be accessed from the outside, which outsiders are permitted access to the permitted inside services, and which outside services may be accessed by insiders.

It can be thought of as a mechanism to block certain types of traffic, plus a mechanism to permit certain types of traffic between untrusted and trusted networks. The desired access policy determines the balance between these two tools for monitoring and filtering both incoming and outgoing traffic, such as access control list, stateful pack inspection (stateful information is derived from past communications), event logging, denial-of-service detection, virus scanning, and probe detection.

Myerson [9] points out that network administrators must often choose from among a dizzying array of specialized hardware and software firewall products to meet their organizations' need for network security. Although individual products from different vendors are attractive as best-of-breed solutions in specific areas such as virus detection or authentication, businesses require assurance that the disparate products will work together to provide seamless, comprehensive network security.

Alternatively, administrators can choose to purchase a broad range of solutions, including firewalls, from a single vendor as part of a product suite. Although this may alleviate some integration concerns, it can also limit the choice of application. It is unlikely any single vendor can provide the desired capabilities across a spectrum of security technologies.

Increasingly, firewall vendors are opening their products to allow the integration of third-party security applications. Some even have very extensive partner programs to strengthen their firewall products. Check Point Software, for example, has over 200 members in its Open Platform for Security (OPSEC) alliance, which includes authentication, encryption, content security, networking infrastructure, application software, and managed service providers. Check Point certifies third-party products as OPSEC-compliant.

The trend is toward personal firewalls that replace all the functions of a corporate firewall with the one that is decentralized while retaining centralized control. Buying a $50,000 enterprisewise firewall is often an overkill for protecting the small RFID infrastructure.

Unlike hardware-based firewalls, personal firewalls are relatively inexpensive software programs that install directly on each PC in the organization.

They take control of the network hardware and perform the same basic functions as corporate firewalls: intrusion detection, access control, and event logging. They filter all network traffic, allowing only authorized communications.

Even after a firewall solution is implemented, it is recommended that a security risk assessment be conducted periodically. This helps network administrators identify and resolve security breaches before they are discovered and exploited by hackers and cause serious problems later.

Although the companies have chosen a firewall product to be installed, firewall security is a full-time endeavor that requires specialized technical staff and appropriate tools. Organizations that lack these resources can outsource firewall management to a third-party firm, even though risk assessment is conducted by in-house security teams.

For example, firewall management is one component of a service launched by Network Associates, who has teamed up with Frontier Communications. The two suppliers provide services built around NAI's global professional services and Internet security products, including the Web-Shield E-ppliance line. WebShield E-ppliance products are Web-enabled versions of NAI's antivirus, firewall, and VPN software, which have been modified as plug-and-play hardware-based security appliances.

Many other companies offer managed firewall solutions, including Cable and Wireless USA, GTE Internetworking, Intermedia Communications, Madge Networks, Netrex (recently acquired by Internet Security Systems), Sprint, Swisscom, and UUNET (a subsidiary of MCI WorldCom).

On September 27, 2000, ICSA.net announced that Unisys Corporation is the first organization to achieve Managed Firewall Provider certification through ICSA.net's TruSecure(TM) Managed Service Provider (MSP) program. This company met or exceeded ICSA.net's firewall security standards for logical and physical security, environmental support, connectivity, internal and remote virus attacks, firewall product certification, confidential data, and employee background checks and authentication procedures.

As part of the certification process, Unisys received physical inspections from a team of TruSecure analysts, as well as assessments of standard configuration vulnerabilities and management controls. Through its Unisys e-@ction Managed Services Centers, Unisys provides remote network and security monitoring and management for clients worldwide. The program also offers the support of ICSA.net's Rapid-Response Team, deployed during times of critical electronic threats.

The bottom line is to choose between personal and corporate firewalls. The choice depends on the size of the enterprise information systems of which the RFID infrastructure is a part.

6.5.3 Risk Assessment Service

A comprehensive risk assessment service is offered by ICSA. The organization's TruSecure is a package of security assurance services to help Internet-connected organizations assess their vulnerabilities. The service was developed in response to data ICSA compiled in a survey of 200 Internet-connected organizations, including small businesses, Fortune 500 companies, and federal government agencies. According to the survey, 93 percent of the responding organizations had security flaws that left them open to malicious attacks, even though they had implemented firewalls.

Using a variety of home-grown, commercial, and underground hacking tools, ICSA performs a remote electronic assessment of an organization's network connections to make it more aware of what devices can be seen by an intruder. ICSA technicians can probe corporate Web servers, routers, and services such as FTP and Telnet.

To achieve TruSecure certification, ICSA clients undergo a six-step process. The first step is the testing and analysis of vulnerabilities. Next, a methodology of best practices is implemented to bring the network and systems up to security standards. Then ICSA conducts an electronic performance review, on-site audits, ICSA perimeter certification, and periodic spot checks. The TrueSecure service starts at about $39,000 per year.

One of the oldest security assessment and reporting services is offered by the Computer Emergency Response Team (CERT) Coordination Center, which is part of the Networked Systems Survivability program in the Software Engineering Institute, a federally funded research and development center at Carnegie Mellon University. The program was set up in 1988 to study Internet security vulnerabilities, provide incident response services to sites that have been the victims of attack, publish a variety of security alerts, research security and survivability in wide-area-networked computing, and develop information to help improve host security.

The Coordination Center issues CERT advisories, documents that provide information on how to obtain a patch or details of a workaround for a known computer security problem. The CERT Coordination Center works with vendors to produce a workaround or a patch for a problem, and does not publish vulnerability information until a workaround or a patch is available. A CERT advisory may also be a warning about ongoing attacks.

Vendor-initiated bulletins contain verbatim text from vendors about a security problem relating to their products. They include enough information for readers to determine whether the problem affects them, along with specific steps that can be taken to avoid problems. The goal of the CERT Coordination Center in creating these bulletins is to help the vendors' security information get wide distribution quickly.

On August 28, 2000, Computer Associates released eTrust Internet Defense, an integrated software package designed to protect companies doing business online from attacks and security breaches. This package allows companies to migrate to the complete software suite and lets E-businesses take advantage of CA's risk assessment services. It includes five programs, which can be licensed separately or as a suite:

- eTrust Firewall, which enables companies to provide authorized users with Internet/intranet/extranet access
- eTrust Content Inspection, which includes real-time attack intervention, and automatic detection, blocking, and notification of all types of malicious content
- eTrust Intrusion Detection, which provides real-time, nonintrusive detection, policy-based alerts, and automatic prevention
- eTrust VPN, which lets companies keep their E-business systems safe from hackers
- eTrust Anti-virus (InoculateIT), which provides real-time protection

REFERENCES

1. Dixon, Dr. Patrick, "RFIDs: Great new business or brave new world?" presentation slides by Global change at http://www.globalchange.com/ppt/rfid/index.htm.
2. *Securing RFID Data for the Supply Chain*, VeriSign.
3. Jackson, William, "New tool demonstrates hacks against RFID tags," *Government Computer News*, July 29, 2004.
4. Suprina, Darren, "Security risks with RFID," *RFID Journal*, May 16, 2005.
5. Johnston, Roger, G., CPP and Jon S. Warner, "The Dr. Who conundrum," *Security Management, ASIS International*, September 2005.
6. WSIS physical security cracked, posted by Cowboy Neal on Thursday December 11, 2003, 10:56 PM at the Slashdot Web site.
7. Juels, Ari, "Minimalist cryptography for low-cost RFID tags," RSA Laboratories, Bedford, MA.
8. Is elliptic-curve cryptography suitable to secure RFID tags? *Workshop on RFID and Light-Weight Crypto*, July 14-15, 2005 Graz (Austria).
9. Myerson, Judith M., *Constructing a Secure Enterprise Network – Firewalls*, JMMyerson, 2004. Note Myerson requires permission to reprint quoted parts of her report for this book.
10. Collins, Jonathan, Study ranks RFID implementors, *RFID Journal*, May 13, 2004 at http://www.rfidjournalc.om/article/articleview/942/1/1.
11. Defense Department taps IBM for RFID rollout, Press releases, March 17, 2004 at http://www-1.ibm.com/press/PressServletForm.wss?MenuChoice=pressreleases&TemplateName=ShowPressReleaseTemplate&SelectString=t1.docunid=6873&TableName=DataheadApplicationClass&SESSIONKEY=any&WindowTitle=Press+Release&STATUS=publish.

Appendix A

PASSIVE RFID TECHNOLOGY

In this section, we briefly cover passive RFID products from Avonwood, Escort Memory Systems, Intermac, Northern Apex, Pillips, SAMsys, Symbol Technologies (formerly Matrics), TAGSYS, and Texas Instruments.

A.1 AVONWOOD (HTTP://WWW.AVONWOOD.COM)

Avonwood offers two passive RFID systems: Eureka 111 that operates between 125 kHz and 134 kHz and Eureka 211 that operates at 13.56 MHz.

A.1.1 Eureka 111 Systems

Eureka 111 tags can be read only, Write Once/Read Many (WORM), or read/write. This passive RFID system is well suited for industrial tracking and quality control applications, asset tracking, and identification and tote bin tracking.

A.1.2 Eureka 211 Systems

The Eureka 211 passive system is particularly useful for parcel/package tagging, supply chain logistics, and brand verification, and hence is often called a "smart label." User memory can be up to 1120 characters (10 kb) and the tag can be read only or read/write (but not WORM). Read speed is 20 tags per second at 1.4 Kbps with additional "Fast Mode" to allow for 25 Kbps. Tag-to-reader communication occurs at 70 Kbps.

The Eureka 13.56 MHz conforms to International Organization for Standardization (ISO) 18000 air interface standard. The Eureka 211 Industrial Decoder reads and writes all manufacturers' 13.56 MHz tags configured to ISO 15693 with support for standard serial interfaces.

A.2 ESCORT MEMORY SYSTEMS (HTTP://WWW.EMS-RFID.COM/)

Escort Memory systems (EMS) offers HMS passive read/write and HMS read-only systems.

A.2.1 HMS Passive Read/Write Systems

EMS offers a complete family of passive read/write RFID tags, handheld reader/writers, antenna, and ancillary equipment. The HMS-Series is the third-generation RFID system developed by EMS with hundreds of installations throughout the world. Submersible antennas for the disk drive industry, 8-mm diameter/high memory tags, high-temperature surviving tags, and conveyor antennas are well suited for tough industrial environments.

- HMS100 – Series Passive Read/Write Tags
- HMS800 – Series Passive Reader/Writers
- HMS827 – Series Passive Reader/Writer
- HMS828 – Series Passive Reader/Writer
- HMS820-04/HMS830-04 Series Passive Conveyor Reader/Writers
- HMS820-08/HMS830-08 Series Passive Wide-Plate Reader/Writers
- HMS820/HMS830 Passive Reader/Writers
- HMS827-04 Passive Conveyor Reader/Writer
- HMS827-05 Passive Tubular Reader/Writer
- HMS814/HMS816 Portable Reader/Writers

A.2.1.1 HMS100 Series Passive Read/WriteTags

EMS' button-size HMS100 Series Tags can withstand high temperature applications up to 464°F (240°C). Paint ovens, hot water rinse stations, and welding stations are some of the applications suited for these tags.

A.2.1.2 HMS800 Series Passive Reader/Writers

The HMS800 Series Passive Reader/Writer is a stand-alone Serial Reader/Writer with an integrated antenna that communicates to the host over an RS232 or RS422 interface with a data transfer rate of 1000 bps. Material handling, sortation systems, work-in-progress monitoring, and quality control are some of the HMS800 Series applications.

A.2.1.3 HMS827 Series Passive Reader/Writer

Selectable horizontal and vertical reading are now possible with the HMS827's patented rotating head. This provides greater flexibility in a factory automation environment where space is limited. For added convenience, the HMS827 is available with an RS485 multidrop interface (MUX32 Protocol) and an RS232 point-to-point interface. In addition, the HMS827 provides a data transfer speed of 1000 bps.

A.2.1.4 HMS828 Series Passive Reader/Writer

Selectable horizontal and vertical reading are now possible with the HMS828's patented rotating head, which provides greater flexibility in a factory automation environment where space is limited. For added convenience, the HMS828 is available with an RS485 multidrop interface (MUX32 Protocol) and an RS232 point-to-point interface. In addition, the HMS828 provides a data transfer speed of 1000 bps and incorporates EMS's patented TCB technology.

A.2.1.5 HMS820-04/HMS830-04 Series Passive Conveyor Reader/Writers

These conveyor reader/writers are designed to collect data for input to demanding material handling and automation applications. The Conveyor Antennas can be snugly mounted underneath the path of the tote and the 14-in. wide Reader/Writer can track any size tote/pallet on the same path without time-consuming adjustments. It also features an integrated DeviceNet interface module and a RS232/RS422 point-to-point interface.

A.2.1.6 HMS820-08/HMS830-08 Series Passive Wide-Plate Reader/Writers

Reading and writing ranges of 81-square-inch field can be attained with the patent-pending Wide-Plate Reader/Writer Series. The HMS830-08 provides the same Read/Writer range as the HMS820-08 but with an integrated DeviceNet Module inside. They are well suited for assembly or production environments that require faster identification/tracking response times and increased memory capabilities.

A.2.1.7 HMS820/HMS830 Passive Reader/Writers

The HMS820/HMS830 Passive Reader/Writers are solid-state devices compactly housed in two-part ABS plastic National Electrical Manufacturers Association (NEMA) 4 enclosures. The HMS820 is available with a RS485 multidrop interface and a RS232/RS422 point-to-point interface. The HMS830 is available with a DeviceNet interface.

The HMS820 and HMS830 are programmable and combine large internal match tables with Input/Output (I/O) to greatly reduce decision and response times from the host Personal Computer (PC) or Programmable

Logic Controller (PLC). The HMS820 and HMS830 have a slave serial port that can serve many purposes including either writing tag information to a marquis or accepting bar-code scanner inputs.

A.2.1.8 HMS827-04 Passive Conveyor Reader/Writer

An HMS100-Series Passive Read/Write Tag can be attached to a tote, pallet, or any carrier. When the tag-mounted carrier travels directly over the HMS827-04 Conveyor Reader/Writer, data is instantly transferred from host PLC or PC to the Tag (or vice versa). Using the frequency of 13.56 MHz and housed in a tough IP65 industrial strength enclosure, the Conveyor Reader/Writer provides an inexpensive alternative to bar-code applications.

A.2.1.9 HMS827-05 Passive Tubular Reader/Writer

The HMS827-05 Passive Reader/Writer is designed to fit into small areas and to work with conveyor work points. It comes with a NEMA 4 rating, and a reading/writing range anywhere from 8 to 36 mm from antenna to tag. The HMS827-05 incorporates a threaded 30-mm diameter tubular antenna with two M30 mounting nuts.

A.2.1.10   HMS814/HMS816 Portable Reader/Writers

HMS814 Portable Reader/Writer can plug directly into Intermec's® Antares handheld terminals to provide portable read/write capabilities. HMS816 Portable Reader/Writer interfaces directly to the host (e.g., laptop, palmtop) via RS232 serial port. Both Portable RFID Reader/ Writers allow flexible handheld identification and tracking solutions to a wide range of industries, such as automotive, material handling, electronics, and food processing.

A.2.2   Passive Read-Only Systems

EMS offers a family of RFID tags and antennas and ancillary equipment. Tags can be attached to a product or carrier and act as an electronic identifier. Tags are read by an EMS Reader (or antenna) suitable for tough industrial environments.

- ES600-Series Read-Only Tags
- RS427 Read-Only Reader
- RS427-04 Passive Read-Only Conveyor Antenna

A.2.2.1 ES600-Series Read-Only Tags

The ES600-Series Read-Only Tags are low-cost electronic identifiers that can be attached to most any object in the harshest environments. They can be read through nonconductive materials, contain no moving parts, and provide practically unlimited life with absolutely no maintenance requirements. For added flexibility the ES620HT and the ES650HT Tags are designed to retain data integrity after exposure to temperatures as high as 401°F or 205°C.

A.2.2.2 RS427 Read-Only Reader

The RS427 is a compact versatile Reader featuring an integrated antenna built inside a NEMA 4 enclosure. The integrated Antenna can be rotated from 90 degrees to 180 degrees to provide Read flexibility for most applications. The RS427 is available with an RS485 multidrop interface (MUX32 protocol), or RS232 point-to-point interface and either a horizontal or vertical read head.

A.2.2.3 RS427-04 Passive Read-Only Conveyor Antenna

In the past, the positioning of an antenna relative to the passing totes was critical. Read range had to accommodate different-sized totes or the totes had to be positioned near the antenna. The RS427-04 Passive Read-Only Conveyor Antenna addresses this concern because it can be substituted for a roller's position or may even be installed between the conveyor rollers. Antenna adjustments are a thing of the past, because the Conveyor Antenna can track any size toe/pallet with its 13-inch-wide reading field. Communicating to the Conveyor Antenna are Escort Memory Systems' low-cost ES600-Series Read-Only Passive Tags.

A.3 INTERMEC (WWW.INTERMEC.COM)

Intermec offers RFID tags and inserts (e.g., smart labels), readers, and printer. Description of these products includes Table A.1 on reading ranges of 915-MHz (UHF) tags in feet in an assortment of materials, such as plastic, cardboard, free space, plywood, glass, and metal (direction application), and Table A.2 on reading ranges of 2.5-GHz (microwave) tags in inches for like materials.

A.3.1 RFID Tags and Inserts

RFID tags and inserts are capable of receiving, storing, and transmitting digital information. The tags themselves are made up of either a transmitter and receiver pair, or a transceiver with an information storage mechanism attached.

- 915 MHz Tag for Reusable Plastic Containers (RPC)
- 2450 MHz Metal Mount Tag
- 915 MHz Reusable Container Insert
- 915 MHz Encapsulated Stick Tag
- 915 MHz Free Space Insert
- 2450 MHz Metal Mount Insert
- 915 MHz Container Tag

Table A.1   Intermec Range of 915-MHz Materials in Feet

	Plastic	Metal, Direct Contact	Metal, .06 in. Stand-Off	Glass	Cardboard	Free Space	Plywood
Container insert	4.5	.5	.5	8	3.5	3.5	6
Container tag	9.5	.25	.75	5	9	13	8
Intelligent ID card	3.5	0	0	1.5	7.5	9	1.5
Reusable plastic container tag	10	1	3.5	4	6.5	6	7
Encapsulated metal mount stick tag	12.5	10	8	13	13	13	12
"Free space" tag	4	0	0	4	11	12	10

Source: Intermec.

The Intermec Series 915-MHz RPC tag is specifically designed to track RPC for the life of the container. Using RFID to store information on a small chip, the Intellitag® technology of the 915 series allows you to track goods along the entire supply chain. Reading range is up to 10 feet.

The 2450 MHz Metal Mount Tag is designed for use on metal or RFre-flective surfaces. The tag combines an impressive range with a rugged package designed for harsh manufacturing environments. The tag includes

Table A.2   Intermec Range of 2450-MHz Materials in Inches

	Plastic	Metal, Direct Contact	Metal, .06 in. Stand-Off	Glass	Cardboard	Free Space	Plywood
CIB Meander tag	22	0	9	5	16	16	17
Metal mount tag	21	38	43	1.5	28	28	29
Metal mount insert	24	0	11	7	19	18	16

Source: Intermec.

mounting holes for mechanical attachment and has a small amount of flexibility that allows for conformance to the mounting surface. Reading range is up to 48 inches.

The Intellitag RPC Insert (915 MHz Reusable Container Insert) is the core of the RPC tag. The insert works well with plastic, is suitable for encapsulation, and has been molded into numerous products for smart container applications. Typical applications include pallet, carton, and container tracking. Reading range is up to 10 feet.

The 915 MHz Encapsulated Stick Tag is a ruggedized design that utilizes a metal back plane to provide consistent performance on a variety of materials. The long dipole design provides superior range performance and is ideal for tracking of metal parts and containers in manufacturing environments. Typical applications include Work In Process (WIP), pallet, carton, and container tracking. Reading range is up to 13 feet.

The 2450 MHz CIB Meander Free Space Insert is designed for maximum performance in open air. It is used in Sensormatic's Sensor-ID RFID/Electronic Article Surveillance (EAS) tags, which combine the security features of EAS with the supply chain management power of RFID. The insert construction includes a rigid substrate and is the smallest RFID transponder in the Intermec portfolio. Inventory management is a typical application. Reading range is up to 12 inches.

The 2450 MHz Metal Mount Insert is the core of the metal mount tag. It is suitable for encapsulation using a variety of molding processes and has been used in several applications requiring optimum performance on metal. WIP is a typical application. Reading range is up to 48 inches.

The 915 MHz Intellitag Container Tag is a high-performance durable product originally designed for use with plastic pallets. Typical applications include pallet, carton, and container tracking. Reading range is up to 13 feet.

A.3.2 RFID Readers

Intermec RFID readers extract and separate information from RFID tags. Readers may also interface to an integral display or provide a parallel or serial communications interface to a host computer or industrial controller.

- IP3 Portable RFID (UHF) Reader
- Microwave Original Equipment Manufacturer (OEM) Reader
- UHF OEM Reader
- UHF PC Reader
- Sabre 1555 Reader/Interrogator
- Intellitag Fixed Readers and Modules: 915 MHz and 2450 MHz

The IP3 Portable RFID (UHF) Intellitag reader, an accessory handle for attachment to the popular Intermec 700 Series Color mobile computers runs under the Microsoft® Pocket PC platform. It is a handheld mobile computing device with three radios—personal area (PAN) or *Bluetooth™, Local Area Network (LAN), and Wide Area Network (WAN)—as well as the area and linear imagers integrated into the handheld device with the ability to read and write to Intellitag RFID tags.

The IP3 can integrate into supply chain management for retail operations, industrial manufacturing, and logistics applications. The IP3 reader is ideal for RFID solutions requiring an extended read range, multi-tag sort, read/write, and memory capacity not provided by "proximity" technology. It works with exception-based scanning, available for UHF frequency band. Its integrated circular-polarized antenna read tags in any orientation.

This reader has met the following standards.

- Automotive Industry Action Group (AIAG) B-11
- American National Standard Institute (ANSI) InterNational Committee for Information Technology Standards (INCITS) 256:1999 (R2001) - Parts 2, 3.1, and 4.2
- ANSI MH10.8.4
- ISO/International Engineering Consortium (IEC) CD18000 Part 4
- ISO/IEC WD18000 Part 6

The Intermec Intellitag Microwave OEM Reader Products include reader/programmer board sets for integration into microwave-band RFID systems requiring read range up to 2.5 meters multi-tag sort, read/write, and memory capacity. These products are useful in applications including transportation, security access, supply chain management, retail, manufacturing, logistics, and healthcare applications. The fixed reader/programmer board set is designed as an option for the Intermec 2100 Universal Access Point (UAP), but it may be integrated into other microcontroller-based systems.

Intermec's Intellitag UHF OEM Reader products include reader/programmer board sets for integration into RFID solutions requiring read range up to 7 meters, multitag sort, read/write, and memory capacity. These products are useful in applications including transportation, security access, supply chain management, retail, manufacturing, logistics, and healthcare applications.

The fixed reader/programmer board set is designed as an option for the Intermec 2100 UAP, but it may be integrated into other microcontroller-based systems. It utilizes wired or wireless connection options through the 2100 UAP.

With Intermec's UHF OEM Reader products, your spread-spectrum frequency-hopping RFID reader/programmer board set can coexist with your RF data collection network. The board sets also provide RFID data collection integrated into a local area network through a configuration option for the Intermec 2100 UAP.

Intermec's Intellitag UHF PC Card (type II PCMCIA) provides integration into RFID solutions requiring read range (within 2 m), multi-tag sort, read/write, and memory capacity. The Intellitag series of products is useful in applications including transportation, security access, supply chain management, retail, manufacturing, logistics, and healthcare. The PC card is designed as an option for Intermec's industrial data terminals and may also be used in laptop PCs. With the Intellitag UHF PC card, a spread-spectrum frequency-hopping RFID reader can coexist with your RF data collection network. An anticollision algorithm allows up to 40 tags per second to be scanned, regardless of the number of tags in the read zone.

The Intermec Sabre™ 1555 Reader/Interrogator is an extremely powerful data collection device capable of scanning bar codes as well as reading/RFID tags and labels. The Sabre 1555 combines a laser scan engine for reliable bar-code scanning up to 5 m (7 ft) with the capacity to read/program RFID tags up to a 2-m (6-ft) range. Using Intellitag technology and support for ANS NCITS 256-1999 (the only approved standard for RFID item management), the Sabre 1555 packs superior power to read/program single or multiple tags and labels. A 40-character display, audio feedback, and single mode key are available.

The Sabre 1555 offers a lithium ion battery option to operate with a variety of Portable Data Terminals (PDTs) without consuming PDT battery power. Each lithium ion battery pack comes with its own integrated charger. The 1555 is ergonomically designed and weighs less than 600 g (16 oz). EasySet® configuration software allows product setup through simple scanning of a series of bar codes. In a matter of minutes, your users can be up and running.

Intellitag Fixed Reader/Module (915 MHz and 2450 MHz) is available as a stand-alone reader or a module for integration into an existing housing and comes with four addressable antenna ports for flexible deployment of RFID across multiple portals or conveyor assemblies. Serial interfaces for connection to programmable logic controller equipment are custom configurable. It is designed for indoor industrial environments.

Intermec introduces a new FCC-approved fixed reader, the ITRFxxx01, and module, the ITRMxxx01, to the existing Intellitag family of RFID tags, scanners, and readers. Packaged in a sturdy extruded aluminum enclosure with an available power supply, the readers are ready for freestanding installation in indoor industrial environments. The modules are supplied without the aluminum housing, making them ready to integrate into other systems and enclosures.

The reader and module, available in either 915-MHz or 2450-MHz frequency bands, are ready for integration into supply chain management for retail operations, industrial manufacturing, and logistics applications. Both units are ideal for RFID solutions requiring an extended read range, multi-tag sort, read/write, and memory capacity not provided by "proximity" technology.

With four antenna ports, users can deploy a single ITRFxxx01 reader or module with four antennas, instead having to install four separate readers with one antenna each. This reduces the "cost per antenna," especially when identifying relatively small numbers of items at a time in multiple locations.

The ITRFxxx01 series Intellitag readers are specifically designed to provide cost-effective solutions for implementing RFID into environments using PLC, where RS232 and RS422 connections dominate. The serial port on the ITRFxxx01 or ITFMxxx01 allows the readers to be directly installed and run under the command of a PLC.

RF power output and duty cycle are programmable with both models. This gives the user the flexibility to configure the reader's operation to meet specific regulatory requirements governing the consumption of RF bandwidth, or to meet specific user requirements, such as the need to coexist with a wireless LAN installation.

Applications standards organizations, such as ANSIMH10, are adopting Intellitag technology used in industrial environments that require identification and data capture from multiple, nonuniformly oriented items at ranges in excess of 1 to 2 meters.

As Table A.1 shows, 915-MHz passive container tags work best with free space, cardboard, and plastic materials in respective order whereas reusable plastic container tags are well suited for plastic, plywood, and cardboard materials. Encapsulated metal mount stick tags work best with glass, cardboard, and "free space" materials and "free space" tags work better with "free space," cardboard, and plywood materials. Container and reusable plastic container tags performed poorly with metallic materials.

Now, let's take a look at the reading range of Intermec 2.5 GHz in inches (Table A.2). Metal mount tags work well with metallic materials whereas the other two tags perform poorly or not as well with other materials. CIB Meander tags and metal mount inserts are well suited for plastic, cardboard, "free space," and plywood materials.

A.3.3 Intellitag PM4i Printer

The multi-function Intellitag PM4i printer integrates into industrial manufacturing, warehouse, and logistics applications ensuring all times are labeled and tracked via RFID for quick and accurate data collection throughout the supply chain. RFID smart labels can be created to give RFID applications without host reprogramming. By using frequency agile RFID tags, the Intellitag PM4i can simultaneously encode and print labels that can be used worldwide, thus enabling the tag to be read via multiple frequencies, dependent on regional standards.

The Intellitag PM4i printer can also act as a "smart client" executing user-defined programs for completely stand-alone printer applications. This means your Intellitag PM4i printer can eliminate the personal computer, operate additional hardware (e.g., scanners, other printers, conveyors), and access information from the network host.

Integrated EasyLAN™ Ethernet, USB, and serial are standard interfaces with the Intellitag PM4i printer. Users also have the option to add additional EasyLAN Wireless or industrial interface boards. The EasyLAN Wireless interface uses an integrated standard 802.11b radio. This radio provides 128-bit WEP encryption of the information relayed through the network. Intermec's wired and wireless technology ensures secure printing and network infrastructure for all environments.

A.3.4 RFID Partners

Rapid proliferation of RFID applications has led to an increasing demand for more qualified sources of RFID integration services. Intermec has authorized that the list of partners shown in Table A.3 may engage in Intemrec RFID implementations, including RFID tag development, and RFID-specific business processes. These partners have the expertise to install custom software at the API level, as well as a thorough understanding of the mechanical and civil work that often accompanies an RFID installation.

A.4 NORTHERN APEX (WWW.NORTHERNAPEX-RFID.COM)

Northern Apex offers inlays, an assortment of tags, readers, and antennas.

A.4.1 Inlays and Tags

The inlays and tags come in two frequency types. They are UHF 900 MHz and 13.56 MHz.

Basic and custom-packaged 900-MHz RFID tags are available. 900-MHz inlays can be incorporated into standard laminated paper or plastic to create inexpensive stick-on labels or embedded in products, boxes, pallets, trays, or totes. The dual dipole inlay comes with the Integrated Circuit (IC) that has two ports allowing for perpendicular antenna construction. As a tag moves past a read point in a distribution center or retail store, its unique ID can be automatically communicated back to a central database, allowing managers to make real-time logistics.

The 13.56-MHz read-only, read/write and anti-collision versions are available to choose from with up to 235 characters on the chip in variable field arrays. They can be embedded, injected, or attached to your product with custom-housing or packing designs. Available are Industrial Smart Labels, and Tags for Calibration System Tracking, Luxury Products

Table A.3 RFID Partners

Acsis, Inc.	Micromation, Inc.
Antreon	Millenium Technologies
Aseco	MobileTech Solutions
Bar Code Specialties	Northrop Grumman Information Technology, Inc.
Business Solutions International (BSI)	Nutech Systems
Catalyst	O'Dell Engineering
Coalescent Technologies	Pathguide
Compendium Technologies (Melrose Data)	Peak
Compu-Power, Inc.	q.data Inc.
Computer Sciences Corporation	Quest Integrated Solutions
Createch	Quest Solutions
Datamax	R4 Global Services
Deloitte (Agesco)	Radcliffe
Deutron Acquisition	Radio Beacon
DSI	RedPrairie
Eagle Consulting and Development, Inc.	Ryzex
EDI	SAVI Technology
EDI Canada	ScanLynx Technologies
Electronic Data Systems	Science Applications International Corporation
Enterprise Information Systems –EIS	Sentinel Business Systems
Foxfire	Spatial Integrated Systems, Inc.
Genco Dist Ctr	St. Louis Business Forms
Genesta	Sundex
GlobeRanger Corporation	Synergistics Systems
High Jump	SYS-TEC
IBM	Systemgroup
IBM Canada	System Concepts, Inc.
ID Micro	Tacit
Imprint	Taylor Data
IMS	Tech Center, L.L.C.
Industrial Marking Systems	Tecsys
Intellimark	Texas Barcode
Irista (HK Systems)	Tolt
KiSP Inc.	Toolworx
Le Groupe Resolution	Worldwide Fiber Optics, Inc.
MagTech	

Authentication, Plastic Container Tracking, Bin Identification, Packaging Tracking, Animal Tags, Production Tracking, Automated Parking, and various other applications.

The AR900 high temperature-resistant tag was developed for those particular industrial applications where the tag is subjected to extended periods of intense heat, temperature swings, or brake-out procedures. The material itself is rated for 1000°F.

A.4.2 Readers and Antennas

The readers and antennas come in two frequency types. They are UHF 900 MHz and 13.56 MHz.

A.4.2.1 900-MHz Readers and Antennas

TSR 222 is a read/write portable data collection device with capabilities to function with a multiple number of PDA and PC devices. It is tethered to serial communication port or if PDA is equipped enables Bluetooth, bar code, Wi-Fi, or IR. The reader communicates with HF tags including Class 0, 0+, and Gen2 EPCglobal-compliant technologies. It is durable in a variety of industrial, commercial, and field service environments.

MLR 8100 is a portable reader is designed to connect with a Symbol SPT 8100 PDA or other offering the most advanced WIN CE/Pocket PC-based operating system scanner. It allows the end user to have tethered network communication, bar code, and external key pad, as well as all other standard Symbol built-in features of the model chosen.

SCR 2400 is a versatile "self-contained reader station" that tracks production of manufactured products and monitors the package for product authentication. It combines Win OS PC, LCD touch-screen, and RFID reader station and is designed to accept up to four remote RFID antennas. For direct user interface or integrated control I/O interface, "drop-in" Manufacturing, Production, and Packaging applications are offered as a stand-alone or interface with existing applications.

NAR 400 is a Multi-Protocol reader providing real-time, seamless integration tag processing for all EPC-compliant and Gen2 tags that collects, writes, processes, and communicates information. It also provides a ready-to-connect network hub connecting to customers' corporate networks via Ethernet or Serial connections. It gives read ranges up to 25 feet while providing security, privilege controls, and full traceability of all operator actions.

NSR 400 is an indoor stationary reader targeted for warehouse or business applications. The reader is anti-collision operation and is ready to be interfaced to a network with a RS 485 connector. Four multiplexers can be attached to one unit supporting up to 32 antennas at one time.

ANT-001 is one of the better indoor antennas (28.25 in. × 12.5 in. × 1.5 in.) for several mounting locations including doorways, overhead, dock doors, shelves, tunnels, and wall mount in a variety of industrial and retail environments. The general-purpose antenna is intended for long-range and large-area RFID tag reading and solid-state devices with no moving parts or mechanical switches and no configuration needed to become operational. Outdoor and NEMA enclosure options are available.

NA-ANT Stand is another indoor antenna that can be mounted on an adjustable aluminum stand. This stand is approximately six pounds with an adjustable height to 5 ft 6 in. You can mount the (28.25 in. × 12.5 in. × 1.5 in.) general-purpose antenna for a height between 3 in. to over 6 ft for long-range reading and easy movement, wherever the antenna is required. An optional 900-MHz reader can be mounted directly onto the stand.

A.4.2.2 13.56-MHz Readers and Antennas

SCR-2400 is a versatile "self-contained reader station" that tracks production and manufactured products and monitors the package for product authentication. This station combines Windows OS PC, LCD touch-screen, and RFID reader station and is designed to accept up to four remote RFID antennas. For direct user interface or integrated control I/O interface, "drop-in" Manufacturing, Production, and Packaging applications are available as a stand-alone or interface with existing applications.

XP 600 is a read/write Palm Pilot reader with sled design for the Palm PDA family. It is capable of converting the standard Palm device into an RFID reader. It allows for easy software development with standard Palm OS development tools.

Stationary L100 or L200 series Readers are suited for multiplexing up to four higher-powered industrial fixed antennas together to read tags in multiple locations at one time. Off-the-shelf antennas up to 16 in. in diameter can result in 10–20 in. read range for passive 13.56-MHz technology.

The TSR-222 reader is a read/write portable data collection device that captures data and transmits to multiple PDA and PC devices via a serial connection or Bluetooth interface with a read range of 2–4 in. It can enable bar code, Wi-Fi, Bluetooth, and IR when interfaced with equipped PDA.

DP120USB is a desktop point-of-sale enabled reader that comes with a USB connection providing for a read range of 2–4 in. The USB-powered connection allows the device to read/write data to PC, laptop, or other notebook devices.

DP 150 is a read/write portable tethered reader that interfaces and attaches to any Palm OS or Windows CE PDA with a read range of 2–4 inches.

DP175BT is a Bluetooth-enabled read/write reader with a capability of about 30–50 ft communication range back to a PDA or computing device. It is self-contained with antenna, RFID coupler, Bluetooth engine, and rechargeable battery pack. The reader enables Bluetooth PDA and PC devices with no cable or serial port connection.

XP8100SM is a portable read/write data collection device designed to connect with the Symbol SPT 8100 PDA interfacing with WIN CE Pocket PC operating system with a read range of 2–4 in. This reader allows for barcode data capture, Wireless LAN (WLAN), or Wireless WAN (WWAN) communications. This device is built for manufacturing, industrial, and field service environments, and is sealed to IP54 standards for protection against rain and dust.

XP1800/1875 is a read/write sled or tethered device designed to interface with the Symbol SPT 1800/PPT 2800 Series Palm OS or WinCE pocket PC-based PDAs to read within the range of 2–4 in. This unit has a built in bar code and is ideal for warehouse and route driver applications.

DP190FM/DP195FM is a read/write Flange Mount reader device that attaches to a door/wall/conveyor to interface with I/O controls and sensors. It can be factory configurable for constant scanning as well as triggered event. The reader includes antenna, RFID coupler with optional wall mount transformer or battery powered, and typically interfaces with PC or PLC controllers.

AR 100 is an extended reach wand reader with variable purchased "reach" length with visual and audible optional indicators. A connector on the end of a coiled cable can attach to any PDA, Palm OS, WIN CE device, or laptop/desktop PC.

AR 250 is a read/write flexible nose Antenna device allows the tag to be read at an extended reach in awkward positions. Coiled cable and connector allow attachment to any PDA, Palm, Handspring, WIN CE device, or laptop/desktop PC.

DP110 is a read/write Industrial reader device with a coiled cable and its connector allows attachment to any PDA, Palm, Handspring, WIN CE device, or laptop/desktop PC.

A.5 PHILIPS (WWW.SEMICONDUCTORS.PHILIPS.COM)

Philips offers I-CODE transponder ICs and MIFARE® reader components.

A.5.1 I·CODE Transponder ICs

I·CODE is an advanced technology for smart labels which are actually thin wafers sewn on foil. A family of on-chip capacitors allows support for different label sizes. This technology performs read/write operation up to one meter, has large memory sizes, is anti-collision, and can be migrated to ISO 15693. Data can be retained for either five or ten years depending on the model type. Not all models are EPC-compliant as shown in Table A.4.

Table A.4 Philips Transponder IC Features

Product Features	I·CODE1 SL1 ICS30	I·CODE 1 HC[a] SL1 ICS31	I·CODESLI SL2 ICS20	I·CODE EPC SL2 ICS10	I·CODE UID SL2 ICS11
Memory					
Size [bit]	512	512	1024	136	192
Write endurance [cycles]	100,000	100,000	100,000	—	10,000
Data retention [yrs]	10	10	10	5	5
Organization	16 blocks of 4 bytes	16 blocks of 4 bytes	32 blocks of 4 bytes	17 blocks of 1 bytes	24 blocks of 1 bytes
RF-Interface					
According to	I·CODE 1	I·CODE 1	ISO 15693, ISO18000	EPC	EPC
Frequency	13.56 MHz	13.56 MHz	13.56 MHz	13.56 MHz	13.56 MHz
Baudrate [kbits]	Up to 26.5	Up to 26.5	Up to 53	Up to 53	Up to 53
Anticollision	Time slot	Time slot	ISO 15693	EPC	EPC
Operating distance [m]	Up to 1.5	Up to 1.5	Up to 1.5	Up to 1.5	Up to 1.5
Security					
Unique serial number [byte]	8	8	8	—	5
Write protection	Blockwise	Blockwise	Blockwise	—	—
Special Features					
EAS	Yes	Yes	Yes	—	—
AFI	Yes	Yes	Yes	—	—
EPC	—	—	Yes	Yes	Yes
Destroy command	—	—	—	Yes	Yes

[a]HC high capacity (97pF).

Source: Philips.

A.5.2 MIFARE Reader Components

Table A.5 provides an overview of the components for the 13.56-MHz smart card reader ICs and modules.

Table A.5 Philips Smart Card Overview

	R/W Distance (mm)	Host Interface	Card Interface	High Data Rates (kbaud)
Reader ICs				
SL RC400	100	Parallel	ISO 15693	1.66/26.5
MF RC500	100	Parallel	ISO 14443A	—
MF RC530	100	Parallel, SPI	ISO 14443A	Up to 848
MF RC531	100	Parallel, SPI	ISO 14443A&B	Up to 848
CL RC632	100	Parallel, SPI	ISO 14443A&B, ISO 15693	Up to 848
Evaluation Kits				
SL EV400	75	USB	ISO 15693	1.66/26.5
MF EV700	100	USB	ISO 14443 A	106
MF EV800	100	USB, RS232	ISO 14443 A	106
SL EV900	up to 600	RS232	ISO 15693	1.66/26.5

Source: Philips.

A.6 SAMSYS

The SAMSys™ MP9210 is a low-cost, multi-protocol RFID proximity reader operating at 13.56 MHz. This reader works well with short-range RFID applications. The MP9210 can be connected to other SAMSys readers operating at any of the supported frequencies to blend their respective functionalities into advanced multi-frequency, multi-protocol solutions. The reader currently supports the following protocols: Philips I-Code, Texas Instruments Tag-It, and ISO 15693.

The MP9210 can be used as a stand-alone solution or in a networked environment using the SAMSys Interrogator Control Module (ICM). This reader is available as a high-feature, board-level module ready for use in your own equipment or as a fully enclosed reader housed within an ABS plastic case. The MP9210 includes an integrated antenna that makes it easy to set up and use. Applications can be built directly onto it for integrated solutions with high performance and reliability.

A.7 SYMBOL TECHNOLOGIES (WWW.SYMBOL.COM; FORMERLY MATRICS)

In September 2004, Symbol Technologies, Inc. completed its acquisition of Matrics, Inc. The company provides EPC-compliant RFID systems for retail, CPG, defense, transportation, and other vertical markets. Included in the Matrics RFID product line are tags, readers, and antennas.

A.7.1 Tags

Matrics tags are passive, operate at 860–960 MHz (UHF) and are compliant with at least RF air protocol of EPC Class 0 standard, version 1. They are available in read-only, read/write, and read/write many versions. All tags are manufactured in one of the four formats: inlays, adhesive inlays, labels, and converted.

Inlay tags consist of RFID chip and antenna mounted on a substrate whereas adhesive inlays are inlays with the substrate having an adhesive backing. Labels are inlays with the substrate attached to printable label material. Converted products are inlays which are then laminated or encapsulated into a specialized package. These packages can be plastic, rubber, or other materials that can be custom designed, molded, or laminated.

Read-only RFID tags come preprogrammed with customer-supplied EPC codes and are available with one or two antennas. These tags have the read rate of up to 1000 tags per second and long read range of up to 30 feet.

Read-only tags with one antenna are available in five types as shown in Table A.6. Each tag type indicates what materials it can be applied to, what forms are available, and what the maximum reading distance is.

Read-only tags with dual antennas can be read at any orientation and are available in three types as shown in Table A.7. Each type indicates what materials it can be applied to, what forms are available, and what the maximum reading distance is.

A.7.2 Readers

Readers are available for multiple and single ports. A multi-port reader (AR 400 RFID) is a fixed reader, well suited for warehouse and other indoor applications. It is designed to process EPC-compliant, Class 0 (Read-Only and Read/Write), and Class 1 (Read/Write) tags and is upgradeable to Class 1, Gen2. This device is a ready-to-connect network element that provides a variety of options for connecting to customers' corporate networks via Ethernet or serial connections and wirelessly via 802.11. One option is the capability to send the reports of events and status using Simple Network Mail Protocol (SNMP) to customers' network

Table A.6 Symbol Technologies Read-Only Tags with One Antenna

Type	Application	Form	Maximum Reading Distance (ft)
General use	General-purpose use on plastic, corrugated cardboard, bagtag, and plastic	Inlay, adhesive inlay, and label	25
Rubber encapsulated	Metal	Converted only	15
UV protected glass	Glass and windshield	UV-protected inlay only	15
Glass bottle	Glass bottles	Inlay, adhesive inlay, and label	5
Concrete	Embedded in concrete floors	Adhesive inlay only	5

Source: Symbol Technologies.

Table A.7 Symbol Technologies Read-Only Tags with Dual Antennas

Type	Application	Form	Maximum Reading Distance (ft)
Carton	Corrugated cardboard, paper, or plastic	Inlay, adhesive inlay, or label	25
General plastic	Plastic or wood pallet	Inlay, adhesive, or label	15
Paper Roll Core II	Garments, paper, wood	Inlay, adhesive, or label	15

platforms. In addition, the AR 400 provides security, privilege controls, and full traceability of all operator actions.

A single-port reader (SR 100 RF Receiver Module) is designed for embedded applications, such as RFID printers and handhelds, and works with passive RFID smart label inlays. It sends the data to your host computer over a variable baud rate serial TTL interface. This device permits tags to be read at a rate of up to 200 tags per second.

A.7.3 Antennas

Matrics High Performance Antennas are solid-state devices that contain no moving parts or mechanical switches. After installation, there is no configuration necessary to become operational, enabling ease-of-use and immediate performance results.

The Matrics dual directional panel antenna is a dual directional/dual polarization panel antenna array. It is designed to cover 900-MHz ISM frequencies with a VSWR of less than 1.5:1.

Dual Directional Panel Antenna can easily be mounted on ceilings and walls to create read zones around shelves, doorways, and dock doors. Up to four general-purpose antennas can be supported by Matrics Stationary Reader.

A.8 TAGSYS (WWW.TAGSYS.COM)

Tagsys offers products for three market segments:

- Industry and logistics market
- Laundry market
- Textile rental market

A.8.1 Industry and Logistics Market

Table A.8 gives a list of TAGSYS RFID chips, tags, antennas, and kits for the logistics and industry market. Following are brief descriptions of each product.

Table A.8 TAGSYS Products for Logistics and Industry

RFID chips	C210
	C240
	C220
RFID tags	ARIO™
	FOLIO™
RFID readers	MEDIO™ S001 and MEDIO™ S002
	MEDIO™ L100 and MEDIO™ L200
	MEDIO™ S011/S013
	MEDIO™ P111
RFID antennas	RFID Antennas
	Antenna Tuning Kit
RFID kits	Basic
	Expert
	Advanced

A.8.1.1 RFID Chips

TAGSYS offers three chip types.

Operating at the speed of 13.56 MHz, the C210 RFID chip is a tamper-proof ID of 64 bits, programmed once at TAGSYS premises. The read-only memory is read as a unique block. The data speed is 26 kbps from tag to reader and from reader to tag. The data on the tag is expected to last for ten years. The application identifier is coded in the identification part of the chip's memory. Programmable security is not available for this chip.

TAGSYS C240 RFID chip has the same architecture as C210 RFID chip. Primarily used for closed loop logistics applications, the read/write memory of the TAGSYS C240 RFID chip has been partitioned into eight blocks. Each block is made again of four pages of 64 bits. The access conditions for both reading and writing can be customized to fit with the application needs.

Four options of security, based on two 64-bit passwords, may be programmed on the chip, depending on customer requirements. The C240 chip's data speed and data durability are the same as those for the C210 chip. A secured database of 2 Kb is allowed. Customers can personalize portions on the memory on access conditions, including passwords.

The TAGSYS C220 RFID chip is field programmable by the user, well suited for the high-volume and low-cost requirements of logistic applications where large numbers of objects need to be identified and tracked. The memory of the chip consists of 128 bits with 73 for the user data, 40 of which are lockable.

The chip enables users to lock static data and modify dynamic data by using the field-programmable feature. It includes an EAS (Electronic Article Surveillance) feature for theft detection applications. The chip has a unique fast read rate of 79 kbps from tag to reader and 200 bps from reader to tag which, coupled with a multi-read feature, allows extremely fast reading of the chip even when multiple articles are simultaneously (up to 40 tags) in the antenna field. The chip is expected to perform 100,000 read/write cycles for ten years. Unlike the other TAGSYS chips, tag ID is not unique. The chip does not allow memory access by password.

The chip comes in four different sizes: small module, large module, small disk module, and disk module. All have read-only and read/write features. All except the small disk module version have programmable multi-read features. Reading distance for the small module is greater than the reading distance for the large module as shown in Table A.9. This is true for the small disk module (except for the field-programmable mode) and disk module.

As shown in the table, the small disk module has the smallest reading distance and is well suited for integration into dense/lightweight items. The shape of the disk module is circular with the hole in the center for easy fixation with such things as rivets.

Table A.9   TAGSYS ARIO RFID Reading Distance for Small and Large Modules

	Read-Only (Ario 10-SM; in.)	Read/Write (Ario 40-SM; in.)	Field-Programmable Anti-collision (Ario 20-SM; in.)
Small module	Up to 12	Up to 13	Up to 6
Large module	Up to 20	Up to 16	Up to 14
Small disk module	Up to 2	Up to 1.2	
Disk module	Up to 18	Up to 14	Up to 12

Source: TAGSYS.

A.8.1.2   RFID Tags

TAGSYS tags come in two flavors: Ario™ and Folio™.

Launched in 1995, the TAGSYS Ario RFID tags are a series of low-cost industrial tags operating at 13.56 MHz specifically designed to withstand high temperature, humidity, dust, shock, washing processes, and other aspects of harsh industrial environments. Made of an RFID chip connected to an etched antenna on an epoxy substrate, the Ario RFID tags are robust enough to be easily embedded in, injected into, or affixed to products.

Millions of TAGSYS Ario RFID tags are used worldwide to track items such as gas cylinders, plastic crates, garments, video tapes, processed food, and waste bins. In all of these applications, the Ario RFID tags have proven to be able to resist difficult and aggressive environments. It reads Tagsys, Tag-it, TI-RFID, Philips iCode, and other ISO15693 or ISO14443 tags. They can also be encapsulated and injected into products to better suit customer applications. All small and thin, TAGSYS Ario RFID tags come in various shapes and sizes and can embed the different TAGSYS chips, offering more than 15 possible combinations of read-only, read/write, and read/write-EAS-Multi-Read features for specific applications. Memory size ranges from 64 bits to 2 Kbits, allowing memory personalization.

Ultra-thin and flexible, the TAGSYS Folio RFID Tag is a 13.56-MHz flexible label especially designed to be laminated in between paper sheets, plastic foils, or cardboard labels. It is the ideal complement to bar-code labels for applications where both usage of traditional human visible information and RFID technology are required. It is widely used to track and manage numerous items, such as retail, express parcel deliveries, logistics/transport, libraries, airline luggage, and pharmaceutical and chemical items.

The TAGSYS Folio RFID Tag also comes as a CD Tag, designed to identify compact disks (CD-ROMs, Audio CDs, and DVDs) for rental and inventory management purposes. The high tack adhesive in the back of the tag prevents

CD Tags from being removed from their support, therefore preventing theft. The TAGSYS Folio RFID Tag is also supplied as a converted label in different formats. The label is self-adhesive and can easily be printed on thermal transfer printers and provides an efficient and reliable solution to end-users.

All Folio RFID Tag formats are delivered on rolls of 1000 units. The tags are available with TAGSYS C220 RFID chips, can be used with TAGSYS C210 RFID chips, and can be electrically personalized. They provide easier identification and tracking of defective products, increase throughput and automatic processes for label appliance, and reduce losses due to faulty labels.

A.8.1.3 RFID Readers

TAGSYS readers are grouped into four Medio™ types.

The TAGSYS Medio S001 and S002, both small in size, are RFID multi-protocol OEM readers specifically designed to be integrated into small devices. Their multi-protocol firmware enables you to read and write any type of 13.56-MHz RFID chip. The firmware of the Medio S002 can be upgraded to the future ISO18000 RFID chips. These readers can read several RFID tags at the same time (multi-read).

The on-board Flash memory of the Medio S002 enables you to automatically store last configurations, eliminating the need for reprogramming each time the unit is turned on. In addition, Medio S002 reader can be programmed for different configurations, either keyboard stand-alone mode or standard STX communication protocol, facilitating installation of the equipment.

The TAGSYS Medio S001 is multi-protocol and able to read/write TAGSYS, Philips I-Code™, and TI Tag-It™ RFID chips. The TAGSYS Medio S002 is multi-protocol, able to read/write all chips supported by the Medio S001 and all ISO 15693 RFID chips. The TAGSYS Medio S002 has an upgradeable firmware. The communication interface for the TAGSYS Medio S001 is TTL or RS232 and the interface for the TAGSYS Medio S002 is TTL, RS232, RD485, and RS 422. Software suites for both versions include S002 Explorer for test and firmware upgrade and Medio STX E Windows® DLLs (for custom application development).

The TAGSYS Medio L100 and L200 with an average weight of 11 pounds are multi-protocol long-range RFID readers designed for applications where 3-D and volume detection are required. They are used in industrial applications where high numbers of items need to be identified at once.

The Medio L100 has two RF channels and the Medio L200 has four RF channels. Both enable you to multiplex antennas and deliver a high-performance rotating field. Their high RF power (up to 4 W on Medio L100 and 7 W on Medio L200) is software adjustable. Their multi-protocol firmware ensures full compatibility with TAGSYS RFID chips and all ISO15693 RFID chips on the market. Their firmware is upgradeable to comply with future ISO18000 RFID chips.

The TAGSYS Medio L100 and L200 readers have four configurable I/O ports to enable end-users to connect a wide choice of sensors. They come with a software suite that includes the L200 Explorer, with a user-friendly interface for on-site testing and firmware upgrade, and Medio STX E Windows DLLs for custom application development under Windows 98, NT®, 2000, and XP operating systems. They integrate a high-speed Digital Speed Processing unit. Communication speed is up to 38.4 kbps for serial interfaces (RS232, RS 485, and RS 422) and up to 200 kbps (test and debug) for parallel interface (bidirectional and enhanced).

The TAGSYS Medio S011 and S013 are 13.56-MHz RFID OEM readers especially designed to be integrated into small devices. Supporting TAGSYS C210 and C240 RFID chips, these short-range RFID readers integrate a high-speed protocol enabling read/write operations. The on-board EPROM memory allows execution of important tasks without direct control from the host. Small in size, these readers can easily be repackaged. The TAGSYS Medio S011 and S013 have low power consumption and can be easily integrated in mobile devices. Communication interfaces are TTL, RS232, or RS485.

The TAGSYS Medio P111 with the weight of almost three pounds is for use in industrial applications with harsh environments. Connected to any type of 50 ohms impedance antenna, it reads and writes any TAGSYS C210 and C240 RFID chip and works best when combined with the TAGSYS Aero™ LA antenna. With networking capabilities for multi-reading point applications, the Medio P111 can be connected to industrial sensors, and therefore can be externally triggered.

The Medio P111 has two built-in external LEDs for visual control of successful reading. Its onboard Flash memory enables you to develop customized tasks. Specific programs can also be developed and downloaded to the reader via the TAGSYS Development tools (especially designed for the Medio P111 Open Reader Operating System: OROS). Communication interfaces include the RS232, RS422, or RS 485 interface. Communication speed starts at 9600 bps with a maximum of 19,200 bps. The reader is universally plug-and-play packaged. OS memory and Flash memory are set at 16 KB and 128 KB, respectively, with an option of 8 KB for additional memory from an external source.

A.8.1.4   RFID Antennas

TAGSYS antennas come in two types.

TAGSYS offers a wide range of 50 ohms impedance off-the-shelf standard RFID antennas. Available either in round, square, or rectangular shapes and in different sizes, TAGSYS antennas allow a variety of reading/writing ranges. They can be packaged in robust material to be used in industrial environments or simply presented as bare boards to be integrated into specific equipment. They enable various reading and writing distances.

The TAGSYS Antenna Tuning Kit is used to fine-tune 50-ohm impedance antennas, operating at the 13.56-MHz frequency. Packaged in a small and robust suitcase, it includes a full set of accessories (antenna cables, field detector, screwdriver, and power supply) as well as a complete and detailed user guide:

- Antenna Tuning Device
- Coaxial cables
- Two field detectors
- Power supply
- Screwdriver
- BNC/BNC adapter
- 2-pin/BNC adapter
- 50-ohm load
- Installation guide

A.8.1.5 RFID Kits

Three RFID kits are available: basic, expert, and advanced.

The TAGSYS Basic RFID Kit has been designed to allow RFID beginners to easily experiment with RFID technology for their item tracking applications. The kit contains everything needed to evaluate RFID technology without the need for custom software or expensive hardware:

- One reader with its antenna (packaged in transparent plastic)
- Four boxes of RFID tags samples (TAGSYS Ario SM, LM, DM, and Folio RFID tags)
- One cable for connection to a PC
- One CD-Rom (Installation guide)

The TAGSYS Expert RFID Kit can be used for industrial applications in noisy environments where many items need to be identified at once. The contents include:

- 1 long-range reader (TAGSYS Medio L100)
- 2 square antennas (TAGSYS Aero LB) for optimizing the detection RFID tag (multiplexing in volumes)
- 4 sets of TAGSYS RFID Tags to test each for capability
- 1 connector cable
- 1 CD-Rom with installation guide, demonstration software and DLLs to develop RFID application
- Optional: additional tags available on demand in quantities of 100, 500, and 1000

The TAGSYS Advanced RFID Kit is designed to program and read RFID tags operating at the 13.56-MHz frequency. Fix a tag to a small object and place it up to five inches over the tabletop RFID station and you'll be able to read its ID number with the inclusive demonstration software that runs on your desktop computer. It contains:

- 1 tabletop RFID Reading Station
- 3 sets of TAGSYS RFID Tags
- 1 connector cable
- 1 CD-ROM with installation guide, demonstration software, and DLLs

The tabletop reading station with a weight of 2.5 pounds is well suited for mid-range applications where reading/writing distances do not exceed five inches. The kit includes a set of TAGSYS RFID tags of various shapes and chip functionalities (read only, read/write, multi-read). The reader has a RS-232 communication interface.

A.8.2 Industry and Logistics Partner Products

In Table A.10, the list of products is sorted by company, then by product type in ascending order. Athelia is the only other company that offers products to set up basic RFID systems: tags, antennas, and readers.

We start with Athelia that offers RFID-encapsulated tags, enabled antennas, and enabled readers. Most vendors offer RFID-enabled handheld terminals: Blackroc Technology, DAP Technologies, EIA, Minec, Nordicid, Northern Apex, System Concepts, and System Touchstar. Northern Apex's handheld terminals come in six flavors. In addition to Athelia, Ichain and ICS offer RFID-encapsulated tags and GIS and Microraab provide RFID-enabled readers. Only two vendors, Teraoka Seiko and Toshiba, offer RFID-enabled printers.

A.8.2.1 Athelia

Table A.11 shows what RFID products Athelia offers.

ADHESIFPACK is a line of encapsulated smart labels from Athelia, designed to be affixed to a variety of surfaces such as nonmetallic, plastic, and glass. These labels can be embedded with a variety of TAGSYS RFID tags. They are flexible, can be affixed to nonflat surfaces and have an extremely durable adhesive on the back. The ADHESIFPACK labels are used in many applications such as Video and DVD rentals, automobile maintenance, and insurance records.

INDUSPACK is a line of encapsulated smart labels from Athelia Solutions, designed to withstand the harsh and varied environments found in industrial

Table A.10   TAGSYS Industry and Logistics Partner Products Sorted by Company

Company	Product Type	Product Name
Athelia	RFID encapsulated tags	ADHESIFPACK
		INDUSPACK
		ATTACHPACK
	RFID-enabled antennas	INDUSTRIAL ANTENNA A-IP67/A-L/IP67
	RFID-enabled readers	LI 200 INDUSTRIAL READER DESKTOP and HANDHELD
Blackroc Technology	RFID-enabled handheld terminals	Gemini HF210
DAP Technologies	RFID-enabled handheld terminals	MICROFLEX CE5320
		MICROFLEX CE8640
EIA	RFID-enabled handheld terminals	STONE
GIS	RFID-enabled readers	TS-HR80R System/TS-R63 System
Ichain	RFID encapsulated tags	TTPlus Tyre Tag
ICS	RFID encapsulated tags	Waste Bin RFID Tag
	RFID-enabled antennas	Waste Bin RFID Antenna
Microraab	RFID-enabled readers	MR010T-SE Contactless Tag Reader
		MR010T and MR010T-RS485 Contactless RFID Tag Readers
		VICTORY-PROX KIT
Minec	RFID-enabled handheld terminals	Memor2000
		4x
Nordicid	RFID-enabled handheld terminals	PiccoLink®2000 RFID
Northern Apex	RFID-enabled handheld terminals	XP600
		DP150
		XP1800
		XPCIA100 PCMCIA Card Slot Reader
		DP150BT
		DP120USB
System Concepts	RFID-enabled handheld terminals	Easy Tag™ RFID Adapter

(continued)

Table A.10 TAGSYS Industry and Logistics Partner Products Sorted by Company (Continued)

Company	Product Type	Product Name
Teraoka Seiko	RFID-enabled printers	LP-S5000
Toshiba	RFID-enabled printers	B482-QP
Touchstar	RFID-enabled handheld terminals	TouchPC Eagle
		TouchPC Voyager

Source: TAGSYS.

applications. The labels are waterproof and able to withstand vibrations, shocks, and extreme temperatures. The labels operate in harsh environments such as dust, frost, mud, humidity, and dirt. INDUSPACK labels are used in a wide range of harsh industrial applications and environments (gas cylinders, beer kegs, plastic crates, pallets, metal racks, storage containers, metal containers, machinery).

ATTACHPACK is a line of encapsulated smart labels from Athelia Solutions, designed to withstand the harsh and varied environments found in industrial applications. These labels are attached to objects via plastic bracelets or plastic smart seals. The identification of the object is permanent until the label's bracelet or seal is severed. The ATTACHPACK labels are used in a wide range of agro-food, industrial, logistic, and medical applications and environments (cured ham, crates, money bags, authentication of products, surgical equipment, and livestock).

Built in a polycarbonate case and equipped with waterproof connectors, the Industrial Antenna A-IP67 and A-L/IP67 models have been especially designed to be fixed directly on conveyor belt and resist to industrial environment. Designed to operate at a 13.56-MHz frequency and connected

Table A.11 Athelia Industry and Logistics Products

Product Type	Product Name
RFID tags	ADHESIFPACK
	INDUSPACK
	ATTACHPACK
RFID antennas	INDUSTRIAL ANTENNA A-IP67/A-L/IP67
RFID readers	LI 200 INDUSTRIAL READER
	DESKTOP and HANDHELD

to the Industrial Reader LI200, it is the ideal combination for reading and writing 13.56-MHz RFID tags applied onto moving packages or containers (boxes, crates, trays, palettes, etc.). Several types of antennas can be realized to better accommodate environment and performances to achieve.

The LI 200 industrial reader from Athelia Solutions is designed to identify moving packages or containers (i.e., boxes, crates, trays, and palettes) in any type of industrial environment. Configured with one or two antennas, it can read or write information on the RFID tags that pass by the antenna(s) located on the conveyor belt. The reinforced housing is designed for hostile environments found in the food-processing industry.

To respond to Desktop/POS (Point Of Sales) demands for RFID tags initialization or reading, Athelia Solutions has developed two models of ergonomic and user-friendly readers. Designed as a PC peripheral, these readers are easy to install thanks to the Industry Standard RS232 DB9 interface and up to 3-m length cable. Small and CE certified, the Desktop reader is equipped with external leads to indicate successful reading/writing operations, ideal for office, workstation, or retail environments. Adapted for use at varying distances, the handheld reader is IP65 certified.

A.8.2.2 Blackroc Technology (www.blackroc.com)

The Gemini HF210 from Blackroc is a handheld terminal that offers dual RFID/bar-code scanning technology. Lightweight and small, it is the ideal companion for users that need instantaneous scanning of bar-code labels and RFID tags. Scanning/reading can be done via the push button or in continuous mode. In addition, writing new data into tags is also feasible with the TAGSYS Medio S001/S002 RFID reader it integrates and via a serial connection to a host. This Blackroc device reads most popular bar-code symbologies plus Codabar, Telepen, and Plessey. It works with a wide range of "legacy" bar-code applications including libraries that will eventually change over to RFID technology.

A.8.2.3 DAP Technologies (www.daptech.com)

DAP Technologies offer two types of RFID-enabled handheld terminals.

The MICROFLEX CE5320 is a rugged handheld computer. Powered by Windows CE 3.0 version, small and light in weight, it offers a large LCD display, a backlight touch-screen and a highly ergonomic 54-key board. Equipped with PC card slots and high-speed IrDA and RS-232 communication interface, it simplifies data transmission and operates up to four working days without the need to recharge the battery. Integrating both a bar-code scanner and a 13.56-MHz RFID reader, it is a suitable device for industrial applications such as utilities, field services, public safety, agribusiness, and supply chain. Programs are easy to develop and to download.

The following are some technical specifications of this handheld computer.

Processor: Intel Strong ARM processor 206 MHz
Memory: Up to 64 MB RAM and 32 MB FLASH
Communication interface: IrDA, Ethernet 10 Mbps, RS-232, Bluetooth, Wi-Fi, GPRS
Expansion ports: PC card slots (2 type I, II or 1 type III)

The new Microflex CE8640 is a rugged tabletop PC, small and light in weight. The battery of the Microflex CE8640 can operate two to three days. Based on the Intel Strong ARM® processor (206 MHz), it includes several communication options (such as cellular and local networks, serial), an expansion bay for customized applications, a bar-code scanner, or an RFID tag reader. Unlike the handheld version, the desktop version has an USB interface. It runs on either the Windows CE.3.0 or Windows CE.net (4.0) operating system. The Microflex CE8640 is suitable in rough environments such as utilities, field services, public safety, agribusiness, and supply chain.

The following are some technical specifications of this desktop computer.

Processor: Intel Strong ARM processor 206MHz
Memory: Up to 128 Mb RAM and 64 Mb FLASH, 1Gostorage
Battery: Lithium-ion battery
Expansion ports: Two PC card slots (2 type II or 1 type III)
Communication Interface:IrDA, RS-232, USB port and Ethernet 10 Mbps via base station, Bluetooth, Wi-Fi, GPRS

A.8.2.4   EIA (www.eia-italia.com)

The STONE terminal from EIA is a simple, easy-to-use dual technology (RFID and bar code) handheld terminal specifically designed for data collection applications such as inventory, order entry, and invoicing. Small in size and light in weight, the STONE terminal is a very functional device able to operate for a long time. The STONE terminal integrates the TAGSYS Medio S002 RFID reader. It runs on a proprietary operating system, although Windows utilities are included.

A.8.2.5   GIS (www.gis-net.de)

Integrating the TAGSYS 13.56-MHZ Medio S002 OEM module, the TS-HR80R System and TS-R63 System from GiT (Gesellschaft für Informatik und Steuerungstechnik) is a compact RFID reader, designed to read and write any tag on the market. With an RS232 interface, it can be used in many applications, in industry (harsh environment), including goods and library administration. It is equipped with external LEDs and visual inspection of successful reading. Made of a robust plastic material, it can be integrated into public/desktop offices (i.e., libraries).

A.8.2.6 ichain (www.ichain.co-za)

The TTPlus Tyre Tag from ichain is a unit especially designed for the tagging and tracking of both industrial and commercial vehicle tires throughout their lifespan. The tag specification is based on the TAGSYS Ario series of RFID tags, housed in a high-heat, pressure- and stress-resisting casing. This is then vulcanized into a rubber tire patch, with special pressure releasing and strengthening mechanisms built into it, to ensure tag rigidity and eliminating any heat bubbling during curing processes or driving conditions. Insertion of the tag is a simple gluing and curing process, so any tire shop, factory, manufacturer, or distributor can tag their tires. The patch is applied onto the tire inner, between the bead and the shoulder, where it can easily be read through the sidewall from the outside on cross ply, radial, and even steel-belted tires.

The TTPlus Tyre Tag's strength can also withstand any processes that may take place on the tire, and the chip may be cut out and recycled at the end of the tire's life, if necessary. The unit is also available in numerous sizes and patch strengths, and so can be used in place of a standard patch to repair tire injuries while providing a unique tagging system to the entire tire industry.

Custom software geared toward the recording, management, control, and verification of tires in any application is also available as a back-end system leveraging off the TTPlus Tyre Tag. The software is written around the use of any of TAGSYS' portable, fixed, or other tag reading systems.

A.8.2.7 ICS (www.ica.nl)

ICS provides Waste Bin RFID Tag and Antenna.

The Waste Bin RFID Tag is part of the Fair Share Solution developed by ICS for the management of waste collections. It is based on the TAGSYS 13.56 MHz RFID Ario tags, a robust set of RFID tags designed to be encapsulated, over-molded, or injected. This special packaging is made of a robust plastic material with appropriate shape to fit exactly into the waste bin cavity and prevents the tag from any shock, pressure, dirt, and damage that could occur during waste bin manipulation.

The truck is equipped with two 13.56-MHz RFID readers developed by TAGSYS (industrial readers Medio C-P11 placed in the rear cabinet at the lifter of the waste truck, and two custom antennas affixed on the right tooth of each comb of the lifter). Information can therefore be automatically collected, with no additional operation required by the operator or truck driver.

Combined with an on-board computer, the system enables you to deliver waste management reports and data files for other (back-office) container management software.

The Waste Bin RFID Antenna is part of the Fair Share Solution developed by ICS for the Management of Waste collections. Using a TAGSYS 13.56-MHz RFID reader (C-P11), it is combined with a TAGSYS custom design antenna that has been specifically designed to be affixed onto the combs on the lifter of the waste truck. The antenna has been carefully studied by ICS and TAGSYS and designed to get rid of the metallic environment and ensure a minimum of 99.9 percent reading rate whatever the conditions (humidity, dust, temperature, etc.) are. The special packaging, made of epoxy and resin, prevents any shock or pressure damage that could occur during waste bin manipulation.

With the RFID tag attached onto the bin, information can therefore be automatically collected, with no additional operation required by the operator or the truck driver. Antennas are connected via coaxial cables to the RFID readers placed in the rear cabinet at the back of the waste truck. Information can therefore be automatically collected, with no additional operation required by the operator or the truck driver. Combined with an on-board computer the system enables you to deliver waste management reports and data files for other (back-office) container management software.

A.8.2.8 Microraab (www.microraab.hu)

Table A.12 shows what RFID products Microraab offers.

The MR010T and MR010T-RS485 Contactless compact RFID tag readers from Microraab are the appropriate choice for tag reader applications in office buildings, banks, and industrial facilities. They read TAGSYS 13.56-MHz RFID tags with a reading distance of 7 cm, providing Wiegand and Magstripe outputs or RS485 interface. A modern design makes them easy to mount in various systems. The readers are equipped with a LED and buzzer with internal or external indication control.

Table A.12   Microraab Industry and Logistics Products

Product Type	Product Name
RFID-enabled readers	MR010T-SE Contactless Tag Reader MR010T and MR010T-RS485 Contactless RFID Tag Readers Victory-Prox Kit

The MR010T-SE Contactless compact tag reader from Microraab is the appropriate choice for tag reader applications in office buildings, banks, and industrial facilities. It reads TAGSYS 13.56 MHz RFID tags with a reading distance of 7 cm, providing Wiegand or Magnetic Stripe outputs. A modern design enables easy mounting in various systems. The reader is equipped with an LED and buzzer with internal or external indication control.

The Victory-Prox Kits from Microraab are a series of unit access control packages. The aim of these kits is to provide an optimum solution for those customers who would like to design and install their own access control system. No special expertise is required for the installation, and the realized system can be easily extended. The surprisingly low price of these professional kits is suitable for any applications requiring a high-quality access control system.

A.8.2.9 Minec (www.minec.com)

Minec offers two RFID products.

The Memor2000 from MINEC, a bar-code/RFID reader, is a handheld data collection terminal that can be held and operated by one and the same hand without requiring use of a shift key (patent pending). Water-resistant with its 27 coated rubber-keys, the Memor2000 is small, light, and offers a full graphic capability, LCD display, making this terminal tough enough to withstand harsh environment applications. Athelia developed and produces the RFID end cap module of the Memor2000, using the TAGSYS Medio S002 reader operating at 13.56 MHz.

This handheld device is used in applications such as warehouse tracking of containers and pallets, production control, inventory control, field service, and automatic identification. It runs with the M/2 DOS operating system, allowing development and downloading of programs, and provides wireless communication with peripherals (PCs, modems, printers).

The 4X terminal from MINEC offers a unique combination of features: speed of data collection communication, and synchronization. The true one-hand-operated computer terminal, based on the latest technologies for harsh environments (water splash and dust resistant), runs with Windows CE or Linux and can offer online data access via GSM/GPRS, WLAN, and Bluetooth.

Athelia Solutions developed and produces the RFID end cap module of the 4X terminal, using the TAGSYS Medio S002 RFID reader operating at 13.56 MHz, and making it the best designed RFID/bar-code reader. It can be used to read and write bar codes, RFID tags, and MIFARE Contactless smart cards. The 4X is used in applications such as warehouse tracking of containers and pallets, production control, inventory control, field service, and automatic identification.

A.8.2.10 Nordicid (www.nordicid.com)

The PiccoLink2000 is the Windows CE 3.0 handheld PC by Nordic ID. It supports a wide range of applications and is easy to program if required. The low power consumption allows long operation time. The high-contrast screen displays graphics clearly in all environments. Integrating the TAGSYS Medio S002 RFID reader, the PiccoLink2000 is able to read and encode ISO15693 tags.

A.8.2.11 Northern Apex (www.northernapex-rfid.com)

Table A.13 shows what products Northern Apex offers.

The Advantage Series from Northern Apex integrates TAGSYS Medio S002 RFID reader operating at 13.56 MHz and was created to provide portable data collection capabilities in a variety of industrial and commercial applications. The handheld models ™Advantage XP600 is designed to cradle with any Palm Pilot to create a portable RFID data collection device. It is compatible with Palm Pilot m125, m130, m500, m515, and i705. It runs with the Palm OS operating system and provides a communication interface with IrDA.

The DP Series from Northern Apex, a touch-screen and push-button application device, was created to provide off-the-shelf, easily implemented RFID communication tools. The DP 150 series embeds TAGSYS Medio S002 RFID reader operating at 13.56 MHz. It is a handheld RFID read/write device compatible with Palm M series and iPAQ/CASIO as well as standard Com port devices.

It runs with Palm OS or Windows CE and connects via a standard serial port, 9-volt battery powered. Memory is PDA dependent. It provides additional connectors for Compaq iPAQ, Cassiopeia™, Symbol™, Toshiba™, Sony™, and Palm™ devices.

The Advantage XP1800 Series from Northern Apex integrates TAGSYS Medio S002 RFID readers operating at 13.56 MHz, and was created to

Table A.13 Northern Apex Industry and Logistics Products

Product Type	Product Name
RFID-enabled handheld terminals	XP600
	DP 150
	XP1800
	XPCIA100 PCMCIA Card Slot Reader
	DP150BT
	DP120USB

provide portable data collection capabilities in a variety of industrial and commercial applications such as warehouse, route delivery, and inspection.

The Advantage XP1875, a touch-screen and push-button application device, has been designed to cradle with the Symbol SPT1800/2800 pen-notepad computer offering the most advanced Palm Powered™ or Pocket PC-based operating system scanner. The XP1875 allows the end-user to have one-dimensioned bar-code data capture, WLAN or WWAN communications, and 13.5-MHz RFID read/write capabilities.

Designed for durable use in almost any environment, the SPT1800/2800 series housing withstands drops to concrete and is sealed for protection against rain and dust. It provides multiple additional configurations exist for Palm, WIN CE, color screen, and WLAN options and has a communication interface of IrDA.

A portable Blue Tooth handheld read/write device (DP150BT) from Northern Apex integrates the TAGSYS Medio S002-AVSA RFID reader operating at 13.56 MHz. It requires no cable or serial port connection. It will function with iPAQ Blue Tooth-enabled PDA or any other Blue Tooth-enabled PDA/Computer.

Northern Apex provides a series of standard RFID communication devices specifically to meet customers' application requirements when integrating RFID solutions. Each RFID device was designed to offer the flexibility to meet a variety of application requirements. Whether the final RFID solution is industrial, portable, desktop, or a combination of environments, the Apex DP series is designed to provide off-the-shelf, easily implemented communication tools.

The DP120USB from Northern Apex integrates the TAGSYS Medio S002-AVSA RFID reader operating at 13.56 MHz. This device is powered by its USB port eliminating need for a separate power supply. It is used as either a handheld or workstation read/write device. It is typically used with portable data collection or PC, laptop, or notebook devices.

A.8.2.12 System Concepts (www.systemconcepts.com)

The Easy Tag™ RFID Adapter from Systems Concepts, Inc. is a custom-designed RFID adapter for Palm III™/VII™ capable of reading and writing to industry standard 125-KHz and 13.56-MHz RFID tags. The 13.56-MHz EasyTag RFID Adapter is integrating the TAGSYS universal Medio S002 RFID reader that supports the main chips of the market (TAGSYS C210, C240, and C220), TI Tag-It™, Philips I-Code™ and most of the ISO15693.

The RFID Adapter is an add-on to the Palm handheld units which quickly snaps together with the Palm device. The RFID scanner is totally self-contained and because of its own rechargeable batteries, does not derive power from the Palm. It has downloading capabilities using a RS232 connection interface for PC and laptop, facilitating quick transfer and update of the database.

A.8.2.13 Teraoka Seiko (teraoka.digi.co.jp)

The SLP-5000 is a tool for on-demand printing applications in a wide variety of markets such as library, apparel, logistics, electrical ticketing, airline luggage ticketing, and membership cards. The SLP-5000 prints paper labels that embed RFID tags from TAGSYS.

A.8.2.14 Toshiba (www.toshibatec-eu.com)

The Toshiba Tec B482-QP prints bar-code labels and encodes RFID tags. It includes faster processing and a larger standard memory capacity. Furthermore, using an optional PCMCIA Ethernet LAN card, it offers Internet Web Printer Control, e-mail, FTP, and XML functionality. Also available is a basic program feature allowing the B-482 to adapt and process data in new ways removing the need to reprogram existing systems.

The Toshiba Tec B482-QP integrates the TAGSYS Medio S002 reader operating at 13.56 MHz, and can therefore read and encode tags while printing labels.

A.8.2.15 Touchstar (www.touchpc.com)

Touchstar offers two types of RFID-enabled handheld terminals.

Packed with massive memory and processing speed, the TouchPC Eagle from Touchstar is efficient, resourceful, and extremely fast. Sealed against water and dust, the Eagle can handle all types of environments and offers a wide range of peripherals and integrated hardware options. The Eagle also has an array of communications solutions, including dial-up networking, LANs, cellular, satellite, and most wireless networks. This handheld device runs with the DRDOS 7 operating system with memory of 8 Mb and 1-Mb Flash and uses RS232, RS485, and IrDA communication interfaces, and PC card slots.

With a specific end cap integrating the TAGSYS Medio S002 reader operating at 13.56 MHz, the Eagle can address new 13.56-MHz RFID data collection opportunities in a powerful manner, thus improving productivity, reducing paperwork, and increasing profits. The Eagle is used in applications such as route accounting, fuel delivery systems, parcel tracking, and inventory management.

Packed with massive memory and processing speed, the TouchPC Voyager from Touchstar is extremely fast. It comes with 32-MB RAM memory (64-MB RAM memory optional) and 16-MB Flash memory. The Voyager Large has a one-half VGA LCD display, touch-screen, backlit and 64-key tactile keyboard (QWERTY type). It provides two or three working days autonomy without the need to be recharged (with a 7.4 V lithium ion rechargeable battery), and offers power management capabilities.

The device runs on the Intel Strong ARM SA1119 RISC processor, with Windows CE 3.0 and has RS232 port, IrDA, and Ethernet interfaces and type II PC card slots.

Sealed against water and dust, the Voyager can handle all types of environments and offers a wide range of peripherals and integrated hardware options. The Voyager also has an array of communications solutions, including dial-up networking, LANs, cellular, satellite, and most wireless networks.

With an RFID end cap integrating the TAGSYS Medio S002 operating at 13.56 MHz, the Voyager can address new RFID data collection opportunities in a powerful manner, thus improving productivity, reducing paperwork and increasing profits.

A.8.3 Products for the Library Market

Table A.14 shows what products TAGSYS offers to the library market. Most integrate with standard library equipment.

TAGSYS' Library Inventory Reader is a handheld device that can be connected to a pocket PC running under Windows 98, NT, 2000, and XP operating systems. This reader stores item data read from the tags and then transfers it to the library database via the Pocket PC cradle or through a wireless connection.

Also of particular interest are RFID stations in three areas: circulation, programming, and security. Each RFID product for the library market will be further explained on what it does. Several books in a stack on a reading station can be read and identified at once without having the librarian open each book.

TAGSYS Folio tags with a memory of 128 bits have been specifically designed to be affixed into library media, including books, CDs, DVDs, and tapes. The RFID chip of the Folio tag has three sections: a lockable section for the item identification, a rewritable section for library specific use, and a security function for the item antitheft (which can be activated or deactivated). The chip also has a "multiyear" function, allowing several tags can be read at once.

Table A.14   TAGSYS Library Market Products

RFID Tags	FOLIO™ for Libraries
RFID Readers	Library Inventory Reader
RFID Stations	Library Circulation Station
	Library Programming Station
	Library Security Gates

Folio tags are adhesive and can be affixed directly onto items. They also come in different forms: rectangular for books (Folio 20 tags) and round for CDs (Folio 20 CD tags). They can be converted either by TAGSYS (into white or preprinted paper labels featuring information such as library logo and bar-code number) or by libraries (by manually placing their own labels over the tags). These tags can be programmed either by the librarian or delivered already programmed by TAGSYS. Folio tags can be used for both the identification and the antitheft of an item. Libraries that have already equipped their collection with an antitheft device can use Folio tags at the same time for identification only.

Folio tags do not need to be visible to be read, so books and other media can be identified quickly and in any orientation without opening them. Several books can be checked out and checked in simultaneously. Used as an identification device only, the Folio tag is compatible with traditional library security systems, offering at the same time the benefits of RFID (i.e., convenience, multiple check-ins, shelf inventories). The TAGSYS Tagging Tool enables you to easily affix Folio CD tags onto CDs or DVDs.

RFID technology speeds and eases material handling, librarians' daily tasks, and also enables patrons to use convenient self-service stations. It reduces the repetitive tasks of librarians, allowing them to spend more time with patrons. In addition, it helps reduce waiting lines, therefore increasing customer satisfaction.

The TAGSYS Inventory Reader is unique in its shape and functionality and enables librarians to easily identify items on the shelves. This RFID Reader has been designed to perform fast and accurate inventory checks and also to search for specific items (re-shelving, weeding, on-hold management, etc.). Items do not have to be handled one by one nor removed from the shelves.

This handheld RFID reader consists of a long lightweight handle with a flexible end-part (the RFID antenna) that rotates to facilitate the identification of items on all shelves, especially hard-to-reach areas. The reader enables instant data capture when passed alongside the items in a continuous movement. Items are identified regardless of their thickness and proximity to the shelf's edge (any type of shelf, even metallic ones).

The TAGSYS Inventory Reader offers a working autonomy of more than seven hours. It is connected to a Pocket PC that stores and displays item data. This data is then transferred to the library database via the Pocket PC cradle or through a wireless connection. No modification to the library database is required.

The reader includes one cable for connection to iPAQ Pocket PC and one cable for connection to a PC with DB9 connector. Software suite includes demonstration software and TAGSYS E DLL's for Windows Pocket PC 2002 Operating System and TAGSYS002 Explorer for Windows 98, NT, 2000, and XP Operating System.

The TAGSYS Circulation Station is a staff station enabling librarians to check out and check in several items at the same time. In addition, it is possible, in one single operation, to identify the item while activating or deactivating the antitheft function.

The TAGSYS Library Circulation Station can be placed under or above the library circulation desk. It is made of a TAGSYS Library Reader L-L100 and a TAGSYS Aero LI antenna (an additional antenna can be added to increase the number of items processed). It can process 1 to 16 items simultaneously, and can also read TAGSYS RFID patron cards.

The Circulation Station can co-exist with any conventional security systems. This is a key feature when a Folio RFID tag is added to an item that is already equipped with an antitheft device. The Circulation Station provides an easy interface with any existing Integrated Library Systems (ILS). It can be integrated into self-check-out equipment.

Reading and writing distances are 7.5 and 5.9 inches, respectively. Aero LI Antenna and Library Reader L-L100 weigh 4.4 and 11 pounds, respectively. The station has one RF with multiplex capability and rotates at 0°/90°/180°. Communications interfaces include RS232, RS485, and RS422 and bidirectional and enhanced parallel cables. Communication speeds are a maximum of 38.4 Kbps for serial and 200 Kbps for parallel interfaces.

The station comes with four independently configurable four I/O ports and updatable firmware, and 512-Kbytes Flash memory. Software suite includes TAGSYS Library DLLs and L200 Explorer.

The TAGSYS Programming Station is designed to allow an efficient conversion of a collection from existing bar codes to TAGSYS Folio RFID tags. It enables to program the bar-code data into the memory of the Folio tag and to activate its antitheft function at the same time. It is also used to program new items.

Read/write antitheft programming is done in one single operation. The Programming Station offers a simple connection to any computer and can be used in parallel with any bar-code scanner. It can co-exist with conventional antitheft equipment.

Converting an entire collection to RFID is fast and easy: bar codes are scanned, RFID tags are programmed, and their security function is activated all at the same time. The Programming Station interfaces easily with installed Information Library System (ILS).

Reading and writing distances are five inches and four inches, respectively. Software suite includes TAGSYS Library DLLs and S002 Explorer Communication protocol is STX-E, specific DLL for library application.

Invented in the late 1990s, the TAGSYS security system benefits from the latest design innovations to merge RFID and antitheft functions into a single device. Therefore, it performs the simultaneous reading/writing into the chip and activation/deactivation of the antitheft function. TAGSYS Security Gates run the most modern detection algorithm that constantly detects nondeactivated items. A visual and audible signal is triggered instantaneously when security is violated.

Being a stand-alone solution, TAGSYS Security Gates do not need to be linked to the library database, and can still operate when the ILS network is down or under maintenance. The security gate does not require additional equipment to operate. It only requires a single RFID tag and a single piece of hardware equipment. The outer shell of TAGSYS Security Gates can be changed to match the library furniture and style.

Open I/O ports include one TTL level for standard electronic counter, Webcam trigger, and two open drain outputs that can be used for any additional security system: CCTV, or locking gates. A TAGSYS Security Gate is composed of two pedestals. Additional pedestals can be added for increased detection surface. Each pedestal is stand-alone and plug-and-play to the main power.

A.8.4 TAGSYS Partner Products for the Library Market

Table A.15 gives the list of TAGSYS' partner products.

We start with Blockroc Technology. It carries one product that can integrate with TAGSYS reader and possibly others. The handheld terminal reads both RFID tags and bar codes, making it easier for a library to make a transition to RFID technology. It works with a wide range of legacy bar code applications.

Like Blockroc Technology, Minec offers a handheld terminal with a dual capability of reading bar codes and RFID tags. It runs with the M/2 DOS operating system, allowing development and downloading of programs,

Table A.15 TAGSYS Partner Products for Library Market

Product Type	Product Name	Company
RFID-enabled handheld terminals	Gemini HF210	Blackroc Technology
	Memor2000	Minec
RFID-enabled stations	RFID Self Check-out	Vernon Library Supplies
	RFID Self Check-out	Gemsys
	RFID Self Check-out	VTLS Inc
	RFID Self Check-Out Station/Combo Station	Tech Logic
RFID-enabled printers	SLP-5000	Teraoka Seiko
	B482-QP	Toshiba

and provides wireless communication with peripherals (PCs, modems, and printers).

Self-check-out systems from Vernon Library Supplies, Gemsys, VTLS Inc., and Tech Logic work with a desktop or pocket PC or via a LAN-Ethernet connection. Most are SIP/SIP2 compliant needed to interface with various library functions, including returns.

RFID-enabled printers from Teraoka Seiko and Toshiba specifically target a variety of markets, not only library and logistics, but also airline luggage ticketing. They either encode RFID tags or print paper labels to embed these tags. The latter offers Internet Web Printer Control, e-mail, FTP, and XML functionality.

A.8.4.1 Blackroc Technology (www.blackroc.com)

The Gemini HF210 from Blackroc is a handheld terminal that offers dual RFID/bar-code scanning technology. Lightweight and small, it is the ideal companion for users that need instantaneous scanning of bar-code labels and RFID tags. Scanning/reading can be done via the push button or in continuous mode.

In addition, writing new data into tags is also feasible with the TAGSYS Medio S001/S002 RFID reader it integrates and via a serial connection to a host. This Blackroc device reads most popular bar-code symbologies plus Codabar, Telepen, and Plessey. It works with a wide range of legacy bar-code applications including libraries that will eventually change over to RFID technology.

A.8.4.2 Minec (www.minec.com)

The Memor2000 from MINEC, a bar-code/RFID reader, is a handheld data collection terminal that can be held and operated by one and the same hand without requiring use of a shift key (patent pending). Water-resistant with its 27 coated rubber keys, the Memor2000 is small, light, and offers a full graphic capability, LCD display, making this terminal tough enough to withstand harsh environment applications. Athelia Solutions developed and produces the RFID end cap module of the Memor2000, using the TAGSYS Medio S002 reader operating at 13.56 MHz.

This handheld device is used in applications such as warehouse tracking of containers and pallets, production control, inventory control, field service, and automatic identification. It runs with the M/2 DOS operating system, allowing development and downloading of programs, and provides wireless communication with peripherals (PCs, modems, and printers).

A.8.4.3 Vernon Library Supplies (www.vernlib.com)

This self-check-out station has a touch-screen monitor with high-speed bar-code and RFID scanning with multiple language features and capability to customize screen and sound features. It has a host system interface with any SIP II or Ethernet-LAN connections. This station can be connected to a Pentium III or greater PC running at least 800 MHz under the XP Professional Environment and offers multiple base and platform options.

A.8.4.4 Gemsys (www.gemsys.no)

This self-check-out station operates with the SIPII (Z39.70) Protocol common in library systems and is ready for bar codes, RFID, or hybrid solution with both. As standard, it uses patron cards with bar codes, but can be retrofitted with magnetic stripe or smart cards. The station is configurable in different languages. It is possible to use as a self-return station.

The station has a Pentium panel PC with capacitive rugged touch-screen (running Windows 2000) and is connected to a receipt printer with presenter. It integrates TAGSYS RFID reader and antenna, and Datalogic bar-code reader for patron cards. As an option, the station integrates Datalogic bar-code raster scanner for books.

A.8.4.5 VTLS Inc. (www.vtls.com)

The system consists of internally enclosed PC with Windows 2000, CD and floppy drives, hard drive with a 12-inch touch-screen monitor, bar-code reader, magnetic swipe reader, and RFID reader. It comes with a receipt printer, keyboard (connected via Infrared link and only used for system configuration), and 10/100 LAN interface, and provides SIP/SIP2 compliant interface for check-out of material. The bar-code reader supports entry of patron bar code plus items without RFID tags.

The check-out station requires a host ILS (Integrated Library System) which supports the SIP/SIP2 protocol for circulation transactions via Telnet. The host address, username, password, and log-in procedure are required to allow patrons to borrow books without assistance from the library staff. RFID allows multiple check-outs.

A.8.4.6 Tech Logic (www.tech-logic.com)

Tech Logic Corporation's self-check-out systems are designed to use RFID and to interface completely with all other library functions including return, inventory, and security. Self-check-out systems work simultaneously with both RFID and bar codes. Tech Logic offers Self-Check-Out and Self and Assist Check-Out. Both systems use the same software and interface on the patron interface and both allow the patron to self-serve all library material that is available for loan. This includes books, periodicals, audiocassettes, Compact Disks (CDs), Digital Versatile Disc (DVDs), and basically any material that can have an RFID tag attached. The systems have a 10/100 LAN interface and is SIP/SIP2 compliant.

A.8.4.7 Teraoka Seiko (teraoka.digi.co.jp)

The SLP-5000 is a tool for on-demand printing applications in a wide variety of markets such as library, apparel, logistics, electrical ticketing, airline luggage ticketing, and membership cards. The SLP-5000 prints paper labels that embed RFID tags from TAGSYS. It provides automatic detection of tag positioning. The printer comes with two PC slots for external font and a LCD for display of various menus.

A.8.4.8 Toshiba (www.toshibatec-eu.com)

The Toshiba Tec B482-QP prints bar-code labels and encodes RFID tags. It includes faster processing and a larger standard memory capacity. Furthermore, using an optional PCMCIA Ethernet LAN card, it offers Internet Web Printer Control, e-mail, FTP, and XML functionality. Also available is a basic program feature allowing the B-482 to adapt and process data in new ways removing the need to reprogram existing systems.

The Toshiba Tec B482-QP integrates the TAGSYS Medio S002 reader operating at 13.56 MHz, and can therefore read and encode tags while printing labels. It is also ideal for harsh and dirty industrial environments. Its enables reading and writing of tags while printing labels. The printer has a RS232 interface with a print speed of up to eight inches per second.

A.8.5 Textile Rental Industry

Table A.16 shows what products TAGSYS offers to the textile rental industry. Most integrate with standard textile rental equipment.

Table A.16 TAGSYS for Textile Rental Industry Products

RFID tags	Laundry RFID tags
RFID readers	Laundry reader
	Laundry handheld reader
RFID antennas	Laundry RFID antennas
RFID stations	Laundry conveyor station
	Laundry station: for check-in and check-out
	Laundry programming station
	RFID-enabled garment chute
	Fast tagging machine

Both fixed and handheld portable readers fit most sorting conveyor systems. They can be integrated into textile handling equipment such as belt conveyors, folding machines, garment dispensers, and so on.

Operating at 13.56 MHz, the radio frequency identification standard for item tracking, TAGSYS RFID Laundry ID tag can be applied directly by the textile manufacturer or in the laundry plant itself using an automatic tag attachment system.

The tag does not require line of sight to be read. Operating at 13.56 MHz, it provides fast reading speed (one read in five milliseconds). Chip unique identification number is laser-printed on the RFID tag itself. The tag is available in single-read and multi-read (up to 20 tags per second), depending on the requirements of the application.

It is designed to withstand the harsh industrial laundry process (water, extreme temperature, chemicals, water extraction pressure). The tag can easily and unobtrusively be affixed onto any piece of laundry (uniforms, mats, and most flat linen): either sewn or thermo-patched. It can be reused on different garments, although removal and attachment are easier when tag is sewn.

Reading is twice as fast as bar codes, although reading speed is 26 Kbps (one read in five milliseconds that are 20 times faster than low frequency). The tag allows the identification of single linen at a time, soil reading in bulk, and clean reading of stacks or bundles. TAGSYS chips can be read by several RFID readers (fixed or portable) on the market.

Memory size is 64 bits in hexadecimal, a format that can be converted in ASCII by the reader software. Reading distance is 9 inches (230 mm) for TR-L100 reader with a typical 300×300 antenna. The tag's size is very small with the dimension of 0.9 inch (22-mm diameter) by 0.11 inch (2.8 mm) and at the same time is lightweight (0.1 ounce or 2.54 grams).

TAGSYS' TR-L100 Laundry Reader allows several RFID chips to be read simultaneously and can operate with most 13.56-MHz-based RFID chips available in the market. The TR-L100 reader fits most sorting conveyor systems and can be integrated into textile handling equipment such as belt conveyors, folding machines, garment dispensers, and so on.

For manual RFID stations, the reader can be applied to tabletop soil check-in, stack station: for multiple assignment, clean check-out (surgeon pack), and clean bag reading (Tuxedo). For automated RFID stations, the reader can be applied to soil bag reading, return chute, clean stack reading on belt conveyor, and clean sorting on conveyor and garment dispenser. For semi-automated RFID stations, the reader can be applied to vacuum soil check-in and computer-assisted clean sorting.

The reader has multi-chip protocol capability, operates with all TAGSYS RFID chips and can be configured to read upcoming ISO 18000 chips (the international standard for asset tracking, defined to allow interoperability between any RFID chip and any RFID reader at a given frequency). It can handle two RFID antennas (any 50-ohm antenna) for two-user station (four antennas possible with TR-L200 version). Phase control by antenna allows several chips to be read simultaneously regardless of the chip orientation. Digital Processing Unit (DPU) is fast and development software suite is available.

The power for each antenna channel is very low, up to four watts and can be adjusted with software. Reading distance varies according to the type of RFID chip and antenna; for instance, is 9 in. with single-read chips and a 12 × 12 in. antenna. Firmware is updatable with battery-backed RAM.

The reader's parallel interface is bidirectional. It comes with two communication interfaces: serial link (RS232, RS422, or RS485) and parallel link for direct connection to a PC. Software can be used to set address for RS485. Communication protocol for the serial link is Universal TAGSYS STX-E (up to 38.4 Kbps) including stand-alone operating mode. The protocol of the parallel link is TAGSYS specified protocol (up to 200 Kbps).

The reader includes a 512-KB Flash memory for on-board application software. Software included are STX-E protocol including stand-alone operating mode (wedge) and DLL working under Windows NT, 2000, XP, 98, and 95. It comes with four software configurable industrial input/output ports, each of which can be set individually either as input or as output or be used for trigger with the STXE standalone mode. The reader's power consumes up to 40 watts. It comes with the size of 11.8 × 9.8 × 1.7 in. and weight of 11 pounds. The following are available as options.

- L200 Development Kit to develop on-board application software, comes with or without compiler
- TAGSYS Synch Box to operate up to four TR-L100 readers less than three meters apart
- TAGSYS Signal Box with LEDs and sound to confirm power-up and read success
- TAGSYS Interconnect Box to connect two different readers (including bar-code scanners and low-frequency RFID readers) and four PCs via RS232
- TR-L200 reader: version with four antenna channels and up to eight watts per channel
- Those available for specific applications requiring more power and larger RF field

Operating at 13.56 MHz, this RFID handheld laundry reader can be used for final check-outs, providing as another way of checking the completion of deliveries before shipment from the plant or just before delivery to the customer site. In addition, it can also be used for complementary reading during the textile handling process. Two versions are available: network

(TR-HR1) and stand-alone (TR-HR2). The handheld reader can be used to read folded laundry, on hangers, and the inventories (in stand-alone mode at customer site).

The reader comes with a lightweight wand with the RFID antenna at the end-part and multi-read capability. The network version (TR-HR1) connects to a desktop PC with onboard reader that stores and displays item data. The stand-alone version (TR-HR2) connects to any Pocket PC with onboard reader and offers a long working autonomy of more than seven hours and rechargeable time of two or three hours.

The handheld reader allows rapid identification of single or multiple garments on hangers and enables multiple reading and reading folded laundry with no individual handling (placing the end-part of the reader on top of, or inside the stack). It also enables rapid identification of bundles before loading in the truck and is suited for final check-outs by the driver before delivery at customer site. All information needed for the inventory management can be downloaded to the unlimited memory of the Pocket PC. No modification to the laundry database is required.

The handheld reader is compatible with TAGSYS Ario single-read and multi-read Laundry chips and any ISO 18000 chips. It includes three cables: one output cable with RS232 connection, one cable for connection to iPAQ Pocket PC, and one RS232 serial cable for connection to PC. Pocket PC Memory with standard 64-MB Flash can be extended via SD card.

TAGSYS Laundry RFID antennas come in various shapes and sizes according to the application and the read rate required. They include a coaxial cable with BNC male/female adapter. They are packaged in a rugged casing that withstands the harsh industrial laundry environment. They can be used in a desktop configuration or be integrated in major textile handling equipment ensuring optimal identification rate.

The TAGSYS Laundry Conveyor Station is an RFID reading system made up of an industrial packaged RFID antenna set connected to an RFID reader. It has been designed to be integrated with all kinds of conveyor systems for automatic sorting. It allows the identification of all types of garments (from pants to shirts) and complies with CE and FCC regulations. The RFID chip affixed to each garment is identified "on-the-fly" when passing by the antenna and its data is sent to a PLC or a PC. Successful read of the chip can be confirmed using TAGSYS Signal Box (including lights and sounds).

The RFID Reader TR L100 can be either mounted onto the conveyor or inserted directly into the PLC. This RFID station can be implemented at each stage of the sorting process (at the loading, inspection station, at the hanger/carrier marrying). TAGSYS Conveyor Station that comes with double antenna mounting has a reading speed of up to 12,000 garments per hour. It can co-exist with alternative identification technologies (low-frequency, bar-code systems) using TAGSYS Interconnect Box to connect two different readers and four PCs via RS232 allowing interoperability between TAGSYS system and alternative identification systems It easily adapts to existing installed information database.

The conveyor station works with TAGSYS Ario single-read and multi-read. Laundry chips have power consumption of up to 50 watts. Its firmware is upgradeable to read any ISO 18000 chips. The station is provided with three communication interfaces: RS232, RS422, and RS485. Available as an option is TAGSYS Signal Box (with lamps and sound to confirm power up and read success).

TAGSYS laundry station has two-antenna capability: one for check-in and the other for check-out. This laundry station enables two workers to use the station at the same time. Some application examples are the single-read of manual soil check-in and clean check-out, and the multi-read of manual check-out of Surgeon/Clean room pack. It requires no line of sight and can co-exist with existing identification technologies (low-frequency RFID readers and bar-code scanners) using TAGSYS Interconnect Box. The station reads TAGSYS and any ISO 15693 chips with an optional upgrade to ISO 18000 chips.

It comes with three communication interfaces: RS232, RS422, and RS485. Included in the package are one RFID reader (TR-L100) with on-board software; one RFID antenna (antenna type varies according to the application), and TAGSYS STXE software along with Modbus protocols. Available as an option are TAGSYS Interconnect Box with two reader inputs (including bar-code scanners and low-frequency RFID readers) and four PC outputs.

The TAGSYS Laundry Programming Station is an ergonomic tabletop reader designed for proximity identification (one item at a time), particularly garment assignment and inventory conversion to RFID. This RFID station performs instantaneous association of the RFID chip with the garment data in the Laundry database. It also enables the easy association of different identification devices (chip and bar code), making inventory conversion to RFID a smooth operation.

This programming station can operate in parallel with any bar-code scanner and co-exist with low-frequency systems (using TAGSYS Interconnect Box). It can read/write any standard RFID chip at 13.56 MHz. It is compatible with TAGSYS Ario single-read and multi-read Laundry chips with upgradeable firmware to read any ISO 18000 chips.

Reading distance is two inches. The station comes with RS232 as the only communication interface and weighs 1.76 pounds. Its communication protocol is Universal TAGSYS STX-E (4.8 up to 38.4 Kbps) including the stand-alone mode. Available as an option is the TAGSYS Interconnect Box to connect up to two different readers and four PCs via RS232.

When deposited in the TAGSYS RFID-enabled Garment Chute (as a stand-alone system), soiled garments are automatically identified and recorded when deposited in the Garment Chute. Each chute comes with a TAGSYS TR-L100 reader and a set of RFID antennas.

When the RFID tag of the soiled garment is read by the antenna of the chute located in the back office, the garment management database is instantly updated. Resupply requests for that item are sent and the departure to the laundry recorded. The RFID technology allows that several items can be placed in the chute at the same time.

The RFID-enabled Garment Chute can also be combined with automatic RFID garment dispensers to create a complete RFID garment management tracking system that provides a garment distribution center with a final check-out station located on site. Applications include casinos for soil collection, hospitals, medical houses, at a rental customer's site, and any other places that require quality certification and regulation compliance on garment collection.

TAGSYS Fast Tagging Machine allows RFID tags to be attached to any type of textile and at a limited cost, either at the textile manufacturing site or in the laundry facility. With TAGSYS' high-speed Fast Tagging Machine (TR-Tagger8), you can install RFID tags (TAGSYS Ario TL tags) on your existing inventory. Sewn tags are easier to remove and reuse than heat-sealed tags.

This machine is a fully automated device that cuts and places a piece of fabric, dispenses the RFID tag on it, and sews both onto the garment or linen. It is available for purchase or for rent and operates up to eight RFID tags per minute. The tagging machine weights 300 pounds and has a dimension of 48 × 48 inches with a power supply of 110/220 V and 50/60 Hz, ten spare needles, a roll of standard fabric, and a list of other compliant fabric.

The above lists of TAGSYS products for the textile rental industry are complete.

A.8.5 TAGSYS Partner Products for Textile Rental Industry

We now proceed to the list of TAGSYS' partner products as shown in Table A.17.

On RFID laundry stations, we start with Laundry Computer Technics, proceed to Jensen, followed by Positek RFID and Metalprogett. Jensen also offers software and Positek RFID provides a fast tagging machine.

All laundry stations have a touch-screen connected in some way to a PC, sometimes functioning almost like a vending machine. Jensen offers software to track the garment with the laundry process and to register new inventory. Unlike Jensen that requires the software be located in two different places, Positek RFID's Computer Assisted Clean Sorting runs software on SQL Server under Windows 2000 using standard network connections.

Table A.17 TAGSYS Partner Products for Textile Rental Industry

Product Type	Product Name	Company
RFID-enabled stations	Automatic Clean Garment Dispenser and Soil Collector	Laundry Computer Technics
	Automatic Clean Sorting	Jensen
	Computer Assisted Clean Sorting	Positek RFID
	Automatic Clean Sorting	Metalprogetti
	Garment Dispenser and Collector	Metalprogetti
Software	Prisma	Jensen
Other partner products	Positek fast tag machine	Positek RFID

A.8.5.1 Laundry Computer Technics (www.LCT.nl)

The CHIPTEX-Liner enables a fully automated 24-hour, seven-day garment distribution (route tracking) at the customer site as well as a stand-alone soil collection. This system integrates TAGSYS RFID products operating at the 13.56-MHz high frequency. This is how it works:

- The user identifies himself or herself with a personalized ID card.
- The system shows the available garments for this individual wearer on the touch-screen.
- The user then selects the garments he or she would like to receive.
- If the user has enough credits available, the system picks the right garment out of its storage conveyor. If there are not enough credits, the user must return soiled garments in the soiled garment collector. Only users with enough credits can order clean garments.

The system can use "first in, first out" policy or the quickest distribution policy. The system has an extremely high distribution speed because the conveyors of the CHIPTEX-Liner can turn both ways.

The loading of the system can be done manually or automatically. In both cases, TAGSYS RFID chips (previously applied to garments) are identified and the system connects each ID code to a position in the system. This ensures secure garment personalization. The system's software automatically updates inventory, and comes with complete management software, which enables control of the logistics of the garments. Garments are distributed in less than a minute.

This system makes it easier to determine who is responsible in case of lost garments, reduce inventories, and provide equal supply of soiled garments from the customer (i.e., scheduling of production). It allows end users to comply with healthcare regulations and better manage linen logistics.

A.8.5.2 Jensen (www.jensen-group.com)

Jensen offers RFID-enabled stations and software.

Jensen has integrated the TAGSYS RFID Conveyor Station into their METRICON conveyor systems allowing improved performance within garment finishing (up to 12,000–15,000 pieces per day). Identification can be performed at different steps of the garment-handling process for optimal sorting and garment traceability. These systems adapt to different conveyor speeds and provide automatic sorting at the hanger or carrier to ensure high-end automation and productivity. Garments are instantaneously identified when passing by the antenna at a near 100 percent read rate, which is absolutely essential for efficient automatic sorting.

Prisma software allows user-friendly and efficient garment tracking within the whole laundry process. All chip numbers together with the data of the pieces they identify are registered in a database. As soon as an RFID chip is read, its number is sent to the Laundry software by the reader. With the unique RFID chip number, the corresponding information can be found in the database and data can be displayed on the computer screen or sent to controls of machinery or sorting systems.

The functions of the laundry software depend on the requirements. A garment database is typically used in at least two locations:

In the soil department where each incoming piece of laundry is registered as returned by the customer.

The shipping department will read each piece again prior to delivery.

This allows accurate tracking of the inventory circulating between customer and laundry. Additional reading points may take place in the stockroom to register new inventory or in the repair area to register changes and repairs.

A.8.5.3 Positek RFID (www.positekrfid.com)

Positek RFID offers two products for the textile industry.

Computer Assisted Clean Sorting station aims at reducing the time required to sort finished garments at a rate in excess of 720 garments per hour, which is twice as fast as standard manual sorting. The route accounting system feeds the garment counts to the CA Sort, usually after the batch invoice run. CA Sort now knows the day, route, and person data and can develop electronic lots based on the size of the final assembly bays.

This is how the system works:

- The user presents the garment to the antenna.
- The antenna automatically identifies it.
- The operator is prompted with a voice command via a wireless headset to put the garment on a specific slot (without looking at the garment ID).
- A red light appears above the appropriate slot and when all items for a person or customer are present, a green light illuminates to indicate that the order is complete.

Ergonomic design of the final bays (semi-circle or V structure) is used to minimize employee movement and keep the sorting area within reaching distance. This eliminates the movement required when reading numbers or scanning bar codes.

This system can be adapted to second sort based on a spider conveyor with light panels placed above slick rails. At final sort, this stand-alone sorting system can be used to assemble either hanging or folded garments.

The RFID chip is compatible with TAGSYS Ario Laundry chips and any ISO15693 chips. The RFID reading station component comes with a TAGSYS L100 RFID Reader and a TAGSYS industrial RFID Antenna.

Software runs on SQL Server under Windows 2000 using standard network connection (including a modem) with a capability for multi-lingual audio. Capability for a battery-powered tape drive and tapes are included for back-up.

Fast tagging machine is manufactured exclusively for POSITEK for use in the dry cleaning market. Each unit's trays are designed to feed POSITEK's patented reusable tags. The machine, entirely air-operated, removes the tag from the magazine and places it on the needle dramatically reducing tagging time. Each tag is affixed per 1.5 seconds.

A.8.5.4 Metalprogetti (metalpro@tin.il)

Automatic Clean Sorting (MetalProgetti RFID-enabled sorting systems) MetalProgetti has integrated the TAGSYS RFID Conveyor Station into its sorting conveyor systems to automate clean garment sorting on conveyor at a high speed. It reads ISO standard RFID chips and allows identification at different steps of the garment handling process for optimal sorting and garment traceability. Garments are instantaneously identified when passing by the antenna. With a set of antennas covering a wide reading area, all kinds of garments can be read.

Garment Dispenser and Collector (MetalProgetti Battista 2000) automates garment distribution to the wearer and at customer site, integrating TAGSYS RFID products operating at the 13.56-MHz frequency. This is how it works:

- Wearer identifies himself with a patron card/smart card and is given automatically and rapidly the uniform (either personalized or size allocated).
- The soiled garment is returned through a deposit trap door where it is identified. Its departure to the laundry is recorded.
- When clean garments are delivered, they are identified while loading onto the conveyor and get automatically into the right delivery position.
- The database is instantaneously updated each time the garment is read.
- RFID stations send data automatically either through PLC or PC (master mode).

TAGSYS RFID stations are located at the Clean Loading point and at the Soil Deposit unit. A portable reader is also available to allow the operator to process garments off-line. This allows end users to comply with health-care regulations, secure garment personalization, and trace garments at each stage of the handling process.

A.9 TEXAS INSTRUMENTS-RFID (WWW.TI-RFID.COM)

Texas Instruments (TI-RFID) offers RFID products operating at 134.2 kHz and standard 13.56 MHz. The higher-frequency tag products have a primary advantage over the lower-frequency counterparts in that the former antenna makes fewer turns than the latter. The higher frequency allows the transponders to penetrate nonmetallic materials and embed the transponders within an object (e.g., case or container). This means radio waves bounce off metal and are absorbed by water. For this reason, RFID tags may not be embedded within metal objects with high water content. One way of getting around this problem is to use lower-frequency tags that have better penetration capabilities.

In this section, we start with high-frequency products and then proceed to low-frequency products.

A.9.1 13.56-MHz Products

Let's take a look at some Texas Instruments' products with a short description for each.

- RI-K10-001A-00 (HF-I Midrange Eval Kit)
- RI-ANT-T01A-00 (Gate Antenna for High Frequency Readers)
- RI-STU-TRDC-02 (S6350 Midrange Reader Module)
- RI-STU-655A-00 [S6550 Long Range Reader (Housed including Power Supply)]

The HF-I Midrange Evaluation Kit (RI-K10-001A-00) is compatible with the worldwide ISO 15693 standard for 13.56-MHz vicinity cards and smart label inlays. The HF-I Midrange Evaluation Kit includes the S6350 Midrange Reader, a getting-started guide, and demo software CD, assorted Tag-it HF and HF-ISO transponders, a serial data cable, and a power supply. The HF-I Midrange Evaluation Kit is ideally suited for applications such as access control, baggage identification, document and item tracking, parcel identification, library tracking, product authentication, and ticketing, or other applications that require low-cost, flexible labels or cards with a typical read range of up to seven inches.

The Gate Antenna RI-ANT-T01A is a 13.56-MHz antenna optimized for the High Frequency Long Range Readers S6500/S6550 Readers. The antenna is a 300 mm × 300 mm single-loop antenna that can be used with other readers having a transmitter frequency of 13.56 MHz and an output impedance of 50 ohms.

The S6350 Midrange reader module (RLSTU-TRDC-02) is a low-profile, low-power device that is designed to be easily integrated or embedded into almost any system. Operating at a frequency of 13.56 MHz and compatible with ISO/IEC 15693 inlays and tags, the S6350 Reader allows for the interoperability of inlays and tags from multiple manufacturers.

The S6500 Long Range Reader Module (RI-STU-650A-00) handles all RF and digital functions required in order to communicate with Tag-it HF, Tag-it HF-I (ISO 15693 compliant), and all other ISO 15693-compliant transponders from various suppliers. The module has two digital inputs, two digital outputs, a relay output, and an asynchronous interface that can be configured as RS232 or RS485. The configurability of the interfaces also allows the module to be operated on an RS485 data bus. The address can be assigned either through software or hardware (3 DIP switches).

The S6550 Long Range Reader (RLSTU-655A-00), housed including power supply, handles all RF and digital functions required in order to communicate with Tag-it HF, Tag-it HF-I (ISO 15693 compliant), and all other ISO 15693-compliant transponders from various suppliers. The Reader Module is encased in a powder-coated sheet steel box (IP54 protection level). This means that the housed reader can be mounted either inside or outside. The reader has two digital inputs, two digital outputs, a relay output, and an asynchronous interface that can be configured as RS232 or RS485. The configurability of the interfaces also allows the reader to be operated on an RS485 data bus. The address can be assigned either through software or hardware (3 DIP switches).

A.9.2 Low-Frequency Products

Now, let's take a look at some low-frequency TI products:

- RI-K3A-001A (LF Micro Eval Kit)
- RI-ANT-G04E (Series 2000 Gate Antenna Large)
- RI-STU-251B (Series 2000 Reader S251B)
- RI-STU-251B (Series 2000 Reader S251B)

Low Frequency Micro Evaluation Kit (RI-K3A-001A) is a development tool for customers requiring small size and low power in their RFID applications. Contents of the kit are based on 134.2 kHz RFID technology and include the S2000 Micro Reader, demo software CD, LF transponders in various form factors, serial data cable, and international power supply.

The Large Series 2000 Gate Antenna (RI-ANT-G04E) is a fully packaged antenna for applications such as vehicle access to parking lots in an outdoor environment. It can be mounted on a pole or a wall. The antenna is optimized for cable lengths between 0.5 and 4 meters.

The Series 2000 Micro-Reader (RI-STU-MRD1) is an intelligent module that provides the RF and control functions to communicate with TI-RFID transponders. It is equipped with a serial communications interface that may be directly connected to commonly used system controllers. The use of low-Q antennas eliminates the need to tune the system to resonance.

The Series 2000 Reader S251B (RI-STU-251B) provides all the RF and control functions to communicate with TI*RFID LF transponders. It includes a Dynamic Auto Tuning (DAT) function that automatically tunes a standard antenna to resonance and keeps it tuned during operation. The reader performs all the tasks necessary according to the commands from the host to send signals to and receive data from a TI RFID transponder. It decodes the received RF signals into the transponder's identification number, checks the validity, and handles the conversion to a standard serial interface protocol.

A.9.3 Software

Here are some software utilities that can be used to configure, set up, tune, and diagnose specified readers, to download new firmware to readers, and to demonstrate all the ISO 15693 commands.

The S6 Reader Utility V1.32 is a Windows-based software program that interfaces to the S61xx Reader and S65xx Reader (FW 3.10). It provides a means to demonstrate the functional capabilities of these readers as the execution of commands such as reading and writing information to and from Tag-it transponders and can be employed to assist in reader configuration or diagnosis. System requirements are 2.7-MB available hard drive space, and Windows 95, 98, 2000, or NT operating system.

The S6 Util software program can be used for both Tag-It and ISO15693 protocols. It was designed to be used with the S6500 (which supports

Tag-It and ISO15693 Protocol) and the S6000 reader-only supports the Tag-It protocol. The software works with WIN 95/98/2000/NT.

The S6350 Utility is a Windows-based application that interfaces with the S6350 reader and provides a means to demonstrate the functional capabilities of the HF-I Midrange Evaluation Kit. It allows the execution of commands such as reading and writing information to and from both Tag-it HF and Tag-it HF-I (ISO compatible) transponders. S6350 Reader Utility is a tool that can be employed to assist in reader setup, tuning, or diagnosis, and can additionally log transponder responses for initial experimentation and testing. System requirements are 1.5-MB available hard drive space, and Windows 95, 98, 2000, or NT operating system.

The S6500/S6550 Program Library Package consists of the program libraries FEISC and FECOM which assist in programming application software and integrating the S6500/S6550 reader into a system and run all the protocols described in the "S6500/S6550 Configuration and Host Protocol" Reference Guide by directly invoking a function.

SIEMENS On-Chip Memory Programming Tool, Version 2.1.2 is a Flash loader program required to download new firmware to the S6500/S6550 Reader. Download instructions are given in Reference Guide "S6500 Reader Module Firmware Upgrade."

S2_UTIL Version 1.2 is a new Windows-based software utility program for the configuration and demonstration of our Series 2000 readers. This program can be used with the following readers (control modules):

RI-STU-MB2A-xx, RI-STU-MB6A-xx (Software version 1.32, 1.4, 1.5)
RI-CTL-MB2A-xx, RI-CTL-MB6A-xx (Software version 1.32, 1.4, 1.5)
RI-STU-251A-xx, RI-STU-251B-00 (Software version 1.1, 1.2)
RI-STU-MRD1

The S6400 Firmware Downloader V2.03 provides a way to update the firmware of the S6410 Vicinity Wallplate and S6420 Vicinity Mullion reader. The file contains a download program and the latest firmware file for the reader which is currently V2.03. The S6400 reference manual provides the instructions for the download.

The S6400 Utility Software is a Windows-based application that interfaces with the S6400 series readers and provides a means to demonstrate all the ISO 15693 commands, for instance, reading and writing information to Vicinity badges and Tag-it HF-I (ISO compatible) transponders. The S6400 Utility software is also designed to download customer-specific DES 64-bit encryption keys to the S6400 series readers for access control applications.

Appendix B

ACTIVE RFID TECHNOLOGY

We briefly cover active RFID products from Alien Technology, Axcess, Escort Memory Systems, Microtec, Samsys, Savi Technology, and WhereNet.

B.1 ALIEN TECHNOLOGY (WWW.ALIENTECHNOLOGY.COM)

Alien Technology produces Ultra-High Frequency (UHF) tags as well as 2450-MHz (microwave) frequency tags for cases and pallets. Alien's EPC class 1 UHF RFID tags can be applied to metal and liquid environments. When used with circularly polarized antennas, all of Alien's RFID tags are orientation insensitive.

Alien Technology offers these active RFID products:

- Reader ALR 9780
- Reader ALR 9640
- Reader ALR 9930-A
- Reader ALR 2759

Reader ALR 9780 is a high-performance, four-port fixed reader with a frequency of 902–928-MHz ISM band. This FCC-certified reader can be easily mounted where tagged objects are inbound or outbound in a logistics supply chain. It has the ability to read a population of tags at high rates in real-world situations. Software-controlled power output provides for performance optimization in a variety of circumstances. An advanced low-noise RF design provides maximum sensitivity to tag signals rendered faint by distance, moisture, or metal. The use of circularly polarized antennas allows tags to be read whether they are vertically or horizontally oriented.

Configuration is accomplished either locally via serial port or remotely via the Local Area Network (LAN) using a human-readable interface.

Software integration is implemented through the use of XML-formatted control data and binary and C-language APIs.

The ability to trigger reads by external event, command, or schedule allows the reader to mold to the business process. The reader can be configured to notify operators of tag events by LAN, input/output (I/O) signal, or even e-mail. With field-upgradeable firmware and a high-performance digital signal processor, the ALR-9780 is designed for maximum upgradeability to future EPC specifications.

Reader ALR 9640 is a fixed reader with integrated antenna with a frequency of 902–928-MHz ISM band for use with UHF Class 1 tags. Some application examples include industrial warehouse and logistic facilities. The reader electronics and antenna reside in a single package, eliminating external antenna cables. Equipped with an Ethernet interface, the ALR-9640 integrates with a network. The ALR-9640 includes basic over-the-network management and control.

This FCC-approved reader reads up to 50 tags per second. Configuration is accomplished either locally via serial port or remotely via the LAN using a human-readable interface. Software integration is easily implemented through the use of XML-formatted control data and binary and C-language APIs. The ALR-9640 is equipped with a flexible mounting system. The antenna is an orientation-insensitive design, allowing tags to be read no matter what their angle of presentation to the reader.

The ALR-9930-A RFID reader/programmer module with a frequency of 902–928-MHz (ISM) band is designed for rapid integration of EPCglobal UHF Class 1 support. It is small enough for integration into handhelds, printers, shelf readers, and more. A library of C-language APIs ensures integration for rapid prototyping and development.

With an anti-collision algorithm, the ALR-9930-A module reads multiple tags in the field of view, regardless of the number of tags, and is designed as an option for printers, handhelds, and others. Software-controllable output power and communications combined with unlicensed operation provide flexibility within diverse end-user applications. Software integration is easily implemented through the use of binary and C-language APIs. A complete software developer's kit with sample code is available. Firmware is upgradeable.

This 2450-MHz ALR 2750 reader uses an Intermediate Frequency (IF) channel to obtain ranges in order of magnitude greater than existing commercial systems. This reader with four I/O ports is targeted at indoor applications, such as pharmaceutical track and trace and textile tagging. This system has the ability to read up to 250 tags in an RF field and at distances of several feet.

The reader can be interfaced either locally or through a LAN interface to remote servers. Input control lines allow for trigger inputs, which turns on RF only when goods are present, thus alleviating interference with other RF sources in a large warehouse or supply chain. Output control lines enable the operation of a gate or door when a valid tag is interrogated.

It is certified for use in Japan and as of Spring 2004, will soon be licensed in the United States.

B.2 AXCESS INC. (WWW.AXCESSINC.COM)

Axcess offers these tags:

■ AT-132-A Standard Asset Tag
■ AT-132-AT Standard Asset Tag with tamper option
■ AT-132-AM Metal Mount Asset Tag

The AT-132-A Stand Asset Tag from Axcess Inc. is a high-performance active RFID tag based on the company's patented automatic identification technology. The tag can be affixed to virtually any asset (laptops, computers, peripherals, electronic equipment, pallets, inventory items, etc.) for long-range asset protection and monitoring throughout the enterprise or supply chain.

Signal transmissions transmit and receive at the operating frequency of 315 MHz and 126 kHz, respectively, and penetrate walls and obstructions, traveling up to 35 feet within a typical facility, with longer ranges possible in open spaces, such as warehouses and computer rooms. Multiple tags can be read simultaneously such that both the asset and its carrier can be identified in an automatic, hands-free manner. This also allows the asset to be linked to one or more owners. Range in excess of 50 feet is achievable with custom antenna designs.

A tamper feature is available (AT-132A-T) that triggers the tag to transmit a beacon alarm signal upon removal. Asset Beacon Tags are also available that automatically transmit on a preprogrammed timed interval to assist in the tracking and monitoring of tagged objects across broad areas.

The AT-132-AM Metal Mount Asset Tag is available for both metallic and nonmetallic surfaces. It is slightly heavier than the Standard Asset Tag.

B.3 ESCORT MEMORY SYSTEMS

Escort Memory Systems (EMS) provides a complete line of high-memory Active Read/Write RFID Antennas, Tags, and Controllers. They are widely used for automotive applications in harsh, noisy, and dusty manufacturing and assembly environments. The HS-Series Tags provide large memory capacity (up to 32 KB), rapid data transfer speeds of 3000 bytes/second, and long read/write range possibilities, up to 29 inches.

EMS offers the following tags.

■ HS200R-Series Read/Write Tags
■ HL200R-Series Read/Write Tags (European)

- HS200XL-Series Read/Write Tags
- HL200XL-Series Read/Write Tags (European)
- HS200LR-Series Long Range Read/Write Tags

The HS200R-Series Tags incorporate from 64 bytes up to 32 KB of fast, random-access memory and are epoxy encapsulated to withstand the harshest industrial environments. Advanced digital signal processing techniques allow data transmission speed of 3000 bps while still using reliable, safe, low-frequency RF. EMS Tags are the low-frequency RF Tags with high-speed data transfer capability.

The European HL200R Series Read/Write Tags incorporate from 64 bytes up to 8 Kbytes of fast, random-access memory and are epoxy encapsulated to withstand the harshest industrial environments. The HL200R Tags contain a replacement battery power source that will power the Tag for 40 million bytes transferred or ten years.

The HS200XL-Series Read/Write Tags incorporate from 64 bytes up to 32 KB of fast, random-access memory and are epoxy encapsulated to withstand the harshest industrial environments. Advanced digital signal processing techniques allow data transmission speeds of 3000 bps and can transfer up to 800 million bytes of data, without the need for battery replacement.

EMS tags are the low-frequency RF tags on the market with high-speed data transfer capability. The six-inch read/write range of the HS200XL-Series Tag works well with pallet-based automated systems. Once the tag is mounted, the pallet can carry with it all information regarding the product or material on the pallet.

The European HL200XL Series Read/Write Tags incorporate from 64 bytes up to 8 Kbytes of fast, random-access memory and are epoxy encapsulated to withstand the harshest industrial environments. The HL200R Tags contain a replacement battery power sources that will power the tag for 210 million bytes transferred or ten years.

The HS200LR-Series Tags offers up to 31 inches of long-range identification capabilities when used with the HS510 Antenna. The Tags have the same durability, memory capacity, and data transfer rate as the HS200R-Series Tags. The longer range makes the HS200LR-Series Tags well suited for attachment to larger pallets or product carriers.

EMS offers the following antennas.

- HS500-Series Read/Write Antennas
- JH510-Series Read/Write Antennas
- HS550A Wide-Field Read/Write Antennas
- HL500-Series Read/Write Antennas (European)

The HS500-Series Read/Write Antennas connect to a Read/Write RFID Controller to provide an interface between a host computer or Programming

Logic Controller (PLC) and the data in the HS-Series Read/Write Tags. The Antennas can transfer data at the astonishing speed of 3000 bps. Most importantly these Tags can read/write data through virtually any nonconductive material and are unaffected by paint, dust, dirt, and solvents. The compact size and long range of the antenna are well suited for factory automation environments where space is at a premium.

The HS510 Long-Range Antenna provides up to 29 inches of read/write range with the HS200LR-Series Read/Write Tags. HS510 has a rapid data transfer speed of 3000 bps and does not have any moving parts or mechanical switches and is unaffected by paint, dust, dirt, and solvents.

The 16-inch-wide RF field of the HS550A is well suited for use in factory automation environments where tags will be moving at great speeds as they pass the antennas. The distance from the controller card to the antenna can be up to 4000 feet. Due to the IP66 enclosure and high immunity to metal, HS550A has been used in many RFID industrial applications.

The European HL500-Series Antennas connected to an EMS Controller provide an interface between a host computer or programmable controller and the data in the HL200-Series Read/Write Tags. The small size and long range of the Antenna is well suited for use in factory automation environments where space is at a premium. Unaffected by paint, dust, dirt, and solvents the HL500-Series Antennas have been used for many years in the toughest of industrial applications.

EMS offers the following reader/writers and controllers.

- HS814/HS816 Portable Reader/Writers
- HL814/HL816 Portable Reader/Writers (European)
- HS850B Series Eurocard Controller
- HS880B-Series Read/Write Controllers
- HS900 PC-Bus Read/Write Controller

The EMS HMS814 Reader/Writer can plug directly into Intermec®'s handheld terminals to provide portable read/write capabilities. For added flexibility, EMSs offers the HMS816 Portable Reader/Writer which interfaces directly to the host (e.g., laptop, palmtop) via RS232 serial port. The Portable RFID Reader/Writers form EMSs allow flexible handheld identification and tracking solutions to a wide range of industries, such as automotive, material handling, electronics, and food processing.

The European HL814/HL816 Portable Reader/Writers provide a portable Reader/Writer to communicate with the HL200-Series Tags. The HL814 Reader/Writer plugs directly into a mini PC terminal to provide mobile RFID capabilities. For added flexibility, the HL816 Portable Reader/Writer interfaces directly to the host (e.g., laptop, palmtop), via an RS232 serial port. The Portable Reader/Writers allow flexible RFID handheld identification and tracking solutions to a wide range of applications, including automotive, material handling, electronics, and food processing.

The HS850B Serial Eurocard Controller interfaces between the serial port of the user's host computer and up to four HS-Series Antennas. Up to 45 HS850B Controller cards can be connected on one RS-485 multi-drop line, allowing a single host to control up to 180 Antennas. The connection between the Eurocard Controller and each Antenna is via two twisted pairs (four wires) with a maximum cable length of 1200 meters.

The HS880-Series Read/Write Controllers used with the HS-Series Read/Write Tags and Antennas are part of the company's Controller line. Incorporating high-level language capability, the HS880 Controllers offer two fully buffered bidirectional serial ports and can control up to four Antennas. These Controllers process data at 3000 bps, contain 32 KB of RAM and have 64 programmable TTL-level I/O points. The HS882 Controller enhances the standard features of the HS880 Controller with a faster processor and the addition of battery backed real-time clock/date capabilities required for data logging.

The HS900 PC-Bus Read/Write Controller is an XT-type PC expansion board which serves as the interface between a PC, XT, AT, or PC-compatible personal computer and up to four HS-Series Antennas. The Antenna cable length can be up to 4000 feet, which is advantageous because the Controller portion of the RFID system is then afforded extra protection from noise that could be generated by electrical equipment positioned near the read/write station.

B.4 MICROTEC (WWW.KSW-MICROTEC.DE)

In addition to standard functions such as reading, writing, and protecting user data, Smart Active Labels offer additional functionality such as a temperature logger. They are:

- KSW—TempSens® as a paper-thin battery enabling the intelligent label to perform its task of autonomously controlling the temperature. The batteries have a life span of up to one year depending on the activity of the label.
- KSW—TempSens that is ISO compatible and can communicate with every standard ISO reader.

Applications include transport and logistics, pharmaceutical monitoring and identification, transportation, and storage of medical products. Transport and logistics applications focus on quality assurance for temperature sensitive products and perishables (e.g., fresh fruit, vegetables, meat, flowers, or chemical products). Pharmaceutical monitoring and identification focuses on pharmaceutical logistics. Transportation and storage of medical products include products requiring temperature monitoring of blood and blood products, medicine, and vaccines.

B.5 SAMSYS (WWW.SAMSYS.COM)

SAMSys offers two types of active RFID readers: MP9320 UHF Long-Range and MP9320 2.0 EPC readers. Each type is described below.

The MP9320 supports a variety of UHF tag protocols and is available in U.S. Federal Communications Commission (FCC) and European Telecommunications Standards Institute (ETSI) configurations. With its extended read range and high data rates, the MP9320 is especially suited for asset management and logistics applications requiring the simultaneous reading of a large number of tags at greater distances. With RF connections for up to four antennas, the MP9320 easily adapts to loading dock and portal installations for aggregated container tracking, pallet tracking, and inventory management.

The MP9320 is upgradeable to new emerging protocols and standards. The first release of the product supports the ISO 18000-6A and 18000-6B protocols, along with the EM Marin 4022 and new 4222 device. Also, the MP9320 can be implemented as a stand-alone UHF solution or included in a networked reader environment using the SAMSys Interrogator Control and Concentrator Module (ICCM).

The MP9320 is supported by a variety of integration tools including development systems, Web interfaces, SOAP messaging, and FORTH interpreters. The reader's scalable architecture allows the support of dozens of UHF readers on one network, so that multi-frequency capability can be added as an organization's RFID needs grow.

The reader provides RS-232 and RS-485EIA/TIA-232F as host interface connection options, and 10BaseT Ethernet LAN support through the SAMSys Concentrator module. The reader supports up to four antennas and three frequency bands:

- 864–870 MHz (25 kHz steps)
- 902–928 MHz (100 kHz steps)
- 869–525 MHz single frequency

This MP9320 2.0 EPC Reader is a UHF device that supports the EPC Class 1, Generation 1 protocol. The MP9320 2.0 EPC supports a variety of UHF tag protocols and is available in FCC and ETSI configurations.

With its extended read range and high data rates, the MP9320 2.0 EPC is especially suited for inventory control and supply chain applications requiring the simultaneous reading of a large number of tags at greater distances. With RF connections for up to four antennas, the MP9320 2.0 EPC easily adapts to loading dock and portal installations for aggregated container tracking, pallet tracking, and inventory management.

The MP9320 2.0 EPC will be upgradeable to the new Class 1, Generation 2 protocol. In addition to EPC, the reader also supports both ISO 18000-6A and 18000-6B protocols, along with the EM Marin 4022 and new 4222 device. Also, the MP9320 2.0 EPC can be implemented as a stand-alone UHF solution or included in a networked reader environment using the SAMSys ICCM.

The reader is the first to incorporate multi-protocol technology for EPC, ISO 18000-6A, 18000-6B, EM Marin 4022, and 4222. It provides RS-232 and RS-485EIA/TIA-232F as host interface connection options, and 10BaseT Ethernet LAN support through the SAMSys Concentrator module. The reader supports up to four antennas and three frequency bands:

- 864–870 MHz (25 kHz steps)
- 902–928 MHz (100 kHz steps)
- 869–525 MHz single frequency

B.6 SAVI TECHNOLOGY (WWW.SAVI.COM)

Savi data collection capabilities include Savi's own active RFID tags, readers, and signposts integrated with other forms of Automatic Identification and Data Collection (AIDC) technologies such as bar codes, passive RFID, sensors, electronic seals, and satellite systems.

Savi Series 600 Tags, Readers, Signposts, and Security products are built on Savi EchoPoint. It is a configurable system using multiple frequencies for spot-level and wide-area locating of assets. EchoPoint products are designed to provide a modular system for maximum flexibility in deploying active RFID-based networks. EchoPoint employs a unique multi-frequency design and three-element system architecture to achieve both reliable long-range communication and short-range locating capability.

Rather than using a traditional tag and reader system architecture, EchoPoint adds a third unique element—the signpost—to create a flexible architecture that can map into your existing business processes. Signposts communicate with tags over a short-range inductive (123 kHz) link, and Savi tags communicate with readers over a long-range UHF link (100 m). Signposts, which can be fixed, mobile, or handheld, notify tags of their location when tagged items pass through dock doors or other portals, or are placed in specific storage locations or parking slots. Tags then communicate their location back to the reader, along with a unique recognition code. This capability enables items to be tracked throughout the supply chain, with the distinct ability to obtain accurate location information.

The SaviTag ST-654 is the next generation of the well-known SaviTag ST-410. The ST-654 tag offers all of the compelling features of the ST-410 tag in a smaller form factor and lower price and spans both the commercial

EchoPoint™ Network, as well as the legacy DoD tracking network. The ST-654 tag also includes a battery that you can replace using a coin or a screwdriver. With a memory of 128 or 240 KB, the tag carries a frequency of 433 MHz with up to 300-feet range for monitor, wake up, and RF write/read. It has a built-in firmware database designed for quick searching by readers for specific items stored in the tag's memory. This tag works well with containers, vehicles, and large assets.

The Savi SR-650 Fixed Reader collects location and status data from RFID tags within an area and forwards this data to the Savi SmartChain® SiteManager, Savi Retriever, or other host platform. The SR-650 provides long-range, omnidirectional communication to enable effective monitoring of thousands of tagged items over a 100-m radius, ideal for yards, terminals, and warehouses. Ethernet network connectivity supports wired and wireless installations, allowing multiple readers to be easily networked together. Savi's Universal Data Appliance Protocol (UDAP) network protocol provides interoperability with other data collection devices, including bar-code scanners and RFID readers.

The Savi Mobile Reader is a lightweight, battery-operated interrogator/reader module that is used in conjunction with off-the-shelf Personal Digital Assistants (PDAs) or a handheld computer for the purpose of commissioning, identifying, and configuring Savi's EchoPoint RFID tags. Its small form factor module attaches to the back of various off-the-shelf PDAs or handheld computers, and includes a captive cable with a serial interface that connects to the serial port of the handheld computer or PDA. The reader has a long-range, two-way UHF receiver/transmitter for tag wakeup, read, and write, and a short-range, low-frequency transmitter for commissioning of Echopoint RFID tags.

The Savi Sentinel ST-646 is the latest device for securing and monitoring ISO container integrity. It enables shippers, carriers, and logistics service providers to actively monitor the security and integrity of shipments as the container moves throughout the supply chain, detecting both tampering and the potential theft, spoilage, or damage of goods. Any unauthorized opening of the container is detected in real-time, alerting security personnel immediately of problems. Any change in temperature, humidity, and shock can also be detected as the container moves through the ports, terminals, and key transportation routes worldwide. The Savi Sentinel also works in conjunction with established ISO container sealing standards and does not interfere with existing processes and procedures.

Signposts activate only those tags within their immediate vicinity, enabling identification of tagged items at specific locations. Signposts can also transmit commands and configuration information to tags, enabling data read/write, adjustment of tag communication rate, and adjustment of tag frequency. In addition, signposts can activate and deactivate tags, a feature especially important for air cargo and other items that must adhere to strict FAA regulations.

The Savi SP-600-111 Signpost is designed for storage areas, loading bays, hallways, and other locations and enables a highly reliable tracking solution within your existing business processes. With an adjustable, well-defined range of up to 2.5 meters (8.2 feet), complete coverage of conveyors, hallways, storage bins, and other locations is possible without unintentional cross-reads.

The Savi SP-600-211 Signpost is designed for dock doors, vehicle gates, and other portals. The SP-600-211 Signpost has an adjustable well-defined range of up to 4 meters (12 feet) enabling coverage of dock doors and other large portals without unintentional cross-reads.

B.7 WHERENET (WWW.WHERENET.COM)

WhereNet includes these RFID products:

■ WhereTag III (TFF-1011)
■ WherePort II (Model WPT-3200)
■ WhereCall (TFF-1610)

The WhereTag III (TFF-1011) is a key component of the WhereNet Real Time Locating System (RTLS) with a frequency range of 2.4 to 2.483 GHz. It is a small device that can be attached to assets of many kinds, such as forklifts and containers, as well as trailers and container chassis's. It is used to manage those assets by allowing them to be identified and located by the system. Typical locate range for indoors and outdoors are 100 m (350 ft) and 300 m (1000 ft), respectively. Typical read range for indoors and outdoors are 200 m (650 ft) and 1000 m (3000 ft), respectively.

The WhereTag III "blinks" an RF transmission at preprogrammed rates ranging from five seconds to nine hours between blinks. The WhereNet RTLS infrastructure receives these blinks and uses sophisticated Differential Time of Arrival (DTOA) algorithms to determine the location of the tag. Accuracy of this determined location can be as low as two meters and is nominally within three meters in most installations.

The WhereTag III complies with the ANSI 371.1 RTLS standard. It operates in the globally accepted 2.4-GHz frequency band and transmits spread spectrum signals in accordance with the standard. The use of spread spectrum technology provides extremely long range: in excess of 300 meters outdoors. The combination of low power output and cutting edge battery technology allows the WhereTag III to operate for a long time without any maintenance. Battery life can be a long as seven years depending upon blink rate.

A receiver is also built into the WhereTag III. The tag can receive low-frequency magnetic signals from an exciter called a WherePort. The WherePort transmissions can be read at distances ranging from one to six meters. The WherePort can modify the pre-programmed blink rate of a WhereTag III and also identify a particular location "zone."

Designed to operate in a wide range of applications, the WhereTag III is fully sealed and will function in both indoor and outdoor environments. The tag's case is also resistant to oils, solvents, and hydraulic fluids.

WherePort II (Model WPT-3200) is a proximity communication device that is used to trigger a WhereTag II to transmit an alternate "blink" pattern. When a WhereTag II passes though the WherePort's field, the tag can initiate a preprogrammed and (typically) faster blink rate to allow more location points as a tagged asset passes through a critical threshold, such as a shipping/receiving dock door or from one zone to another. When the WhereTag II is sending WherePort-initiated blinks, the tag includes the identification number of the WherePort II. More than 32,000 unique identification numbers are available.

The WherePort II's field is nearly spherical and its range is adjustable from approximately 1 m (3 ft) to 6 m (20 ft). For especially large thresholds (such as very large dock doors) or areas where there may be signal blockage, multiple WherePorts can be interconnected to provide a larger coverage area. Designed for fixed indoor and outdoor applications, the WherePort II is sealed against dust and water. Each WherePort II includes an adjustable mounting bracket and requires only AC or DC power; there are no data cables to install.

The WhereWand is used to configure the identification number, range, and other attributes of the WherePort II. The WherePort II's effective range for a WhereTag II tag is configurable to one of eight levels. Table B.1 shows approximate values assuming voltage inputs of either 24 or 36 VAC.

Table B.1 Eight Levels of Configurable Ranges

Level	Effective Range
8	4.5 to 6 m (15 to 20 ft)
7	4 to 5 m (13 to 16 ft)
6	2.5 to 3 m (8 to 10 ft)
5	2.1 to 2.7 m (7 to 9 ft)
4	1.8 to 2.5 m (6 to 8 ft)
3	1.7 to 2.1 m (5.5 to 7 ft)
2	1.5 to 1.8 m (5 to 6 ft)
1	1.1 to 1.2 m (3.5 to 4 ft)

The WhereCall (TFF-1610) is a key component of the WhereNet Wireless Parts Replenishment System, which provides a highly flexible wireless solution that eliminates the need for wired line-side infrastructure and can replace paper based Kanban Systems. It has a frequency range of 2.4 to 2.483 GHz. Typical read ranges for indoors and outdoors are 100 m (350 ft) and 300 m (1000 ft), respectively.

Each container of parts is associated with a wireless WhereCall, which transmits its unique identification when the call button is pressed by the operator. This transmission is received by a network of WhereNet antennas that are strategically installed at ceiling height within a customer's manufacturing area. The WhereNet Wireless Parts Replenishment System then processes the received signal, confirms that a valid request has been made and forwards a material call to a third party's system software. From there the call can be forwarded to vehicle-mounted terminals, floor-mounted workstations, or paging systems.

WhereCall II is a compact unit, with a call button. The WhereCall uses a LCD to display elapsed time since the last time each button activated. The LCD is visible to operators at their workstations so they know how much time has passed since their last call.

A variant of WhereCall II, WhereCall II PLC, provides for automated call requests by replacing the call button with a sealed connector that can be interfaced to intelligent shop floor equipment. The WhereCall II provides two areas for users to attach their own part numbers or other information.

Appendix C

SEMI-PASSIVE RFID TECHNOLOGY

Here are some semi-passive products offered by Alien Technology, Avonwood, and KSW Microtec.

C.1 ALIEN TECHNOLOGY (WWW.ALIENTECHNOLOGY.COM)

Alien's long-range, high-performance battery-powered backscatter system fills the gap between short-range passive systems and high-cost active RFID systems. Battery-powered passive RFID technology extends the range over which a tag can be read by providing the tag with its own battery power source. With a typical range of over 30 meters, this technology is ideal for applications such as:

- Long-range identification
- Sensor monitoring
- Immobilizer
- Vehicle-asset tracking
- Supply chain automation
- Tamper detection
- Security/access systems
- Time temperature monitoring
- Access control
- Passive tag data storage for hierarchical asset tracking systems

Equipped with this small backscatter system, a tag can store 4 KB of data, including locally acquired sensor data. In one available configuration, the system can monitor and record temperatures at user-defined time intervals. With this system, tags can be applied to temperature-sensitive products at production or shipment, and the temperature history of the product can be downloaded wirelessly at the final destination or at any point along the way. Because it still uses the low-power backscatter technology, a small battery will provide many years of operation.

C.2 AVONWOOD

Avonwood provides these RFID systems:

- Eureka 311 – Active Tag and Readers
- Eureka 411 – Active Tags and Readers
- Eureka 511 – Active Tags and Readers
- Eureka 811 – High Speed Tag

The Eureka 311 is a small active (semi-passive) tag operating at 132 kHz. It is particularly useful for asset tracking and the livestock industry. It can be programmed with an encoder and then is read only with 36 bits of usable memory. The tag is powered by a small internal battery. However, the tag goes to sleep if it is not within the decoder field, hence the life of the tag is typically five years.

The Eureka 411 is an active (semi-passive) tag operating at 132 KHz. Up to 119 characters may be read or written to the tag up to a range of one meter with a standard industrial antenna. The antenna is connected to a Eureka decoder/reader that controls and monitors communications with both the tag and the user's equipment, usually through an RS-232 or RS-485 port. The tag communicates at high speed with a data rate of 1 Kbps with full anti-collision.

The Eureka 511 tag is based on the technology used in the 411 system, and is operating at 132 kHz. The 511 tag is designed specifically for industrial applications to give a longer read range than the standard version of the tag. The 511 tag has read/write and anti-collision capabilities.

The high-speed Eureka 811 tag is a long-range version of the 411 tag, used typically in the rail industry. It operates with vehicles moving up to 110 km per hour at ranges of up to 1.9 meters. It is an active (semi-passive) tag operating at 132 kHz. Up to 118 characters may be read or written to the tag. The tag is read through an antenna that is connected to a Eureka decoder controlling and monitoring communications with both the tag and the user's equipment, usually through an RS-232 or RS-485 port.

C.3 KSW MICROTEC (WWW.KSW-MICROTEC.COM)

KSW Microtec offers TempSens® as a paper-thin battery enabling the intelligent label to perform its task of autonomously controlling the temperature. The batteries have a life span of up to one year depending on the activity of the label. KSW Microtec received a nonexclusive, worldwide license to manufacture and distribute Power Paper's batteries for smart active RFID label products.

Appendix D

RFID MIDDLEWARE

Because data collected by various RFID readers come in different formats, integrating data in a common format with enterprise systems is accomplished via the route of middleware. Most middleware products act as traffic cops or a bridge between disparate systems.

Table D.1 shows a partial list of middleware vendors, firms, and companies.

Table D.1 RFID Middleware, Vendors, Firms, and Companies

Acsis	Axcess	Blue Vector Systems
ConnecTerra	Data Brokers	EPCglobal
Franwell	GlobeRanger	i2 Technologies
Manhattan Associates	OATSystems	Oracle
RF Code	Savi Technology	Sun
T3Ci	TIBCO	VeriSign
		webMethods

D.1 ACSIS INC. (WWW.ACSIS.COM)

Acsis' newest product offering is an RFID interface to SAP R/3® with a focus on supply chain management. It integrates data collected from its partners' 2.4-GHz RFID devices (900 MHz also supported) into a company's SAP R/3 system using DataPass™, a Certified Interface for SAP™ R/3. DataPass operates through Intermec, Symbol, Telxon, LXE, and Techlogix Palmtop CE and Palm™ devices and works with existing LAN or WAN, allowing real-time data collection from warehouse, distribution center, manufacturing location, or any auxiliary site within a supply chain.

DataPass passes data to Microsoft SQL Server as a local database and works with all standard SAP R/3 interfaces. In addition, it allows the use of intelligent RF devices, Windows-enabled PCs, and CE products, all running within the same environment. Visual Basic and Visual C/C++ can be used to build custom local applications.

D.2 AXCESS INC. (WWW.AXCESSINC.COM)

ActiveTrac™ Software provides an enterprisewide personnel, asset, and equipment monitoring solution, with integrated logging, tracking, alert notification, status monitoring, and reporting functions. The software combines operator-friendly displays, flexible configuration, and instantaneous query functions to offer a tool for tracking movements and automatically controlling remote devices. ActiveTrac has a range of applications, including resource management, asset protection, personnel time and attendance, status monitoring, and inventory logistics.

ActiveTrac™, coupled with the company's ActiveTag™ automatic identification products, offers customers the ability to easily monitor and track asset and personnel movements throughout a facility. The system is based on a flexible control point architecture that allows the user to activate and identify tags at specific locations within the facility. Identification and location data broadcast by the tags are gathered by network receivers and forwarded to the ActiveTrac application. The software time-stamps, displays, and logs the event information in a general-purpose database where it can be accessed via standard queries and reports, including quick retrieval of "last seen" location and movement history. Additional reports and queries can be customized to the user's specifications.

The software operates stand-alone or in background with logical interfaces to legacy applications via relay control and ASCII scripts. It runs on the Windows 2000 platform, communicating with devices over the LAN/WAN using minimal bandwidth, and connects directly to network devices via industry standard RS-232 serial port or Ethernet TCP/IP network interfaces. Event data is stored in an ODBC database for flexible customized report/query using an off-the-shelf report generator.

D.3 BLUE VECTOR SYSTEMS
(WWW.BLUEVECTORSYSTEMS.COM)

The X-3000 RFID Configuration System is a Web-based interface that is launched from the Operations Dashboard. This dashboard is a window into the RFID network, allowing customers to centrally manage and control their RFID network by providing a real-time view and system status of the entire RFID network. The structure of the dashboard can be customized to suit the needs of the customer.

The RFID Configuration System allows customers to map their actual physical supply chain network into a logical representation that they can

RFID-enable. It essentially allows businesses to convert physical structures such as dock doors or warehouse shelves into logical entities that can be configured, modified, and outfitted with RFID.

The System includes a large library of behaviors that can be readily used to create or modify parameters, assign functionality to certain network elements, or develop new functionality. One functionality example is pre-integrated EPCglobal's Object Name Service (ONS) and prototype EPC Information Services (EPCIS) solution from VeriSign that you can drag and drop in any implementation.

The RFID Configuration System contains a drag-and-drop functionality to allow replicating a configuration by simply copying and pasting it across a business' entire distribution network. This capability enables customers to scale their operations from a single dock door in a warehouse to a nationwide deployment across their supply chain.

D.4 CONNECTERRA (WWW.CONNECTERRA.COM)

ConnecTerra offers middleware RFTagAware 1.0, the first version of its EPC Savant and reader management software. This software provides an Application Programming Interface (API) for data filtering and integration in various formats with enterprise software. This is accomplished by interacting with RFID readers and performing various operations on data these readers collect from scanning the tags. RFTagAware also monitors the health of remote readers, upgrades software, runs diagnostics, and performs other maintenance operations.

RFTagAware 1.0 supports readers from ThingMagic, Alien Technology, Matrics, Symbol Technologies, Intermec Technologies, AWID, and SAMSys. With the exception of the Matrics model for which the tags are read as EPC Class 0, all readers are capable of reading EPC Class 1 tags.

RFTagAware software can be used in the many non-EPC RFID systems and can support some non-EPC tags and readers such as those from Escort Memory Systems. RFTagAware 1.0 runs on Sun Solaris, Linux, or Microsoft's Windows NT servers.

D.5 DATA BROKERS (WWW.DATABROKERS.COM)

Data Brokers offers three layers of RFID implementation that can be used together or by themselves. The first layer is the foundation and an abstract interface, Driver, which enables direct control of the RFID device. The current version provides device-independent control and includes manufacturers such as Texas Instruments, TagSys, Intermec, Symbol, Sensormatic, and others. The public interface includes methods that enable tag read/write and use of multiple antennas. To facilitate the plug-and-play behavior, Data

Brokers developed a module that maintains a list of known drivers. When executed, it sequentially "tests" each of the drivers and executes specific operations with the connected device. Once it obtains a match, it loads the appropriate driver and makes it available to the rest of the system. It is simple, efficient, and very effective. Using the Driver Factory, one generic configuration may be used.

The second layer defines an "abstract transponder," a software analogue of a physical transponder. A driver reads using the hardware device and produces zero, one, or many transponder software objects in the memory of the program.

The third layer is comprised of standard business logic, common among logistical systems including operations such as inbound/outbound shipping, receiving, put-away, inventory control, sales, and security.

PIRF (Platform Independent Radio Frequency), the core product, uses the first layer to provide a middleware solution for RFID systems integration. The primary benefit is eliminating the tedium of determining how various devices work. Data Brokers provides them with simple function calls for most RFID devices. We also provide support as hardware evolves, as it invariably does. This will protect their investment in time and resources.

VITAL (Virtual Independent Tag Array Logic) is based on the second layer and provides interoperability of tags from different sources. VITAL allows systems architects and developers to focus on the data requirements. For example:

- Company A put on a pallet with a 2.45-GHz tag with a related data.
- Company B receives palletized cartons from Company A and updates the 2.45-GHz tag with data relevant to its systems and processes.
- The items in the carton are tagged at the manufacturing source with 13.56-MHz tags and initialized with SKU data.
- The item tags are updated with price before being shipped to the store.
- The outbound cartons are tagged with a 13.56-MHz tag carton level data, a different "record layout" than the item tag.

VITAL shields the developer from the complexities of "transposing" each data source and type. Throughout the product flow, tag-data is processed from external suppliers, different tag manufacturers, different suppliers, and within the same company. Developers focus on using the data as "record types" in a relational database and functional applications.

SCOPE (Supply Chain Optimization Process Engineering) is based on the third layer. It is targeted as a finished product for small retail companies. It builds on the first two layers to provide solutions for businesses that want to adopt RFID and combine it with other technologies (RFDC, bar code) with minimum investment and risk.

D.6 EPCGLOBAL (WWW.EPCGLOBALINC.ORG)

EPC Middleware acts as the central nervous system of the EPCglobal Network. EPC Middleware manages real-time read events and information, provides alerts, and manages the basic read information for communication to EPCIS or the company's other existing information systems.

EPCIS is the gateway to EPCglobal Network. It receives tag events from EPC Middleware, generates track and trace events based on information which is coming from the EPC Middleware and stores it on local data store for future use. It also serves as a hub for information aggregation for a given EPC (see the section on Verisign).

D.7 FRANWELL (WWW.FRANWELL.COM)

With minimal effort, rfid> Genesis utilizes data from your existing warehouse management system to produce the case and pallet RFID tags that are required. When a customer order requiring RFID tags is released for shipment, it is directed to rfid> Genesis for processing. The inventory for the order is physically brought to the rfid> Genesis station to print the case and pallet tags. When the tags are printed and "slapped" onto the cases, the cases are then restacked onto the pallet. The completed pallet is passed through an rfid> Genesis portal to scan and verify the tags for shipment. The RFID tag data is transmitted to the EPC network for customer receipt. At the customer's site, the product tags can be scanned and verified against the data transmitted to the EPC network.

rfid> Genesis can be integrated or it can operate as a stand-alone system. Additional features are the ability to manage readers attached to a portal and provision for event notification for hardware errors or shipping exceptions.

D.8 GLOBERANGER (WWW.GLOBERANGER.COM)

GlobeRanger's iMotion platform serves as the foundation for both RFID and mobile solutions, providing a platform runtime, software development kit (SDK), application components, and tools for rapid application development and development. Based on Microsoft's .NET Framework, iMotion enables business consultants, application developers, and systems engineers to rapidly configure and manage RFID solutions.

Key Platform Features include event runtime, SDK, Tools, Visual Workflow Center, and the most interesting part, RFID Reader Emulator. Each is briefly described as follows.

GlobalRanger also offers Application Component Libraries that are bundled with the iMotion platform; prebuilt application components provide a head start for rapid applications development. They include RFID Reader Adapters, Event Filters, Event Consumers, Event Monitor, and Service Manager. Each is described as follows.

D.9 I2 TECHNOLOGIES (WWW.I2.COM)

i2 Technologies' Supply Chain Operating Services allows companies to collaborate with one another across their supply chains and to leverage existing legacy systems while supporting new applications. It supports for optimization modules: fulfillment, logistics, production, revenue, and profit-and-spend.

Fulfillment Optimization capabilities include solutions from the i2 Supply Chain Management (SCM) and i2 Service and Parts Management (SPM) solution sets which include demand fulfillment, inventory management, supply chain event management, and replenishment planner. Logistics Optimization capabilities include Supply Chain Strategist, Transportation Bid Collaboration, Transportation Manager, and Warehouse Manager.

Production Optimization capabilities include i2's Production Optimization capabilities along with the i2 Six Supply Chain Management suite. This suite features products such as Supply Chain Strategist, Demand Manager, Demand Fulfillment, Factory Planner, Supply Chain Planner, Profit Optimization, and Supply Collaboration.

Revenue and Profit Optimization is particularly useful when competition acts, demand swings, or fashion changes: supply plans are not immediately adjustable. Spend Optimization is the process of sourcing from an optimal set of suppliers to increase profitability, assist companies drive supply base configuration to future requirements, and align the inbound supply chain with the outbound supply chain.

D.10 MANHATTAN ASSOCIATES (WWW.MANH.COM)

At the heart of RFID in a Box™ is Manhattan Associates' Integration Platform for RFID. This platform-independent middleware eases deployment across RFID devices that work directly with other Manhattan Associates solutions as well as legacy or custom applications. Also included is the EPC Manager, designed for companies requiring quick deployment of RFID/EPC technology with existing supply chain solutions.

D.11 OATSYSTEMS (WWW.OATSYSTEMS.COM)

OATSystems' RFID software suite consists of the middleware Senseware Platform, the Senseware Visibility Server application, and the Senseware EPC Commissioning Module application, providing standards-based RFID solution for companies in the retail, Consumer Packaged Goods (CPG), manufacturing, pharmaceutical, and logistics markets.

The Senseware Platform collects data from leading RFID readers, printers, programmable logic controllers, and hardware devices, and transforms it into actionable business objects and then integrates it into enterprise applications such as Enterprise Relationship Planning (ERP), warehouse management, supply chain management, and manufacturing execution systems. It provides Web-based configuration management and support for Simple Network Management Protocol (SNMP).

The Senseware Platform also serves as the base for Edge Visibility Server and EPC Commissioning Module. The first application uses ruled-based workflows and exception management to improve operational efficiency of following supply items and the integration of shipping and receiving operation with real-time validation. The second application aims to improve management of electronic product codes throughout the enterprise.

D.12 ORACLE (WWW.ORACLE.COM)

Oracle offers Sensor-Based Services which draw on capabilities of its 10*g* database and application server to help companies to better respond to data from RFID tags (and other sensor tools). Warehouse Management software and Oracle Application Server 10*g* Wireless Client will include support for RFID capabilities to accommodate large transactional data.

The next release of Oracle Application Server 10*g* will offer out-of-the-box integration and device management for RFID readers and provide compatibility with RFID tags, reading and printing devices from Alien Technology Corporation, Intermec Technologies Corp., and Zebra Technologies. Oracle's Compliance Assistance Package (CAP) contains built-in adapters to help companies to develop compliance policies and integrate them into back-end systems.

D.13 RF CODE (WWW.RFCODE.COM)

RF Code's TAVIS offers data collection middleware system running on Linux embedded systems, Windows CE, and Windows platforms. It provides support for all Auto-ID types including bar code, active RFID, passive RFID, Remote Tracking Location System (RTLS), and Global Positioning System (GPS)/Cellular Location and is scalable at the enterprise or supply chain level through hierarchical, fault-tolerant central or distributed management.

The TAVIS platform supplies the first and second layers between devices and application-specific software such as Inventory Control, ERP, and Manufacturing Resource Planning (MRP) as well as applications that need instant response such as Access Control and Personnel Tracking.

As of Spring 2004, this enterprise scale data collection platform has been in commercial use for over two and one half years in combination with RF Code's active RFID hardware offering.

D.14 SAVI TECHNOLOGY (WWW.SAVI.COM)

Savi Technology offers Smart Chain middleware in three areas: Site Manager, Mobile Manager, and Client tools. In defining supply chains as a series of activities across multiple locations that connect business partners and processes to deliver goods from one point to another, Savi goes one step higher by providing information via middleware about supply chain activities and the status and location of shipments.

To make this information available, each middleware product must be deployed on a network that various business partners and processes can access and share across the supply chain. It must be able to integrate various Automatic Identification Data Collection technologies used to capture data from different sources in different formats in real-time as physical events change (e.g., loading onto and unloading from a truck). This is made possible by middleware support for Savi's Universal Data Appliance Protocol (UDAP™), an open data format and protocol that allows multiple EPC-client devices, applications, and entities to share information.

D.15 SUN (WWW.SUN.COM)

Sun's version of Savant, an EPC Network middleware technology for its RFID-enabled Supply Chain Execution (SCE) Infrastructure, is available for managing the flow of RFID information between the readers of RFID tags and back-end enterprise system and contains reader failover features to allow the RFID information to continue to flow to its intended destination. The original version of this software running on distributed servers was designed by the Auto-ID Center for its EPC network infrastructure.

Savant software fixes incorrect or duplicate data gathered from readers, before it stores and forwards data to any point of the chain. It also monitors for event changes and sends alerts to their intended recipients. Savants then forward data to the ERP systems through a full-time connection to the readers, or synchronize data on an "as needed" basis. The information the Savant collects for each tag includes EPC of the tag read, EPC of the reader scanning the tag, time stamp of the reading, and temperature or location position.

Savants are not directly connected to EIS applications such as Manugistics, i2, SAP, Oracle, and Provia. They send data to an operations data bus where data can be further processed when requirements change before they pass the resulting data via the adapters to legacy systems. This bus layer can be used to do data warehousing, or to apply business logic to events. Some Sun's iForce partners offer software components to enhance RFID-enabled SCEInfrastructure.

D.16 T3CI (WWW.T3CI.COM)

T3Ci, the RFID analytics and applications company, develops and markets software and subscription services for leaders of RFID initiatives at major retail suppliers and pharmaceutical companies who are responsible for delivering business value from their company's RFID investment. T3Ci's enterprise-class solutions, including inventory intelligence, brand protection, and order execution performance management, represent the most comprehensive RFID application vision in the industry.

T3Ci has worked with "Wal-Mart 8" on developing RFID applications. The "Wal-Mart 8" includes Gillette, Hewlett-Packard, Johnson & Johnson, Kimberly-Clark, Kraft Foods, Nestlé Purina PetCare Co., Procter & Gamble, and Unilever. On October 2004, T3Ci announced it received an investment from SAP Ventures, a division of SAP AG.

D.17 TIBCO (WWW.TIBCO.COM)

TIBCO, a business integration software company, and Alien Technology, a manufacturer of EPC tags, are collaborating on RFID solutions to integrate real-time events generated by Alien's hardware with the TIBCO business integration software. The core of TIBCO software is to analyze RFID events as business conditions change. A manufacturer of EPC tags, Alien partners with more than 35 companies on tags, antennas, readers, handhelds, printers, and software integration.

D.18 VERISIGN (WWW.VERISIGN.COM)

VeriSign provides intelligent infrastructure services for EPCglobal network including Managed ONS, EPCIS, and EPC Discovery Services. As explained in Chapter 2, the ONS is the authoritative directory of manufacturers and products for the EPCglobal Network. When an RFID-tagged object is scanned, ONS identifies the network location of the item's product data.

Verisign hosts its EPCISs in highly secure facilities for supply chain members to store and share product data with their partners. Verisign's EPC Discovery Services enables the secure discovery of EPC track and trace data, providing a listing of all information services that are available for a given EPC. This creates a unified view of data across the supply chain.

The EPC Starter Service provides for access to private, fee-based, hosted EPC-IS and ONS services. The Application Developers Program is free.

D.19 WEBMETHODS (WWW.WEBMETHODS.COM)

The webMethods Integration Platform offers companies to connect an RFID system to SCM and other core back-end systems, such as ERP and Customer Relationship Management (CRM). It links business processes, enterprise systems, databases, workflows, and Web services, and integrates J2EE, .NET, and legacy systems.

The webMethods Integration Platform is the foundation of Global Business Visibility, providing the capability to unify the disparate, heterogeneous IT assets inherent to any organization. With the webMethods Integration Platform, business processes can be integrated and managed across the network of business partners. Business processes then can be managed on a server via a console using webMethods' Open Management Interface Specifications.

Appendix E

NETWORK/SERVER INTERFACES

In this appendix, we cover network or server interfaces for:

- Escort Memory Systems providing programmable interface modules for the network of various RFID products
- WhereNet providing software solutions to link various points of supply chains
- Blue vector systems

E.1 ESCORT MEMORY SYSTEMS (WWW.EMS-RFID.COM)

EMS provides Network Interface Modules for over 95 percent of the world's industrial networks. Profibus, DeviceNet, and Interbus-S are just a few of the industrial networks for which EMS offers general-purpose programmable interface modules. These modules can be used to give a presence to a wide range of existing equipment, such as bar-code readers, RFID antennas, bar-code verifiers, sensors, and switches.

The modules EMS offers include:

- CM01 Module
- CM11/CM12 DeviceNet Interface Modules
- CM21 InterBus-S Module
- CM30-Series Profibus Modules
- CM40-Series Modbus Plus Modules
- CM52 Remote I/O Module
- CM81 ControNet Modules
- CM900 Automatic ID Module

- CM1000 Automatic ID PLC Module
- CM1746 Module
- MM80MicroMux Bus Module

The CM01 Module is a general-purpose programmable interface that can be connected between any standard serial com port or Programmable Logic Controller (PLC) serial communications module to the CM01 and reads/writes to HS-Series RFID Antennas.

EMS CM11/CM12 are external modules that allow any serial device to interface with a Controller Area Network (CAN) bus communications protocol on a master/slave basis. The CM11 contains two serial ports. One serial port can be configured for RS232, RS422, or RS485(MUX32). An additional RS232 serial port is available for downloading programs and configurations. The CM12 has one RFID port compatible with the HS500-Series Antennas.

The CM21 InterBus-S Module is a general-purpose programmable interface device between the InterBus-S network and up to two HS500-Series Antennas, or as many as 32 HMS-Series Reader/Writers, RS-Series Readers, or bar-code scanners on a MUX32 line. The CM21 features a durable NEMA 4 enclosure.

The CM30-Series Profibus Modules are general-purpose programmable interface devices between the Profibus network and up to two HS500-Series Antennas, or as many as 32 HMS-Series Reader/Writers, RS-Series Readers, or bar-code scanners on a MUX32 line. The CM31 features a durable NEMA 4 enclosure whereas the CM32 is encased in an ABS NEMA 2 shell. These modules work with a 386 microprocessor and a real-time DOS compatible operating system.

The CM40-Series Modbus Plus Modules are general-purpose programmable interface devices between the Modbus Plus network and up to two HS500-Series Antennas, or as many as 32 HMS-Series Reader/Writers, RS-Series Readers, or bar-code scanners on a MUX32 line. The CM41 features a durable NEMA 4 enclosure whereas the CM42 is encased in an ABS NEMA 2 shell. These modules work with a 386 microprocessor and a real-time DOS compatible operating system.

The CM52 Remote I/O Module is a general-purpose programmable module that provides an interface between Allen-Bradley Remote I/O Networks and up to two HS500-Series Active RFID Antennas or as many as 32 HMS-Series Reader/Writers, and even bar-code scanners on a MUX32 line. The CM52 can be used to give a remote I/O presence to a wide range of existing equipment, such as bar-code readers, RFID controllers, bar-code verifiers, sensors, and switches.

The CM81 ControlNet Modules are general-purpose programmable interfaces between the ControlNet network and up to two HS/SL500-Series Antennas, or as many as 32 HMS-Series Reader/Writers, RS-Series Readers, or bar-code scanners on a MUX32 line. They offer two general-purpose serial ports and one industrial-level input. The CM81 unit is contained in a NEMA 4 (IP66) enclosure.

The CM900 Automatic ID Module, developed together with AEG Modicon through the ModConnect Partners program, provides ASCII data-handling capabilities for interfacing with Compact and Micro PLCs. The standard program of the CM900 can be configured to work with most serial devices and includes features such as two serial ports for interface to bar-code scanners or other serial devices. This module is C programmable for custom/ unique applications, includes 32 KB of battery-backed RAM, and is compatible with all EMS HS-Series Read/Write RFID Antennas.

The CM1000 Automatic ID PLC Module developed together with AEG Modicon, connects EMS Read/Write RFID Products and bar-code scanners directly to the backplane of Modicon's 800-Series I/O Housings. Eight serial ports on the CM1000 allow direct connection with bar-code scanners or third-party serial interface devices. Other features include three micropro- cessors for maximum performance, 32-KB battery-backed RAM for system storage, a 32-KB EEPROM for program storage, a 32-KB serial buffer, and C language programmability.

The CM1746 RFID Module is specifically designed to integrate our prod- ucts with Allen-Bradley's 1746 I/O backplane and SLC500 PLCs. The CM1746 is mounted in a standard 1746 module enclosure that plugs directly into the 1746 backplane. The CM1746 integrates up to two HS500-Series Antennas, or as many as 32 HMS-Series Reader/Writers, RS-Series Readers, or bar-code scanners on a MUX32 line. This module works with a 386 microprocessor and a real-time DOS compatible operating system.

The MM80 MicroMux Module uses RS232 to RS485 multidrop bus con- troller. It provides the unique advantage of eliminating the need for multiple serial ports. Subsequently, the MicroMux can be quickly configured for network operations, enabling as many as 32 HMS-Series Reader/Writers, RS-Series Readers, or bar-code scanners to be multi-dropped off of one RS232 serial port. Configuration is accomplished via dipswitches and soft- ware commands.

E.2 WHERENET (WWW.WHERENET.COM)

WhereNet offers the following products.

- WhereLAN
- WhereNet Visibility Server Software

WhereNet's WhereLAN Location Sensor and Locating Access Point (LSLAP) comprise Real Time Locating Service (RTLS) 802.11b Wi-Fi infrastructure in a distributed architecture. When configured as a Location Sensor, the device provides distributed RTLS receivers to track assets. The Locating Access Point (LAP) configuration provides RTLS coverage with an integrated wireless LAN access point to connect with mobile workers.

The LSLAPs track a large number of WhereTags simultaneously to ensure location accuracy over a very large coverage area. They forward tag signal information to the WhereNet Visibility Server Software where information can be graphically displayed, used for report generation, or accessed through the Internet.

The LSLAPs communicate with each other and the Visibility via standard wired Ethernet cables or via 802.11b-compliant wireless LANs on the same IT infrastructure. The LAP serves as both as a RTLS Location Sensor and an 802.11b Wi-Fi access point for wireless LAN clients and applications.

WhereNet's Visibility Server Software is an integrated software package that provides all the tools required to effectively manage assets and resources as well as the RTLS. It is a comprehensive package of software that runs on a Microsoft Windows NT and 2000 Server with connection to SQL Server databases. It provides corporations with the ability to exercise control and configuration flexibility from the WhereNet RTLS.

Among Visibility's software components is WhereSoft Locate, which is a distributed Windows Service. When WhereSoft Locate is combined with Visibility and any of the many applications available from WhereNet, it is now possible to locate assets, know their status, and react to any number of user configurable alert conditions. Visibility also provides the tools required to control and monitor the Real-Time Location System. It includes configuration tools, diagnostics, system alerts, an interface manager, and installation tools.

The Alert System allows for e-mail and paging notifications. One of the key components included within Visibility is WhereSoft Launcher providing a single point of entry to all the components of Visibility. Residing as a tray icon, the launcher can be easily accessed and includes the following groups of software modules: Operation, Administration, Diagnostics, Installation, and Documentation.

WhereNet offers a number of applications, which in combination with Visibility, are made to enhance the RTLS system. They include WhereSoft Yard, WhereSoft Container, and WhereSoft Vehicle. Let's take a brief look at each.

WhereSoft Yard is a set of resource management tools for planning, scheduling, and utilization of yard resources. The system enables companies to achieve more efficient movement of trailers and product through supply chains. Common problems such as spoiled cargo, late departures, line shutdowns, and demurrage disputes can be avoided using WhereSoft Yard.

WhereSoft Container is a set of resource management tools for planning, scheduling, and utilization of manufacturing resources. By revolutionizing asset management, WhereSoft Container provides users with the ability to actually see the location and status of their resources on a real-time basis. This "total resource visibility" is the asset management tool, enabling customers to guide their resources throughout supply chains in a more efficient manner.

WhereSoft Vehicle is a set of resource management tools for managing vehicles within a manufacturing and distribution environment. WhereSoft Vehicle allows companies to locate and maintain vehicles in a more efficient manner. Common problems, such as vehicle search times, late deliveries, and shipment quality issues that could affect the efficiency of supply chains can be avoided using WhereSoft Vehicle.

E.3 BLUE VECTOR SYSTEMS (WWW.BLUEVECTORSYSTEMS.COM)

Blue Vector Systems offers these network products:

- X-3000 RFIDrouter
- X-3000 Network Manager Appliance (NMA)
- X-3000 Configuration System

The RFIDrouter™ is the intelligent end-point of the distributed Blue Vector RFID network infrastructure. The RFIDrouter links RFID readers together to create RFID subnets. Its distributed router intelligence makes it possible to deploy large-scale, centrally managed RFID networks. These networks can be used to scale RFID implementations from a single installation to a nationwide deployment. It is self-configuring for new processes, events, and devices.

RFIDrouters controlling certain readers assigned to specific dock doors will receive the new configuration. The RFIDrouter's flexible storage options allow for data buffering in an event of network outages with remote restart functionality. For network design focused on creating reliability and survivability, the RFIDrouter has warm or hot standby functionality allowing it to automatically switch to a redundant set of readers should one set go down.

The RFID NMA enables centralized management and operations by providing a global view of the entire RFID system deployment with the ability to control and modify system parameters centrally. The NMA links RFID subnets created by the RFIDrouter to form a community of RFID domains creating a network infrastructure layer between IT/ERP systems and RFID tags/readers. The NMA's Web-based configuration system allows businesses to convert their physical structures such as dock doors or warehouse shelves into logical entities that can be configured, modified, and outfitted with RFID. The NMA also supports an Application Development Layer to create vertical specific applications that are tightly coupled with Blue Vector's RFID network infrastructure.

The X-3000 RFID Configuration System is a Web-based interface that is launched from the Operations Dashboard. It allows customers to centrally manage and control their RFID network by providing a real-time view and system status of the entire RFID network. The structure of the Dashboard can be customized to suit the needs of the customer.

The RFID Configuration System allows customers to map their actual physical supply chain network into a logical representation that they can RFID-enable. The customers can scale their operations from a single dock door in a warehouse to a nationwide deployment across their supply chain. The RFID Configuration System also allows businesses to convert physical structures such as dock doors or warehouse shelves into logical entities that can be configured, modified, and outfitted with RFID.

The System includes a large library of behaviors that can be readily used to create or modify parameters, assign functionality to certain network elements, or develop new functionality. Functionality such as EPCglobal's ONS and prototype EPC Information Services solution from VeriSign is preintegrated, taking the form of a behavior that can be dragged and dropped into any implementation.

Appendix F

PHYSICAL MARKUP LANGUAGE FOR RFID APPLICATIONS

EPC Network standards consist of Electronic Product Code (EPC) and Physical Markup Language (PML). Whereas the EPC describes how a physical object should be described, PML standardizes the content of messages exchanged between Savant servers and RFID readers (and other sensors), and between Savant/EPC Information Service and an external application, such as Supply Chain Management (SCM).

In the following, we give examples with five XML file instances and two XML schemas in PML format [1].

F.1 XML FILE INSTANCES

We give the following instances to show:

- How a RFID reader reads multiple tags
- How a RFID reader reads the tag ID and data from such a tag
- How a RFID reader reads from the tag ID and data from such a tag with a memory chip
- How data observed by a mounted sensor on the tag is read when such a tag is in the vicinity of a RFID reader
- How a RFID reader reads data in hexbinary format of observations by a sensor

The data in each instance may be captured using PML Core messaging between two PML-enabled systems in the EPC Network system. Data communication in the core messaging can be accomplished as the bridge between Savant and EPC Information Service (EPCIS) or Enterprise Applications in the EPC Network system. These XML Instance files are based on the PML Core schema documented in F.2.

F.1.1 Instance 1: Multiple Tags with No Data

In one example, we show how an RFID reader detects multiple tags and identifies an EPC in each tag.

Listing F.1 RFIDReaderAndTags.xml

```
<?xml version="1.0" encoding="UTF-8"?>
<pmlcore:Sensor
xmlns:pmlcore="urn:autoid:specification:interchange:
PMLCore:xml:schema:1"
xmlns:pmluid="urn:autoid:specification:universal:
Identifier:xml:schema:1"
xmlns:xsi="http://www.w3.org/2001/XMLSchema-instance"
xsi:schemaLocation="urn:autoid:specification:
interchange:PMLCore:xml:schema:1
../SchemaFiles/Interchange/PMLCore.xsd">
    <pmluid:ID>urn:epc:1:4.16.36</pmluid:ID>
    <pmlcore:Observation>
        <pmluid:ID>00000001</pmluid:ID>
        <pmlcore:DateTime>2002-11-06T13:04:34-06:00
        </pmlcore:DateTime>
        <pmlcore:Command>READ_PALLET_TAGS_ONLY</pmlcore:
Command>
    <pmlcore:Tag>
        <pmluid:ID>urn:epc:1:2.24.400</pmluid:ID>
    </pmlcore:Tag>
    <pmlcore:Tag>
        <pmluid:ID>urn:epc:1:2.24.401</pmluid:ID>
    </pmlcore:Tag>
    <pmlcore:Tag>
        <pmluid:ID>urn:epc:1:2.24.402</pmluid:ID>
    </pmlcore:Tag>
    <pmlcore:Tag>
        <pmluid:ID>urn:epc:1:2.24.403</pmluid:ID>
    </pmlcore:Tag>
```

```
    <pmlcore:Tag>
        <pmluid:ID>urn:epc:1:2.24.404</pmluid:ID>
    </pmlcore:Tag>
  </pmlcore:Observation>
 </pmlcore:Sensor>
```

F.1.2 Instance 2: Tags with Data

We give an example of how a reader reads the tag ID and data from such a tag and show how a different identification scheme other than EPC is used.

Listing F.2   RFIDReaderAndTags2NoEPC.xml

```xml
<?xml version="1.0" encoding="UTF-8"?>
<pmlcore:Sensor
xmlns:pmlcore="urn:autoid:specification:interchange:
PMLCore:xml:schema:1"
xmlns:pmluid="urn:autoid:specification:universal:
Identifier:xml:schema:1"
xmlns:xsi="http://www.w3.org/2001/XMLSchema-instance"
xsi:schemaLocation="urn:autoid:specification:
interchange:PMLCore:xml:schema:1
../SchemaFiles/Interchange/PMLCore.xsd">
    <pmluid:ID schemeID="MyScheme" schemeAgencyID=
    "http://sensor.example.org/"
schemeVersionID="v1">10023453</pmluid:ID>
    <pmlcore:Observation>
      <pmlcore:DateTime>2002-11-06T13:04:34-06:00
      </pmlcore:DateTime>
      <pmlcore:Tag>
        <pmluid:ID schemeID="MyScheme"
schemeAgencyID="http://sensor.example.org/"
schemeVersionID="v1">21114444</pmluid:ID>
    </pmlcore:Tag>
    <pmlcore:Tag>
      <pmluid:ID schemeID="MyScheme"
schemeAgencyID="http://sensor.example.org/"
schemeVersionID="v1">21114400</pmluid:ID>
    </pmlcore:Tag>
```

```
        </pmlcore:Observation>
    </pmlcore:Sensor>
```

F.1.3 Instance 3: Memory Tags with Data

The following illustrates how an RFID reader can be used to read from the tag ID and data from such a tag with a memory chip. An example showing how the reader can write data to the tag is excluded.

Listing F.3 RFIDReaderAndTagsWithMemory.xml

```xml
<?xml version="1.0" encoding="UTF-8"?>
<pmlcore:Sensor
xmlns:pmlcore="urn:autoid:specification:interchange:
PMLCore:xml:schema:1"
xmlns:pmluid="urn:autoid:specification:universal:
Identifier:xml:schema:1"
xmlns:xsi="http://www.w3.org/2001/XMLSchema-instance"
xsi:schemaLocation="urn:autoid:specification:
interchange:PMLCore:xml:schema:1
../SchemaFiles/Interchange/PMLCore.xsd">
    <pmluid:ID>urn:epc:1:4.16.36</pmluid:ID>
    <pmlcore:Observation>
        <pmluid:ID>00000001</pmluid:ID>
        <pmlcore:DateTime>2002-11-06T13:04:34-06:00
        </pmlcore:DateTime>
        <pmlcore:Tag>
          <pmluid:ID>210000A8900016F000169DC1</pmluid:ID>
          <pmlcore:Data>
           <pmlcore:XML>
             <EEPROM xmlns="http://sensor.example.org/">
               <FamilyCode>12</FamilyCode>
               <ApplicationIdentifier>123
               </ApplicationIdentifier>
               <Block1>FFA0456F</Block1>
               <Block2>00000000</Block2>
             </EEPROM>
           </pmlcore:XML>
          </pmlcore:Data>
        </pmlcore:Tag>
```

```
          </pmlcore:Observation>
      </pmlcore:Sensor>
```

F.1.4 Instance 4: Tags with Mounted Sensors

Let's suppose a temperature sensor is mounted on an active tag that measures the temperature at certain times and stores the resulting data even when the reader is not in use. Here is the example showing the tag ID and the data observed by the sensor being read once the tag is in the vicinity of the RFID reader.

Listing F.4   RFIDReaderAndTagsWithSensor.xml

```
<?xml version="1.0" encoding="UTF-8"?>
<pmlcore:Sensor
xmlns:pmlcore="urn:autoid:specification:interchange:
PmlCore:xml:schema:v1_0"
xmlns:pmlunv="urn:autoid:specification:universal:
ComplexType:Identifier:xml:schema:v1_0"
xmlns:xsi="http://www.w3.org/2001/XMLSchema-instance"
xsi:schemaLocation="urn:autoid:specification:
interchange:PmlCore:xml:schema:v1_0
PmlCore_1.xsd">
    <pmlunv:ID>urn:epc:1:4.16.36</pmlunv:ID>
    <pmlcore:Observation>
      <pmlunv:ID>00000001</pmlunv:ID>
      <pmlcore:DateTime>2002-11-06T13:04:34-06:00
      </pmlcore:DateTime>
      <pmlcore:Tag>
        <pmlunv:ID>urn:epc:1:2.24.400</pmlunv:ID>
        <pmlcore:Sensor>
          <pmlunv:ID>urn:epc:1:12.8.128</pmlunv:ID>
          <pmlcore:Observation>
            <pmlcore:DateTime>2002-11-06T11:00:00-
06:00</pmlcore:DateTime>
              <pmlcore:Data>
                <pmlcore:XML>
                  <TemperatureReading
xmlns="http://sensor.example.org/">
                    <Unit>Celsius</Unit>
```

```
                    <Value>5.3</Value>
                  </TemperatureReading>
                </pmlcore:XML>
              </pmlcore:Data>
            </pmlcore:Observation>
            <pmlcore:Observation>
              <pmlcore:DateTime>2002-11-06T12:00:00-
  06:00</pmlcore:DateTime>
                <pmlcore:Data>
                  <pmlcore:XML>
                    <TemperatureReading
  xmlns="http://sensor.example.org/">
                      <Unit>Celsius</Unit>
                      <Value>5.3</Value>
                    </TemperatureReading>
                  </pmlcore:XML>
                </pmlcore:Data>
              </pmlcore:Observation>
            </pmlcore:Sensor>
          </pmlcore:Tag>
        </pmlcore:Observation>
  </pmlcore:Sensor>
```

F.1.5 Instance 5: Observed Data in Hexbinary Format

The following shows how an RFID reader can read observations made by
a sensor and can be represented in hexbinary format.

```
<pmlcore:Sensor
xmlns:pmlcore="urn:autoid:specification:interchange:
PMLCore:xml:schema:1"
xmlns:pmluid="urn:autoid:specification:universal:
Identifier:xml:schema:1"
xmlns:xsi="http://www.w3.org/2001/XMLSchema-instance"
xsi:schemaLocation="urn:autoid:specification:
interchange:PMLCore:xml:schema:1
../SchemaFiles/Interchange/PMLCore.xsd">
    <pmluid:ID>urn:epc:1:4.16.36</pmluid:ID>
    <pmlcore:Observation>
      <pmlcore:DateTime>2002-11-06T13:04:34-06:00
      </pmlcore:DateTime>
```

```
    <pmlcore:Data>
<pmlcore:Binary>0FB8A0F5CB0F11000FB8A0F5CB0F11000FB8A0F5CB0
F1100</pmlcore:Binary>
    </pmlcore:Data>
  </pmlcore:Observation>
</pmlcore:Sensor>
```

F.2 XML SCHEMAS

The XML Instance file examples in Section F.1 are based on the following two PML Core schemas [1]. The first schema, PmlCore, imports the second schema, Identifier.

Listing F.5 PmlCore.xsd

```
<?xml version="1.0" encoding="UTF-8"?>
<schema
targetNamespace="urn:autoid:specification:
interchange:PMLCore:xml:schema:1"
xmlns="http://www.w3.org/2001/XMLSchema"
xmlns:autoid="http://www.autoidcenter.org/2003/xml"
xmlns:pmlcore="urn:autoid:specification:interchange:
PMLCore:xml:schema:1"
xmlns:pmluid="urn:autoid:specification:universal:
Identifier:xml:schema:1"
elementFormDefault="qualified"
attributeFormDefault="unqualified" version="1.0">
    <import namespace="urn:autoid:specification:
    universal:Identifier:xml:schema:1"
schemaLocation="../Universal/Identifier.xsd"/>
    <annotation>
      <documentation>
        <autoid:copyright>Copyright ©2003 Auto-ID Center.
All Rights Reserved.</autoid:copyright>
        <autoid:disclaimer>Auto-ID Center, its members,
officers, directors, employees, or agents shall not be
liable for any injury, loss, damages, financial or
otherwise, arising from, related to, or caused by the
use of this document. The use of said document shall
constitute your express consent to the foregoing
exculpation.</autoid:disclaimer>
        <autoid:program>Auto-ID version 1.0</autoid:program>
```

```
    <autoid:purpose>PML Core Specification version
1.0</autoid:purpose>
  </documentation>
 </annotation>
 <element name="Sensor" type="pmlcore:SensorType"/>
 <complexType name="AnyXMLContentType">
   <annotation>
     <documentation>
       <autoid:definition>The AnyXMLContentType
provides localized openess </autoid:definition>
     </documentation>
   </annotation>
   <sequence>
     <any namespace="##any" processContents="skip">
       <annotation>
         <documentation>
           <autoid:definition>Any content</autoid:
definition>
         </documentation>
       </annotation>
     </any>
   </sequence>
</complexType>
   <complexType name="DataType">
     <annotation>
       <documentation>
         <autoid:definition>The Data element holds
text, binary or XML data.</autoid:definition>
       </documentation>
     </annotation>
     <choice>
       <element name="Text" type="string">
         <annotation>
           <documentation>
             <autoid:definition>Text value</autoid:
definition>
           </documentation>
         </annotation>
```

```
      </element>
      <element name="Binary" type="hexBinary">
        <annotation>
          <documentation>
            <autoid:definition>Binary value</autoid:
definition>
          </documentation>
        </annotation>
      </element>
      <element name="XML" type="pmlcore:
AnyXMLContentType">
        <annotation>
          <documentation>
            <autoid:definition>The XML element holds any
XML elements the instance author would like to include.
It is provided to enable localized openness and to allow
instance document authors to create instance documents
containing elements above and beyond what is specified
by the PML CORE schema</autoid:definition>
          </documentation>
        </annotation>
      </element>
    </choice>
  </complexType>
  <complexType name="ObservationType">
    <annotation>
      <documentation>
        <autoid:definition>Information related to an
observation/measurement by a sensor in the EPC Network.
Observations represent measurements by the sensor.
They associate the actual observed data with the sensor.
</autoid:definition>
      </documentation>
    </annotation>
    <sequence>
      <element ref="pmluid:ID" minOccurs="0">
        <annotation>
          <documentation>
```

```
                <autoid:definition>The observation ID element
is a number assigned to this specific observation.
</autoid:definition>
                </documentation>
            </annotation>
        </element>
        <element name="DateTime" type="dateTime">
            <annotation>
                <documentation>
                    <autoid:definition>The Observation DateTime
element denotes the date and time stamp when the observation
was made.</autoid:definition>
                </documentation>
            </annotation>
        </element>
        <element name="Command" type="string"
minOccurs="0">
            <annotation>
                <documentation>
                    <autoid:definition>The observation command
element denotes the command was issued to the sensor to
trigger the observation.</autoid:definition>
                </documentation>
            </annotation>
        </element>
        <element name="Tag" type="pmlcore:TagType"
minOccurs="0"
maxOccurs="unbounded">
            <annotation>
                <documentation>
                    <autoid:definition>The Observation Tag element
denotes tags observed by a sensor as part of the observa-
tion.</autoid:definition>
                </documentation>
            </annotation>
        </element>
        <element name="Data" type="pmlcore:DataType"
minOccurs="0"
maxOccurs="unbounded">
            <annotation>
```

```
      <documentation>
            <autoid:definition>The Observation Data
element denotes any data captured by the sensors as part
of the observation.</autoid:definition>
            </documentation>
         </annotation>
      </element>
   </sequence>
</complexType>
<complexType name="SensorType">
   <annotation>
      <documentation>
            <autoid:definition>Information related to a
sensor in the EPC Network. A sensor is any device that
is capable of making measurements, e.g., RFID readers,
temperature sensors, humidity sensors.</autoid:definition>
            </documentation>
         </annotation>
         <sequence>
            <element ref="pmluid:ID">
               <annotation>
                  <documentation>
                        <autoid:definition>The Sensor ID element
is the number assigned to this particular sensor in the
EPC network. It is by default an EPC. If a different
identification scheme is to be used, the identification
scheme must be specified using the attributes of the
identifier type.</autoid:definition>
                     </documentation>
                  </annotation>
               </element>
            <element name="Observation" type="
pmlcore:ObservationType"
maxOccurs="unbounded">
                  <annotation>
                     <documentation>
                        <autoid:definition>The Sensor Observation
element denotes observations/measurements made by this
particular sensor.</autoid:definition>
                        </documentation>
```

```
            </annotation>
          </element>
        </sequence>
      </complexType>
      <complexType name="TagType">
        <annotation>
          <documentation>
            <autoid:definition>Information related to a
tag in the EPC Network. A tag is any electronic or
nonelectronic device that carries at least an identifier.
</autoid:definition>
          </documentation>
        </annotation>
        <sequence>
          <element ref="pmluid:ID">
            <annotation>
              <documentation>
                <autoid:definition>The Tag ID element is
a unique number assigned to the tag.</autoid:definition>
              </documentation>
            </annotation>
          </element>
          <element name="Data" type="pmlcore:DataType"
minOccurs="0">
            <annotation>
              <documentation>
                <autoid:definition>The Tag Data element
contains any data stored on the tag.</autoid:definition>
              </documentation>
            </annotation>
          </element>
          <element ref="pmlcore:Sensor" minOccurs="0"
maxOccurs="unbounded">
            <annotation>
              <documentation>
                <autoid:definition>The Tag Sensor ele-
ment denotes any sensor that is mounted on the tag
</autoid:definition>
              </documentation>
```

```
        </annotation>
      </element>
    </sequence>
  </complexType>
</schema>
```

Listing F.6 Identifier.xsd

```
<?xml version="1.0" encoding="UTF-8"?>
<schema targetNamespace="urn:autoid:specification:
universal:Identifier:xml:schema:1"
xmlns:pmluid="urn:autoid:specification:universal:
Identifier:xml:schema:1"
xmlns:autoid="http://www.autoidcenter.org/2003/xml"
xmlns="http://www.w3.org/2001/XMLSchema"
elementFormDefault="qualified" attributeFormDe-
fault="unqualified" version="1.0">
  <annotation>
    <documentation>
      <documentation>
        <autoid:copyright>Copyright ©2003 Auto-ID Center,
All Rights Reserved.</autoid:copyright>
        <autoid:disclaimer>Auto-ID Center, its members,
officers, directors, employees, or agents shall not be
liable for any injury, loss, damages, financial or oth-
erwise, arising from, related to, or caused by the use
of this document. The use of said document shall constitute
your express consent to the foregoing exculpation.
</autoid:disclaimer>
        <autoid:program>Auto-ID version 1.0
</autoid:program>
        <autoid:purpose>PML Core Specification version
1.0</autoid:purpose>
      </documentation>
    </documentation>
  </annotation>
  <element name="ID" type="pmluid:IdentifierType"/>
  <annotation>
    <documentation>
      <autoid:definition>A reusable element of type
'IdentifierType'</autoid:definition>
```

```
        </documentation>
     </annotation>
     <complexType name="IdentifierType">
        <annotation>
           <documentation>
              <autoid:definition>A character string to identify
and distinguish uniquely, one instance of an object in an
identification scheme from all other objects within the
same scheme</autoid:definition>
           </documentation>
        </annotation>
        <simpleContent>
           <extension base="token">
              <attribute name="schemeID" type="token"
use="optional">
                 <annotation>
                    <documentation>
                       <autoid:definition>The identifier of the
identification scheme</autoid:definition>
                    </documentation>
                 </annotation>
              </attribute>
              <attribute name="schemeAgencyID" type="token"
use="optional">
                 <annotation>
                    <documentation>
                       <autoid:definition>The identifier of the
agency that maintains the identification
scheme</autoid:definition>
                    </documentation>
                 </annotation>
              </attribute>
              <attribute name="schemeVersionID" type="token"
use="optional">
                 <annotation>
                    <documentation>
                       <autoid:definition>The version of the
identification scheme</autoid:definition>
                    </documentation>
```

```
        </annotation>
      </attribute>
      <attribute name="schemeURI" type="anyURI"
use="optional">
        <annotation>
          <documentation>
            <autoid:definition>The Uniform Resource
Identifier that identifies where the Identification Scheme
is located</autoid:definition>
          </documentation>
        </annotation>
      </attribute>
    </extension>
  </simpleContent>
  </complexType>
 </schema>
```

REFERENCES

1. Floerkemier, Christian, Dipan Anarkat, Ted Osinski, and Mark Harrison, "PML Core Specification 1.0 (Recommended)," *Auto-ID Center*, 15 September 2003.

Appendix G

WAREHOUSE MANAGEMENT SYSTEMS

Companies offering Warehouse Management Systems (WMSs) include RT-Systems' RT-LOCATOR, Robocom, HighJump, KARE Technologies, and Daly Commerce.

G.1 RT-SYSTEMS: RT-LOCATOR

RT-Systems started its warehouse management system (WMS) called RT LOCATOR, on DOS platforms, migrated to UNIX-based systems, and now offer Windows-based SQL applications using PowerBuilder to build them.

RT LOCATOR provides WMS tools for receiving, putaway, inventory control, order fulfillment, data collection, RFID, pick bin replenishment, automated worker direction, cycle counting, customized reports, and communications with a host computer. The following is a list of industries in which RT-Systems have implemented.

- Automotive suppliers
- Auto assembly component sequencing
- Consumer goods manufacturing
- Education supplies distribution
- Government publication distribution
- Lawn and garden supplies distribution, and chemical manufacturing
- Food manufacturing
- Foodservice distribution
- Office supplies distribution
- Printing services distribution

G.2 ROBOCOM

RIMS® (Robocom's Inventory Management System) is an off-the-shelf WMS that integrates with E-commerce/E-business front ends and provides visibility into a warehouse and overall supply chain of which it is a part. This system operates in an open system environment and interfaces with an organization's existing information systems infrastructure. It runs on UNIX, Windows NT, Windows 2000, Linux, and Sun OS, and provides host interfaces with QAD's MFG/PRO, SAP, Baan, other ERP and legacy systems, and XML documents or transaction-based interfaces. It offers the capability of monitoring the flow of material in and out of a warehouse, as well as tracking current stock.

RIMS is a user-friendly, menu-driven application designed to satisfy the requirements of virtually any warehouse operation from a simple paper-driven VDT (Video Display Terminal) system, to a paperless RDT (Radio Data Terminal) system. This system optionally integrates with external material handling devices (carousels, conveyors, and so on), any of which might use RFID scanning for verification and tracking. In addition to RF devices and bar-code scanners, it interfaces with:

- Conveyors
- Sortation systems
- Label applicators
- Automated Storage and Retrieval Systems (AS/RS)
- Carousels
- Automated Guides Vehicles (AGV)
- Voice technology
- Pick-to-light
- Transportation systems
- Crystal Reports
- RIMS.Alert
- RIMS.Vision

RIMS will continue to evolve with technological and functional refinements. Robocom's maintenance customers benefit from upgrading to the latest release and using functional enhancements that are generally built into the standard offering. Its many features and functions of RIMS can be categorized as follows.

- Management control
- Inbound
- Inventory management
- Outbound
- RDT subsystem
- Other RIMS modules

Let's take a look at each category.

G.2.1 Management Control

This feature is concerned with the management control of security and system parameters. It provides history/archiving, QA/item status, and compliance labels. While the inventory changes, RIMS gives a reason code or two. ABC tracking, product class groupings, and workload planning are some of other things that fall under the category of management control.

G.2.2 Inbound

Inbound is of two types: receiving and putaway. The receiving inbound type is concerned with:

■ Purchase orders, returns, ASNs, blind receipts
■ Variable pack sizes
■ Lot-controlled/serialization
■ Cross cocking

The putaway inbound type is concerned with directed putaway, stored as received/staged after receipt, and cross docking.

G.2.3 Inventory Management

This feature involves inventory counting, re-warehousing, quality assurance, and reports. Inventory counting is of three types: cycle counting, physical inventory, and opportunistic counting whereas re-warehousing can be automatic or manual replenishment or demand replenishment by order or by item re-branding. Quality assurance is concerned with user-defined QA status and optional default QA for returns.

G.2.4 Outbound

Picking and packing/shipping are the two major outbound features. Outbound picking includes the following.

■ Batch/order/wave picking
■ Metering product to production lines/work centers
■ Bill of material/kitting
■ FIFO/LIFO or FEFO/LEFO
■ Pick priorities/requested lots/operators assignments
■ Stage/load in reverse delivery sequence
■ RIMS/host backorders

Outbound picking is concerned with:

- Hierarchical innerpacks/outerpacks
- Interface to carrier label/shipping systems
- Compliance labeling
- Serialized Shipping Container Codes (SSCC)
- Fluid loading
- ASN generation
- Shipping documents

G.2.5 RDT Subsystem

This feature pertains to any hardware (e.g., truck-mounted or handheld), real-time and on-board/network printers.

G.2.6 Other RIMS Modules

They include interfaces, toolkit, RIMS Hostlink, RIMS Chainlink, RIMS.Voice, RIMS.Alert, and RIMS.Vision. These interface modules fall into the following groups.

- Generic
  - ASCII file data transfer
  - Defined transaction layouts
  - Triggered by changes to inventory
- Dedicated certified interface to QAD's MFG/PRO
- Certified to interface with SAP R/3

The toolkit module contains a RIMS customization utility and has the capability to change field names and lengths, and screen position as well and to hide unused fields. The RIMS Hostlink works with XML API and has the capability of consolidating multiple transactions in a single document, receiving and sending data elements and handling variable field lengths. The Chainlink module, on the other hand, works with the XML API tool for interfaces from other systems, allows visibility of information without logging on a RIMS system, and is capable of adding a link to a Web page.

RIMS.Voice provides voice-directed picking, interfaces to Vocollect's Talkman, and stand-alone RIMS picking. It is in combination with RIMS RDT/paper-based picking and translatable to any language. RIMS.Alert interfaces with RIMS or any other system and receives alertable event information via XML documents. It provides predefined alert messages to predefined recipient(s) and can communicate throughout entire enterprise or to a separate external system. RIMS.Vision uses Blueprint of Warehouse, interfaces with RIMS via XML documents, and displays RIMS information graphically on Blueprint.

G.3 HIGHJUMP

HighJump's WMS contains these components:

- Warehouse Advantage
- Advantage Fulfillment Optimizer
- Slotting Advantage
- Container Advantage

Warehouse Advantage is the core of the WMS, providing intelligent work direction (RF-directed processes) and detailed audit trail. Advantage Fulfillment Optimizer provides an interface with Warehouse Advantage and consolidation and sequencing of multiple orders into truckloads or waves. It also provides real-time update of total weight and volume, and other metrics related to a wave or shipment for multi-users.

Slotting Advantage works well with the environment of frequently reconfiguring fulfillment to meet changing demands from customers, and is fully integrated with warehouse operations. This provides the capability to reslot a warehouse or distribution center without the time-consuming changes to a slotting plan for the Warehouse Advantage with the goal of optimizing warehouse layout, material handling, and space efficiency. Slotting Advantage provides tools to analyze product history, demand, lead time, velocity, and special handling situations. The analytic results are then used to compute bin size and location for a given product based on the required service level with the required service level within the available physical space. More advanced algorithms may be used to determine the most efficient material flow paths and reorder points for each product.

Container Advantage comes into play when changes in order profiles are driving more full-case and split-case picking, and rules surrounding carton and pallet builds are getting more complex. It has the capability of selecting the number and size of cartons needed to pack orders for shipment based on each item's dimensional cube, orientation restrictions, stacking factors, weight, and compatibility with other items. Container Advantage permits configurable constraints to reduce shipping damage (and returns) and prevent worker injury.

G.4 KARE TECHNOLOGIES

KARE Technologies' Visual Warehouse utilizes RF handheld terminals to perform all warehouse functions, enabling real-time data collection and validation. It operates as a stand-alone system, or can work in conjunction with your existing enterprise system. Unlike other WMSs, Visual Warehouse comes in a modular design to permit automation of tasks that you only need, such as:

- Receiving, putaway
- Order picking, packing, and shipping
- Physical inventory and cycle count
- Replenishment

Let's take a look at each task.

The Receiving module lets you track the receipt of material from vendors or from internal production operations. Received material is immediately available to fill customer orders. Material may be set aside for crossdock, received directly to a storage location, or placed in a temporary staging location to be handled later with the Putaway transaction.

The Putaway module is used to move material from staged receiving locations to final storage locations. Based on system configuration, material may be moved to prime locations, locations holding like items, or empty locations in a certain system-directed or user-specified sequence.

The Picking module provides an extremely flexible and efficient method for picking orders without any paperwork. Among the options are order picking, group picking, and zone picking. Orders may be picked by priority or user-defined type (customer order, production order, and so on). The Packing and Shipping modules are used to box, verify, and ship orders that have been picked.

The Physical Inventory and Cycle Count module can be used to verify inventory for a specific item or location, or it can be used to perform a complete physical inventory. Cycle counts may be performed in user-directed and system-directed modes. Inventory discrepancies may be corrected automatically and immediately, or they may be flagged for later review.

The Replenishment module lets you move material from bulk storage to forward pick locations that are running low on material. As an on-hand quantity falls below the defined minimum, Visual Warehouse creates a replenishment requirement for that item and location.

G.5 DALY COMMERCE

Daly Commerce's WMS has four components: warehouse management, shipyard management, RF component, and value-added service. The warehouse management component aims at managing warehouse receiving, put-away, moving, replenishment, counting, picking, packing, and shipping. The shipyard management focuses on shipyard integration. Rate, ship, and manifest customer orders on as many as eleven major small parcel carriers can be done at one time.

The RF component allows the receipt, movement, and tracking of inventory using a handheld or vehicle-mounted radio receiver. The value-added service component supports light manufacturing operations in both Made-to-Stock and Made-to-Order environments. It may be used for assembly/disassembly, in-house repair/refurbishment, and other value-added operations.

Appendix H

SUPPLY CHAIN EXECUTION SYSTEMS

Companies offering Supply Chain Execution Systems (SCEs) include HighJump, Provia, Softeon, ClearOrbit, and PeopleSoft.

H.1 HIGHJUMP

HighJump's RFID technology-enabled SCE product suite includes solutions for warehouse management, yard management, transportation management, supply chain visibility, event management, trading partner enablement/collaboration, automated data collection, mobile solutions, and system integration. We have already covered warehouse management advantages and take a brief look at other aspects of the product suite.

Yard Advantage facilitates the exchange of real-time information across the enterprise on mobile computing devices to enable managers in prioritizing even the busiest yards with accurate data. Whether implemented as a stand-alone module or as part of a wider warehouse management or supply chain execution solution, Yard Advantage accomplishes operational efficiency by coordinating and optimizing physical product movement as it arrives in the yard, and is introduced into the warehouse or distribution center, and as it departs from the yard.

Transportation Advantage performs detailed route analysis and optimization to help ensure orders are shipped more efficiently and faster. It includes an option to provide your carriers with a self-service Web portal for tendering and tracking responses. Transportation Advantage provides flexible tracking and proof of delivery requests and responses and comes with two components: Parcel Manifesting and International Trade Documentation.

Parcel Manifesting leverages Clippership®'s Windows-based functionality to manage your multi-carrier requirements, including E-manifesting, compliance label generation, and countless reporting capabilities. Clippership performs rate shopping to determine optimal shipment rates and routing. Parcel Manifesting organizes vendor compliance requirements to help eliminate noncompliance penalties on a daily basis.

Supply Chain Visibility provides two levels of password-protected visibility: order visibility via Customer Service Advantage and management visibility via Advantage Dashboard. Using Customer Service Advantage's password-protected Web portal, you can access order life-cycle information to take advantage of its demand-planning capabilities. What this means is that the customers can access real-time on the status of their orders, such as order receipt, time to delivery, picking status, and shipping information: all done via the Web. Customer Service Advantage acts a secure portal through which customers, partners, and customer service personnel can access information based on the privileges assigned to them. All Web pages can be viewed on wireless PDA devices.

With Advantage Dashboard, managers and executives need visibility to updated data about inventory levels, order volumes, order status, and employee productivity, so they can make real-time decisions. As is Customer Advantage, it is a Web-based portal that they can access over the Internet or corporate intranet. It can be viewed on wireless PDA devices.

Event Advantage focuses on providing intelligent notification of and response to the events in one part of the supply chain as they occur. It provides proactive alerts by measuring and monitoring supply chain processes for exceptions and bottlenecks. Communications means to receive the alerts include phone, fax, numeric pager, and e-mail. Event Advantage can be implemented as either a stand-alone module or as part of a wider warehouse management or supply chain execution solution.

Trading Partner Enablement/Collaboration provides the suppliers, carriers, and customers with a range of collaboration capabilities from a simple Web portal collaboration to complete supply chain information synchronization. All aim at reducing inventory carrying costs and stock-outs. This is accomplished through:

- Collaborative inventory management via Collaboration Advantage
- Supplier execution management via Supplier Advantage
- Customer order visibility via Customer Service Advantage

With Collaboration Advantage, you can avoid supply chain inventory exceptions, increase fill rates and forecast upcoming demand spikes for suppliers. Supplier Advantage aims at increasing the speed of receiving operations. Through the portal, your suppliers are able to acknowledge purchase orders, enter shipping information, and generate item and Advance Shipping Notice (ASN) labels. Customer Service Advantage provides customers the order status and inventory information they want. All Web pages can be viewed on wireless PDA devices.

Data Collection Advantage is a RFID-enabled data collection solution that can be integrated into PeopleSoft, Oracle, MAPICS, SAP, and any other ERP system thus automating inventory tracking, picking, putaway, and other aspects of business improvement processes.

Data Collection Advantage for PeopleSoft offers PeopleSoft-certified data collection solution for the PeopleSoft Manufacturing, Inventory, and Purchasing applications (versions 7.5 and 8). Most common transactions can be entered into PDAs that in turn send the results to PeopleSoft. Data Collection Advantage for PeopleSoft Transactions offers the options shown in Table H.1.

Data Collection Advantage for Oracle ERP leverages real-time information exchange, often reducing transaction time by 80 percent. Integrated into Oracle ERP's standard interfaces and APIs, it can be used for Work In Process (WIP), Inventory Control, Order Management, Purchasing, and Quality. It works with Oracle 10.7 or 11.0 and easily migrates to 11i later on with few or no interfaces.

More than HighJump's 30 preconfigured transactions are available that you can modify or extend existing transaction suites using personalized menus with no programming experience. Oracle's stored procedures help ensure continuous data capture when Oracle is down and eliminates re-entry of data after network failures.

Data Collection Advantage for SAP ERP deals with the issue of data entry on the shop floor by connecting material handling and shop floor personnel to the enterprise R/3 system. Many shop floor or material handling

Table H.1   Data Collection Advantage Options

Purchase order receipts	Shipping container management
Advanced shipping notification receipts	Physical inventories
Inter-unit business receipts	Container management
Putaway confirmation	Single and multiple output completions
Picking confirmation	Scrap reporting
Shipping confirmation	Flow manufacturing
Inventory adjustments	Production picking confirmation
Cycle counts	Kit issues
Bin-to-bin transfers	

procedures are unique to the company. Many companies have special operational requirements that are not easily met by R/3. Data Collection Advantage for SAP ERP fills in the gaps by providing SAP with the data while keeping the R/3 system intact.

Data Collection Advantage for MANAGE 2000 allows data collection from the warehouse and shop floor and real-time visibility of production conditions for managers and decision makers.

Here are some MANAGE 2000 transaction sets included in the Data Collection Advantage for MANAGE 2000.

- Time and attendance
- Labor tracking (direct, indirect, and repetitive)
- Receiving (work order, purchase order, repetitive production, repetitive group order, cash receipts)
- Sales order shipment
- Work order issues
- Material moves (planned)
- Unplanned physical inventories/cycle counts
- Miscellaneous adjustments
- Stock inquiries

Data Collection Advantage for other ERPs can extend the functionality of any type of ERP system on the market with the data collection you can configure. You can use menu-driven screens to meet your application needs and it allows you to leverage the power of the Internet to capture and view data anywhere.

Shop floor visibility is accomplished with Vision Information Station that allows you to view, collect, and report manufacturing information from a single source. As a PC-based extension to Data Collection Advantage, Vision IS enhances shop floor operations through paperless data collection, one-touch information access, and hardware integration. You will be able to see all the information you need quickly and accurately, such as CAD drawings, order information, and operating instructions.

Vision IS can be deployed over existing LAN/WAN infrastructure and interfaced with other systems. It facilitates real-time information sharing with back-office databases and allows customization of each Vision workstation to match each worker's needs.

HighJump's mobile solutions provide stand-alone data collection applications that optimize inventory management, provide overall business process improvement, and extend HighJump's supply chain execution suite with both connected and disconnected applications. They provide three advantages: proof of delivery, asset inventory management, and remote replenishment. We now take a look at each.

Delivery Advantage is a Pocket PC-based application that directs and confirms deliveries and pick-ups for internal (campus) or external (route/customer) packages, and provides last mile tracking to extend visibility of products within the supply chain. It gives many businesses the visibility and control within their delivery and pick-up processes. Delivery Advantage guides delivery and pick-up personnel through their route, allowing them to confirm package pick-up/drop-off and capture signatures to confirm activity completion.

Asset Advantage manages asset inventories with flexible, efficient counting processes. It is a batch-automated data collection solution for companies with ERP already in place and runs on a handheld device. Asset Advantage also records asset transfers, performs asset additions, and records asset attribute changes.

Par Inventory Advantage automates and manages replenishment inventories for remote storage locations (carts, trucks, etc.). It offers multiple replenishment options and reduces counting time, eliminating paper-based processes, and improving replenishment accuracy. This HighJump software also manages cart inventories in industries such as healthcare and trucking where the scope of replenishment is contained on a mobile "container." It utilizes menu-driven screens and handheld PDA terminals to direct users through the entire counting process, providing continual work direction and verification that help ensure data accuracy at every step.

Advantage Link aims at integrating Web-based solutions with enterprise and E-commerce applications and between business and order fulfillment systems. It supports the following methods: ODBC, flat file, XML, Oracle Open Interface, TCP/IP sockets, AS/400 On-Line, Advantage Link for PeopleSoft, Advantage Link for SAP, and IBM MQ Series. In addition, certified interfaces include PeopleSoft, MAPICS, Oracle, and SAP.

Although not part of the HighJump supply chain execution suite, RFID Configuration gives you the option to flexibly deploy RFID or bar codes at multiple points within the supply chain through:

- RFID Compliance via Compliance Advantage
- RFID-Enabled Warehouse Management
- RFID-Enabled Container and Asset Tracking
- RFID-Enabled Container, Asset Tracking via Tracking Advantage
- RFID-Enabled Data Collection

Compliance Advantage™ offers you the ability to comply with current mandates from retailers such as Wal-Mart and the Department of Defense while easily adapting to future requirements. This solution can be implemented on either a stand-alone basis or in conjunction with your existing fulfillment systems to tag items, cases, and pallets, as well as generate accurate advance shipping notices for your customers.

RFID-Enabled Warehouse Management has extended its Warehouse Advantage to include Electronic Product Code (EPC) compliance as well as workflows that support RFID. Customers now have the option of selecting which activities they want to perform with RFID, bar codes, or both.

Tracking Advantage provides tracking for returnable containers and other high-value assets in closed-loop environments. In addition to hands-free recognition of inbound and outbound containers, Tracking Advantage offers Internet-based visibility of these assets throughout the supply chain. Through Data Collection Advantage, manufacturers can now track work in process and finished goods with RFID technology, which is especially important for tracking items in lots or by serial number.

H.2 PROVIA

Provia's ViaWare suite of supply chain execution solutions includes ware-housing, transportation, order, and yard management products seamlessly integrated together with Web-based visibility tools to create a real-time order-to-delivery fulfillment solution. The heightened level of visibility turns data into information, information into knowledge, and knowledge into a competitive advantage.

ViaWare WMS manages the real-world change in your distribution environment by improving inventory accuracy, maximizing space utilization, and increasing labor performance whereas ViaWare TMS auto-mates and optimizes the difficult and time-consuming processes associated with truckload and LTL (Less-Than-Truckload) shipping. Via Ware SPS (Small Parcel) automates the difficult and time-consuming pro-cesses associated with parcel shipping and ViaWare OMS (Order Man-agement) for third-party logistics (3PL) providers manages products, orders, shipments, and delivery information by customer for multi-client environments. ViaWare YMS (Yard Management) extends the warehouse beyond the physical four walls by controlling the activities of trailers on the dock and in the yard.

H.3 SOFTEON

Softeon's Enterprise Logistics Information Technology (ELITE) is a supply chain management system built on a scalable, Web-based architecture that provides maximum application portability and reusability. Its open XML-based Web services architecture allows integration with existing legacy system(s). ELITE provides reports in multiple formats, each of which can be distributed though e-mail.

The ELITE Modules include:

- Warehouse Management System (WMS)
- Order Management System (OMS)
- Distribution Management System (DMS)
- Forecast Management System (FMS)
- Resource Management System (RMS)
- Assembly and Kitting Management System (AMS)
- Transportation Management System (TMS)
- Yard Management (YMS)

The WMS offers robust, flexible, real-time warehouse management functionality and provides complete control over every aspect of warehouse operations, from location management to receiving/putaway operations as well as inventory control. The graphical warehouse layout tools allow real-time inventory visibility and user-defined queries to view and manage inventory.

Here are some other key features of WMS:

- Real-time graphical view of warehouse inventory
- Flexible location management
- Planned and blind receiving with ASN, PO interface
- User-defined putaway rules
- Staged putaway
- Cross-docking
- Inventory tracking by license plate, lot number, expiration date, and so on
- SKU-level FIFO/LIFO/FIFO/LIFO methodologies with user overrides
- Inventory hold/reservations
- Rule-based flexible replenishment
- Returns processing
- Cycle count and physical inventory
- Extensive transaction audit trail
- Role-based security model
- Powerful, user-friendly query screens
- Productivity analysis/reporting

The OMS is an order entry and processing system that provides complete control of each stage of the order process, including order entry, pricing and promotion, credit processing, allocation, and shipment invoicing. The OMS interface supports extensive tax calculation using software like Taxware®. The OMS module can be installed by itself or with any combination of other ELITE modules.

The ELITE Distribution Management System uses optimal, accurate fulfillment processes to pick and ship orders to customers in a timely manner. Functionality ranges from inventory control, shipping, and accounting to order fulfillment and tracking. It is also integrated with voice picking and RFID and provides full support for various material-handling equipment such as ASRS, conveyor, and pick-to-light.

The FMS allows users to predict future orders and budgets, as well as measure forecast accuracy. By providing an accurate forecast, the correct products and quantities can be available to meet sales demand. Adequate production or purchasing can then be scheduled, leading to a reduction in out-of-stocks as well as lower costs to the customer. FMS supports a variety of forecasting methods and statistical models. Here are other key features:

- Multiple levels of forecasting: Stock Keeping Unit (SKU), SKU group, region
- Planning for multiple ranges of time (week, month, quarter, year, etc.)
- Multiple statistical methods: regression, smoothing and seasonal smoothing
- Import and export of forecast data from external sources
- Roll-forward forecast data
- Forecast versus actual analysis
- Comparison analysis
- Month-end processing to freeze forecast data
- Graphical and textual representation through visual tools
- User/group-level security

The RMS gives you control of your material-handling equipment and labor. Its seamless interfaces to the Order and Distribution Management Systems give you graphical tools that provide you the information needed to determine which orders can be released and where labor is needed, and can warn you of pending overtime conditions. Here are other key features:

- Task and activity definition
- Task time and cost definition
- Resource allocation and tracking
- Resource estimation/simulation
- Real time resource activity visibility
- "What if" analysis
- Track the time needed for various tasks (gauging productivity)
- Resource cost estimation (including overtime)
- Actual versus plan analysis

The ELITE Assembly & Kitting System (AMS) uses a bill of materials to define the relevant items to be assembled or kitted, and can also automatically generate purchase orders for raw materials. The advanced material requirement-planning tool helps to analyze the material requirements of finished goods. AMS allows extensive planning and control features thorough project or program planning, product costing, work order management, and actual versus plan analysis. Other key features include:

- Project/program planning
- Bill of materials management
- Work order management
- Requirements planning
- Line production management
- Inventory control and replenishment
- Activity-based costing
- Actual versus plan analysis
- Allocation of SKUs for assembly
- Purchase order generation for raw materials needed, either manually or automatically
- Unused SKUs (due to cancellation of work orders) are returned to the warehouse
- Defective SKUs can be returned to vendor
- De-kitting

The TMS optimizes the inbound/outbound process through planning, execution, and visibility. The planning tool provides functionality for automated carrier selection, routing, and opportunity-for-shipment consolidation. The execution tool provides functionality for carrier-compliant labels, shipment documents, export documents, and EDI/XML interfaces. Real-time reporting for carrier performance analysis, carrier cost comparison, and shipment tracking allows for analysis and visibility functionality. Here are other key features:

- Carrier rates by zones
- Automated routing to select best carrier and load type (LTL, TL, etc.)
- Shipment consolidation based on carrier contracts, rates, and tariffs
- Zone skipping
- Multi-carrier, multi-leg, multi-stop
- Pooled shipments
- Rate calculation based on route/zones, rate contracts (discounts), and so on
- "What if" analysis for alternate hubs/carriers, and so on
- Carrier-compliant labels
- Shipping documents

- Shipment manifest
- Export documents
- Hazmat labels
- Exchange BOL, freight invoice, shipment status with carriers through EDI/XML
- Shipment status and tracking
- Carrier performance analysis
- Cost comparison

The YMS offers accurate management of the trailers and containers in your shipping yard. YMS handles every yard-related function, including appointment scheduling, trailer check-in, trailer audit, age-analysis, and check-out functionality. Some other features include:

- Appointment scheduling/management
- Inbound/outbound in-transit visibility
- Trailer check-in and check-out
- Trailer audit
- Trailer movement
- Analysis report and query
- Graphical visibility tool
- External interfaces

H.4 CLEARORBIT

ClearOrbit, an E-supply chain software vendor offers a software suite that "layers" RFID capabilities on top of existing ERP systems with the need for custom programming or the removal of existing bar-coding software. Unlike most other products offering supply chain execution and collaboration extensions, ClearOrbit products do not pull transactional data from a proprietary duplicate data model which must then be synchronized with the ERP data model on the back end. With Pro Series, your ERP remains the enterprise system of record. All key supply chain and financial data—purchase orders, inventory records, item definitions, sales orders, and so on—are maintained in your ERP, and accessed in real-time by ClearOrbit products.

The ClearOrbit Pro Series consists of the following configurations, based on your ERP platform:

- Pro Series for any ERP
- Pro Series for Oracle Applications 10.7
- Pro Series for Oracle Applications 11.0
- Pro Series for Oracle E-Business Suite (11i)
- Pro Series for SAP R/3

We now take a look at each.

H.4.1 Pro Series for Any ERP

This offering comes in two parts, Connected Pro and Xtended Pro Series. They are followed by Pro Series Technology Standards and compatible environments.

The Connected Pro Series is the infrastructure layer of Pro Series for any ERP, consisting of the following modules.

ClearOrbit Connect 5.0 serves as an ERP device integration operating system, allowing direct access to key material handling and manufacturing devices such as bar-code printers, scales, inventory carousels, RF/RFID, and conveyors. Connect provides direct integration to the ERP and does not store key data on proprietary middleware databases. This enables a real-time connection and allows sophisticated interaction between ERP business events and physical devices. By avoiding duplication of data, accuracy problems, material shortages, and significant inventory write-offs are avoided.

ClearOrbit's Compliance Label Manager is a rules-based engine to identify and manage user-defined bar-code label format and RFID tags to ensure compatibility with customer shipping requirements. It offers a comprehensive solution to the problem of vendor-compliant labels. This provides a standard product solution for any ERP to a problem that is typically solved by costly third-party consulting or dedicated in-house IT staff. Industry standard label formats (GM 1421A, AIAG, UCC) are supported.

Collaborative Print Manager utilizes the Compliance Label Manager Rules engine and can be integrated into ERP supplier portals to allow customers to publish their label definitions to the supplier base. Any supplier on the system gains instant access to the label library via the Internet and can print bar-code labels to correspond to orders received and accepted.

ProView provides real-time event management and charting to manage supply chain events. It includes a rules engine to define message escalation to the proper decision makers, based on event severity.

The Xtended Pro Series is the business application layer of Pro Series for ERP.

Advanced Collaborative Replenishment (A.CR) automates the direct materials replenishment process with your suppliers. A.CR closes the loop between the demand information published to suppliers and the physical shipments sent by suppliers in response to the demand signal. A.CR eliminates most invoice disputes and enables companies to implement Evaluated Receipt Settlement (ERS) in their ERP. A.CR integrates directly to the ERP data model, avoiding duplicate PO or inventory data that can drive integration costs and delay implementation.

Advanced Contract Manufacturing (A.CM) enables companies to better manage contract manufacturers to increase efficiency. A.CM provides contract manufacturers and their OEM customers with immediate visibility to required production orders, while automating the drop shipment process. This allows contract manufacturers to ship directly to end customers while the OEM maintains invoicing, ASN, and labeling control.

The native J2EE architecture and use of industry standards gives Pro Series customers a variety of deployment options and supported environments. Let's take a look at the standards and application servers.

Pro Series technology standards consist of the following.

- Primary applications developed in J2EE (Java 2 Platform, Enterprise Edition).
- Handheld applications developed in J2ME (Java 2 Platform, Micro Edition).
- Database/ERP calls developed in JDBC (Java Database Connectivity), providing database independent connectivity from Java.
- JAAS (Java Authentication and Authorization Service) provides pluggable authentication and authorization services for Java.
- JSP (Java Server Pages) and Servlets provide server-side scripting for Web pages.

Pro Series compatible application servers, consist of the following.

- BEA WebLogic
- IBM WebSphere
- Oracle 9iAS
- Apache Tomcat (JSP/Servlet engine)—Open Source
- JBoss—Open Source
- Jonas—Open Source
- Jetty (JSP/Servlet engine)—Open Source

Pro Series compatible JDBC databases consist of the following.

- Oracle 8, 8i, 9i, 10g
- IBM DB2
- MS SQL Server
- MySQL
- ADABAS
- IBM AS/400
- IMS
- Informix
- OS/390 Sequential files

Pro Series compatible JAAS modules consist of the following.

- Oracle 8*i* Authentication
- LDAP
- NT Authentication
- Database Authentication

Pro Series compatible operating systems consist of the following.

- Windows 9.X, NT, 2000, XP
- HPUX
- Solaris
- Linux
- IBM AS/400
- IBM OS/390

H.4.2 Pro Series for Oracle 10.7/11.0/11i

The information on Connected Pro Series is similar to that for the same in Section 3.12.4.1 on Pro Series for ERP.

The Xtended Pro Series is the business application layer of Pro Series for Oracle, consisting of the following.

- Advanced Collaborative Replenishment (A.CR) to automate the direct materials replenishment process with your suppliers
- Advanced Contract Manufacturing (A.CM) to enable you to better manage contract manufacturers to increase efficiency
- Advanced Fixed Assets (A.FA) to improve tracking of your fixed assets through integrated bar coding and scanning
- Advanced Order Fulfillment (A.OF) to optimize outbound processes using advanced shipping and manifesting extensions
- Gemini Simplified Interfaces (G.SI) for Mobile and Desktop Automation to provide an interface to Oracle's manufacturing transactions

H.4.3 Pro Series for SAP R/3

The ClearOrbit Pro Series extends SAP R/3 to control material movement within manufacturing, warehousing, and fulfillment operations, and, in collaboration with trading partners, at key process points of inventory ownership transfer.

Pro Series is completely compatible with the following versions of SAP.

SAP R/3 3.1H
SAP R/3 4.0B
SAP R/3 4.5B
SAP R/3 4.6C
SAP R/3 Enterprise Edition (4.70)

The Connected Pro Series is the infrastructure layer of Pro Series for SAP, consisting of the following.

ClearOrbit's SAP Certified Integration Product, Connect 5.0, serves as an ERP device integration operating system, allowing direct access to key material handling and manufacturing devices such as bar-code printers, scales, inventory carousels, RF/RFID, and conveyors. Connect provides direct integration to SAP R/3 and does not store key data on proprietary middleware databases. This enables a real-time connection and allows sophisticated interaction between SAPConsole business events and physical devices. By avoiding duplication of data such as inventory records, the SAP R/3 production planning (PP) and materials management (MM) modules gain real-time visibility to that data in the SAP enterprise system. Data accuracy problems, material shortages, and significant inventory write-offs are prevented.

ClearOrbit's Compliance Label Manager is a rules-based engine to identify and manage user-defined bar-code label format and RFID tags to ensure compatibility with customer shipping requirements. It offers a comprehensive solution to the problem of vendor-compliant labels. This provides SAP R/3 customers a standard product solution to a problem that is typically solved by costly third-party consulting or dedicated in-house IT staff. Industry standard label formats (GM 1421A, AIAG, UCC) are supported.

Collaborative Print Manager for mySAP Supplier Relationship Management (SRM) utilizes the Compliance Label Manager Rules engine and can be integrated into SAP's Supplier Self Service product to allow customers to publish their label definitions to the supplier base. Any supplier on the system gains instant access to the label library via the Internet and can print bar-code labels to correspond to orders received and accepted during their Supplier Self Service session. Customers are assured 100 percent label accuracy on incoming shipments, and suppliers avoid the costs associated with programming and maintaining label changes on their system.

ProView provides real-time event management and charting to manage supply chain events in SAP. It includes a rules engine to define message escalation to the proper decision makers, based on event severity.

The Xtended Pro Series is the business application layer of ProSeries for SAP R/3, consisting of the following.

Advanced Collaborative Replenishment (A.CR) automates the direct materials replenishment process with your suppliers. A.CR closes the loop between the demand information published to suppliers and the physical shipments sent by suppliers in response to the demand signal. A.CR eliminates most invoice disputes and enables companies to implement Evaluated Receipt Settlement (ERS) in SAP. A.CR integrates directly to the SAP R/3 data model, avoiding duplicate PO or inventory data that can drive integration costs and delay implementation.

Advanced Contract Manufacturing (A.CM) enables companies to better manage contract manufacturers to increase efficiency. A.CM provides contract manufacturers and their OEM customers with immediate visibility to required production orders, while automating the drop shipment process. This allows contract manufacturers to ship directly to end customers while the OEM maintains invoicing, ASN, and labeling control.

Advanced Inventory Management (A.IM) extends SAP Warehouse Management and Production Control by providing key automated shop/warehouse floor transactions currently beyond the scope of the SAP R/3 RF solution, such as PO receiving, Kanban, and Confirmation transactions. It augments standard SAPConsole transactions with enhancements such as "list of values" and field-level data validations. A.IM operates directly from the enterprise data model and never duplicates transactional data in a separate data model, truly enabling the real-time enterprise. This approach ensures data integrity and reduces ownership costs by utilizing all configuration, setup, and tolerances already defined in SAP R/3.

H.5 PEOPLESOFT (FORMERLY JD EDWARDS, NOW PART OF ORACLE)

Let's take a look at PeopleSoft's EnterpriseOne SCM application before we talk a little about its Warehouse Management Logistics. The SCM application contains 20 modules, each assigned to its appropriate group as follows.

- Advanced Planning
  - Demand Consensus
  - Demand Forecasting
  - Production and Distribution Planning
  - Production Scheduling: Discrete
  - Production Scheduling: Process
  - Strategic Network Optimization
  - Tactical Network Optimization

- Customer Order Management
  - Advanced Pricing
  - Agreement Management
  - Base Configurator
  - Order Promising
  - Product Variants
  - Sales Order Management

- Logistics
  - Advanced Inventory Management
  - Bulk Stock Logistics
  - Inventory Management Base
  - Transportation Management
  - Warehouse Management

- Manufacturing
  - Quality
  - Requirements Planning

In the Logistics group, Warehouse Management and Transportation Management are the most important in that order of importance as they pertain to RFID technology. Warehouse Management, fully Web-enabled, allows integration with radio frequency (and bar-code) data collection devices and optimization of pick, putaway, and replenishment functions. It establishes rules for each type of material movement based on factors such as unit measure or minimum/maximum levels and sets up zones for various storage areas, such as bulk, high rack, flock, pick, and returns.

Warehouse Management module provides integration with other aspects of EnteptiseOne: Sales Order Management, Procurement and Subcontract Management, Manufacturing Management, Inventory Management, Quality, Transportation Management, Requirements Planning, General Accounting, Order Processing, Sales Management Analytics, and Inventory Analytics.

Transportation Management supports inbound and outbound movement, and is adept at handling discrete or bulk loads, in parcel, less than truckload, or full truckload environments. When used with a private fleet, it offers full integration with the general ledger, accounts receivable, and asset life-cycle management systems for detailed cost analysis, multi-tiered pricing, integrated preventive maintenance scheduling, and complete asset management. It provides integration with Sales Order Processing, Procurement and Subcontract Management, Shop Floor Management, Inventory Management, Quality Management, Warehouse Management, Accounts Payable, Accounts Receivable, General Accounting, Advanced Cost Accounting, and Customer Relationship Management.

Appendix I

ENTERPRISE INTELLIGENCE: WEBFOCUS

This appendix looks at WebFOCUS as an example of enterprise intelligence.

Let's briefly cover five aspects of this software: data sources, Reporting Server, data management, Microsoft integration, portal integration, and Web services.

I.1 DATA SOURCES

WebFOCUS provides comprehensive native access to more than 85 data sources, including relational, legacy, ERP, and CRM. It can provide both direct user access and data warehousing services. Table I.1 shows a list of direct data interfaces.

I.2 REPORTING SERVER

The WebFOCUS Reporting Server, the "hub" of the WebFOCUS architecture, enables highly efficient reporting, query, and analysis from any data on any platform in any file structure. The server can deliver content in HTML, DHTML, XML, Excel, and PDF for Web browsers and wireless devices. Table I.2 shows a list of platforms supported by WebFOCUS.

Java™ Server environment provides support for:

- Major application servers, such as IBM WebSphere, BEA WebLogic, Sun/Netscape iPlanet, and Microsoft IIS
- Multi-threaded Java Servlet implementation
- Web services used to create and publish reports as a J2EE or .NET Web service

Table I.1   Direct Data Interfaces

Adabas	IMS/DC	Proprietary Files
ALLBASE/SQL	IMS/TM	PROGRESS
ALL-IN-1	INFOAccess	QSAM
ASCII	Informix	Rdb
BPICS	IMS/DB	Red Brick
Btrieve	Ingres	RMS
C-ISAM	Integral	Sands RDBMS
CA-DataCom/DB	ISAM	SAP R/3
CA-IDMS	IVISoft	SAP BW
CA-Ingres	JDBC	ShareBase
CICS Reporting and	J.D. Edwards (now part	Shared Medical
Transactions	of PeopleSoft)	Systems Siebel
Cloudbase	KSAM	SQL/DS
D&B Millennium	Lawson	SUPRA
DB2	Lotus	Sybase
DB2/2	Lotus Notes	SYSTEM 2000
DB2/400	ManMan	System/36 Files
DB2/6000	Model 204	Tandem Non-Stop
DBMS	MS-SQL Server	Teradata
dBASE	MS-OLAP Services	TOTAL
DL/1	MUMPS	TurboIMAGE
DMS	Net-ISAM	UDB
DSM/MUMPS	NOMAD	UFAS
ENSCRIBE	NonStop SQL	ULTRIX/SQL
Essbase	ODBC	UNIFY
Excel	OLE/DB	VSAM
Flat files	Omnidex	Walker Interactive
FOCUS	Oracle	WDS
FOCUS Fusion	PeopleSoft	WIIS
Hogan Financials	PickSystems	WP
IDS-II		XML

Table I.2   Platforms Supported

IBM	Compaq	HP	Microsoft	Sun	Other
z/OS	Tru64 UNIX	HP-UX	Windows XP	Sun Solaris	Linux
OS/390	VMS/VAX		Windows NT		Dynix (Sequent)
OS/400	OpenVMS/Alpha		Windows 2000		
AIX	NonStop Himalaya				
VM					
MVS					

WebFOCUS server clusters with built-in load-balancing. Its multi-tiered processing provides the partitioning of application logic over multiple platforms and fail-over automatically reroutes users to other servers if problems occur.

I.3 DATA MANAGEMENT

Data management solutions for any database could be used with RFID-based data automatically captured from tags affixed to items, cases, pallets, and containers. They include:

- ETL Manager
- Resource Analyzer
- Resource Governor
- Metadata Manager

The choice of one or more solutions depends on the supply chain enterprise's requirements on complying with RFID mandates and infrastructure technologies used to implement the same.

ETL Manager provides fully automated Extract, Transform, and Load (ETL) tools to simplify the creation, maintenance, and expansion of data warehouses, data marts, micro marts, and operational data stores. Its interface enables fast end-to-end ETL process creation involving heterogeneous data structures across disparate computing platforms. ETL Manager provides the following capabilities.

- Aggregate, join, merge, and apply selection criteria to information from any combination of back-office systems.
- Simplify data movement from back-office systems to E-business platforms using automatically generated and managed FTP scripts or most native transport protocols.
- Transform data from raw forms into structures that are more suited to an application.
- Simplify loading of data into a target database through the automatic invocation of bulk loaders or row-at-a-time inserts.
- Execute, schedule, review, manage, audit, and create dependencies among ETL requests.
- Load only changed records via "change data capture" capability into a data source, dramatically reducing the time needed to refresh data and making it easy to achieve a near-real-time data warehouse.

Resource Analyzer—the second data management solution—helps in monitoring resource consumption, so you can identify inefficiencies in an information architecture, eliminate bottlenecks and resource contentions, achieve peak performance, and maximize ROI. This analyzer tool provides the following capabilities.

- Provide more than 80 detailed reports and graphs that give a clear picture of how your information assets are being utilized.
- Optimize long-running requests to speed up access and minimize resource consumption.
- Identify dormant data that can be eliminated to speed up response times.
- Identify heaviest resource consumption times by hour, day, week, or month, so you can plan accordingly.
- Limit query volumes by showing users how to request just the data required and by choosing optional delivery methods.

Resource Governor, the WebFOCUS' third data management solution, aims at enhancing control over an enterprise's business intelligence environment via empowerment and resource consumption management. It provides the following capabilities.

- Technology can predict required system resources before a request is executed and stop problem queries before they use up too many resources that result in long waits for consumers.
- Query cancellation occurs before any data resources are unnecessarily or improperly used.
- Graphical wizards or unique business rules language make it easy to define what constitutes problem queries.

Metadata Manager provides an environment for managing metadata from all your enterprise information sources. It provides the following capabilities.

- Store, browse, edit, and organize metadata from virtually any information source.
- Combine metadata from many sources, including ETL mappings, database and application schemas from all data sources, and third-party tools.
- Display information in both technical and business views to make it easier for users with varying levels of expertise to understand.
- Store metadata in an Open Information Model (OIM)-compliant repository, which provides better third-party integration.

I.4 MICROSOFT INTEGRATION

OnLine Analytic Processing (OLAP) is increasingly being used against data warehouses and data marts, and Microsoft makes this technology widely available via Analysis Services. WebFOCUS offers integration with Microsoft Office 2000, Office XP, and SQL Server for enterprise business intelligence reporting solutions.

These integration capabilities provide the following features and benefits.

- Ability to save a complex WebFOCUS report into Excel 2000 and XP while preserving report formatting and drill-downs to detail data via hyperlinks active in the spreadsheet.
- Simple automatic generation of Excel PivotTables from WebFOCUS reports, an alternative way to create PivotTables to using the native Microsoft interface.
- Ability to report against data stored in the Microsoft Analysis Services cube, as well as joining this information with other data files within a single report.
- High-performance direct-access drivers to read and update Microsoft Access and SQL Server databases from within WebFOCUS.

Through comprehensive support for .NET, any WebFOCUS report can be exposed as a service that is callable from Visual Studio .NET, so report output can be integrated within any application an unlimited number of times. Developers can take advantage of flexible drill-down and report output options, as well as on-demand paging and ad hoc capabilities. Additionally, the WebFOCUS viewer control for Visual Studio .NET integrates tool bars specific to the report output from directly within the browser. With WebFOCUS and .NET, developers can rapidly deploy real-time business intelligence applications that scale to meet enterprise demands, regardless of architecture.

I.5 PORTAL INTEGRATION

Portal integration enables developers to create comprehensive reporting portals and dashboards, or incorporate robust business intelligence content into existing third-party portal infrastructures. As part of the overall portal strategy, WebFOCUS Business Intelligence Dashboard and WebFOCUS Open Portal Services are provided with regard to universal data connectivity and personalized access to information sources.

WebFOCUS Open Portal Services provide users of third-party portal products with the ability to add WebFOCUS business intelligence capabilities to their portal interface. This functionality is achieved through a set of reusable EIP components that are built in a number of formats, such as ASP, JSP, Java™, JavaScript, and HTML/XML.

The WebFOCUS Business Intelligence Dashboard is a customizable interface delivering business intelligence content to meet individual user needs. The dashboard enables administrators to maintain tight security and company control over the data, and users can choose the reports they want in the style they want to see them.

Supported portals include:

- IBM WebSphere
- Microsoft SharePoint
- Plumtree
- BEA
- Vignette Portal Services (formerly Epicentric)
- CA CleverPath
- Oracle-PeopleSoft
- mySAP

Obviously IBM WebSphere, Microsoft SharePoint, PeopleSoft, Oracle, and mySAP are database vendor-specific. Plumtree, BEA, Vignette Portal Services, and CA Cleverpath enable customers to add business intelligence content to their portal initiatives without any need for additional programming. Developers gain the ability to quickly and easily integrate any enterprise data—more than 85 sources across 35 platforms—and distribute it to employees, partners, and customers via a personalized portal page that incorporates users' e-mails, sales leads, inventory reports, and market news.

I.6 REPORTS AS WEB SERVICES

WebFOCUS exposes reports as Web services, allowing external applications built with Web services-supported languages (such as VB.NET, C#, and Java) to consume them via standard Simple Object Access Protocol (SOAP). WebFOCUS' data access and integration capabilities provide access to relational data sources, legacy, multidimensional, SCM, ERP, and CRM via Web services. WebFOCUS reports can incorporate information from any enterprise system and then be published as a Web service.

WebFOCUS provides the following features.

- Ability to build new procedures that can be published as J2EE or .NET calls
- A utility for automatic generation of WSDL
- Exposed functionality, such as security, report execution, application management, user administration, and delivery/scheduling

I.7 WEB SERVICES ADAPTER

The WebFOCUS Web Services Adapter enables Web services created and deployed using any Web services authoring tool to be directly consumed by the WebFOCUS report server and manipulated as though it were relational data. Once defined, WebFOCUS enables metadata describing the Web service to be automatically created, catalogued, and made directly accessible for reporting or analytical purposes. WebFOCUS can then integrate both internal and external data sources to create combined reports.

The same Web service may be manipulated in conjunction with RDBMSs, DBMSs, and legacy file systems accessible through the WebFOCUS enterprise adapter architecture. WebFOCUS can also read a Web service as a data source when creating a data warehouse or mart using WebFOCUS ETL Manager. Enterprises can conduct ad hoc reporting against these Web services.

WebFOCUS supports the following features.

- Creation of metadata for any Web service via its WSDL.
- Drill down from any report to any other data available via Web services.
- The ability to join data from Web services or a real database to a Web service.
- Output of any Web services data as Excel spreadsheets, Excel PivotTables, PDF files, or standard HTML.
- Scheduled or event-driven e-mail alerts containing data from a Web service.

I.8 MISCELLANEOUS

It also provides an object-oriented 4GL for structured, object-oriented, and hybrid programming. Its Excel write-back feature allows Excel 97, Excel 2000, and Excel XP users to:

- Simplify distribution of budgeting, production, and operational spreadsheets to users inside and outside the organization.
- Automate the update of operational data—in any database on any platform—directly from an Excel spreadsheet.
- Utilize rich formatting options, including calculations, numeric and date formatting, and styling control from templates.
- Work within their current WebFOCUS reporting environment and plug into any Web server environment.
- Leverage complete Web deployment, so any user with a browser can view and update data.
- Deliver user-customized macros—from simple to sophisticated—with Excel worksheets.

- Utilize full security, so users can see and update only the data to which they have access via Excel.

WebFOCUS Maintain provides some more capabilities, such as:

- A shared application server for persistent data and communications, user connection pooling, and workload balancing
- A graphical interface that completely avoids complex languages such as C or Java or complex standards such as COM or CORBA
- Relational data, XML, and ERP connectors
- CICS and IMS connectors, for access to legacy transactional data
- Connection and context/state management, for operational efficiency
- Resource governing, to prevent runaway queries
- Mobile solutions that allow developers to build and deploy applications for offline data collection through Palm, Blackberry, and other handheld devices

Appendix J

ENTERPRISE DATABASES

Base/One and CodeBase are covered in this appendix.

J.1 BASE/ONE

Base/One Internet Server (BIS), a middleware for distributed (grid and cluster) computing (U.S. Patent pending), runs secure, highly graphical Windows database applications efficiently over the Internet. These applications can operate without a browser, using only a regular dial-up connection to the Internet, through Base/One's high-speed peer-to-peer Rich Client architecture (see Section 4.2.2) via PCs.

For fault-tolerant grid computing, BIS includes Batch Job Servers that can be used locally or remotely from PCs on a LAN or across the Internet, and greatly speed up long-running tasks by scheduling identifiable parts of the batch for distribution. BIS supports coordinated parallel processing by a dynamic pool of PCs, useful, for example, for repetitive database-intensive tasks such as data loads and transformations.

BIS mixes well with Thin Client Web technologies and includes the Base/1 Foundation Application, which reduces the work needed to build and operate commercial Web sites. It also supports industrial-strength security and user administration and a database command processor for running complex scripts. BIS also works well with Crystal Web Report Server, ColdFusion, IIS/ASP/COM, and ASP.NET.

Interactive and Batch Windows applications built with the Base/One Foundation Classes (BFC) Database Library can be used whether the database is located across the Internet or on a laptop, LAN, or WAN. Through messages to the Base/One's Internet Server, these high-efficiency Windows applications can work without change to access remote databases, communicating automatically (using TCP/IP).

The remaining portion of this section covers Base/One Foundation Class Library, Data Command Processor, Database Library, and systems requirements.

J.1.1 Base/One Foundation Class Library

The Base/One Foundation Class Library (BFC) is an object-oriented framework for building Windows applications, especially Internet-enabled database applications. BFC is based on the Microsoft Foundation Class Library (MFC), which is an extensive Visual C++ framework for doing general-purpose software development under Windows.

BFC is broken down into multiple components, which can be used in part or as an integrated whole. BFC has about 100 classes and 2000 functions that have been designed to be reused. Almost all BFC classes are derived from MFC classes and add significant extensions to MFC. BFC includes:

- An integrated collection of utility, database, screen, and administrative classes
- State-of-the-art screen controls easily connected to the database classes
- A customizable distributed computing facility for executing long-running tasks in parallel over multiple machines
- Integrated support for leading reporting and graphics packages, crystal reports, and pinnacle graphics

J.1.2 Database Command Processor

Database Command Processor runs a complex script of command files (scripts) that can include SQL, DOS, and Windows commands, plus special BFC database commands, for example, for viewing, loading, and unloading large databases. Command files can be run interactively, using the Command Processor Dialog, and can also be run (without change) in unattended "batch" mode, using the Batch Facility. The databases being manipulated can be local (two-tier) or remote (three-tier), through the Internet Server (BIS).

The Command Processor supports a variety of commands. The processing done for a command line depends on the type of command line. Here are the types of commands accepted by the command processor.

- Common SQL commands
- Built-in basic commands
- Built-in commands that use the data dictionary
- DOS and WIN command lines
- Error suppression commands
- Database buffer commands

- Database manager commands
- Custom commands
- Macro assignment command lines
- Any other command line

J.1.2.1   Common SQL Commands

If the first token is one of the recognized SQL commands, the command line is passed to the SQL engine, possibly after some modest processing to simplify entry. For example, prefixing the qualifier (schema) of the table name is done automatically in the FROM clause of insert, update, and delete statements.

The recognized SQL commands are:

INSERT, UPDATE, DELETE, CREATE, DROP, GRANT, REVOKE, and COMMIT

SELECT is not one of the directly supported SQL commands. Instead, you formulate queries and return results through Database Buffer commands (see below).

Also introduced below are other, friendlier, alternative, Database Library commands that can be used instead of the standard SQL commands. For example, you can use AddRec instead of INSERT, ChgRec instead of UPDATE, and CreatDbRecTyp instead of CREATE.

J.1.2.2   Built-In Basic Commands

If the first token is one of the recognized basic built-in commands, then the appropriate Command File is executed or Command Processor function is invoked. "Built-in" basic commands are an integral part of the Command Processor and are available exclusively through its command line interface.

The Command Processor's built-in basic commands include:

```
Run, GoToCmdFil, DefMacro, UndefMacro,
OpenOutputCmdFil, ClosOutputCmdFil
```

The Command Processor can create an Output Command File listing all commands that will be executed when the command file is executed. Macros and nested command files are expanded for a total picture of what will happen at runtime. All statements are listed, but are not executed, providing a tool for understanding, testing, and maintaining command files.

J.1.2.3   Built-In Commands That Use the Data Dictionary

If the first token is one of the recognized "built-in" commands that take advantage of the presence of the Data Dictionary that is part of the Rich Client database architecture, then the appropriate Command Processor function is invoked in combination with access to the current database's data dictionary.

The Command Processor's built-in commands that use the data dictionary include:

```
LoadRecs, UnloadRecs, DefMacroFromDb
CreatDbRecTyp, DropDbRecTyp, CreatDbIdx, DropDbIdx
CreatDbRefIntegrity, DropDbRefIntegrity
GrantDbRights, RevokeDbRights
```

J.1.2.4 DOS and WIN Command Lines

If the first token is "DOS" or "WIN", then the rest of the command line is passed for DOS or Windows command line execution. (For DOS paths, because backslash, \, is considered the general "escape" character, remember to double any backslashes, \\, and the Command Processor will automatically convert them back into a single backslash, \, before passing the command line on for execution.)

J.1.2.5 Error Suppression Commands

If the first token is SuppressDbErrsBegin or SuppressDbErrsEnd, then this command line marks the start or the end of a sequence of commands in which all but fatal errors are ignored, and only the most severe errors cause processing to stop.

J.1.2.6 Database Buffer Commands

A database buffer represents an area of main memory used for retrieving data from and transmitting data to a database. For each type of database buffer, there is a separate Create command (e.g., CreatRecBuf, CreatRecSetScrlCacheBuf, CreatProcBuf), which appears first on the command line, and the second token is the name to be given to the new database buffer. Thereafter, if the first token of a command line is a user-created Database Buffer Name, then this must be followed by "dot", that is, ".", followed by a function name that is valid for the type of Database Buffer. The rest of the command line is treated as parameters to that function. Most operations on a database buffer require using the "BufferName – dot – command" syntax (e.g., "recStudent.GetNextRec").

The Database Buffer commands are described in the Database Library manual. The ones that can be used in a Command processor command line include:

```
CreatRecBuf, CreatRecSetBaseBuf, CreatRecSet
ScrlCacheBuf
```

```
CreatProcBuf, CreatRecSetFilBuf
```

```
InitRec, InitRecSet, InitProc, InitRecSetFil,
AddRec, ChgRec, DelRec, SetData, SetParamData,
SetPrepareDbCmdFlag
ExecProc, BuildRecSetFil, WriteRec
GetRecSet, GetRec, GetFirstRec, GetLastRec,
GetNextRec, GetPrevRec
SetSelItmLst, SetSelFromLst, SetSelCriteria,
SetSelDistinctFlag
SetSelFromLstAndJoinExpr, SetGrpByColLst,
SetGrpHavingCondition
SetSortOrder, SetSortKey, SetSearchVal, FindRec,
GetData, GetAttObj, SetAttObj, SetDbBufNam
```

J.1.2.7 Database Manager Commands

The Database Manager provides the Command Processor with most important functions for operating on databases as a whole. Whatever follows the command name in the command line is passed as parameters to the Database Manager function. There are commands for opening and closing additional databases or switching between databases. There are other useful commands, such as CopyData, which copies data from one database buffer to another, DelResultSet, which is used for deleting large numbers of database records from a record type based on a criterion, and DelRecSetFil for deleting a record set file.

The Database Manager commands are described in the Database Library manual. The ones that can be used in a Command processor command line include:

```
OpenDb, ClosDb, SwitchDb, SetDbTyp, SetLogonUsr
Commit, SuppressDbErrsBegin, SuppressDbErrsEnd
CopyData, DelResultSet, DelRecSetFil, InitDbLog,
LogStr
StartDbTrace, StopDbTrace, SetDbTraceLvl,
SetDbTraceOutputOpt
```

J.1.2.8 Custom Commands

If the first token in a command line is on the list of "custom" commands in that application's "global definitions," then the associated, application-supplied, Custom Command Function is invoked, with the rest of the command line passed as a parameter. ShowStr and ShowDbBuf are sample, useful, custom display commands, and their C++ source code can be changed to suit the application. Such global definitions are not available through the BFCCOM interface, and Custom Commands are not available through BFCCOM.

Besides adding new commands, the Custom Command facility can also be used by C++ programmers to deny access to any of the known commands that can appear as the first token in a command line. The search to determine if the first token is a Custom Command precedes all other lookups. This permits the programmer to prevent the use of any command simply by making an entry that launches a custom function that returns an access-denied message.

J.1.2.9   Macro Assignment Command Lines

If the first token of a command line is not recognized, and the second token is the equal sign, then the first token is taken as the name of a macro to be set with the return value of the command specified by the rest of the command line (i.e., starting with the third token).

J.1.2.10   Any Other Command Line

If the first token is not recognized by the Command Processor and the second token is not the equal sign, =, then the entire command line is passed without change for execution to the SQL processor of the current database.

To see exactly what is being passed to the database engine, use the Trace facility. This allows display of all database function calls, the values of passed parameters, SQL statements, and processing start and completion times.

The low-level programmer's (as opposed to operator's) interface to the command processor is the Command Processor class (clsCmdProc) (as opposed to dialog). The Command Processor class is derived directly from MFC CObject and is used to execute commands directly or to run files containing commands. (Many of the commands used in command files are available directly as C++ functions, with equivalent parameters.) Besides the direct MFC C++ interface, the Command Processor class can be used through COM and .NET interfaces, and there are C++, C#, Visual Basic, VB.NET, ASP, and ASP.NET examples.

J.1.3 Database Library

Rich Client applications are built using either the Database Library of BFC (Base/One Foundation Classes) or the full BFC framework. An existing Windows MFC (Microsoft Foundation Classes) program or Visual Basic program can be turned into a Rich Client application by substituting direct calls to the database with calls to the Database Library. The Database Library supports databases from IBM, Microsoft, Oracle, and Sybase, the top vendors of high-performance database software.

The Database Library is built on a Data Dictionary, which provides a complete description of record layouts and indexes of the database for validation and to ensure efficient data access. You can choose to use automated database creation, including building of tables, indexes, and referential constraints, and granting access rights to individual users and groups. Data dictionary records (regions, records, fields, and indexes) are the most basic examples of built-in record types. The System Region consists of all the built-in record types. It is broken down into subregions, such as the Data Dictionary Region, the Security Region, and the Batch Region, which group the built-in record types by function.

The data dictionary describes all the other database regions and contains the description of all the other record types, both built-in and application-specific. For example, within the Security Region, there is one User Master Record for each user allowed to access the database. The User Master Record contains fields that identify the user such as the user's name, log-on ID, security group, and unique number (User Code).

The data dictionary can define every field, record type, region, and index in the database using these built-in records:

Database Region Dictionary records (logical hierarchy)—DbRegDic
Database Record Type Dictionary records (lists relational tables)—
    DbRecTypDic
Database Field Dictionary records (lists columns within tables)—DbFldDic
Database Index Dictionary records—DbIdxDic

The Database Field Dictionary describes each field and is used for allocating the database buffer's main memory. The Database Record Type Dictionary provides sufficient information about record types to dynamically create database record types. The Database Region Dictionary breaks the database down into convenient logical groupings of record types.

The Database Index Dictionary is used to ensure that queries are done efficiently. Each record contains information about an index in the database, such as the list of key fields, the record type (table) from which index entries are taken, whether the index keys are unique, and the storage dictionary record that defines the CREATE parameters used when the index is created.

There is a single set of data dictionaries that exists for each Rich Client database. This means that all applications running against the same database share the same set of data dictionaries.

The data dictionary also contains records used for the optional parameters that most database systems support in their CREATE TABLE and CREATE

INDEX commands. These built-in records are used for specifying storage parameters:

Database Storage Dictionary records—DbStorDic
Database Macro Dictionary records—DbMacroDic

The Database Storage Dictionary defines the storage parameters that will be used when each record type table and index is created. There is a complete set of all the database creation parameters available for the back-end databases. (For example, there are entries for the Sybase SQL Anywhere DBSPACE parameter and for the Oracle TABLESPACE and PCTFREE parameters.)

Every record type (table) and index can be associated with a Storage Dictionary record. If no Storage Dictionary record is provided for a given record type or index, then the CREATE SQL commands use the back end's defaults. Record types and indexes can use the same Storage Dictionary record, which lets them share the same storage parameters and groups them logically for the DBA. The fields in the Storage Dictionary records contain macros rather than actual values.

Each Storage record is associated with a set of macros. Each macro equates to a parameter. This allows enormous flexibility and control in setting creation parameters.

The Database Macro Dictionary specifies the value to be substituted for each storage parameter. The use of macros in the storage dictionary (rather than actual values) allows for the greatest flexibility at database creation time. An application is free to use the Macro Dictionary to store any of its own macros as well as those required for database creation.

Once the data dictionary information has been entered, it can be unloaded and used to automatically regenerate the full database creation instructions (SQL), including CREATE TABLE, CREATE INDEX, ALTER TABLE, GRANT, etc. The data dictionary information created under one database system can easily be used to generate the same database layout on any of the other database systems BFC supports (Oracle, MS SQL Server, Access, DB2, Sybase, SQL Anywhere, etc.).

Getting and setting a record's attached objects is similar to getting and setting other types of database fields, such as numbers, dates, and character strings. GetAttObj( ) is used to retrieve an attached object from a database buffer containing data fetched from the database. SetAttObj( ) is used to place or replace an attached object in a database buffer before the data is sent to the database. The programmer does not specify "M" or "B" because the database field dictionary stores whether an attached object is in memo or binary format.

Attached objects are not retrieved until the last moment. That is, when the record is retrieved, the AttObj ID is returned but the attached object itself is not retrieved until GetAttObj( ) is called. Each time GetAttObj( ) is called the database is accessed. Because an attached object can be large, the database subsystem does not try to hold onto a copy of the object. Multiple calls to GetAttObj( ) will go to the database each time, even if the same attached object is being retrieved. (This avoids potentially large amounts of disk space being grabbed to cache the objects temporarily and has the additional minor benefit of detecting up to the last minute whether other users have made modifications before the user starts making changes.)

If the same attached objects are likely to be accessed repeatedly and unlikely to be changed, the application programmer can cache them in local files to avoid extra database accesses. Note that for text fields that have a maximum length of 1975 (MAX_DbFldLenChar), the database designer has the option of making these CHAR fields instead of memo or bin attached object fields. (CHAR fields are completely retrieved at the time the record is fetched and are stored locally in the database buffer.)

J.1.4 Systems Requirements

Here are systems requirements for BFC programming:

- Microsoft Visual C++ or Visual Basic (version 6.0 or .NET2003) or C# (.NET2003)
- Windows 2003, XP, 2000, NT 4.0, 98
- 32 MB RAM, at least 128 MB recommended
- 500 MB free hard drive space for development (for class libraries, help system, third party libraries, plus debug and release builds of Demo & Starter Applications, Internet Server demo, and room for your own application, along with optional sample local database)
- 32-bit database software (one or more of the following versions or higher)
  - IBM DB2 Universal (v 8.1) (Windows, AS400, and OS/390)
  - Microsoft Access 2000 and 97
  - Microsoft SQL Server (v. 2000 and 7)
  - Oracle (v. 9.2, 8.1.7 and 8.04) (network version and Personal Oracle)
  - Sybase Adaptive Server (v. 12.5.1)
  - Sybase SQL Anywhere (v. 6.0)

Tools such as Crystal and Pinnacle Graphics are built into BFC, so it is not necessary to install these packages. The required headers, libraries, and DLLs are installed as part of BFC.

J.2 CODEBASE

The Sequiter software's CodeBase family of database programming tools works with all popular operating systems (Windows, UNIX, Linux, OS/2, Macintosh, DOS) and programming languages. It also provides supports for Excel and PowerBasic. With it, you can access a database locally, in a shared network environment, or over the Internet.

CodeBase permits query of millions of records and bulk appends on the fly. You can execute SQL queries in your application or through any tool that supports ODBC, use ADP or ADO.NET with CodeBase SQL product, and call CodeBase engine functions directly from a source code.

CodeBase is not limited to desktop computer platforms. It can run on constrained environments such as PDAs or embedded devices. Applications built with CodeBase for Windows CE 4.0, CodeBase for Pocket PC, or CodeBase for J2ME load fast and use a minimum of system resources.

CodeBase supports multi-user file compatibility with the data, index, and memo files of FoxPro, dBASE, and Clipper. Thousands of commercial applications directly use or import/export data in the xBASE format.

The maximum table size is 4.2 billion gigabytes (4,611,686,018,427,387,904 bytes) under both 32-bit and 64-bit operating systems. This is large enough for any application today or in the foreseeable future.

The remaining portion of this section covers CodeBase for Windows CE 4.0, J2ME, JDBC. Linux, and UNIX, bundle for Windows and .NET, Delphi, and Kylix, SQL 2.02 for Windows, 64-bit add-on, slow query performance, windows registry, MS Access, VB example, and C++ example.

J.2.1 Windows CE 4.0

CodeBase for Windows CE 4.0 supports the various Windows CE/Pocket PC operating systems and hardware. Developers can now create fully functional and robust database applications for Windows CE devices with very few memory requirements. You can create a fully functional database application that adds as little as 150 kB to your executable.

CodeBase for Windows CE includes CodeBase for Windows, enabling the development of applications for the desktop as well. CodeBase data files are compatible between CE and desktop applications.

Also included in CodeBase for Windows CE is the full source code allowing programmers to reduce the library size even further by removing other functional modules that are not required. Table J.1 shows what features Windows CE supports.

Table J.2 shows what processors are supported for specific CE platforms.

Table J.1   Features Supported by Windows CE

MS IDE support	Microsoft Visual Studio .NET 2003
	Microsoft Windows CE Toolkit for
	  Visual Basic 6.0
	Microsoft Windows CE Toolkit for
	  Visual C++ 6.0
	Microsoft eMbedded Visual Tools 3.0
	Microsoft eMbedded Visual Tools 4.0

Includes CodeBase Bundle for Windows and .Net	YES
Includes full source code	YES
Concurrency	Single User
Foxpro file format support	YES
CodeBase API support	C# C/C++ Visual Basic
Major CodeBase Function groups supported	Data file Expression evaluation Error Field Field information Index Query & Join Tag
Linking method	Dynamic Link Library Static Library (C/C++ only)

J.2.2   J2ME

CodeBase® for J2ME (Java 2 Platform, Micro Edition) is a high-speed database engine for the Java constrained environment. Developers can create database applications for embedded and constrained systems. It includes the following.

■ Royalty-Free CodeBase distribution for the constrained Java environment.
■ A Pure Java Thin Client implementation for use with the CodeBase Database Server for Windows.

Table J.2 Processors Supported by Mobile PCs

	Handheld PC (ver 2.0)	Handheld PC Pro (ver 2.11)	Palm-sized PC (ver 2.11)	Pocket PC (ver 3.0)	Pocket PC 2002	Pocket PC 2003	CE .NET (ver. 4.0)
Arm		VB C/C++		VB C/C++	VB C/C++ C# VB.Net	C/C++ C# VB. Net	C/C++
MIPS	VB C/C++	VB C/C++	VB C/C++	VB C/C++			C/C++
SH-3	VB C/C++	VB C/C++	VB C/C++	VB C/C++			C/C++
SH-4		VB C/C++					C/C++
x86					C# VB. Net	C/C++ C# VB.Net	C/C++
x86 emulator	VB C/C++	VB C/C++	VB C/C++	VB C/C++	VB		C/C++

■ A small footprint stand-alone JNI implementation of CodeBase. This JNI library is a completely self-contained database that does not require any external databases or servers.

■ CodeBase for Linux, including full source code. This allows you to reduce the library used in the stand-alone JNI implementation by removing functional modules that are not required, and rebuilding the shared library.

CodeBase for J2ME uses the small footprint CodeBase API that minimizes resource requirements. For JDBC support under the constrained environment use our separately available CodeBase for JDBC 2.1. Table J.3 is a chart comparing J2ME implementations.

In addition to the Linux operating system using J2ME, Sequiter is working on support for additional constrained operating systems and Java development environments.

J.2.3 JDBC 3.0

CodeBase for JDBC 3.0 provides a client-side component, the CodeBase JDBC Driver, a pure Java, JDBC 2.1 driver capable of connecting from Java

Table J.3   Comparing J2ME Implementations

	Pure Java Thin Client	Stand-Alone JNI
Includes full source code	Yes	Yes
Concurrency	Multi-user	Single-user or multi-user
File format support	CodeBase, FoxPro, dBase, Clipper	CodeBase, FoxPro, dBase, Clipper
CodeBase API support	Java	Java
Major CodeBase function groups supported	Data File Error Field	Data File Error Field Query & Join
Linking method	Pure Java	JNI, Dynamic Link Library
Code footprint	Less than 60 k to include all classes	Starts at 150 k for DLL
Additional requirements	CodeBase Server for Windows	None

applets or JDBC-enabled applications. It can connect to the server-side component over Local Area Networks (LAN), Wide Area Networks (WAN), intranets, or the Internet. It is installed on your users' workstations (of any platform, including UNIX, Windows, and Mac), although the most common setup is a PC running a Java-enabled Web browser. CodeBase for JDBC works with all platforms.

Javasoft's JDBC, a type 3 driver, is a set of standard interfaces that enable Java applications and applets to access multiple database management systems using Structured Query Language (SQL). The JavaSoft JDBC Driver Manager handles multiple drivers connecting to different databases and provides the capability for users to define stored procedures.

The server-side component, the CodeBase Database Server, is an application installed on a Windows operating system and provides data source management and administration tools, in addition to database connectivity services. It supports data access also via ODBC, OLE-DB, and the CodeBase native API and works with Windows 2003, XP, 2000 or 2000 Advanced Server, NT Server, or Workstation. (Java applets using JDBC must connect through a Web server.)

All of the standard xBASE data types (Character, Numeric, Logical, etc.) have been logically mapped to corresponding JDBC data types, assuring full xBASE file compatibility. CodeBase for JDBC 3.0 also includes support for new enhanced xBASE field types that map directly to OLE DB data types, eliminating the need for data conversions, and improving read/write performance by avoiding conversion routine overhead.

CodeBase for JDBC also provides support for isolation levels that provides developers well-defined control over how multiple users access shared databases. CodeBase supports these isolation levels:

- Read Uncommitted
- Read Committed
- Repeatable Read
- Serializable

J.2.4 UNIX

CodeBase for UNIX permits developers to build database applications in single- or multi-user configurations with features including transaction processing, logging, backup, and queries. It has very low disk and memory requirements which translates to fast loading applications using fewer system resources.

CodeBase for UNIX is available in two versions, one for Intel-based systems, and one for non-Intel systems. Both versions include CodeBase for Windows.

CodeBase is well suited for the UNIX platforms shown in Table J.4. CodeBase for UNIX also supports C and C++.

J.2.5 Linux

CodeBase for Linux allows developers to build stand-alone applications in single- or multi-user configurations or take advantage of the client/server support and create database solutions accessible over a network or the

Table J.4   UNIX Platforms

Non-Intel UNIX	Intel-Based UNIX
AIX	BSDI
Dec Alpha	DGUX
HP-UX	Linux
IRIX	SCO
Solaris	Solaris x86
SunOS	Unisys
	UnixWare

Internet. It contains enterprise-level features including transaction processing, security, logging, backup, and intelligent queries. It goes beyond the xBASE file size limitations to create huge table, index, and memo files.

Language Support includes C/C++ (Java add-on available) on most Linux distributions including RedHat, Caldera, Debian, SuSe, and Turbolinux.

J.2.6 Bundle for Windows and .NET

CodeBase Bundle for Windows and .NET includes the features shown in Table J.5.

J.2.7 Delphi and Kylix

CodeBase for Kylix was specifically designed for Kylix users developing on Linux systems. Because CodeBase is available for both Kylix and Delphi, you can use the same source code to develop applications for either Linux or Windows.

CodeBase for Kylix features the same functionality and small footprint as CodeBase for Delphi with the exception of a few differences. CodeBase for Kylix is currently available only in stand-alone configuration and file compatibility support is limited to the FoxPro file format. CodeBase for Delphi supports FoxPro, Clipper, and dBASE file formats in both client/server and stand-alone.

J.2.8 SQL 2.0 for Windows

Under Windows, you can use CodeBase SQL 2.0 with all popular development tools and applications. This includes Visual Basic, ADO, VB.NET, ADO.Net, ODBC, ODBC.NET, C/C++, C++.NET, C# (Csharp), Visual C++, Delphi, Borland C++ Builder, ASP .NET, PHP, Crystal Reports, Access, and more. CodeBase SQL 2.0 can also be used with the flexible CodeBase Engine API to boost performance and provide low-level database access.

CodeBase SQL 2.0 currently supports the following configurations.

- Single-user
- Networked multi-user
- Client/server

J.2.9 64-Bit Add-On

The CodeBase for 64-bit Add-On uses a 64-bit version of the CodeBase library. However, the same API and data files from other versions of CodeBase 6 can still be used, making the transition from 32-bit to 64-bit that much easier.

Table J.5   Windows and .NET Bundle

Languages supported	CodeBase .NET • Visual Basic .NET • C# (Csharp) • C++.NET CodeBase for Windows • Visual Basic • C • C++ • Delphi
Configurations supported	• Single-user • File-sharing multi-user • Client/Server
Components included	• CodeBase Administrator • CodeReporter • CodeControls
Operating systems supported	• Windows Server 2003 • Windows XP • Windows 2000 • Windows NT • Windows Me • Windows 98/95 • Windows 3.x
Compilers supported	CodeBase for Windows • Microsoft Visual Basic • Microsoft Visual C++ • Borland C++ Builder • Borland Delphi CodeBase .NET • Microsoft Visual Basic.NET • Microsoft C# .NET • Microsoft Visual C++.NET

Complete source code and scripts are included for building the Code-Base C and C++ libraries under 64-bit environments. CodeBase for 64-bit Add-On has been successfully tested under various platforms. Table J.6 shows some features of the 64-bit add-ons.

J.2.10 Maximum Limits

Table J.7 lists the maximums for CodeBase, including maximums for retaining xBase file compatibility.

Table J.6 Add-On Features

Concurrency	Single-user and multi-user
File formats	FoxPro 2.x and up
CodeBase API support	C/C++
Function groups	Data file
	Expression error
	Field
	Index
	Query & Join
	Transactions
Linking method	Static Library
Supported platforms	AIX 4.3
	HP-UX 11.0
	Solaris 8 (SPARC version)
	SuSE Linux (IBM zSeries, Intel Itanium)
	Windows XP 64-bit Edition (Intel Itanium)

J.2.11 Slow Query Performance

Here are some common problems and solutions for when query optimization does not work.

J.2.11.1 Unique Tag

In order for CodeBase to optimize a query with an index tag, that tag must contain an entry for *every* record in the table. Therefore, a tag created as is r4uniqueContinue cannot be used for query optimization.

Even if a tag is created as r4unique or e4unique, you must ensure that CodeBase recognizes that fact when it opens the table later. Index files do not store the type of unique; they only store whether the tag is unique. So you must set CODE4.errDefaultUnique before opening the table or t4unique after opening the table.

This means that if you open a table with a unique tag and do not explicitly set the tag's unique type to r4unique or e4unique, CodeBase will think that the tag is r4uniqueContinue and will not use the tag for optimizing a query.

J.2.11.2 Filtered Tag

As mentioned above, CodeBase can only optimize a query with an index tag if that tag contains an entry for every record in the table. Therefore, a

Table J.7   Maximum Limits

Description	Limit
Number of open files	Constrained only by the compiler and the operating environment.
Data file size	1,000,000,000 bytes with large file support turned off. Limited only by maximum number of records with large file support turned on.
Number of records	2,147,483,647 (2.1 billion)
Record width	Limited only by maximum number of fields and maximum field width. 65500 bytes for FoxPro compatibility. 128 bytes for dBase IV compatibility. 1022 bytes for Clipper 5.x compatibility.
Number of fields	2046 255 for FoxPro compatibility. 128 for dBase IV compatibility. 1022 for Clipper 5.x compatibility.
Field width	65533 bytes 254 bytes for FoxPro or dBase IV compatibility.
Floating point/numeric field width	19
Memo file size	(2,147,483,647 memo blocks) * (Memo Block Size) with large file support turned on. 4 GB with large file support turned off.
Memo block size	32768 bytes (32 kB).
Memo entry size	(Maximum value of an unsigned integer) minus (overhead). The overhead may vary depending on compiler or platform but should never exceed 100 bytes. Therefore, if the system uses a 32-bit unsigned integer, the memo entry size is: $4,294,967,296 - 100 = 4,294,967,196$ bytes (approximately 4 GB).

(continued)

Table J.7   Maximum Limits (Continued)

Description	Limit
Number of tags per index file	Unlimited when using the FoxPro file format. 47 when using the dBASE IV file format. 1 when using the Clipper 5.x file format.
Index file size	2048 GB with 512-byte index blocks and large file support turned on. 4096 GB with 1024-byte or larger index blocks and large file support turned on. 4 GB with large file support turned off and multi-user support disabled. 1 GB with large file support turned off and multi-user support enabled.
Index key size	240 bytes when using the FoxPro file format. 102 bytes when using the dBASE IV file format. 388 bytes when using the Clipper 5.x file format.

tag that has a filter cannot be used for query optimization, even if the filter is ".NOT. DELETED( )".

To ensure that a query is optimizable but does not find deleted records:

1. Make sure your index includes an unfiltered tag indexed on the field you wish to query. It is perfectly acceptable to have two tags with the same sort expression but different filter expressions. For example, your index might have tags called *L_NAME* and *L_NAMEA*. *L_NAME* indexes on the *L_NAME* field and filters out deleted records. *L_NAMEA* indexes on the *L_NAME* field and has no filter (the "A" is for "ALL").
2. Add the ".NOT. DELETED( )" statement to your query expression. For example,

```
L_NAME = 'SMITH' .AND. .NOT.DELETED()
```

J.2.11.3 Tag Using General Collating Sequence

In versions of CodeBase after version 6.50, tags that are sorted according to the general collating sequence are ignored, by default, when the relation module attempts to optimize a query. Therefore, a query expression that was optimizable in previous versions of CodeBase because such a tag will not be automatically optimized in the newer versions.

To optimize queries of these tags, CodeBase can take advantage of the code4useGeneralTagsInRelate( ) function to change the behavior of the relation module.

J.2.12 Windows Registry

If stand-alone CodeBase SQL/ODBC does not return more than 254 columns, you can make changes to the Windows registry settings of the driver to increase the number of columns that it returns.

The following steps show you how to do it.

1. Open the Windows Registry Editor.
2. If you are using the default DSN CodeBaseOdbcStand, go to

   ```
   HKEY_CURRENT_USER\Software\ODBC\ODBC.INI\
   CodeBaseOdbcStand
   ```

   where you will find several values already there (e.g., DBQ, Locking Attempts).
3. Add a new string value called MaxColSupport, and assign it a number no greater than the limits given for column support in the CodeBase ODBC help file.
4. If you have created your own DSN, you will need to make the change to your DSN's registry settings, located under either

   ```
   HKEY_CURRENT_USER\Software\ODBC\ODBC.INI\  or
   HKEY_LOCAL_MACHINE\Software\ODBC\ODBC.INI\
   ```

J.2.13 Using CodeBase from Microsoft Access

Here is one way of using CodeBase from Microsoft Access. These instructions apply specifically to Microsoft Access 2000 and above.

1. In MS Access, open the Visual Basic editor (Alt-F11).
2. In the Visual Basic editor, open the *File* menu and select *Import File...*
3. In the *Import File* dialog that appears, browse to the CodeBase module, **codebase.bas**.
4. In an existing module (or in a new module), write a function (not a sub) containing CodeBase function calls.
5. Back in MS Access, create a macro with a "RunCode" action which calls the function that contains the CodeBase function calls.

J.2.14 Running Visual Basic Example

The project Example.vbp that included with CodeBase references a module called Example.bas. This module does not actually exist. The reference in the project is there as placeholder for whichever example you wish to run. To run an example, do one of the following.

- Replace the reference with a reference to an example module that does exist.
  1. In Visual Basic, open Example.vbp. Visual Basic will prompt you with the message, File not found: "Example.BAS"--Continue Loading Project? Click "Yes".
  2. Open the **Project** menu and select **Add Module**.
  3. Browse for and select a file whose name is exN.bas, where N is a number.

- Rename one of the existing examples to Example.bas.

  1. In the Examples directory, locate the example you wish to run. Examples designed to run in Example.vbp are named exN.bas, where N is a number.
  2. Rename the .bas file to **Example.bas**.
  3. Open **Example.vbp** in Visual Basic.

To rebuild an example project, follow these steps.

1. Open Visual Basic.
2. Create a new **Standard EXE** project. Make sure that the name of the main form is **Form1**.
3. Add codebase.bas and exN.bas (where N is a number) to your project.
4. Add a CommandButton to the form.
5. In the Click event of the CommandButton, call the **ExCode** subroutine.

J.2.15 Running Visual C++ Example

To build a project that will run a simple CodeBase example, follow these steps.

1. Open Visual C++.
2. Create a new Win32 Console Application project.

   - From the File menu, select New...
   - In the dialog box that appears, click on the Projects tab.

- In the project type list, select Win32 Console Application and click OK.
- In the dialog that appears, select an empty project.

3. Add an example source file and c4lib.lib.

- From the Project menu, select Add To Project and Files...
- Browse for any source file in the CodeBase examples directory.
- Repeat for c4lib.lib, which can be found in the msc60 directory.

4. Open the project settings dialog box. From the Project menu, select Settings...

5. Set the project to use a multi-threaded run-time library.

- Click on the C/C++ tab.
- Under Category, select Code Generation.
- Under Use run-time library, select Debug Multithreaded.

This is for the Debug configuration. If you want to build with the Release configuration, follow these same steps, but select Multi-threaded instead of Debug Multithreaded.

6. Set the CodeBase source directory as an additional include directory.

- Click on the C/C++ tab.
- Under Category, select Preprocessor.
- Under Additional include directories, type in the location of the CodeBase source directory. e.g., c:\codebase\cpp\source.

7. Set the working directory to the CodeBase examples directory. This step is necessary if the example you intend to run opens an existing data file. The CodeBase examples that open an existing data file do not specify an explicit path. Therefore, the executable you build must be running from the directory where the example data files reside.

- Click on the Debug tab.
- Under Working directory, type in the location of the CodeBase examples directory, for example, c:\codebase\cpp\examples.

8. Your example project is now ready to compile and run.

Appendix K

DATA SYNCHRONIZATION: GOLDENGATE

GoldenGate 7 is a good example of data synchronization. It is a software platform for capturing, transforming, integrating, and delivering data across the enterprise and beyond to customers, partners, vendors, and elsewhere. The software provides synchronization capabilities for the widest range of databases in the industry.

GoldenGate employs a decoupled architecture to provide maximum flexibility in choice of hardware, operating system, and database for sources and targets. GoldenGate 7 works on all major databases, including Oracle, DB2 (OS/390 and UDB), Microsoft SQL, Sybase, Informix, SQL/MP, SQL/MX, MySQL, IMS/VSAM, Teradata, Enscribe, and all ODBC databases. It runs on most operating systems and platforms: UNIX, Windows NT/2000/XP, Linux, and Sun Solaris, HP/UX, IBM AIX, IBM OS/390, and TRU64.

Let's take a look at three aspects of this software: primary modules, software modules (add-on), and database replication.

K.1 PRIMARY MODULES

GoldenGate 7 is made up of three primary modules: Capture, Delivery, and Manager. Capture and Delivery perform most processing functions, and these two modules are decoupled in order to provide maximum processing flexibility, modularity, and performance.

K.1.1 GoldenGate Capture Core

This module is for extracting data from source systems. Capture also provides a host of flexible functions for queueing, formatting, and transforming data.

- Retrieves inserts, updates, and deletes from a database change source
- Filters out unnecessary data
- Selects specific columns and transforms the data (optionally)
- Outputs changes to one or more queues

K.1.2 GoldenGate Delivery Core

This module's powerful capabilities enable users to:

- Read queues for the latest database changes
- Execute mapping and transformation rules according to custom specifications
- Apply changes to designated tables in target databases

K.1.3 GoldenGate Manager Core

This module constantly monitors the operations and status of the Capture and Delivery modules and executes a number of data management tasks:

- Collector processes
- Threshold reporting
- Log resource management
- Purging of old queues
- Preallocation of log trail space
- Manager reporting

K.2 SOFTWARE MODULES

GoldenGate also provides several software modules that support and extend the capabilities of our core offerings.

- Activity Console
- Syncfile
- Rollback

The GoldenGate Activity Console is a Web-based application that provides complete administrative control over all GoldenGate modules and synchronization management and reporting functions. With its dashboard-style GUI, the Activity Console allows database administrators and even nontechnical users to proactively monitor performance from virtually any workstation on your network. In short, it simplifies and expedites your data movement and management activities, from viewing and processing events to initiating processes and executing processing requests. In addition, anyone in the IT organization can now access data synchronization activity from a browser anywhere, alleviating pressure and time constraints on database administrators.

Syncfile is a fully fault-tolerant software module that is ideal for situations where there is a need to duplicate configuration files or other infrequently changed files, but where incremental change capture is not appropriate. Providing the ability to copy and deliver nearly any type of file across an organization. Syncfile supports a wide range of synchronization scenarios, including daily, weekly, and off-hours copying. Using GoldenGate's browser-based GUI, users can easily execute a number of file synchronization tasks, such as:

- Replicate files over Expand and TCP/IP using FUP and FTP
- Make changes to EDIT file contents on the fly
- Accommodate differences between source and target platforms
- Duplicate TACL macros, object, obey, and source code

For organizations with mission-critical systems, GoldenGate Rollback is well suited for the solution for fast recovery from downtime. Integrated with GoldenGate 7, Rollback provides effective tools for performing selective backout processing on enterprise databases, and eliminates the need for full restore operations that usually require several hours or more. GoldenGate Rollback is ideal in situations where data becomes corrupted or is deleted due to human error.

K.3 DATABASE REPLICATION

Database replication-supported environments come in two types:

- Enterprisewide data synchronization
- Bidirectional replication, data capture, and transformation

Technology environments within most large organizations are made up of a wide range of applications, databases, operating systems, and hardware platforms. Having the capability to move data across all these heterogeneous systems has long been a goal of IT professionals: Oracle replication to DB2, DB2 replication to Sybase, and so on.

GoldenGate realizes this goal by enabling data capture, transformation, and bidirectional replication between virtually all major databases, including any combination of Oracle, DB2, Microsoft SQL Server, Sybase, Informix, NonStop SQL, MySQL, Times Ten, Enscribe, and other databases. By leveraging native interfaces GoldenGate eliminates the need for additional middleware when capturing, transforming, and mapping data between these diverse databases.

Appendix L

PARTITIONING LARGE DATABASES: ORACLE

Dividing large historical tables and associated indices into time-related partitions allows users to add, delete, and manage records in a partition independently of other partitions. Let's take a look at the code example creating a table in Listing L.1. Then we take a look at another code example in Listing L.2.

LISTING L.1 CREATE TABLE EXAMPLE

```
CREATE TABLE RFID_item (acct_no NUMBER(5),
                  supplier_name CHAR(30),
                  number_of_items NUMBER(10),
                  week_no INTEGER)
      PARTITION BY RANGE (week_no) ...
          (PARTITION VALUES LESS THAN (10) TABLESPACE
             rfid0,
           PARTITION VALUES LESS THAN (20) TABLESPACE
             rfid1,
           PARTITION VALUES LESS THAN (30) TABLESPACE
             rfid2;
          ...
           PARTITION VALUES LESS THAN (100) TABLESPACE
             rfid100;
```

What this is saying is that we have an RFID_ITEM table partitioned by week. The first partition covers items for week 0–9 and the second partition includes items for week 10–19. The third partition covers items for week 20–29 and the final partition includes items for week 90–99.

The time-related partitions we just gave are arbitrary. We can change the way time is divided. We can divide the time into 12 partitions to conform to a calendar year. This means one partition to represent each month of the year.

As a matter of fact, partitions need not be time-related; they could be used to divide exception items into smaller and more manageable parts. The partitioning rules state that every table and index partition must have a noninclusive upper bound, as specified by the VALUES LESS THAN clause to satisfy the criterion that every table and index partition have an upper bound. This means that VALUES LESS THAN is always on the next-lower partition. The first partition is the partition with the lowest VALUES LESS THAN clause and the last or highest partition is the partition with the highest VALUES LESS THAN clause. One word of caution that if we attempt to insert a value greater than or equal to the partition bound for the highest partition in the table, we will see the insert will fail.

The first step in writing out the partitioning clause is to arbitrarily assign letter values to each item in each category: item unavailability, item delivery, item security, packaging of items, excess items, item exception, item administration, and item returns.

We assign codes to each item type in the item unavailability category, as follows.

AA   Backlogged items
AB   Cannibalized items
AC   Damaged items
AD   Discontinued items

We assign codes in the item delivery category, as follows:

BA   Backordered items
BB   Bullwhip Items
BC   Late items
BD   Unusable items due to late delivery

For the item security category, we assign the following codes:

CA   Degaussed items
CB   Lost items
CC   Improperly classified items
CD   Misplaced items
CE   Returned items
CF   Stolen items

In the packing of items category are the assigned codes:

DA   Improperly packaged items
DB   Items without required hazardous instructions
DC   Items without required instructions
DD   Missing item parts
DE   Spoiled items
DF   Tampered items

For the excess items category, we assign the following codes:

EA   Duplicate items
EB   Excess items
EC   Idle items

For the item inspection category, each item type is assigned a code:

FA   Counterfeited items
FB   Poor quality Items
FC   Recalled items

We assign codes in the item administration category, as follows:

GA   Cancelled items
GB   Misconfigured items
GC   Misrecorded items
GD   Mis-shipped items
GE   Over-shipped items
GF   Under-shipped items
GG   Late recorded items
GH   Unshipped items

The item returns category shows the following codes:

HA   Unwanted (returned) items
HB   User-dissatisfied items
HC   Vapor items
HD   Wrong items

Then we specify the upper bound for each partition with the VALUES LESS THAN clause for each item category, like this:

BA   Unavailability items
CA   Late item delivery
DA   Item security
EA   Packaging of items
FA   Excess items
GA   Item inspection
HA   Item administration
IA   Item returns

The next step is to use an upper bound value to represent a partition in the following CREATE TABLE clause. Although we can add some more item categories, the last partition must have a value, for example, ZZ, higher than the codes assigned to the items of the last category, as in Listing L.2.

LISTING L.2 CREATE TABLE FOR CODED UNUSABLE ITEMS

```
CREATE  TABLE  RFID_item  (acct_no  NUMBER(5),
                supplier_name  CHAR(30),
                number_of_items  NUMBER(10),
                unusable_type  CHAR(10))
        PARTITION  BY  RANGE  (item_type)  ...
        PARTITION  VALUES  LESS  THAN  ('BA')  TABLESPACE
            rfidu0,
        PARTITION  VALUES  LESS  THAN  ('CA')  TABLESPACE
            rfidu1,
        PARTITION  VALUES  LESS  THAN  ('DA')  TABLESPACE
            rfidu2;
        PARTITION  VALUES  LESS  THAN  ('EA')  TABLESPACE
            rfidu3;
        PARTITION  VALUES  LESS  THAN  ('FA')  TABLESPACE
            rfidu4;
        PARTITION  VALUES  LESS  THAN  ('GA')  TABLESPACE
            rfidu5;
        PARTITION  VALUES  LESS  THAN  ('HA')  TABLESPACE
            rfidu6;
        PARTITION  VALUES  LESS  THAN  ('IA')  TABLESPACE
            rfidu8;
            ...
        PARTITION  VALUES  LESS  THAN  ('ZZ')  TABLESPACE
            rfidu100;
```

What the first partition says is it collects all item types falling under the unavailability items category (BA): backlogged items (AA), cannibalized items (AB), damaged items (AC), and discontinued items (AD), each with the value of less than BA. This is also true for other exception item type categories: late item delivery (CA), item security (DA), packaging of items (EA), excess items (FA), item inspection (GA), item administration (HA), and item returns (IA). This means the item delivery category as an exception type category (CA) collects the following items assigned less than CA: backordered items (BA), bullwhip items (BB), and late items (BC).

Appendix M

SOFTWARE ENGINEERING STANDARDS

This appendix contains IEEE, ISO, and related software engineering standards.

M.1 IEEE STANDARDS

IEEE software engineering standards are implemented in an array of disciplines, including: computer science, quality management, project management, systems engineering, dependability, and safety. Table M.1 is a list of some approved standards unless otherwise noted.

Table M.1   IEEE Standards

Pub No.	Issue Date	Title
IEEE STD 610.12	1990	Standard Glossary of Software Engineering Terminology
IEEE STD 730	2002	Standard for Software Quality Assurance Plans
IEEE STD 828	1998	Standard for Software Configuration Management Plans
IEEE STD 829	1998	An American National Standard, IEEE Standard for Software Test Documentation
IEEE STD 830	1998	Recommended Practice for Software Requirements
IEEE STD 982.1	1988	IEEE Recommended Practice for Software Requirements Specifications

(continued)

Table M.1 IEEE Standards (Continued)

Pub No.	Issue Date	Title
IEEE STD 982.2	1988	IEEE Standard Dictionary off Measures to Produce Reliable Software
IEEE 990	1987	IEEE Recommended Practice for ADA as a Program Design Language
IEEE1002	1987	Standard Taxonomy for Software Engineering Standards
IEEE 1008	1987 (r-1993)	IEEE Standard for Software Unit Testing
ANSI/IEEE 1012	1998	An American National Standard, IEEE Standard for Software Verification and Validation Plans
IEEE 1016	1998	IEEE Recommended Practice for Software Design Descriptions
IEEE 1016.1	1993	IEEE Guide to Software Design Descriptions
IEEE STD 1028	1988	Standard for Software Reviews and Audits
IEEE STD 1042	1987	An American National Standard, IEEE Guide to Software Configuration Management
IEEE STD 1044	1993	IEEE Standard Classifications for Software Anomalies
IEEE STD 1045	1992	IEEE Standard for Software Productivity Metrics
IEEE STD 1058	1998	IEEE Standard for Software Project Management Plans
IEEE STD 1059	1993	IEEE Guide for Software Verification And Validation Plans
IEEE STD 1061	1998	IEEE Standard for Software Quality Metrics Methodology
IEEE STD 1062	1993	IEEE Recommended Practice for Software Acquisition
IEEE STD 1063	2001	IEEE Standard for Software User Documentation
IEEE STD 1074	1997	IEEE Standard for Developing Software Life Cycle Processes
IEEE STD 1029	1992	IEEE Recommended Practice for the Evaluation and Selection of CASE Tools
IEEE STD 1175.1	2002	Guide for CASE Tool Interconnections— Classifications and Description
IEEE STD 1219	1993	IEEE Standard for Software Maintenance

Table M.1   IEEE Standards (Continued)

Pub No.	Issue Date	Title
IEEE STD 1220	1998	Standard for the Application and Management of the Systems Engineering
IEEE STD 1228	1994	IEEE Standard for Software Safety Plans
IEEE STD 1233	1998	Guide for Developing System Requirements Specifications
IEEE STD 1298	1992	Standard for Software Quality Management System, Part 1: Requirements
IEEE STD 1320.1	1998	Standard for Functional Modeling Language—Syntax and Semantics for IDEF0
IEEE STD 1320.2	1998	Standard for Conceptual Modeling Language Syntax and Semantics
IEEE STD 1362	1998	Guide for Information Technology—System Definition—Concept of Operations
IEEE STD 1420.1	1995	Standard for Information Technology—Software Reuse—Data Model for Reuse
IEEE STD 1420.1a	1996	Supplement to Standard for Information Technology—Software Reuse—Data
IEEE STD 1420.1b	1999	IEEE Trial-Use Supplement to Standard for Information
DRAFT J-STD.2, IEEEP1448 - EIA PN 3764	1/31/1997	U.S. Implementation of ISO/IEC 12207 International Standard, Guide, Standard for Information Technology—Software Life Cycle Processes—Implementation Considerations
IEEE STD 1462	1998	Standard—Adoption of International Standard ISO/IEC 14102: 1995; 1465-1998, Standard—Adoption of International Standard ISO/IEC 12119: 1994(E)
IEEE STD 1471	2000	Recommended Practice for Architectural Description of Software Intensive
IEEE STD 1490	1998	Guide—Adoption of PMI Standard—A Guide to the Project Management Body of Knowledge
IEEE STD 1517	1999	IEEE Standard for Information Technology—Software Life Cycle Processes—Reuse

(continued)

Table M.1   IEEE Standards (Continued)

Pub No.	Issue Date	Title
IEEE STD 1540	2001	Standard for Software Life Cycle Processes—Risk Management
IEEE STD 2001	2002	Recommended Practice for Internet Practices—Web Page Engineering
IEEE 14143.1	2000	Adoption of ISO/IEC 14143-1:1998 Information Technology—Software
IEEE STD 15288	In progress 2006	Adoption of the OSO/IEC 15288 —Systems Engineering System Life Cycle Processes

M.2   ISO/IEC STANDARDS

Table M.2 shows some standards that have been or will be approved.

Table M.2   ISO/IEC Standards

Pub No.	Issue Date	Title
ISO/IEC 9126-1	2001	Software engineering—Product quality—Part 1: Quality model
ISO/IEC TR 9126-2	2003	Software engineering—Product quality—Part 2: External metrics
ISO/IEC TR 9126-3	2003	Software engineering—Product quality—Part 3: Internal metrics
ISO/IEC TR 9126-4	2004	Software engineering—Product quality—Part 4: Quality in use metrics
ISO/IEC TR 14471	1999	Information technology—Software engineering—Guidelines for the adoption of CASE tools
ISO/IEC 14598	2000	Software engineering—Product evaluation—Part 2: Planning and management
ISO/IEC 14598-3	2000	Software engineering—Product evaluation—Part 3: Process for developers
ISO/IEC 14598-4	1999	Software engineering—Product evaluation—Part 4: Process for acquirers

Table M.2 ISO/IEC Standards (Continued)

Pub No.	Issue Date	Title
ISO/IEC 14598-6	2001	Software engineering—Product evaluation—Part 6: Documentation of evaluation modules
ISO/IEC TR-14759	1999	Software engineering—Mock up and prototype—A categorization of software mock up and prototype models and their use
ISO/IEC 15504-2	2003	Information technology—Process assessment—Part 2: Performing an assessment
ISO/IEC 15939	2002	Software engineering—Software measurement process
ISO/IEC TR 16326	1999	Software engineering—Guide for the application of ISO/IEC 12207 to project management
ISO/IEC TR 19759	2005	Software engineering—Guide to the Software Engineering Body of Knowledge (SWEBOK)
ISO/IEC 19761	2003	Software engineering—DOSMIC-FFP—A functional size measurement method
ISO/IEC 20926	2003	Software engineering—IFPUG 4.1 Unadjusted functional size measurement method—Counting practices manual
ISO/IEC 20968	2002	Software engineering—Mk II Function Point Analysis—Counting Practices Manual
ISO/IEC 24570	2005	Software engineering—NESMA functional size measurement method version 2.1—Definitions and counting guidelines for the application of Function Point Analysis
ISO/IEC 25000	2005	Software engineering—Software product Quality Requirements and evaluation (SQuaRE)—Guide to SQuaRE.
ISO/IEC 90003	2004	Software engineering—Guidelines for the application of ISO 9001_2000 to computer software

M.3 RELATED STANDARDS

Table M.3 lists some IEEE/EIA standards.

Table M.3   Related Standards

Pub No.	Issue Date	Title
IEEE/EIA 12207.0	1996	Industry Implementation of International Standard ISO/IEC 12207: 1995
IEEE/EIA 12207.1	1996	Industry Implementation of International Standard ISO/IEC 12207: 1995
IEEE/EIA 12207.2	1997	Industry Implementation of International Standard ISO/IEC 12207: 1995

Appendix N

BUSINESS PROCESS AUTOMATION: IBM PRODUCTS

Here are some IBM products to automate and integrate business processes, information, workflows, and applications.

WebSphere® Business Integration Server allows customers to integrate business information. This server is the third element of the IBM RFID product. The other two elements are Devices and WebSphere RFID Premises Server.

WebSphere Process Server is based on Service-Oriented Architecture that simplifies the integration and automation of enterprise business processes.

WebSphere Business Modeler is useful for analyzing complex business scenarios before business processes are automated and implemented.

WebSphere Business Monitor V6.0 uses a graphical business dashboard to view and monitor performance. When the performance drops below the user-defined thresholds, the users will get an alert.

WebSphere Message Broker connects with both standard and nonstandard-based applications and services.

WebSphere MQ exchanges messages with business applications across different platforms.

IBM WebSphere MQ Workflow V3.6 automates processes and business workflows for interaction with any external application program and Web services.

IBM Rational Portfolio Manager is a real-time Project Portfolio Management (PPM) solution designed to optimize the business side of IT. This allows organizations to track projects and identify internal resource supply/ project demand. Executives can use real-time multidimensional views, graphs, and reports to identify which projects have the greatest potential to contribute to the business and which projects justify the commitment of limited resources.

IBM WebSphere® Adapters allow users to integrate processes to exchange information among ERP, HR, CRM, and supply chain systems. Adaptors are grouped in application and technology. The list of application adapters is shown in Table N.1.

Table N.1   IBM WebSphereR Adapters (Application)

Ariba Buyer	SAP Software	Centricity Gateway
Nightfire Applications	Clarify CRM	Oracle Applications
eMatrix	PeopleSoft Enterprise	ESRI Spatial Database
Portal Infranet	I2	QAD MFG/PRO
I2 Active Data Warehouse	SAP Exchange Infrastructure	IndusConnect Framework
Siebel Business Applications	JD Edwards OneWorld	Spirent Applications
JD Edwards World	SunGard FRONT ARENA	Manugistics
Telcordia Applications	Maximo MEA	Websphere Commerce Adapter
MetaSolv Applications		

IBM WebSphere® Technology Adapters provide connectivity to access data, technologies, and protocols that enhance integration infrastructure. The list of adapters is given in Table N.2.

Table N.2   IBM WebSphereR Technology Adapters

ACORD XML	iSoft Commerce Suite Express	Adapter for Enterprise JavaBean (EJB)
JDBC	COM	JMS
CORBA	Flat Files	Data Handler for Complex Data
Lotus Domino	Data Handler for EDI	SWIFT
Data Handler for XML	TPI On-Ramp	Microsoft Exchange
TPI Solo	FIX Protocol	TPI Trading Networks
Web Services	HTTP Adapter (Java-Based)	WebSphere MQ Adapter
iSeries (integration broker IBM iSeries)	WebSphere Message Broker	iSoft Commerce Suite Advanced
WebSphere MQ Workflow Adapter	iSoft Commerce Suite Enterprise	

Development tools to provide a framework for development of custom adapters include *WebSphere Adapter Toolkit* and *WebSphere Business Integration Adapter Development Kit*.

IBM WebSphere® Partner Gateway V6.0 is capable of serving multiple B2B protocols and standards, including traditional EDI, FTP scripting for WAN connectivity, as well as XML-based documents and partner interface processes, and allows the addition of protocols and standards.

The gateway leverages WebSphere Application Server V6.0 in Express, Advanced, and Enterprise Editions. The Express Edition is available on Microsoft® Windows®, Linux® SUSE and Red Hat, IBM OS/400, and i5/OS. The Advanced and Enterprise Editions are targeted for B2B exchanges and hubs to integrate large trading partner communities. They are available on Microsoft Windows, Linux SUSE and Red Hat, Sun® Solaris, and IBM AIX®.

Appendix O

COMMERCIAL ASSESSMENT PRODUCTS

The following is a list of some commercial assessment products: Netective, now called HackerShield v2.0, and NetRecon.

O.1 HACKERSHIELD

Among these tools is Netective developed by Netect, a provider of network scanning and response software. Netect was acquired by BindView in January 1999. Netective (now called HackerShield) is a software solution that scans and detects networks for potential security holes, and offers the user patches or corrective actions to fix the breaches before they become a threat. Netective identifies and resolves security vulnerabilities at both the operating system level and the network level. It also monitors key system files for unauthorized changes and, by referencing a one-million-word dictionary, identifies vulnerable user passwords through a variety of password cracking techniques.

A detailed report provides network administrators with a description of each vulnerability and corrective action as well as a ranking of vulnerabilities by the risk they pose to a site's security. Network administrators are also presented with a high-level overview of the vulnerability and its solution with an option to link to a more detailed explanation and reference materials.

Employing an implementation model similar to anti-virus products, Netect provides ongoing security updates via the Internet to ensure that users are protected from the latest threats. Netect uses secure push technology to broadcast the vulnerability updates. Users are not required to reinstall the software in order to integrate the updates.

O.2 NETRECON

Axent Technologies offers NetRecon, a tool that checks for vulnerabilities from various points within the network and reports them in real-time. NetRecon employs a scanning technique that allows it immediately to display vulnerabilities as they are detected and quickly performs deeper probes. Multiple objectives are executed in parallel, checking each network and attached device for common vulnerabilities. For example, one objective looks for password information from a server, another objective tries to crack passwords, and another looks for servers with rlogin (remote log-in) services to see if the cracked user passwords will provide access. The results from the first objective are loaded into the second and from the second into the third as soon as some results are available.

NetRecon can scan a company's networks from the outside or the inside. Scanning from the outside shows how a network looks to an external attacker, and scanning from the inside reveals which parts of the network can be exploited internally or by an external attacker who has gained local network access.

Appendix P

RISK-RELATED SOFTWARE

Acertus™, Securac's Enterprise Risk Management (ERM) software solution enables organizations to identify, measure, manage, and mitigate risk and compliance in all aspects of the organization. The software is designed to improve how organizations assess risk, security, and regulatory compliance.

Contact information:

Bryce Mitchell, Executive V-P Sales at Securac Inc.
877-328-7220
info@securac.net, http://www.securac.net

Integrated Computer Engineering, Inc. (ICE), a wholly owned subsidiary and directorate within American Systems Corporation's System Division since January 2002, has developed Risk Radar, a risk management software designed by project managers for project managers. This tool helps program and project managers—at all levels and in all industries and project types—quickly categorize, prioritize, track, report, and manage their project risk.

Contact information:

http://www.iceincusa.com

Bayesian Systems, Inc. is a leading provider of software for managing uncertainty based on a long-overlooked but powerful principle called Bayes theorem. This theorem is the fundamental principle governing the process of logical inference. It determines what conclusions can be made with what degree of confidence based on the totality of relevant evidence available.

The company offers WinAward™, a business development decision and management system; Risk Assessment Software and Consulting, a product that helps solve risk, decision, and communication problems and includes methods development, custom software development, and application of the Bayesian software engine; and BayesEngine™ Technology.

Contact information:

Bayesian Systems, Inc.
18310 Montgomery Village Avenue, Suite 615
Gaithersburg, MD 20879
301-987-5400 (V); 301-987-9387 (F)
helpdesk@bayes.com, http://www.bayes.com

Computer Sciences Corporation offers RISKMASTER software family for risk management claims: RISKMASTER/World™, a Windows-based risk management information system; its new browser-based system RISKMAS-TER.net™; and Global Risk Systems, a tool for implementing and optimizing business risk strategies that covers traditional insurance and loss data, as well as enterprise risk management data.
Contact information:

CSC's Corporate Headquarters
2100 East Grand Avenue
El Segundo, CA 90245
310-615-0311
http://www.csc-fs.com/

C/S Solutions, Inc. offers integrated analytical tools for cost, schedule, and risk management. Their software tools integrate with existing earned value and scheduling systems, and there is no need to re-engineer the current automation environment. The firm provides high-quality program management software, consulting services, and training for organizations interested in proactive program management. The company offers many products, including wInsight which is the tool for analyzing, sharing, consolidating, and reporting earned value management data. wInsight functions as a user-friendly MS Windows interface to engage technical managers, senior managers, and program control professionals in proactive project management.
Contact information:

C/S Solutions
111 N. Sepulveda, Suite 333
Manhattan Beach, CA 90266
310-798-6396 (V); 310-798-4226(F)
info@cs-solutions.com, http://www.cs-solutions.com

Entegra Corporation provides software for reputation risk management, incident reporting/tracking, investigation/case management, and issue management. They offer Ki4 which is an enterprise reputation-risk solution that "listens" and "measures" reputation risk across all stakeholders, internal and external. Ki4 provides the information and knowledge that executives need in order to build, maintain, manage, and protect the most fragile asset: the corporate reputation.

Contact information:

Entegra Corporation
One Lincoln Center
18W140 Butterfield Road, 15th Floor
Oakbrook Terrace, IL 60181
630-613-7661 (V); Sales Info: 630-613-7635 (V)
info@entegracorp.com, http://www.entegracorp.com/

Envision Technology Solutions has developed advanced risk management information systems software for a wide variety of businesses, including self-insured and self-administered corporations; insurance agencies, brokerages, and companies; third-party claims administrators; and other financial intermediaries. Their products include: RiskEnvision, a fully integrated risk management information system that assists with claim data management for property and casualty lines of insurance; WebEnvision, a Web-enabling product featuring elaborate browser technology for RiskEnvision; and CompVision, a risk management information system for workers compensation claim management and cost containment.

Contact information:

Envision Technology
6975 Union Park Center, Suite 120
Midvale, UT 84047
801-568-1818 (V)
sales-info@envision-ts.com

For the past 20 years Galorath Incorporated (also known as GA SEER™ Technologies) has provided a comprehensive set of decision-support and production optimization tools. Combined with extensive consulting and support services, these estimation and analysis tools help manage product design and manufacturing operations, driving out costs and building in quality.

Contact information:

info@galorath.com

The GIFIC Corporation is the original developer of the GIFIC® display language, a revolutionary new graphing/plotting paradigm that allows the creation of "picture" displays of most databases of information. Whether your interest is data fusion, data visualization, or data compression, GIFIC shows large amounts of information in a small space.

Contact information:

GIFIC
405 Atlantic St
Melbourne Beach, FL 3295
321-724-8420 or 800-37-GIFIC; 321-724-8420(V)
info@gific.com, http://www.gific.com/

High Tower Software is a pioneer in visual data discovery solutions for Global-1000 companies who need to turn massive amounts of rapidly changing business data into knowledge and results. By automatically detecting any data element or trend that requires immediate analysis, the Tower-View product allows companies to prevent costly problems and capitalize on opportunities. TowerView was designed to address the more advanced needs of enterprises tracking changes to huge quantities of data, either from real-time sources, data warehouses, or large data files, enterprises that need to perform the critical task of data discovery.

Contact information:

High Tower Software
19712 MacArthur Blvd., Suite 120
Irvine, CA 92612
949-852-2233; 877-448-6937; 949-852-2230 (F)
info@high-tower.com

Asvaco™ Assessment Software, produced by Idealsoft, Inc., can assess anything, at any time, covering any topic. It includes Asvaco ScriptWriter, which allows anyone to create an assessment from scratch or add on to an existing set of questions, and Asvaco Engine, which runs the newly scripted assessment produced in the Asvaco ScriptWriter (sold separately).

Contact information:

Idealsoft, Inc.
2060-D Avenue
De Los Arboles #161
Thousand Oaks, CA 91362
805-523-8434
info@asvaco.com

International Security Technology, Inc. offers CORA® (Cost-of-Risk Analysis), a risk management decision support system that helps risk managers to optimize strategies for mitigation and transfer of, and recovery from operational risks of all kinds. CORA risk management projects are two-step processes. First, it provides a convenient context for risk analysts to organize, collect, store, validate, and collate the data that describes the risks and loss exposures of an organization. It then uses sophisticated algorithms to construct a quantitative risk model using these data.

Specifically it calculates Single Occurrence Loss (SOL), and Annualized Loss Expectancy (ALE) for the organization, and then displays the results in tabular and graphic form. Second, risk managers use the CORA quantitative risk model to evaluate the cost/benefit of proposed risk management measures to identify the optimum package. It can estimate the Return On Investment (ROI) of risk mitigation and risk transfer actions.

For example, CORA can identify insurance policies with a positive ROI, and it can also estimate IT system availability, taking into account all the threats that cause service interruptions. Finally, CORA can analyze alternate business continuity plans and determine the optimum Recovery Time Objective for IT systems taking into account both loss reduction and implementation costs.

Contact information:

Robert V. Jacobson CISSP, CPP
International Security Technology, Inc.
99 Park Avenue, 11th Floor
New York, NY 10016-1501
888-478-2672; 212-808-5206(F)
info@ist-usa.com

Legacy Systems Research is a software development and management consulting firm based in Idaho. The firm offers CostBenefit.ComCentric software which assesses financial risks from business operations.

Contact information:

G. Johnson
Legacy Systems Research
P.O. Box 52115
Idaho Falls, ID 83405-2115
208-522-5401; 208-246-1018(F)
info@costbenefit.com

Lumenaut is a software design company that specializes in developing out-of-the-box analytical applications for business. The company has developed "Lumenaut," a statistical and decision analysis software add-in for Excel, featuring parametric and nonparametric statistics, decision trees, and sensitivity analysis.

Contact information:

Lumenaut
inquiry@lumenaut.com
http://www.lumenaut.com

Lumina Decision Systems, Inc., of Los Altos, California, is a computer software and services company that develops and markets software for modeling and decision support, such as Analytica™, which is a visual modeling tool incorporating hierarchical influence diagrams for building and managing complex risk models. In addition to information about the company itself, sources of information, both on and off the Web, are listed for categories such as management software, risk and insurance, medical decision making, and decision sciences.

Mainstay Software Corporation was established to continue developing and marketing MAINSTAY, a one-of-a-kind OLAP (On-Line Analytical Processing) database and when the company began to focus its attention on the aerospace/defense industry, it developed (using MAINSTAY) PPAS (Proposal Pricing and Analysis System), the company's flagship product. As the first PC-based proposal pricing tool, PPAS received much attention.

Today, it is used by many government contractors for preparation, analysis, and presentation of proposals, as well as for the analysis and evaluation of proposals by government agencies themselves. In addition to the PPAS product, Mainstay Software offers a parametric estimating program, Para-Model, and a risk assessment and management software product, STAR, which are both designed with flexibility in mind to accommodate the requirements of government requests for proposals.

Contact information:

Mainstay Software Corporation
7853 East Arapahoe Court Suite 2500
Denver, CO 80112
303-220-8780

A SW-CMM Level 5 and P-CMM Level 3 global Information Technology (IT) applications outsourcing company with nearly two decades of experience, Mastek Ltd. offers application management, application development, risk management solution, system integration for financial services, insurance, manufacturing, telecom, and retail sectors. Mastek offers offshore software development, applications management, risk management, CRM/eCRM, and consulting services. Its solutions use technologies such as Java™, EJB™, J2EE™, JSP™, Sun Solaris, UNIX, C and C++, XML, and TCP/IP, among others.

Developed by David Vose and his team at Vose Consulting, ModelAssist can be used as a "personal risk analysis expert," giving you a complete roadmap to risk analysis. With over 150 example models and more than 500 risk analysis topics, ModelAssist will not only help beginners produce accurate, defensible, and clear risk analyses, but also offer advanced risk analysts an opportunity to expand and improve their risk analysis skills. ModelAssist is available in four versions, of which two are for Crystal Ball and two for @RISK users.

Contact information:

609-279-0882
huybert@risk-modelling.com

M-Tech International, Inc. offers software tools for the food industry. The Hazard Analysis Tools (HAT) system is a total electronic solution to managing HACCP in the food industry. It includes comprehensive HACCP planning, record keeping, and plant floor data collection using radio frequency handheld devices.

Contact information:

M-Tech International, Inc.
P.O. Box 666
Conway, AR 72033
501-328-9178; 501-328-9148(F)
sales@myhaccp.com

The Navy's Best Manufacturing Practices Center of Excellence offers free risk management software (Technical Risk Identification and Mitigation System, TRIMS) as part of its Program Manager's WorkStation (PMWS). This tool primarily focuses on risk management in systems engineering.

Contact information:

info@bmpcoe.org

NeuralWare is a leading supplier and developer of neural network software for the development and deployment of innovative, intelligent, on-line solutions for commercial, industrial, government, and scientific applications. NeuralWare combined the expertise of mathematics, engineering, and computer science within their product line to produce powerful computation environments beyond standard statistical models for engineers and scientists.

The company's products form a high-performance technical computing environment providing nonlinear mathematics through neural networks to produce some of the most state-of-the-art software solutions possible.

Contact information:

NeuralWare
230 E. Main St., Suite 200
Carnegie, PA 15106
412-278-6280; 412-278-6289 (F)
info@neuralware.com

Optial™ is a leading supplier of Web-based audit, compliance, and risk management solutions for business and government. Their products have been implemented by Fortune 500 organizations in almost 50 countries. Optial offers a platform for managing key business assurance activities generating operational cost reductions and delivering transparency and confidence in the management of corporate risks.

The Optial system is developed as a flexible platform to support risk management and compliance methodologies within global corporations. The applications are accessed via a standard Web browser from any computer connected to the Internet or intranet as applicable.

Contact information:

info@optial.com

Palisade Corporation is a world leader in risk analysis, decision analysis, optimization, and statistical analysis software products. Since 1984 Palisade has used Monte Carlo simulation and genetic algorithm technologies to help analysts, researchers, and managers make better decisions.

Palisade products include: @RISK (risk analysis add-in for Excel), PrecisionTree (decision analysis add-in for Excel), StatTools (statistics add-in for Excel), @RISK for Project (risk analysis add-in for Microsoft Project), Evolver (genetic algorithm optimizer for Excel), RISKOptimizer (genetic algorithm and Monte Carlo simulation optimizer), and the DecisionTools Suite.

Contact information:

607-277-8000
sales@palisade.com, http://www.palisade.com

ProRisk is an interactive, graphically based decision support tool for project managers to assist in the identification, management, and mitigation of risks associated with project management tasks.

Contact information:

Geoffrey G. Roy
School of Engineering

Murdoch University
Perth, WA 6150, Australia
618-9360 7103; 618-9360 7104(F)
geoff@eng.murdoch.edu.au

The Q5AIMS Audit & Inspection Management System enables you to conduct your audits, behavior-based observations, and corrective actions. Integrating desktop, laptop, tablet, Palm, or Pocket PC technology, Q5AIMS is your total audit management solution. Q5AIMS is multidimensional. It is used for security, risk management, health and safety, environmental, and all quality auditing.

Contact information:

John Lukins
709-739-8801, 8803; 866-737-7574
jlukins@q5systems.com, http://www.q5systems.com

Quantalytics, Inc. offers a remote automatic computer backup solution named Q-Back. This software runs a computer backup job unattended at night, after business hours, and transfers the compressed, password-protected files via FTP to Quantalytics' backup server.

Contact information:

Michael Lukin
516-295-5121
mlukin@quantalytics.com

Reliability Analysis Center, an information analysis center chartered by the U.S. Department of Defense and operated by Alion Science and Technology (formerly IIT Research Institute), serves as a government and industry focal point that provides technical expertise and information to improve the reliability, maintainability, quality, and supportability of manufactured components and systems. RAC offers a complete product line of reliability, maintainability, quality, and supportability publications, automated databases, and software, including PRISM, a new software tool that ties together several tools into a comprehensive system reliability prediction methodology.

Contact information:

http://rac.alionscience.com/Help/Rac_ContactUs.html
http://rac.alionscience.com/PRODUCTS/index.html

Risk Services & Technology of Amherst, New Hampshire offers their Risk-Trak Risk Management Software and consulting services in risk management for government, military, and commercial entities. RiskTrak is fully compatible with Windows and features; an SQL engine for database management, network interface, and e-mail functionality. RiskTrak imports from, and exports to, any fully ODBC-compliant database.

Contact information:

RST
17 Old Nashua Road, #6
Amherst, NH 03031-2839
603-673-9907; 603-673-9913 (F)
RST@stgrp.com

RiskWatch Inc., a leading risk assessment software company since 1990, provides quantitative risk analysis software that produces accurate results for better decision making on security measures. Based in Annapolis, Maryland, with a sales and engineering office in San Jose, California, its clients include U.S. federal agencies and departments, states, and corporations. The software is available in versions for information systems, for physical security, for school security, and for security planning.

Contact information:

http://www.riskwatch.com

CERT® Coordination Center, Software Engineering Institute, Carnegie Mellon University offers the Operationally Critical Threat, Asset, and Vulnerability Evaluation[SM], or OCTAVE®, approach. It is a self-directed information security risk evaluation method that offers a systematic way for an organization to address its information security risks, sorting through the complex web of organizational and technological issues. The OCTAVE method and its implementation guide can be downloaded from the CERT Coordination Center Web site at http://www.cert.org/octave/.

Taknosys Software Corporation focuses on developing solutions that aid users in their decision-making processes. Taknosys Software offers both custom and packaged software solutions as well as training in the art/science of decision making.

Contact information:

Taknosys Software Corporation
229 Martin Street
Sharon, WI 53585
262-736-2824; 262-736-2825 (F)
info@taknosys.com

U.S. Design designs, manufactures, and markets high-capacity and high-performance optical storage products for the computer industry. U.S. Design has solutions for applications such as data archival, imaging, backup, multimedia, and data distribution.

Contact information:

http://www.usdesign.com

Appendix Q

SAMPLE SECURITY POLICY TEMPLATES

SANS has received permission to provide the following sanitized security policies from a large organization that you adapt to the security needs of your organization.

- Acceptable Use Policy
- Acquisition Assessment Policy
- Audit Vulnerability Scan Policy
- Automatically Forwarded E-Mail Policy
- Database Password Policy
- E-Mail Retention Policy
- Extranet Policy
- Information Sensitivity Policy
- Password Policy
- Remote Access Policy
- Risk Assessment Policy
- Router Security Policy
- Server Security Policy
- Virtual Private Network (VPN) Policy
- Wireless Communications Policy

Q.1 ACCEPTABLE USE POLICY

Abstract: This policy defines acceptable use of equipment and computing services, and the appropriate employee security measures to protect the organization's corporate resources and proprietary information.

Q.1.1 Overview

InfoSec's intentions for publishing an Acceptable Use Policy are not to impose restrictions that are contrary to <Company Name> established culture of openness, trust, and integrity. InfoSec is committed to protecting <Company Name>'s employees, partners, and the company from illegal or damaging actions by individuals, either knowingly or unknowingly.

Internet/intranet/extranet-related systems, including but not limited to computer equipment, software, operating systems, storage media, network accounts providing electronic mail, WWW browsing, and FTP, are the property of <Company Name>. These systems are to be used for business purposes in serving the interests of the company, and of our clients and customers in the course of normal operations. Please review Human Resources policies for further details.

Effective security is a team effort involving the participation and support of every <Company Name> employee and affiliate who deals with information or information systems. It is the responsibility of every computer user to know these guidelines, and to conduct their activities accordingly.

Q.1.2 Purpose

The purpose of this policy is to outline the acceptable use of computer equipment at <Company Name>. These rules are in place to protect the employee and <Company Name>. Inappropriate use exposes <Company Name> to risks including virus attacks, compromise of network systems and services, and legal issues.

Q.1.3 Scope

This policy applies to employees, contractors, consultants, temporaries, and other workers at <Company Name>, including all personnel affiliated with third parties. This policy applies to all equipment that is owned or leased by <Company Name>.

Q.1.4 Policy

Q.1.4.1 General Use and Ownership

1. Although <Company Name>'s network administration desires to provide a reasonable level of privacy, users should be aware that the data they create on the corporate systems remains the property of <Company Name>. Because of the need to protect <Company Name>'s network, management cannot guarantee the confidentiality of information stored on any network device belonging to <Company Name>.

2. Employees are responsible for exercising good judgment regarding the reasonableness of personal use. Individual departments are responsible for creating guidelines concerning personal use of Internet/intranet/extranet systems. In the absence of such policies, employees should be guided by departmental policies on personal use, and if there is any uncertainty, employees should consult their supervisor or manager.

3. InfoSec recommends that any information that users consider sensitive or vulnerable be encrypted. For guidelines on information classification, see InfoSec's Information Sensitivity Policy. For guidelines on encrypting e-mail and documents, go to InfoSec's Awareness Initiative.

4. For security and network maintenance purposes, authorized individuals within <Company Name> may monitor equipment, systems, and network traffic at any time, per InfoSec's Audit Policy.

5. <Company Name> reserves the right to audit networks and systems on a periodic basis to ensure compliance with this policy.

Q.1.4.2 Security and Proprietary Information

1. The user interface for information contained on Internet/intranet/extranet-related systems should be classified as either confidential or not confidential, as defined by corporate confidentiality guidelines, details of which can be found in Human Resources policies. Examples of confidential information include but are not limited to: company private, corporate strategies, competitor sensitive, trade secrets, specifications, customer lists, and research data. Employees should take all necessary steps to prevent unauthorized access to this information.

2. Keep passwords secure and do not share accounts. Authorized users are responsible for the security of their passwords and accounts. System-level passwords should be changed quarterly; user-level passwords should be changed every six months.

3. All PCs, laptops, and workstations should be secured with a password-protected screensaver with the automatic activation feature set at ten minutes or less, or by logging-off (control-alt-delete for Win2K users) when the host will be unattended.

4. Use encryption of information in compliance with InfoSec's Acceptable Encryption Use policy.

5. Because information contained on portable computers is especially vulnerable, special care should be exercised. Protect laptops in accordance with the "Laptop Security Tips."

6. Postings by employees from a <Company Name> e-mail address to newsgroups should contain a disclaimer stating that the opinions expressed are strictly their own and not necessarily those of <Company Name>, unless posting is in the course of business duties.

7. All hosts used by the employee that are connected to the <Company Name> Internet/intranet/extranet, whether owned by the employee or <Company Name>, shall be continually executing approved virus-scanning software with a current virus database. Unless overridden by departmental or group policy.

8. Employees must use extreme caution when opening e-mail attachments received from unknown senders, which may contain viruses, e-mail bombs, or Trojan horse code.

Q.1.4.3 *Unacceptable Use*

The following activities are, in general, prohibited. Employees may be exempted from these restrictions during the course of their legitimate job responsibilities (e.g., systems administration staff may have a need to disable the network access of a host if that host is disrupting production services).

Under no circumstances is an employee of <Company Name> authorized to engage in any activity that is illegal under local, state, federal, or international law while utilizing <Company Name>-owned resources.

The lists below are by no means exhaustive, but attempt to provide a framework for activities that fall into the category of unacceptable use.

Q.1.4.3.1 *System and Network Activities*

The following activities are strictly prohibited, with no exceptions.

1. Violations of the rights of any person or company protected by copyright, trade secret, patent, or other intellectual property, or similar laws or regulations, including, but not limited to, the installation or distribution of "pirated" or other software products that are not appropriately licensed for use by <Company Name>.

2. Unauthorized copying of copyrighted material including, but not limited to, digitization and distribution of photographs from magazines, books, or other copyrighted sources, copyrighted music, and the installation of any copyrighted software for which <Company Name> or the end user does not have an active license is strictly prohibited.

3. Exporting software, technical information, encryption software, or technology, in violation of international or regional export control laws, is illegal. The appropriate management should be consulted prior to export of any material that is in question.

4. Introduction of malicious programs into the network or server (e.g., viruses, worms, Trojan horses, e-mail bombs, etc.).

5. Revealing your account password to others or allowing use of your account by others. This includes family and other household members when work is being done at home.

6. Using a <Company Name> computing asset to actively engage in procuring or transmitting material that is in violation of sexual harassment or hostile workplace laws in the user's local jurisdiction.

7. Making fraudulent offers of products, items, or services originating from any <Company Name> account.

8. Making statements about warranty, expressly or implied, unless it is a part of normal job duties.

9. Effecting security breaches or disruptions of network communication. Security breaches include, but are not limited to, accessing data of which the employee is not an intended recipient or logging into a server or account that the employee is not expressly authorized to access, unless these duties are within the scope of regular duties. For purposes of this section, "disruption" includes, but is not limited to, network sniffing, pinged floods, packet spoofing, denial of service, and forged routing information for malicious purposes.

10. Port scanning or security scanning is expressly prohibited unless prior notification to InfoSec is made.

11. Executing any form of network monitoring that will intercept data not intended for the employee's host, unless this activity is a part of the employee's normal job/duty.

12. Circumventing user authentication or security of any host, network, or account.

13. Interfering with or denying service to any user other than the employee's host (e.g., denial-of-service attack).

14. Using any program/script/command, or sending messages of any kind, with the intent to interfere with, or disable, a user's terminal session, via any means, locally or via the Internet/intranet/extranet.

15. Providing information about, or lists of, <Company Name> employees to parties outside <Company Name>.

Q.1.4.3.2 E-Mail and Communications Activities

1. Sending unsolicited e-mail messages, including the sending of "junk mail" or other advertising material to individuals who did not specifically request such material (email spam).

2. Any form of harassment via e-mail, telephone, or paging, whether through language, frequency, or size of messages.

3. Unauthorized use, or forging, of e-mail header information.

4. Solicitation of e-mail for any other e-mail address, other than that of the poster's account, with the intent to harass or to collect replies.
5. Creating or forwarding "chain letters,""Ponzi," or other "pyramid" schemes of any type.
6. Use of unsolicited e-mail originating from within <Company Name>'s networks of other Internet/intranet/extranet service providers on behalf of, or to advertise, any service hosted by <Company Name> or connected via <Company Name>'s network.
7. Posting the same or similar non-business-related messages to large numbers of Usenet newsgroups (newsgroup spam).

Q.1.5 Enforcement

Any employee found to have violated this policy may be subject to disciplinary action, up to and including termination of employment.

Q.1.6 Definitions

Term Definition
Spam Unauthorized or unsolicited electronic mass mailings.

Q.2 ACQUISITION ASSESSMENT POLICY

Abstract: Defines responsibilities regarding corporate acquisitions, and defines the minimum requirements of an acquisition assessment to be completed by the information security group.

Q.2.1 Purpose

To establish InfoSec responsibilities regarding corporate acquisitions, and define the minimum security requirements of an InfoSec acquisition assessment.

Q.2.2 Scope

This policy applies to all companies acquired by <Company Name> and pertains to all systems, networks, laboratories, test equipment, hardware, software, and firmware, owned or operated by the acquired company.

Q.2.3 Policy

Q.2.3.1 General

Acquisition assessments are conducted to ensure that a company being acquired by <Company Name> does not pose a security risk to corporate networks, internal systems, or confidential/sensitive information. InfoSec will provide personnel to serve as active members of the acquisition team throughout the acquisition process. The InfoSec role is to detect and evaluate information security risk, develop a remediation plan with the affected parties for the identified risk, and work with the acquisitions team to implement solutions for any identified security risks, prior to allowing connectivity to <Company Name>'s networks. Below are the minimum requirements that the acquired company must meet before being connected to the <Company Name> network.

Q.2.3.2 Requirements

Q.2.3.2.1 Hosts

1. All hosts (servers, desktops, laptops) will be replaced or re-imaged with a <Company Name> standard image.
2. Business critical production servers that cannot be replaced or re-imaged must be audited and a waiver granted by InfoSec.
3. All PC-based hosts will require <Company Name> approved virus protection before the network connection.

Q.2.3.2.2 Networks

1. All network devices will be replaced or re-imaged with a <Company Name> standard image.
2. Wireless network access points will be configured to the <Company Name> standard.

Q.2.3.2.3 Internet

1. All Internet connections will be terminated.
2. When justified by business requirements, air-gapped Internet connections require InfoSec review and approval.

Q.2.3.2.4 Remote Access

1. All remote access connections will be terminated.
2. Remote access to the production network will be provided by <Company Name>.

Q.2.3.2.5 Labs

1. Lab equipment must be physically separated and secured from non-lab areas.

2. The lab network must be separated from the corporate production network with a firewall between the two networks.

3. Any direct network connections (including analog lines, ISDN lines, T1, etc.) to external customers, partners, etc., must be reviewed and approved by the Lab Security Group (LabSec).

4. All acquired labs must meet with LabSec lab policy, or be granted a waiver by LabSec.

5. In the event the acquired networks and computer systems being connected to the corporate network fail to meet these requirements, the <Company Name> Chief Information Officer (CIO) must acknowledge and approve of the risk to <Company Name>'s networks.

Q.2.4 Enforcement

Any employee found to have violated this policy may be subject to disciplinary action, up to and including termination of employment.

Business Critical Production Server A server that is critical to the continued business operations of the acquired Company.

Q.3 AUDIT VULNERABILITY SCAN POLICY

Abstract: Defines the requirements and provides the authority for the information security team to conduct audits and risk assessments to ensure integrity of information/resources, to investigate incidents, to ensure conformance to security policies, or to monitor user/system activity where appropriate.

Q.3.1 Purpose

The purpose of this agreement is to set forth our agreement regarding network security scanning offered by the <Internal or External Audit Name> to the <Company Name>. <Internal or External Audit Name> shall utilize <Approved Name of Software> to perform electronic scans of Client's networks or firewalls or on any system at <Company Name>.

Audits may be conducted to:

■ Ensure integrity, confidentiality, and availability of information and resources.
■ Investigate possible security incidents ensure conformance to <Company Name> security policies.
■ Monitor user or system activity where appropriate.

Q.3.2 Scope

This policy covers all computer and communication devices owned or operated by <Company Name>. This policy also covers any computer and communications device that are present on <Company Name> premises, but which may not be owned or operated by <Company Name>. The <Internal or External Audit Name> will not perform Denial of Service activities.

Q.3.3 Policy

When requested, and for the purpose of performing an audit, consent to access needed will be provided to members of <Internal or External Audit Name>. <Company Name> hereby provides its consent to allow of <Internal or External Audit Name> to access its networks or firewalls to the extent necessary to allow [Audit organization] to perform the scans authorized in this agreement. <Company Name> shall provide protocols, addressing information, and network connections sufficient for <Internal or External Audit Name> to utilize the software to perform network scanning.

This access may include:

- User-level or system-level access to any computing or communications device.
- Access to information (electronic, hardcopy, etc.) that may be produced, transmitted, or stored on <Company Name> equipment or premises.
- Access to work areas (labs, offices, cubicles, storage areas, etc.).
- Access to interactively monitor and log traffic on <Company Name> networks.

Q.3.3.1 Network Control

If Client does not control their network or Internet service is provided via a second or third party, these parties are required to approve scanning in writing if scanning is to occur outside of the <Company Name's> LAN. By signing this agreement, all involved parties acknowledge that they authorize of <Internal or External Audit Name> to use their service networks as a gateway for the conduct of these tests during the dates and times specified.

Q.3.3.2 Service Degradation or Interruption

Network performance or availability may be affected by the network scanning. <Company Name> releases <Internal or External Audit Name> of any and all liability for damages that may arise from network availability restrictions caused by the network scanning, unless such damages are the result <Internal or External Audit Name>'s gross negligence or intentional misconduct.

Q.3.3.3 Client Point of Contact during the Scanning Period

<Company Name> shall identify in writing a person to be available if the result <Internal or External Audit Name> Scanning Team has questions regarding data discovered or requires assistance.

Q.3.3.4 Scanning Period

<Company Name> and <Internal or External Audit Name> Scanning Team shall identify in writing the allowable dates for the scan to take place.

Q.3.4 Enforcement

Any employee found to have violated this policy may be subject to disciplinary action, up to and including termination of employment.

Q.3.5 Revision History

29 September 2003, updated to include National Association of State Auditors, Comptrollers, and Treasurers; the National Association of Local Government Auditors; the U.S. General Accounting Office; and U.S. Inspectors General Legal and Reporting Considerations.

Q.4 AUTOMATICALLY FORWARDED E-MAIL POLICY

Abstract: Documents the requirement that no email will be automatically forwarded to an external destination without prior approval from the appropriate manager or director.

Q.4.1 Purpose

To prevent the unauthorized or inadvertent disclosure of sensitive company information.

Q.4.2 Scope

This policy covers automatic e-mail forwarding, and thereby the potentially inadvertent transmission of sensitive information by all employees, vendors, and agents operating on behalf of <Company Name>.

Q.4.3 Policy

Employees must exercise utmost caution when sending any e-mail from inside <Company Name> to an outside network. Unless approved by an employee's manager InfoSec, <Company Name> e-mail will not be automatically forwarded to an external destination. Sensitive information, as defined in the *Information Sensitivity Policy*, will not be forwarded via any means, unless that e-mail is critical to business and is encrypted in accordance with the *Acceptable Encryption Policy*.

Q.4.4 Enforcement

Any employee found to have violated this policy may be subject to disciplinary action, up to and including termination of employment.

Q.4.5 Definitions

E-mail	The electronic transmission of information through a mail protocol such as SMTP. Programs such as Eudora and Microsoft Outlook use SMTP.
Forwarded e-mail	E-mail resent from internal networking to an outside point.
Sensitive information	Information is considered sensitive if it can be damaging to <Company Name> or its customers' dollar value, reputation, or market standing.
Unauthorized Disclosure	The intentional or unintentional revealing of restricted information to people who do not have a need to know that information.

Q.5 DATABASE PASSWORD POLICY

Abstract: Defines requirements for securely storing and retrieving database usernames and passwords.

Q.5.1 Purpose

This policy states the requirements for securely storing and retrieving database usernames and passwords (i.e., database credentials) for use by a program that will access a database running on one of <Company Name>'s networks.

Computer programs running on <Company Name>'s networks often require the use of one of the many internal database servers. In order to access one of these databases, a program must authenticate to the database by presenting acceptable credentials. The database privileges that the credentials are meant to restrict can be compromised when the credentials are improperly stored.

Q.5.2 Scope

This policy applies to all software that will access a <Company Name>, multi-user production database.

Q.5.3 Policy

Q.5.3.1 General

In order to maintain the security of <Company Name>'s internal databases, access by software programs must be granted only after authentication with credentials. The credentials used for this authentication must not reside in the main executing body of the program's source code in clear text. Database credentials must not be stored in a location that can be accessed through a web server.

Q.5.3.2 Specific Requirements

Q.5.3.2.1 Storage of Data Base User Names and Passwords

- Database user names and passwords may be stored in a file separate from the executing body of the program's code. This file must not be world readable.
- Database credentials may reside on the database server. In this case, a hash number identifying the credentials may be stored in the executing body of the program's code.
- Database credentials may be stored as part of an authentication server (i.e., an entitlement directory), such as an LDAP server used for user authentication. Database authentication may occur on behalf of a program as part of the user authentication process at the authentication server. In this case, there is no need for programmatic use of database credentials.
- Database credentials may not reside in the documents tree of a Web server.
- Pass through authentication (i.e., Oracle OPS$ authentication) must not allow access to the database based solely upon a remote user's authentication on the remote host.
- Passwords or pass phrases used to access a database must adhere to the *Password Policy*.

Q.5.3.2.2 Retrieval of Database User Names and Passwords

■ If stored in a file that is not source code, then database user names and passwords must be read from the file immediately prior to use. Immediately following database authentication, the memory containing the user name and password must be released or cleared.

■ The scope into which you may store database credentials must be physically separated from the other areas of your code; for example, the credentials must be in a separate source file. The file that contains the credentials must contain no other code but the credentials (i.e., the user name and password) and any functions, routines, or methods that will be used to access the credentials.

■ For languages that execute from source code, the credentials' source file must not reside in the same browseable or executable file directory tree in which the executing body of code resides.

Q.5.3.2.3 Access to Database User Names and Passwords

■ Every program or every collection of programs implementing a single business function must have unique database credentials. Sharing of credentials between programs is not allowed.

■ Database passwords used by programs are system-level passwords as defined by the *Password Policy.*

■ Developer groups must have a process in place to ensure that database passwords are controlled and changed in accordance with the *Password Policy.* This process must include a method for restricting knowledge of database passwords to a need-to-know basis.

Q.5.3.2.4 Coding Techniques for Implementing This Policy

[Add references to your site-specific guidelines for the different coding languages such as Perl, Java, C, or Cpro.]

Q.5.4 Enforcement

Any employee found to have violated this policy may be subject to disciplinary action, up to and including termination of employment.

Q.5.5 Definitions

Term	Definition
Computer language	A language used to generate programs.
Credentials	Something you know (e.g., a password or pass phrase), or something that identifies you (e.g., a user name, a fingerprint, voiceprint, retina print). Something you know and something that identifies you are presented for authentication.
Entitlement	The level of privilege that has been authenticated and authorized. The privileges level at which to access resources.
Executing body	The series of computer instructions that the computer executes to run a program.
Hash	An algorithmically generated number that identifies a datum or its location.
LDAP	Lightweight Directory Access Protocol, a set of protocols for accessing information directories.
Module	A collection of computer language instructions grouped together either logically or physically. A module may also be called a package or a class, depending upon which computer language is used.
Name space	A logical area of code in which the declared symbolic names are known and outside of which these names are not visible.
Production	Software that is being used for a purpose other than when software is being implemented or tested.

Q.6 E-MAIL RETENTION POLICY

Abstract: Defines standards to prevent tarnishing the public image of the organization.

Q.6.1 Purpose

The E-Mail Retention Policy is intended to help employees determine what information sent or received by email should be retained and for how long.

The information covered in these guidelines includes, but is not limited to, information that is either stored or shared via electronic mail or instant messaging technologies.

All employees should familiarize themselves with the email retention topic areas that follow this introduction.

Questions about the proper classification of a specific piece of information should be addressed to your manager. Questions about these guidelines should be addressed to Infosec.

Q.6.2 Scope

This e-mail retention policy is secondary to <Company Name> policy on Freedom of Information and Business Record Keeping. Any email that contains information in the scope of the Business Record Keeping policy should be treated in that manner. All <Company Name> e-mail information is categorized into four main classifications with retention guidelines:

Administrative Correspondence (four years)
Fiscal Correspondence (four years)
General Correspondence (one year)
Ephemeral Correspondence (Retain until read, destroy)

Q.6.3 Policy

Q.6.3.1 Administrative Correspondence

<Company Name> Administrative Correspondence includes, though is not limited to clarification of established company policy, including holidays, time card information, dress code, workplace behavior, and any legal issues such as intellectual property violations. All e-mail with the information sensitivity label Management Only shall be treated as Administrative Correspondence. To ensure Administrative Correspondence is retained, a mailbox admin@<Company Name> has been created, if you copy (cc) this address when you send e-mail, retention will be administered by the IT Department.

Q.6.3.2 Fiscal Correspondence

<Company Name> Fiscal Correspondence is all information related to revenue and expense for the company. To ensure Fiscal Correspondence is retained, a mailbox fiscal@<Company Name> has been created, if you copy (cc) this address when you send e-mail, retention will be administered by the IT Department.

Q.6.3.3 General Correspondence

<Company Name> General Correspondence covers information that relates to customer interaction and the operational decisions of the business. The individual employee is responsible for e-mail retention of General Correspondence.

Q.6.3.4 Ephemeral Correspondence

<Company Name> Ephemeral Correspondence is by far the largest category and includes personal e-mail, requests for recommendations or review, e-mail related to product development, updates, and status reports.

Q.6.3.5 Instant Messenger Correspondence

<Company Name> Instant Messenger General Correspondence may be saved with logging function of Instant Messenger, or copied into a file and saved. Instant Messenger conversations that are Administrative or Fiscal in nature should be copied into an e-mail message and sent to the appropriate e-mail retention address.

Q.6.3.6 Encrypted Communications

<Company Name> encrypted communications should be stored in a manner consistent with <Company Name> Information Sensitivity Policy, but in general, information should be stored in a decrypted format.

Q.6.3.7 Recovering Deleted E-Mail via Backup Media

<Company Name> maintains backup tapes from the e-mail server and once a quarter a set of tapes is taken out of the rotation and they are moved off site. No effort will be made to remove e-mail from the offsite backup tapes.

Q.6.3.8 Enforcement

Any employee found to have violated this policy may be subject to disciplinary action, up to and including termination of employment.

Q.6.3.9 Definitions

Approved Electronic Mail	Includes all mail systems supported by the IT Support Team. These include, but are not necessarily limited to, [insert corporate supported mailers here…]. If you have a business need to use other mailers contact the appropriate support organization.
Approved Encrypted E-Mail and Files	Techniques include the use of DES and PGP. DES encryption is available via many different public domain packages on all platforms. PGP use within <Company Name> is done via a license. Please contact the appropriate support organization if you require a license.

Approved Instant Messenger	The Jabber Secure IM Client is the only IM that is approved for use on <Company Name> computers.
Individual Access Controls	Individual Access Controls are methods of electronically protecting files from being accessed by people other than those specifically designated by the owner. On UNIX machines, this is accomplished by careful use of the chmod command (use *man chmod* to find out more about it). On Macs and PCs, this includes using passwords on screensavers, such as Disklock.
Insecure Internet Links	All network links that originate from a locale or travel over lines that are not totally under the control of <Company Name>.
Encryption	Secure <Company Name> Sensitive information in accordance with the *Acceptable Encryption Policy.* International issues regarding encryption are complex. Follow corporate guidelines on export controls on cryptography, and consult your manager or corporate legal services for further guidance.

Q.6.3.10 Revision History

28 July, 2003 Added discussion of backup media.

Q.7 EXTRANET POLICY

Abstract: Defines the requirement that third-party organizations requiring access to the organization's networks must sign a third-party connection agreement.

Q.7.1 Purpose

This document describes the policy under which third-party organizations connect to <Company Name> networks for the purpose of transacting business related to <Company Name>.

Q.7.2 Scope

Connections between third parties that require access to non-public <Company Name> resources fall under this policy, regardless of whether a telco circuit (such as frame relay or ISDN) or VPN technology is used for the connection. Connectivity to third parties such as the Internet Service Providers (ISPs) that provide Internet access for <Company Name> or to the Public Switched Telephone Network does not fall under this policy.

Q.7.3 Policy

Q.7.3.1 Prerequisites

Q.7.3.1.1 Security Review

All new extranet connectivity will go through a security review with the Information Security department (InfoSec). The reviews are to ensure that all access matches the business requirements in a best possible way, and that the principle of least access is followed.

Q.7.3.1.2 Third-Party Connection Agreement

All new connection requests between third parties and <Company Name> require that the third party and <Company Name> representatives agree to and sign the *Third Party Agreement*. This agreement must be signed by the Vice President of the Sponsoring Organization as well as a representative from the third party who is legally empowered to sign on behalf of the third party. The signed document is to be kept on file with the relevant extranet group. Documents pertaining to connections into <Company Name> labs are to be kept on file with the [name of team responsible for security of labs].

Q.7.3.1.3 Business Case

All production extranet connections must be accompanied by a valid business justification, in writing, that is approved by a project manager in the extranet group. Lab connections must be approved by the [name of team responsible for security of labs]. Typically this function is handled as part of the *Third Party Agreement*.

Q.7.3.1.4 Point of Contact

The Sponsoring Organization must designate a person to be the Point of Contact (POC) for the Extranet connection. The POC acts on behalf of the Sponsoring Organization, and is responsible for those portions of this policy and the *Third Party Agreement* that pertain to it. In the event that the POC changes, the relevant extranet Organization must be informed promptly.

Q.7.3.2 Establishing Connectivity

Sponsoring Organizations within <Company Name> that wish to establish connectivity to a third party are to file a new site request with the proper extranet group. The extranet group will engage InfoSec to address security issues inherent in the project. If the proposed connection is to terminate within a lab at <Company Name>, the Sponsoring Organization must engage the [name of team responsible for security of labs]. The Sponsoring Organization must provide full and complete information as to the nature of the proposed access to the extranet group and InfoSec, as requested.

All connectivity established must be based on the least-access principle, in accordance with the approved business requirements and the security review. In no case will <Company Name> rely upon the third party to protect <Company Name>'s network or resources.

Q.7.3.3 Modifying or Changing Connectivity and Access

All changes in access must be accompanied by a valid business justification, and are subject to security review. Changes are to be implemented via corporate change management process. The Sponsoring Organization is responsible for notifying the extranet management group or InfoSec when there is a material change in their originally provided information so that security and connectivity evolve accordingly.

Q.7.3.4 Terminating Access

When access is no longer required, the Sponsoring Organization within <Company Name> must notify the extranet team responsible for that connectivity, which will then terminate the access. This may mean a modification of existing permissions up to terminating the circuit, as appropriate. The extranet and lab security teams must conduct an audit of their respective connections on an annual basis to ensure that all existing connections are still needed, and that the access provided meets the needs of the connection. Connections that are found to be depreciated, or are no longer being used to conduct <Company Name> business, will be terminated immediately. Should a security incident or a finding that a circuit has been deprecated and is no longer being used to conduct <Company Name> business necessitate a modification of existing permissions, or termination of connectivity, InfoSec or the extranet team will notify the POC or the Sponsoring Organization of the change prior to taking any action.

Q.7.4 Enforcement

Any employee found to have violated this policy may be subject to disciplinary action, up to and including termination of employment.

Q.7.5 Definitions

Circuit	For the purposes of this policy, circuit refers to the method of network access, whether it is through traditional ISDN, Frame Relay etc., or via VPN/Encryption technologies.
Sponsoring Organization	The <Company Name> organization who requested that the third party have access into <Company Name>.
Third Party	A business that is not a formal or subsidiary part of <Company Name>.

Q.8 INFORMATION SENSITIVITY POLICY

Abstract: Defines the requirements for classifying and securing the organization's information in a manner appropriate to its sensitivity level.

Q.8.1 Purpose

The Information Sensitivity Policy is intended to help employees determine what information can be disclosed to non-employees, as well as the relative sensitivity of information that should not be disclosed outside of <Company Name> without proper authorization.

The information covered in these guidelines includes, but is not limited to, information that is either stored or shared via any means. This includes: electronic information, information on paper, and information shared orally or visually (such as telephone and video conferencing).

All employees should familiarize themselves with the information labeling and handling guidelines that follow this introduction. It should be noted that the sensitivity level definitions were created as guidelines and to emphasize common sense steps that you can take to protect <Company Name> Confidential information (e.g., <Company Name> Confidential information should not be left unattended in conference rooms).

Please Note: The impact of these guidelines on daily activity should be minimal.

Questions about the proper classification of a specific piece of information should be addressed to your manager. Questions about these guidelines should be addressed to Infosec.

Q.8.2 Scope

All <Company Name> information is categorized into two main classifications:

- <Company Name> Public
- <Company Name> Confidential

<Company Name> Public information is information that has been declared public knowledge by someone with the authority to do so, and can freely be given to anyone without any possible damage to <Company Name> Systems, Inc.

<Company Name> Confidential contains all other information. It is a continuum, in that it is understood that some information is more sensitive than other information, and should be protected in a more secure manner. Included is information that should be protected very closely, such as trade secrets, development programs, potential acquisition targets, and other information integral to the success of our company. Also included in <Company Name> Confidential is information that is less critical, such as telephone directories, general corporate information, personnel information, and so on, which does not require as stringent a degree of protection.

A subset of <Company Name> Confidential information is "<Company Name> Third Party Confidential" information. This is confidential information belonging or pertaining to another corporation which has been entrusted to <Company Name> by that company under non-disclosure agreements and other contracts. Examples of this type of information include everything from joint development efforts to vendor lists, customer orders, and supplier information. Information in this category ranges from extremely sensitive to information about the fact that we have connected a supplier/vendor into <Company Name>'s network to support our operations.

<Company Name> personnel are encouraged to use common sense judgment in securing <Company Name> Confidential information to the proper extent. If an employee is uncertain of the sensitivity of a particular piece of information, he or she should contact their manager.

Q.8.3 Policy

The Sensitivity Guidelines below provides details on how to protect information at varying sensitivity levels. Use these guidelines as a reference only, as <Company Name> Confidential information in each column may necessitate more or less stringent measures of protection depending upon the circumstances and the nature of the <Company Name> Confidential information in question.

1. **Minimal Sensitivity:** General corporate information; some personnel and technical information.

   i. Marking guidelines for information in hardcopy or electronic form.

   ii. *Note:* Any of these markings may be used with the additional annotation of "3rd Party Confidential".

   iii. Marking is at the discretion of the owner or custodian of the information. If marking is desired, the words "<Company Name> Confidential" may be written or designated in a conspicuous place on or in the information in question. Other labels that may be used include "<Company Name> Proprietary" or similar labels at the discretion of your individual business unit or department. Even if no marking is present, <Company Name> information is presumed to be "<Company Name> Confidential" unless expressly determined to be <Company Name> Public information by a <Company Name> employee with authority to do so.
      a. Access: <Company Name> employees, contractors, people with a business need to know.
      b. Distribution within <Company Name>: Standard interoffice mail, approved electronic mail and electronic file transmission methods.
      c. Distribution outside of <Company Name> internal mail: U.S. mail and other public or private carriers, approved electronic mail and electronic file transmission methods.
      d. Electronic distribution: No restrictions except that it be sent to only approved recipients.
      e. Storage: Keep from view of unauthorized people; erase whiteboards, do not leave in view on tabletop. Machines should be administered with security in mind. Protect from loss; electronic information should have individual access controls where possible and appropriate.
      f. Disposal/Destruction: Deposit outdated paper information in specially marked disposal bins on <Company Name> premises; electronic data should be expunged/cleared. Reliably erase or physically destroy media.
      g. Penalty for deliberate or inadvertent disclosure: Up to and including termination, possible civil or criminal prosecution to the full extent of the law.

2. **More Sensitive:** Business, financial, technical, and most personnel information.

   i. Marking guidelines for information in hardcopy or electronic form.

ii. *Note:* Any of these markings may be used with the additional annotation of "3rd Party Confidential". As the sensitivity level of the information increases, you may, in addition or instead of marking the information "<Company Name> Confidential" or "<Company Name> Proprietary", wish to label the information "<Company Name> Internal Use Only" or other similar labels at the discretion of your individual business unit or department to denote a more sensitive level of information. However, marking is discretionary at all times.

  a. **Access:** <Company Name> employees and non-employees with signed non-disclosure agreements who have a business need to know.

  b. **Distribution within <Company Name>:** Standard interoffice mail, approved electronic mail and electronic file transmission methods.

  c. **Distribution outside of <Company Name> internal mail:** Sent via U.S. mail or approved private carriers.

  d. **Electronic distribution:** No restrictions to approved recipients within <Company Name>, but should be encrypted or sent via a private link to approved recipients outside of <Company Name> premises.

  e. **Storage:** Individual access controls are highly recommended for electronic information.

  f. **Disposal/Destruction:** In specially marked disposal bins on <Company Name> premises; electronic data should be expunged/cleared. Reliably erase or physically destroy media.

  g. **Penalty for deliberate or inadvertent disclosure:** Up to and including termination, possible civil or criminal prosecution to the full extent of the law.

3. **Most Sensitive:** Trade secrets and marketing, operational, personnel, financial, source code, and technical information integral to the success of our company.

   i. Marking guidelines for information in hardcopy or electronic form.

   ii. *Note:* Any of these markings may be used with the additional annotation of "3rd Party Confidential". To indicate that <Company Name> Confidential information is very sensitive, you should label the information "<Company Name> Internal: Registered and Restricted", "<Company Name> Eyes Only", "<Company Name> Confidential" or similar labels at the discretion of your individual business unit or department. Once again, this type of <Company Name> Confidential information need not be marked, but users should be aware that this information is very sensitive and be protected as such.

a. **Access:** Only those individuals (<Company Name> employees and non-employees) designated with approved access and signed non-disclosure agreements.

b. **Distribution within <Company Name>:** Delivered direct-signature required, envelopes stamped confidential, or approved electronic file transmission methods.

c. **Distribution outside of <Company Name> internal mail:** Delivered direct; signature required; approved private carriers.

d. **Electronic distribution:** No restrictions to approved recipients within <Company Name>, but it is highly recommended that all information be strongly encrypted.

e. **Storage:** Individual access controls are very highly recommended for electronic information. Physical security is generally used, and information should be stored in a physically secured computer.

f. **Disposal/Destruction:** Strongly Encouraged: In specially marked disposal bins on <Company Name> premises; electronic data should be expunged/cleared. Reliably erase or physically destroy media.

g. **Penalty for deliberate or inadvertent disclosure:** Up to and including termination, possible civil or criminal prosecution to the full extent of the law.

Q.8.4 Enforcement

Any employee found to have violated this policy may be subject to disciplinary action, up to and including termination of employment.

Q.8.5 Definitions

Appropriate Measures	To minimize risk to <Company Name> from an outside business connection. <Company Name> computer use by competitors and unauthorized personnel must be restricted so that, in the event of an attempt to access <Company Name> corporate information, the amount of information at risk is minimized.
Configuration of <Company Name>-to-other business connections	Connections shall be set up to allow other businesses to see only what they need to see. This involves setting up both applications and network configurations to allow access to only what is necessary.
Delivered Direct; Signature Required	Do not leave in interoffice mail slot, call the mail room for special pick-up of mail.

Approved Electronic File Transmission Methods	Includes supported FTP clients and Web browsers.
Envelopes Stamped Confidential	You are not required to use a special envelope. Put your document(s) into an interoffice envelope, seal it, address it, and stamp it confidential.
Approved Electronic Mail	Includes all mail systems supported by the IT Support Team. These include, but are not necessarily limited to, [insert corporate supported mailers here…]. If you have a business need to use other mailers contact the appropriate support organization.
Approved Encrypted email and files	Include the use of DES and PGP. DES encryption is available via many different public domain packages on all platforms. PGP use within <Company Name> is done via a license. Please contact the appropriate support organization if you require a license.
Company Information System Resources	Include, but are not limited to, all computers, their data and programs, as well as all paper information and any information at the Internal Use Only level and above.
Expunge	To reliably erase or expunge data on a PC or Mac you must use a separate program to overwrite data, supplied as a part of Norton Utilities. Otherwise, the PC or Mac's normal erasure routine keeps the data intact until overwritten. The same thing happens on UNIX machines, but data is much more difficult to retrieve on UNIX systems.
Individual Access Controls	Methods of electronically protecting files from being accessed by people other than those specifically designated by the owner. On UNIX machines, this is accomplished by careful use of the chmod command (use *man chmod* to find out more about it). On Macs and PCs, this includes using passwords on screensavers, such as Disklock.
Insecure Internet Links	All network links that originate from a locale or travel over lines that are not totally under the control of <Company Name>.
Encryption	Secure <Company Name> Sensitive information in accordance with the *Acceptable Encryption Policy*. International issues regarding encryption are complex. Follow corporate guidelines on export controls on cryptography, and consult your manager or corporate legal services for further guidance.

One Time Password Authentication	Accomplished by using a one time password token to connect to <Company Name>'s internal network over the Internet. Contact your support organization for more information on how to set this up.
Physical Security	Either having actual possession of a computer at all times, or locking the computer in an unusable state to an object that is immovable. Methods of accomplishing this include having a special key to unlock the computer so it can be used, thereby ensuring that the computer cannot be simply rebooted to get around the protection. If it is a laptop or other portable computer, never leave it alone in a conference room, hotel room or on an airplane seat, etc. Make arrangements to lock the device in a hotel safe, or take it with you. In the office, always use a lockdown cable. When leaving the office for the day, secure the laptop and any other sensitive material in a locked drawer or cabinet.
Private Link	An electronic communications path that <Company Name> has control over its entire distance. For example, all <Company Name> networks are connected via a private link. A computer with modem connected via a standard land line (not cell phone) to another computer have established a private link. ISDN lines to employee's homes is a private link. <Company Name> also has established private links to other companies, so that all email correspondence can be sent in a more secure manner. Companies which <Company Name> has established private links include all announced acquisitions and some short-term temporary links

Q.9 PASSWORD POLICY

Abstract: Defines standards for creating, protecting, and changing strong passwords.

Q.9.1 Overview

Passwords are an important aspect of computer security. They are the front line of protection for user accounts. A poorly chosen password may result in the compromise of <Company Name>'s entire corporate network. As such, all <Company Name> employees (including contractors and vendors with access to <Company Name> systems) are responsible for taking the appropriate steps, as outlined below, to select and secure their passwords.

Q.9.2 Purpose

The purpose of this policy is to establish a standard for creation of strong passwords, the protection of those passwords, and the frequency of change.

Q.9.3 Scope

The scope of this policy includes all personnel who have or are responsible for an account (or any form of access that supports or requires a password) on any system that resides at any <Company Name> facility, has access to the <Company Name> network, or stores any non-public <Company Name> information.

Q.9.4 Policy

Q.9.4.1 General

- All system-level passwords (e.g., root, enable, NT admin, application administration accounts, etc.) must be changed on at least a quarterly basis.
- All production system-level passwords must be part of the InfoSec administered global password management database.
- All user-level passwords (e.g., e-mail, Web, desktop computer, etc.) must be changed at least every six months. The recommended change interval is every four months.
- User accounts that have system-level privileges granted through group memberships or programs such as "sudo" must have a unique password from all other accounts held by that user.
- Passwords must not be inserted into email messages or other forms of electronic communication.
- Where SNMP is used, the community strings must be defined as something other than the standard defaults of "public," "private," and "system" and must be different from the passwords used to log in interactively. A keyed hash must be used where available (e.g., SNMPv2).

■ All user-level and system-level passwords must conform to the guidelines described below.

Q.9.4.2   Guidelines

Q.9.4.2.1   General Password Construction Guidelines

Passwords are used for various purposes at <Company Name>. Some of the more common uses include: user level accounts, web accounts, email accounts, screen saver protection, voicemail password, and local router logins. Because very few systems have support for one-time tokens (i.e., dynamic passwords which are only used once), everyone should be aware of how to select strong passwords.

Poor weak passwords have the following characteristics.

■ The password contains less than eight characters.
■ The password is a word found in a dictionary (English or foreign).
■ The password is a common usage word such as:
  ■ Names of family, pets, friends, co-workers, fantasy characters, etc.
  ■ Computer terms and names, commands, sites, companies, hardware, software.
  ■ The words "<Company Name>", "sanjose", "sanfran," or any derivation.
  ■ Birthdays and other personal information such as addresses and phone numbers.
  ■ Word or number patterns like aaabbb, qwerty, zyxwvuts, 123321, etc.
  ■ Any of the above spelled backward.
  ■ Any of the above preceded or followed by a digit (e.g., secret1, 1secret).

Strong passwords have the following characteristics.

■ Contain both upper and lower case characters (e.g., a-z, A-Z).
■ Have digits and punctuation characters as well as letters e.g., 0-9, !@#$%^&*()_+|~-=\`{}[]:";'<>?,./).
■ Are at least eight alphanumeric characters long.
■ Are not a word in any language, slang, dialect, jargon, etc.
■ Are not based on personal information, names of family, etc.
■ Passwords should never be written down or stored on-line. Try to create passwords that can be easily remembered. One way to do this is create a password based on a song title, affirmation, or other phrase. For example, the phrase might be: "This May Be One Way

To Remember" and the password could be: "TmB1w2R!" or "Tmb1W>r~" or some other variation.

Note: Do not use either of these examples as passwords!

Q.9.4.2.2 Password Protection Standards

Do not use the same password for <Company Name> accounts as for other non-<Company Name> access (e.g., personal ISP account, option trading, benefits, etc.). Where possible, do not use the same password for various <Company Name> access needs. For example, select one password for the Engineering systems and a separate password for IT systems. Also, select a separate password to be used for an NT account and a UNIX account.

Do not share <Company Name> passwords with anyone, including administrative assistants or secretaries. All passwords are to be treated as sensitive, Confidential <Company Name> information.

Here is a list of "don'ts":

- Don't reveal a password over the phone to anyone.
- Don't reveal a password in an e-mail message.
- Don't reveal a password to the boss.
- Don't talk about a password in front of others.
- Don't hint at the format of a password (e.g., "my family name").
- Don't reveal a password on questionnaires or security forms.
- Don't share a password with family members.
- Don't reveal a password to co-workers while on vacation.

If someone demands a password, refer them to this document or have them call someone in the Information Security Department.

Do not use the "Remember Password" feature of applications (e.g., Eudora, OutLook, Netscape Messenger).

Again, do not write passwords down and store them anywhere in your office. Do not store passwords in a file on any computer system (including Palm Pilots or similar devices) without encryption.

Change passwords at least once every six months (except system-level passwords which must be changed quarterly). The recommended change interval is every four months.

If an account or password is suspected to have been compromised, report the incident to InfoSec and change all passwords.

Password cracking or guessing may be performed on a periodic or random basis by InfoSec or its delegates. If a password is guessed or cracked during one of these scans, the user will be required to change it.

Q.9.4.2.3 Application Development Standards

Application developers must ensure their programs contain the following security precautions. Applications:

- Should support authentication of individual users, not groups
- Should not store passwords in clear text or in any easily reversible form
- Should provide for some sort of role management, such that one user can take over the functions of another without having to know the other's password
- Should support TACACS+, RADIUS and/or X.509 with LDAP security retrieval, wherever possible

Q.9.4.2.4 Use of Passwords and Passphrases for Remote Access Users

Access to the <Company Name> Networks via remote access is to be controlled using either a one-time password authentication or a public/private key system with a strong passphrase.

Q.9.4.2.5 Passphrases

Passphrases are generally used for public/private key authentication. A public/private key system defines a mathematical relationship between the public key that is known by all, and the private key, that is known only to the user. Without the passphrase to "unlock" the private key, the user cannot gain access.

Passphrases are not the same as passwords. A passphrase is a longer version of a password and is, therefore, more secure. A passphrase is typically composed of multiple words. Because of this, a passphrase is more secure against "dictionary attacks."

A good passphrase is relatively long and contains a combination of upper and lowercase letters and numeric and punctuation characters. An example of a good passphrase:

```
"The*?#>*@TrafficOnThe101Was*&#!#ThisMorning"
```

All of the rules above that apply to passwords apply to passphrases.

Q.9.5 Enforcement

Any employee found to have violated this policy may be subject to disciplinary action, up to and including termination of employment.

Q.9.6 Definitions

Application Administration Account	Any account that is for the administration of an application (e.g., Oracle database administrator, ISSU administrator).

Q.10 REMOTE ACCESS POLICY

Abstract: Defines standards for connecting to the organization's network from any host or network external to the organization.

Q.10.1 Purpose

The purpose of this policy is to define standards for connecting to <Company Name>'s network from any host. These standards are designed to minimize the potential exposure to <Company Name> from damages which may result from unauthorized use of <Company Name> resources. Damages include the loss of sensitive or company confidential data, intellectual property, damage to public image, damage to critical <Company Name> internal systems, etc.

Q.10.2 Scope

This policy applies to all <Company Name> employees, contractors, vendors and agents with a <Company Name>-owned or personally owned computer or workstation used to connect to the <Company Name> network. This policy applies to remote access connections used to do work on behalf of <Company Name>, including reading or sending e-mail and viewing intranet web resources.

Remote access implementations that are covered by this policy include, but are not limited to, dial-in modems, frame relay, ISDN, DSL, VPN, SSH, and cable modems, and so on.

Q.10.3 Policy
Q.10.3.1 General

1. It is the responsibility of <Company Name> employees, contractors, vendors and agents with remote access privileges to <Company Name>'s corporate network to ensure that their remote access connection is given the same consideration as the user's on-site connection to <Company Name>.
2. General access to the Internet for recreational use by immediate household members through the <Company Name> Network on personal computers is permitted for employees that have flat-rate services. The <Company Name> employee is responsible to ensure the family member does not violate any <Company Name> policies, does not perform illegal activities, and does not use the access for outside business interests. The <Company Name> employee bears responsibility for the consequences should the access be misused.

3. Please review the following policies for details of protecting information when accessing the corporate network via remote access methods, and acceptable use of <Company Name>'s network:
   a. Acceptable Encryption Policy
   b. Virtual Private Network (VPN) Policy
   c. Wireless Communications Policy
   d. Acceptable Use Policy
4. For additional information regarding <Company Name>'s remote access connection options, including how to order or disconnect service, cost comparisons, troubleshooting, and so on, go to the Remote Access Services Web site.

Q.10.3.2 Requirements

1. Secure remote access must be strictly controlled. Control will be enforced via one-time password authentication or public/private keys with strong pass-phrases. For information on creating a strong pass-phrase see the Password Policy.
2. At no time should any <Company Name> employee provide their login or email password to anyone, not even family members.
3. <Company Name> employees and contractors with remote access privileges must ensure that their <Company Name>-owned or personal computer or workstation, which is remotely connected to <Company Name>'s corporate network, is not connected to any other network at the same time, with the exception of personal networks that are under the complete control of the user.
4. <Company Name> employees and contractors with remote access privileges to <Company Name>'s corporate network must not use non-<Company Name> email accounts (i.e., Hotmail, Yahoo, AOL), or other external resources to conduct <Company Name> business, thereby ensuring that official business is never confused with personal business.
5. Routers for dedicated ISDN lines configured for access to the <Company Name> network must meet minimum authentication requirements of CHAP.
6. Reconfiguration of a home user's equipment for the purpose of split-tunneling or dual homing is not permitted at any time.
7. Frame Relay must meet minimum authentication requirements of DLCI standards.
8. Non-standard hardware configurations must be approved by Remote Access Services, and InfoSec must approve security configurations for access to hardware.

9. All hosts that are connected to <Company Name> internal networks via remote access technologies must use the most up-to-date anti-virus software (place url to corporate software site here), this includes personal computers. Third party connections must comply with requirements as stated in the *Third Party Agreement*.

10. Personal equipment that is used to connect to <Company Name>'s networks must meet the requirements of <Company Name>-owned equipment for remote access.

11. Organizations or individuals who wish to implement non-standard Remote Access solutions to the <Company Name> production network must obtain prior approval from Remote Access Services and InfoSec.

Q.10.4 Enforcement

Any employee found to have violated this policy may be subject to disciplinary action, up to and including termination of employment.

Q.10.5 Definitions

Cable Modem.	Cable companies such as AT&T Broadband provide Internet access over Cable TV coaxial cable. A cable modem accepts this coaxial cable and can receive data from the Internet at over 1.5 Mbps. Cable is currently available only in certain communities.
CHAP	Challenge Handshake Authentication Protocol is an authentication method that uses a one-way hashing function. DLCIData Link Connection Identifier (DLCI) is a unique number assigned to a Permanent Virtual Circuit (PVC) end point in a frame relay network. DLCI identifies a particular PVC endpoint within a user's access channel in a frame relay network, and has local significance only to that channel.

Dial-in Modem	A peripheral device that connects computers to each other for sending communications via the telephone lines. The modem modulates the digital data of computers into analog signals to send over the telephone lines, then demodulates back into digital signals to be read by the computer on the other end; thus the name "modem" for modulator/demodulator.
Dual Homing	Having concurrent connectivity to more than one network from a computer or network device. Examples include: Being logged into the Corporate network via a local Ethernet connection, and dialing into AOL or other Internet service provider (ISP). Being on a <Company Name>-provided Remote Access home network, and connecting to another network, such as a spouse's remote access. Configuring an ISDN router to dial into <Company Name> and an ISP, depending on packet destination.
DSL	Digital Subscriber Line (DSL) is a form of high-speed Internet access competing with cable modems. DSL works over standard phone lines and supports data speeds of over 2 Mbps downstream (to the user) and slower speeds upstream (to the Internet).
Frame Relay	A method of communication that incrementally can go from the speed of an ISDN to the speed of a T1 line. Frame Relay has a flat-rate billing charge instead of a per time usage. Frame Relay connects via the telephone company's network.

ISDN	There are two flavors of Integrated Services Digital Network or ISDN: BRI and PRI. BRI is used for home office/remote access. BRI has two "Bearer" channels at 64kbit (aggregate 128kb) and 1 D channel for signaling info.
Remote Access	Any access to <Company Name>'s corporate network through a non-<Company Name> controlled network, device, or medium.
Split-tunneling	Simultaneous direct access to a non-<Company Name> network (such as the Internet, or a home network) from a remote device (PC, PDA, WAP phone, etc.) while connected into <Company Name>'s corporate network via a VPN tunnel. VPN Virtual Private Network (VPN) is a method for accessing a remote network via "tunneling" through the Internet.

Q.11 RISK ASSESSMENT POLICY

Abstract: Defines the requirements and provides the authority for the information security team to identify, assess, and remediate risks to the organization's information infrastructure associated with conducting business.

Q.11.1 Purpose

To empower InfoSec to perform periodic information security risk assessments (RAs) for the purpose of determining areas of vulnerability, and to initiate appropriate remediation.

Q.11.2 Scope

Risk assessments can be conducted on any entity within <Company Name> or any outside entity that has signed a *Third Party Agreement* with <Company Name>. RAs can be conducted on any information system, to include applications, servers, and networks, and any process or procedure by which these systems are administered or maintained.

Q.11.3 Policy

The execution, development, and implementation of remediation programs is the joint responsibility of InfoSec and the department responsible for the systems area being assessed. Employees are expected to cooperate fully with any RA being conducted on systems for which they are held accountable. Employees are further expected to work with the InfoSec Risk Assessment Team in the development of a remediation plan.

Q.11.4 Risk Assessment Process

For additional information, go to the Risk Assessment Process.

Q.11.5 Enforcement

Any employee found to have violated this policy may be subject to disciplinary action, up to and including termination of employment.

Q.11.6 Definitions

Entity	Any business unit, department, group, or third party, internal or external to <Company Name>, responsible for maintaining <Company Name> assets.
Risk	Those factors that could affect confidentiality, availability, and integrity of <Company Name>'s key information assets and systems. InfoSec is responsible for ensuring the integrity, confidentiality, and availability of critical information and computing assets, while minimizing the impact of security procedures and policies upon business productivity.

Q.12 ROUTER SECURITY POLICY

Abstract: Defines standards for minimal security configuration for routers and switches inside a production network, or used in a production capacity.

Q.12.1 Purpose

This document describes a required minimal security configuration for all routers and switches connecting to a production network or used in a production capacity at or on behalf of <Company Name>.

Q.12.2 Scope

All routers and switches connected to <Company Name> production networks are affected. Routers and switches within internal, secured labs are not affected. Routers and switches within DMZ areas fall under the *Internet DMZ Equipment Policy.*

Q.12.3 Policy

Every router must meet the following configuration standards.

1. No local user accounts are configured on the router. Routers must use TACACS+ for all user authentication.
2. The enable password on the router must be kept in a secure encrypted form. The router must have the enable password set to the current production router password from the router's support organization.
3. Disallow the following:
   a. IP directed broadcasts
   b. Incoming packets at the router sourced with invalid addresses such as RFC1918 address
   c. TCP small services
   d. UDP small services
   e. All source routing
   f. All Web services running on router
4. Use corporate standardized SNMP community strings.
5. Access rules are to be added as business needs arise.
6. The router must be included in the corporate enterprise management system with a designated point of contact.
7. Each router must have the following statement posted in clear view:

   "UNAUTHORIZED ACCESS TO THIS NETWORK DEVICE IS PROHIBITED. You must have explicit permission to access or configure this device. All activities performed on this device may be logged, and violations of this policy may result in disciplinary action, and may be reported to law enforcement. There is no right to privacy on this device."

Q.12.4 Enforcement

Any employee found to have violated this policy may be subject to disciplinary action, up to and including termination of employment.

Q.12.5 Definitions

Production Network	The "production network" is the network used in the daily business of <Company Name>. Any network connected to the corporate backbone, either directly or indirectly, which lacks an intervening firewall device. Any network whose impairment would result in direct loss of functionality to <Company Name> employees or impact their ability to do work.
Lab Network	A "lab network" is defined as any network used for the purposes of testing, demonstrations, training, etc. Any network that is stand-alone or firewalled off from the production network(s) and whose impairment will not cause direct loss to <Company Name> nor affect the production network.

Q.13 SERVER SECURITY POLICY

Abstract: Defines standards for minimal security configuration for servers inside the organization's production network, or used in a production capacity.

Q.13.1 Purpose

The purpose of this policy is to establish standards for the base configuration of internal server equipment that is owned or operated by <Company Name>. Effective implementation of this policy will minimize unauthorized access to <Company Name> proprietary information and technology.

Q.13.2 Scope

This policy applies to server equipment owned or operated by <Company Name>, and to servers registered under any <Company Name>-owned internal network domain.

This policy is specifically for equipment on the internal <Company Name> network. For secure configuration of equipment external to <Company Name> on the DMZ, refer to the *Internet DMZ Equipment Policy*.

Q.13.3 Policy

Q.13.3.1 Ownership and Responsibilities

All internal servers deployed at <Company Name> must be owned by an operational group that is responsible for system administration. Approved server configuration guides must be established and maintained by each operational group, based on business needs and approved by InfoSec. Operational groups should monitor configuration compliance and implement an exception policy tailored to their environment. Each operational group must establish a process for changing the configuration guides, which includes review and approval by InfoSec.

- Servers must be registered within the corporate enterprise management system. At a minimum, the following information is required to positively identify the point of contact:
  - Server contact(s) and location, and a backup contact.
  - Hardware and Operating System/Version.
  - Main functions and applications, if applicable.
- Information in the corporate enterprise management system must be kept up-to-date.
- Configuration changes for production servers must follow the appropriate change management procedures.

Q.13.3.2 General Configuration Guidelines

- Operating System configuration should be in accordance with approved InfoSec guidelines.
- Services and applications that will not be used must be disabled where practical.
- Access to services should be logged or protected through access-control methods such as TCP Wrappers, if possible.
- The most recent security patches must be installed on the system as soon as practical, the only exception being when immediate application would interfere with business requirements.
- Trust relationships between systems are a security risk, and their use should be avoided. Do not use a trust relationship when some other method of communication will do.
- Always use standard security principles of least required access to perform a function.
- Do not use root when a nonprivileged account will do.
- If a methodology for secure channel connection is available (i.e., technically feasible), privileged access must be performed over secure channels, (e.g., encrypted network connections using SSH or IPSec).
- Servers should be physically located in an access-controlled environment.
- Servers are specifically prohibited from operating from uncontrolled cubicle areas.

Q.13.3.3 Monitoring

All security-related events on critical or sensitive systems must be logged and audit trails saved as follows:

- All security related logs will be kept online for a minimum of one week.
- Daily incremental tape backups will be retained for at least one month.
- Weekly full tape backups of logs will be retained for at least one month.
- Monthly full backups will be retained for a minimum of two years.

Security-related events will be reported to InfoSec, who will review logs and report incidents to IT management. Corrective measures will be prescribed as needed. Security-related events include, but are not limited to:

- Port-scan attacks.
- Evidence of unauthorized access to privileged accounts.
- Anomalous occurrences that are not related to specific applications on the host.

Q.13.3.4 Compliance

- Audits will be performed on a regular basis by authorized organizations within <Company Name>.
- Audits will be managed by the internal audit group or InfoSec, in accordance with the *Audit Policy*. InfoSec will filter findings not related to a specific operational group and then present the findings to the appropriate support staff for remediation or justification.
- Every effort will be made to prevent audits from causing operational failures or disruptions.

Q.13.4 Enforcement

Any employee found to have violated this policy may be subject to disciplinary action, up to and including termination of employment.

Q.13.5 Definitions

DMZ	De-Militarized Zone. A network segment external to the corporate production network.
Server	For purposes of this policy, a Server is defined as an internal <Company Name> Server. Desktop machines and Lab equipment are not relevant to the scope of this policy.

Q.14 VIRTUAL PRIVATE NETWORK (VPN) POLICY

Abstract: Defines the requirements for Remote Access IPSec or L2TP Virtual Private Network (VPN) connections to the organization's network.

Q.14.1 Purpose

The purpose of this policy is to provide guidelines for Remote Access IPSec or L2TP Virtual Private Network (VPN) connections to the <Company Name> corporate network.

Q.14.2 Scope

This policy applies to all <Company Name> employees, contractors, consultants, temporaries, and other workers including all personnel affiliated with third parties utilizing VPNs to access the <Company Name> network. This policy applies to implementations of VPN that are directed through an IPSec Concentrator.

Q.14.3 Policy

Approved <Company Name> employees and authorized third parties (customers, vendors, etc.) may utilize the benefits of VPNs, which are a "user managed" service. This means that the user is responsible for selecting an Internet Service Provider (ISP), coordinating installation, installing any required software, and paying associated fees. Further details may be found in the *Remote Access Policy*.
 In addition,

1. It is the responsibility of employees with VPN privileges to ensure that unauthorized users are not allowed access to <Company Name> internal networks.
2. VPN use is to be controlled using either a one-time password authentication such as a token device or a public/private key system with a strong passphrase.
3. When actively connected to the corporate network, VPNs will force all traffic to and from the PC over the VPN tunnel: all other traffic will be dropped.
4. Dual (split) tunneling is not permitted; only one network connection is allowed.
5. VPN gateways will be set up and managed by <Company Name> network operational groups.

6. All computers connected to <Company Name> internal networks via VPN or any other technology must use the most up-to-date anti-virus software that is the corporate standard (provide URL to this software); this includes personal computers.

7. VPN users will be automatically disconnected from <Company Name>'s network after thirty minutes of inactivity. The user must then logon again to reconnect to the network. Pings or other artificial network processes are not to be used to keep the connection open.

8. The VPN concentrator is limited to an absolute connection time of 24 hours.

9. Users of computers that are not <Company Name>-owned equipment must configure the equipment to comply with <Company Name>'s VPN and Network policies.

10. Only InfoSec-approved VPN clients may be used.

11. By using VPN technology with personal equipment, users must understand that their machines are a de facto extension of <Company Name>'s network, and as such are subject to the same rules and regulations that apply to <Company Name>-owned equipment; that is, their machines must be configured to comply with InfoSec's Security Policies.

Q.14.4 Enforcement

Any employee found to have violated this policy may be subject to disciplinary action, up to and including termination of employment.

Q.14.5 Definitions

IPSec Concentrator A device in which VPN connections are terminated.

Q.15 WIRELESS COMMUNICATION POLICY

Abstract: Defines standards for wireless systems used to connect to the organization's networks.

Q.15.1 Purpose

This policy prohibits access to <Company Name> networks via unsecured wireless communication mechanisms. Only wireless systems that meet the criteria of this policy or have been granted an exclusive waiver by InfoSec are approved for connectivity to <Company Name>'s networks.

Q.15.2 Scope

This policy covers all wireless data communication devices (e.g., personal computers, cellular phones, PDAs, etc.) connected to any of <Company Name>'s internal networks. This includes any form of wireless communication device capable of transmitting packet data. Wireless devices or networks without any connectivity to <Company Name>'s networks do not fall under the purview of this policy.

Q.15.3 Policy

Q.15.3.1 Register Access Points and Cards

All wireless Access Points/Base Stations connected to the corporate network must be registered and approved by InfoSec. These Access Points/Base Stations are subject to periodic penetration tests and audits. All wireless Network Interface Cards (i.e., PC cards) used in corporate laptop or desktop computers must be registered with InfoSec.

Q.15.3.2 Approved Technology

All wireless LAN access must use corporate-approved vendor products and security configurations.

Q.15.3.3 VPN Encryption and Authentication

All computers with wireless LAN devices must utilize a corporate-approved Virtual Private Network (VPN) configured to drop all unauthenticated and unencrypted traffic. To comply with this policy, wireless implementations must maintain point to point hardware encryption of at least 56 bits. All implementations must support a hardware address that can be registered and tracked (i.e., a MAC address). All implementations must support and employ strong user authentication which checks against an external database such as TACACS+, RADIUS, or something similar.

Q.15.3.4 Setting the SSID

The SSID shall be configured so that it does not contain any identifying information about the organization, such as the company name, division title, employee name, or product identifier.

Q.15.4 Enforcement

Any employee found to have violated this policy may be subject to disciplinary action, up to and including termination of employment.

Q.15.5 Definitions

User AuthenticationA method by which the user of a wireless system can be verified as a legitimate user independent of the computer or operating system being used.

Q.15.6 Revision History

July 10, 2003, Section 3.4 Added
July 6, 2003, expanded to support CDI Initiative

INDEX

1

13.56 MHz, 42, 59, 185

8

802.11, 195, 202

A

antenna
  adjusting positions, 145
  conveyor, 29, 53, 186
  docking door, 70
  dual, 53–54, 202
  geographical zone, 45
  improper positioning, 30, 45
  orientation, 5, 29
  perpendicular, 4, 30
  ports, 193–194
  random orientation, disadvantages, 5, 29
  reading area limits, 70
anti-collision, 200, 206
arranging cases
  odd vs even, 51
  problems, 51

B

backup site, 114
Backscatter, 253–254
bandwidths
  loading times, 111
  mixing, 120
battery, paper-thin, 246, 255
Bayes theorem, 365
blocking transmitter in a cat, 173
business process reengineering
  network level, 126, 131
  object hierarchy, 157
  organizational maturity, 132
  package level, 126
  site level, 127

C

Capability Maturity Model, 41, 370
cable, 107
  coaxial, 199
  antenna, 209
CERT advisories, 182
chicken
  spoiled, 45, 110
  temperature changes, 109
chips
  memory size, 44
  voltage threshold, 44
circuitry
  insufficient power, 175
  thermostat, 144
Class 1, Gen2, 202
close-loop system, 134
COMPTIA RFID+ certification, 20
concerns
  business executives, 75
  database migration, 112
  IT executives, 75
configuration
  European Telecommunications Standards
    Institute, 247
  FCC, 247. See Elliptic Curve Cryptography
container tag, 52, 190, 194
conveyance units
  active and passive, 4, 55
  white noise, 51, 55–56
conveyors, 55–56, 186–199
  antenna, 29, 53, 186
  verification and tracking, 290

corporate spy, 17, 171
cost/benefit analyses, 15
cryptography
   active tags, security, 170
   defense-in-depth, 176
   minimalist, 173
   pseudonym throttling, 175
   weak, risks of, 176
   cyber-attacker, 130

D

data requirements, 47, 116, 260
database performance
   loading times, remote, 111
   RAID and filegroup options, 113
database physical design, 114
deployment
   METRO Group, 27, 40, 82, 110, 155
   Target, 41, 98, 121, 133
digital signature, 173
dipole, 191, 195
dual shipping faces, 123

E

EAI, loosely vs tightly coupled, 118
electromagnetic fog, 173
Elliptic Curve Cryptography, 173
EPC
   64-bits, three versions, 33
   other bit codes, 33
   partitions, 95
EPC Information Services
   PML, 93. See Physical Markup Language
   Middleware, 62
EPC number, not properly recorded, 130
EPC-compliant, 60, 64, 71, 149
EPCglobal members, 98
eTrust Internet Defense, 183

F

firewall security
   standards, 181
   weak spots, 179
fluidic self-assembly, 41
forecasting methods, 304
FoxMeyer Drug, bankruptcy, 89
frequency
   bands, de facto, 59
   interference, 5
   liquids, 128, 149
Future Store, 82–87, 139, 155

G-H

gray market, 130
harsh manufacturing environment, 190
hierarchy of objects, 157
high carbon content, 51
hybrid reader, 30, 45

I

IBM
   DB2 for SAP, 27, 117
   DB2 UDB, 114
   Department of Defense, 178
   label placements, 129, 144
   Emerging Technologies Toolkit, 94
   METRO Group, 27, 69, 110
   Oracle/PeopleSoft, 27, 117
   SAP customer, 117
   Sensor and Actuator Solutions, 66
   WebSphere® Adapters, 360
idle items, 129
iMotion, Device Emulator, 145
impedance, 208–209, 237
inductive link, 248
incremental models, risk management, 160
interference problem, bundling products, 51
interview findings, 102
investments in infrastructure, 41
ISO
   15693, 48, 185, 199–207, 231–239
   15961, 60
   18000, 48, 228–248
   18185, 60
   22389, 60
item
   exception, 348
   falling out of truck, 110
   security, 348, 351
   unavailability, 348
   return reasons, 78

L

lithium ion, 193, 220
load balancing, 119
loading dock, 247
   forklift truck drivers, 7, 23, 71, 127
   resolving bottlenecks, 7
loading times, remote database, 111
log resource management, 344
logistics maturity
   high, 78
   low, 78
loosely coupled, 134

M

map flags
  military application
  RFID-based items, 111
  temperature changes, 111
metrics, 91, 156
measured limits, logistics visibility,
    78, 154
Medicare cuts, 80
maturity factor, 91, 156
METRO Group, 40, 82–89, 140, 155
  first retailer in rolling out, 68
  Future Initiative, 86
  hybrid technology, 57
  IBM, 69
  maturity, 139
migration
  issues, 112
  planning, 107, 116
minimum voltage threshold, 44
microwave, 189
model
  Capability Maturity, 41
  linearity, 159
  SCM Logistics Maturity, 76,
    153, 159
  statistical, 304, 371
monitoring sensor, 253
multidrop interface, 187, 189
multiple customers, 11, 121
multiple tables, vertical partitioning,
    113
multi-protocol, 191, 201, 207, 248
multi-tag sort, 192

N-O

normalization, vertical partitioning.
    See row splitting, 113
OASIS standards, 36
offending materials 3, 27–30, 61, 72–73,
    121
  13.56 MHz vs lower-frequency, 42
  detune or attenuate tag signals, 4
OLAP, 114, 314, 317, 370
operational requirements
  database physical design, 114
optimal reads, factors of, 30
Oracle, combining tags with sensors, 67
organizational maturity
  adaptive RFID technology, 156
  business process reengineering, 132
  culture, 89–90

P

Palm OS, 198–199, 218
partitioning
  generating ROIs, 113
  increasing throughputs, 114
  multiple tablespaces, 114
  vertical, 113
partitions
  EPC, 95
  number of, 107
  overflowing and reorganizing, 115
  static and dynamic, 106
  time-related, 347–348
password
  64-bit, 170, 176
  protection policy, 167
PCMCIA, 193
performance, remote database, 111
Physical Markup Language, 93
PKI, 173, 176–177
PML examples, 35, 94
Pocket PC, 192–199, 219–230
policies, confusing, 174
privacy issues, 16

Q-R

query parallelism, 115
RAID, 113
readers
  four types, 30
  hybrid, 30, 45, 55–57
  METRO Group, 57
  multi-protocol, multi-frequency, 55
  strategic points, 5, 31
reasons for item returns, 78
refrigeration breakdown, 45
regulatory compliance, 365
reshipping items, 129
RFID
  active tags, cryptography, 170
  advantages, 1
  attacks, 170
  benefits, 138
  consumer item-level tracking, 71, 149
  database middleware, 108
  data on spoiled chicken, 109
  denial-of-service, 173
  differences from bar-code scanner, 2
  drastic temperature changes, 111
  early implementation, 66
  electromagnetic fog, 173
  emulating tag read speed, 145

event alert, 12
fewer insurance claims, 127
forklift truck drivers, 7, 23, 71, 127
IBM, 27, 110
idle items, 129
implementation approaches, 156
infrastructure in hospitals, 81
jamming radio signals, 173
limited real-time recalls, 128
linking with Web services, 91
nested tags, 90
passive, when appropriate, 4
programmability, 43
quality of input readers, 18, 30, 70, 131, 144
real-time recovery, 128
reshipping, 129
reusable smart labels, 71, 149
scanner-equipped cell phones, 8
scanning on conveyors, 290
sensor-based services, 26, 108
service attributes, 178
standard types, 20
tag and ship approach, 124
tag deactivation, 16
tag vulnerability, 170
tracking physical movement, 6
unsecured tags, 169
Visual Device Emulator, 145
voluntary compliance, 141
Web services, 7
RIED, 25, 97
risks
separated items, 110
contributing factors, 102
incremental models, 160
ROI
partitioning types, 113
risk mitigation, 369
time-value, 15
row splitting, vertical partitioning, 113
RS232, 26, 44, 186–189
RS422, 194, 207–208
RS485, 26, 187–189, 197

S

safety, 353
SANS, 377
SAP
IBM customer, 117
RFID application, 64, 152
scanner-equipped cell phones, 8
SCE applications

major players, 63, 151
SCM Logistics Maturity Model, 76, 153, 159
sensor
monitoring, 253
temperature, 44–45
sensor-based services
Oracle, 26–27, 83, 108, 109
RFID technology, 26, 108
servers
three Savant modules, 97
sleep/wake commands, 174–175
smart labels, 66, 71, 149, 189
smart shelves, 8, 75, 82, 87
solid state, 187, 197, 203
spiral models
sidetracking difficult problems, 162
statistical models, 304, 371

T

tags
active, weaker signal, 45
add-on memory, 59
amount of data, 3, 6, 27
anti-theft deterrance, 44
awakened, 174
chip to sleep, 174
classes, 24, 28, 38, 47
incorporating ISO standards, 60
migrating to EPC, 60
combining with sensors, 67
counterfeiting, 172
detune or attenuate signals, 4
digital signature, 173
dual antenna, read-only, 29
ECC-enabled, 175
high carbon content, 51
interior case wall, 56
memory size, 3, 6, 27
metal beams in warehouse, 52
nested, 90
one antenna, read-only, 29
optimal tag location, 50
PKI, 173
product shape and size, 51, 70, 126
refrigeration breakdown, 45
sawing or etching, 17, 171
security stamp, 173
sending an alert, 45
shape and size of the product, 128, 149
smart appliances, 174
storage capacity, 43
testing reading ranges, 53

two-active, 59
unsecured, 169
user privileges, 3
very short range passive, 59
vulnerability to alteration, 170
when they work, 3, 27
wrong data, 128, 149
Target, 41, 98, 121, 133
technology maturity, 134
temperature
    drastic changes, 27, 44, 111, 249
    high, 109, 186, 197, 206
    sensor, 44–45
thermostat circuitry, 144
threshold, minimum voltage, 44
Threshold reporting, 344
throughputs
    docking loading problem, 68
    benchmarks for partitioning, 114
tightly-coupled, 118
time-related partitions, 347–348
time-value ROI, 15
tradeoffs, 47, 63, 151
traffic bottlenecks, 89, 105, 120

transponder, abstract, 260
triggering alert event, 118

U-W

U.S. Federal Drug Administration, 84
uncertainty, 84
vertical partitioning, examples 113
voluntary compliance, 141
war driving, wireless LAN driving, 170
warehouse
    items falling off, 109
    metal of a lift truck, 56
    problems with metal beams, 52
    separated items, 111
Warehouse Management System, 12, 62, 151,
    289–303
war-driving, 170
war-walking, 17, 171
waterfall models, risk management, 160
Wide-Plate Reader, 186–187
Win CE, 57, 66, 83, 19
wireless LAN driving. See war-driving